Voices from the Negro Leagues

VOICES FROM THE NEGRO LEAGUES

Conversations with 52 Baseball Standouts of the Period 1924–1960

BY BRENT KELLEY

McFarland & Company, Inc., Publishers
Jefferson, North Carolina, and London

British Library Cataloguing-in-Publication data are available

Library of Congress Cataloguing-in-Publication Data

Kelley, Brent P.
    Voices from the Negro leagues : conversations with 52 baseball
standouts of the period 1924–1960 / by Brent Kelley.
      p. cm.
    Includes bibliographical references (p.) and index.
    ISBN 0-7864-0369-1 (case binding : 50# alkaline paper) ∞
    1. Baseball players — United States — Interviews. 2. Afro-
American baseball players — Interviews. 3. Negro leagues —
History. I. Title
GV865.A1K446   1998
796.357'089'96073 — dc21   97-37332
                                       CIP

Manufactured in the United States of America

McFarland & Company, Inc., Publishers
  Box 611, Jefferson, North Carolina 28640

TO THE MEMORY OF CELIA GRAHAM

Contents

Introduction

My stepfather grew up in a small town in Oklahoma. It was so small that, if a boy wanted to play baseball, he couldn't be choosy about the color of his teammates; there just wasn't enough of any one color to field a team, so he played with black boys, white boys, even red boys.

In the 1930s when he was in his teens, he remembered black barnstorming teams coming through the area. When a game was nearby — in the next town, which was larger — his town would close down and everyone would go watch the game.

After he married my mother (we lived in Atlanta), he asked me one day — the year was perhaps 1950 — "Do you want to see a type of baseball you've never seen?" He took me to Ponce de Leon Park and we watched a game between the Atlanta Black Crackers (I guess) and the Birmingham Black Barons (I know; I remember the "BBB"). I had no idea who the players were, although one of them may have been Willie Mays in his last days with Birmingham. I didn't know much about baseball then; the only games (maybe two or three) I had ever seen were Southern Association games involving the Atlanta Crackers. And those guys were all *white*. Until that point, I didn't know that black people could play baseball.

But, boy, could they *ever* play baseball!

This year, 1997, marks the 50th anniversary of the "official" breaking of the color barrier in Major League Baseball. When Jackie Robinson played a game for the Brooklyn Dodgers on April 15, 1947, baseball changed forever. Before that, there were white leagues and there were Negro leagues. Now there are major leagues.

Today, decades after the Negro leagues ceased, many — most? — people, even solid baseball fans, know that there were some good black ballplayers — Satchel Paige, Josh Gibson, and a handful of others — but that was about it. They never stop to think that there had to be nine men on the field and nine men on the team they were playing.

It's like saying the 1950 American League consisted of Joe DiMaggio, Yogi Berra, Phil Rizzuto, and Whitey Ford — the Yankees' Hall of Famers. Who played first base for the Yankees? Second base? Left field? Who pitched when Ford didn't? And who did they play against? Those guys weren't out there by themselves.

Just as the American and National leagues are major leagues, the Negro leagues were major leagues. The debate over whether Hideo Nomo was a true rookie in 1995 because he had played in the Japanese major leagues could have had precedence, although no one thought about it when Jackie Robinson, Don Newcombe, Sam Jethroe, Willie Mays, Joe Black, and Junior Gilliam — all Negro major league graduates — were chosen as rookies of their years in the '40s and '50s. And many of the Negro league graduates who later played in the major leagues had *better* statistics than they did in the Negro leagues, which may well be a commentary on the respective qualities of play.

Sure, there were superstars in black baseball, just as in the white game. And just as Babe Ruth and Dizzy Dean would

Jackie Robinson being congratulated by George Shuba after hitting a home run on Opening Day, 1946, Montreal vs. Jersey City, International League, Robinson's first game in organized ball (author's collection).

have been stars against any competition, so would have Willie Wells and Hilton Smith. It's safe to say that a major league star — black or white — would be a star anywhere, a regular a regular anywhere, and a scrub a scrub anywhere.

Negro league baseball ceased to exist after the 1960 season, but it had been dying since that day late in 1945 when Branch Rickey and the Brooklyn Dodgers signed the Kansas City Monarchs' shortstop, Robinson, to an "organized" ball contract;

because once the color line was broken, Major League Baseball put a constant drain on the black leagues, buying (or taking) the best young players who came along. The quality of Negro baseball decreased from the point of Robinson's signing and by the late 1940s, with the brightest young players having been taken by the major leagues, the level of play was well below what it had been only a few years earlier. Still, black baseball produced. In the late '40s and early '50s, Willie Mays, Henry Aaron, Ernie Banks, and several others began their careers in the "dying" Negro leagues.

Now, five decades after Robinson, it's hard to imagine what baseball would have been like without him or Mays or Aaron or Roy Campanella or any of the many others who started out in the Negro leagues. And, following them, we've had Roberto Clemente, Willie Stargell, Bobby and Barry Bonds, Frank Thomas, and so many more who, 60 years ago, would have been unable to play in the major leagues.

The way had to be paved for Ken Griffey and Reggie Jackson and it was, by men who were every bit as good — maybe better — but whom few baseball fans saw or even heard of. Josh Gibson may have been the most powerful hitter of all time. Surely few men could pitch as well as Smoky Joe Williams or Verdell Mathis. One has to wonder how Ty Cobb would have fared against his contemporary Williams, Stan Musial against Mathis, Lefty Grove against Gibson.

In 1995, at the time of the celebration of the 75th anniversary of the founding of the Negro National League, there were estimated to be 290 men still alive who played Negro league baseball. And they were *old* men. There may be no 100th anniversary celebration because there may be no one left to celebrate. Recently there has been a great deal of work done, trying to put together information on the black leagues and the black players, but most of it has centered on the stars: Josh Gibson, Satchel Paige, Monte Irvin, Buck Leonard, and so

on. These were great players without question and their stories make the reader long to have seen them play, but their stories alone do not tell the tale of Negro league baseball.

Here, in their own words, 52 former Negro league players — from the greats such as Buck Leonard, Max Manning, and Wilmer Fields to some who only passed through briefly — tell what the games and the players were like, how they traveled and the problems they encountered.

The Reverend Harold Tinker tells how he discovered 16-year-old Josh Gibson in the 1920s; Josh Johnson tells of his teammates passing the hat to take up a collection to enable him to attend college; Thomas Turner describes the superb treatment he received from the fans in Mexico when he played there; and Gene Collins describes the abuse heaped on the players when barnstorming through our own southern states.

You may see a few discrepancies here from what has appeared in other books — years played, teams played for, records — but what is in these pages is from the players themselves, and one must feel they know better than anyone else when, where, and how well they played. Every attempt has been made to obtain photographs of each man from his playing days, but some are just not available.

Complete, correct statistics for Negro league baseball do not exist today. They may never have. Some have been unearthed in recent years by researchers, and some more will undoubtedly be in the future, but it's safe to say that there will always be a gap — we'll never have them all.

And that's too bad. Baseball lends itself to statistical analysis as nothing else, but that's only a part of the reason. There are people who will tell you that Negro baseball was inferior, and one of the reasons they say this is the lack of hard, black-and-white, statistical proof.

(One of my favorite arguments by those who put down Negro baseball as inferior is the one that goes something like this: "They only played against other blacks." Well, the whites only played against other whites, so what's the point?)

Sure, Ted Williams has great career "numbers," but even without them, anyone who ever saw him swing a bat knew he was a marvelous hitter. You could tell Rickey Henderson was fast without checking his stats. Stand at the plate for a Nolan Ryan fastball and you didn't need a list of his strikeout victims to know he could bring it.

And so it is with men such as Buck Leonard, Cool Papa Bell, and Bill Foster. Stats only verify what all who saw them already knew. Unfortunately, not enough saw them and those who did are literally a dying breed.

With that said, some statistics are presented following the interviews. For some seasons and for some players, nothing exists; for others (seasons and players), there is something, but it is likely incomplete. Statistics from Latin America and Canada are likewise incomplete; in fact, records of years played and teams played for in many cases do not exist, but what is known is included here.

For some players in some years, there may be only a few numbers. There may be stats from some league games but not all, or there may be stats from games against all competition. There may be complete totals in some categories but only partial in others; for instance, a pitcher may have a correct number of innings in a season, but only a partial total of strikeouts.

Also confusing are the sources of the stats. One source frequently differs from another, and both claim to be accurate. Perhaps they both are, perhaps neither is. And some of what is listed is hearsay, based on the memories of the men themselves.

An asterisk (*) denotes a league leader in a given category.

Too many people have said, and still say, "They came along too early."
None of these men believe that.
As Cool Papa Bell said, "They opened the door too late."

Part One

BEFORE JACKIE ROBINSON ENTERED ORGANIZED BALL

Before 1946, Negro baseball was a separate entity from the white game. A few men began their careers in black baseball and then went on to organized ball, but these were Cubans who reputedly had no black ancestry and could "pass." If, however, a player carried African characteristics — color, features, hair, and so on — he played in the Negro leagues if he wanted to play baseball.

The Negro teams signed players on ability and potential, knowing that they would not be lured to organized ball. Over the years, minor attempts and a few queries were made by white teams into the availability of or desire by certain black players to perhaps play white ball but, although many knew the day would someday come, nothing materialized.

Finally, Baseball Commissioner Kenesaw Mountain Landis died and A. B. "Happy" Chandler took the office. It was a new world, and Jackie Robinson's signing is one of the most important events of the 20th century. It was too late, however, for the veterans of the black game. Their abilities may have still been there, but their ages were against them.

Cowan "Bubba" Hyde

Leadoff Hitter

NEGRO LEAGUE DEBUT: 1924

Bubba Hyde was the leadoff batter for the Memphis Red Sox for more than a decade, all the more amazing when you consider he was 30 years old when he joined the club on a permanent basis.

And when he joined the Red Sox, he had already been around for many years. Today he holds the distinction of having played in the Negro leagues earlier than anyone else still living. In 1924, at the age of 15, Bubba Hyde played briefly for the Red Sox before returning to school.

After two years of college, he came back to professional baseball and remained active through 1954, when he was in his mid–40s. In 1949, he played briefly in organized ball for Bridgeport, Connecticut, in the Boston Braves system, batting .327. He was scheduled for promotion to the big league club, but at the time he received the call his daughter, Almerth, was being born and he rightfully considered her birth to be more important, so he left the club to be with his family. He did not reveal this in the interview, nor did he ever tell his daughter; rather, she learned it years later from two of his friends, Verdell Mathis and Ted "Double Duty" Radcliffe. He rounded out his career playing in Canada.

Why did you choose professional baseball?

I was just interested in it because I liked the game and I played in school. I just got attached to it and I stayed with it.

You first played professionally at the age of 15.

I really didn't sign with the team, but I went up to Birmingham — I was in school down at Morris Brown in Atlanta — but I didn't like it and I went back to school. I didn't finish [college], just the sophomore year.

Most of your playing days were spent with the Memphis Red Sox. How did you join them?

I played with several teams. I played with Cincinnati in 1936 and the manager over there was Double Duty Radcliffe. He asked me about going [to Memphis] in 1937, so I agreed and signed a contract over there and I stayed there through '49, with exceptions of '40 and '41. I went down to Mexico, he and I both.

Everything was pretty nice [in Mexico]. I didn't like the food. [Laughs] Mexico City had a beautiful park and the facilities and everything were okay. Monterrey was nice, but the rest of the teams weren't up to par on the conditions of the field and other conditions, either.

You were an All-Star.

I was on there three times. I did all right.

Every year they had a team of Negro ballplayers to go to California and play against the major leaguers, so I was picked

This page and opposite: *Cowan "Bubba" Hyde (courtesy of Cowan Hyde).*

four or five years there. We made good money at it because we drew well when we played there. We played out there about two-and-a-half months. I did well. Pitchers like Feller, Bob Lemon, [Mike] Garcia, Johnny Sain, Bo Newsom — all these guys.

Yeah, I did all right down there. I was the leadoff man and I stayed on the bases.

You were fast.

Yeah, that's why they kept me there so long. If I couldn't run, they wouldn't've had me up there. I led off for Memphis from '37

to '49. And I had some power. I hit
quite a few home runs.

Does one game stand out?

There were a lot of games. In 1938
there were several games. We played
Kansas City in the playoffs and we
knocked them out. A single game is
hard to do.

I do remember one game. We
were playing the major leaguers in
the Hollywood park [Gilmore Field]
and we had a good crowd. They were
leading us, 4 to 1, in the ninth inning
and we got three men on and I came
to bat on Bo Newsom and the second pitch he threw me, I hit it on
top of the left field fence — it didn't
go out — and bounced back in the
park, so I got a double and we
cleared the bases. That made us 4–4
and we had a man playing with us
from New York — he was an Arkansas
boy but lived in New York — Little
Splo Spearman. They called him Little Splo. He came to bat and he singled me in and we beat them, 5 to 4. We
played against the best they had up in the
majors at that time.

Who was the best player you saw?

Willie Wells, Senior. Some people say
Josh and that, but Willie Wells was the
greatest player that I ever saw. He didn't
have a strong arm. He hurt his arm the first
year he came up to play, but he played a
shallow infield — shortstop — but he didn't
have any bad hops. He'd come in there to
field a ground ball and it'd hop up and he'd
put his glove on it. He threw everybody out
that ever went to bat that hit to short and
he hit 25 to 35 home runs a year and he hit
.325 or .330 every year. And he was a *smart*
ballplayer. He's the best ballplayer I ever
knew.

*Most people say he belongs in the Hall of
Fame.*

I think he does. He belongs there.

Who was the best pitcher?

Let's see. The best pitcher might not be
the pitcher that had the reputation of being

the best pitcher. I hit against Feller. Feller
or Satchel didn't give me too much trouble,
nor did Lemon or Garcia. Two pitchers
that come to my mind that I would rate the
best that I ever hit against — well, there
were three pitchers: I would say Bill Foster — he was a lefthander, Chicago American Giants; and I would say Johnny Sain —
he played for the Boston Braves; and the
next one would be Hilton Smith with the
Kansas City Monarchs. Satchel would come
in and pitch three innings and go and
Smith would pitch six. I might rate him the
greatest pitcher that I know. He was as
good as Satchel. He should be in the Hall of
Fame. Sure, he should.

*There was a great pitcher you didn't have
to bat against there with you in Memphis:
Verdell Mathis.*

He was great! I'd put him with anybody.
He pitched in three or four All-Star games
and he never lost. He was a great lefthander.

Talk about the travel.

To be honest about our traveling, the man that I played for in Memphis, he was a doctor and he was very, very wealthy. There were four doctors, all of them brothers. Dr. Martin. I couldn't say anything bad about Dr. Martin. He owned the bus and every year he would have the bus gone over, *everything* fixed, even the paint job. Just telling you the truth, we didn't have it as bad as some of the other players in the league because we had a man with some money. We weren't stuck out on the road or anything like that.

Now, I'll tell you about the places we went for food. A lot of places we were turned down, you know, but there were some places that accepted us. We used to go down to Texas — Greenville, Texas — and they would accept us there. Then there's several other places — we used to play the white teams all the time in Duncan, Texas, and Enid, Oklahoma.

We just grew accustomed to going to the black restaurants and hotels and we were pretty well satisfied with that because we had some nice hotels in Memphis, Chicago, Kansas City, and New York. We had nice colored hotels and restaurants and it didn't bother us. Once in a while we might be going through the countryside or something and stop and there'd be a problem, but it wasn't very many times because we would make it our business to not stop. You know what I mean?

How much money were you paid?

We made pretty good money — well, at that time [it] was good money. I got $375 a month and my expenses down in Memphis during that span. I didn't have to worry about my money because it was always there.

Then, sometimes, I was overdrawn at the end of the season, but the man I played for — you might ask Verdell Mathis about that, too; he was there — he was a good man. He would draw a line through that overdrawn business and leave a check for me in the offices. He was a good man.

I went up to Canada for about four years after that and made more money than that, but it wasn't too bad I didn't think at the time. That's what I made all those years.

The level of baseball in Canada was very good.

They started off pretty good. The first time I went up there I made $1,100, but they didn't last too long — three or four years — because they cut that down — the classification of the league — from A ball to C and didn't pay as much money.

Some of us were in eastern Canada and some of us were in western Canada. I was in western Canada — Winnipeg in the Man-Dak League. Winnipeg in 1951, then I played in Brandon about '53. I was there three or four years. I played center field and left field.

How much did you receive for meal money?

With Memphis? We got three dollars for meal money. And when we went to the All-Star game, we got more because I was player representative along there about 1943 or 1944. We didn't play one game, we played two games — one in Chicago and one in Washington. We played the game in Chicago; we were playing the Grays and we beat them in Chicago and then we went to Washington. We struck in Washington and that's when they changed; we won our suit. We were getting $150 for the All-Star games — $150 for both places, Chicago and Washington. Then we got $150 for Chicago and $150 for Washington and $15 for eating money. That was for the All-Star game.

You played a long time. Did you enjoy it?

Oh, yeah. I played with Bridgeport in organized ball. They accepted us in the game after '47 when Jackie went up to Brooklyn — and Bankhead and them. I played under Jimmie Foxx at Bridgeport. I did all right. He was a good man to play for.

Would you go back and play baseball again?

Oh, yeah. Yeah, I'd go back. I don't regret my play at all.

COWAN F. "BUBBA" HYDE
Born 4-10-08, Pontotoc, MS
Ht. 5' 8½"   Wt. 155   Batted and Threw R

Year	Team, league	Pos	G	AB	R	H	2B	3B	HR	RBI	SB	BA
1924	Memphis Red Sox, NNL	OF										
1927		OF										.190
1930	Birm. Black Barons, NNL	OF										.237
1937	Indianapolis Athletics, NAL	OF										
	Cincinnati Clowns, NAL	OF										
1938	Memphis Red Sox, NAL	OF										
1939		OF										
1940		OF										
1941		OF		28		10						.357
1942		OF	16	67		21	4	1	0		0	.313
1943		OF		42		17	2	1	0		0	.405
1944		OF	66	245	37	68	11	5	2		14	.278
1945		OF	39	152	17	39	9	1	0	8	5	.257
1946		OF										.298
1947		OF										
1948		OF	73	252	43	69	9	7	1	28	11	.274
1949	Memphis Red Sox, NAL	OF										
	Bridgeport, COlL	OF	25	98	13	32	6	0	1	21	4	.327
1950	Memphis-Chicago, NAL	OF	17	72	16	21	4	2	0	8	7	.292
	Elmwood, MnDkL	OF	33	143		45				5		.315
1951	Chi. American Giants, NAL	OF										
	Elmwood, MnDkL	OF	30	132		46			2	10		.348
	Farnham, ProvL	OF	15	57	5	11	3	0	0	5	2	.193
1952	Winnipeg, MnDkL	OF										
1953	Brandon, MnDkL	OF	62	271		79			0	30		.292

Record in Latin America.

Year	Team, league	Pos	G	AB	R	H	2B	3B	HR	RBI	SB	BA
1940	Santa Rosa, MexL	OF	11	49	10	15	4		1	5	4	.306

Harold Tinker

Josh and the Crawfords

NEGRO LEAGUE DEBUT: 1929

Men have become famous for recognizing star qualities in others. Paul Krichell discovered Lou Gehrig. Cy Slapnicka found Bob Feller. Ed Katalinas scouted and signed Al Kaline.

Fame such as that is unlikely to occur anymore. With the sophisticated scouting and cross-checking and amateur baseball publications, no one man will ever again receive credit for the discovery of a star. Generally, the world knows all there is to know about a high draft pick long before he turns pro. Seventy years ago, however, super amateur ballplayers often played in obscurity, and a man with an eye for talent and who happened to be in the right place at the right time could find one of these kids and surprise the baseball world.

Harold "Hooks" Tinker, now the Reverend Harold Tinker, was such a man. As the first-ever manager of the legendary Pittsburgh Crawfords, he spotted a 16-year-old kid whom he felt the Crawfords could use. The kid was Josh Gibson, and there are those who will tell you he was the greatest hitter baseball has ever seen. Tinker invited the youthful Gibson to become a member of his team, and a legend was born.

Tinker himself was only 22 at the time, but even at that age he was recognized as a superior leader. He guided the Crawfords from anonymity as a semi-pro team to a level of play so good they were able to schedule the great Homestead Grays.

Harold Tinker's career was not very long, but his baseball knowledge and player evaluation was recorded for posterity when Josh Gibson was elected to the Hall of Fame.

Reverend Tinker is in his 90s now, but he still remembers young Josh and other aspects of baseball from 65 to 70 years ago.

How old were you when you began playing for the Crawfords?

Oh, let's see. It was 1927 so I had to be 22 years old. I was born in 1905. I played with several teams before I played with the Crawfords. I played first of all with one of the company teams in the Pittsburgh area. It was called WEMCO. It was a sandlot team for Westinghouse Electric. I was 15 years old then.

I played one year with a kid team called Keystone Juniors. That was the first team after I left WEMCO. And then I went to the Pittsburgh Monarchs. I was the field captain there for four years, 'til 1926. I played '26 and '27 with a team from Edgar Thompson's Field. They called them Edgar Thompson Community. I went from there to the Crawfords in 1927. I played there 'til '31.

John King (left), owner of the Pittsburgh Crawfords, and Harold Tinker, Crawfords manager, circa 1928 (courtesy of Harold Tinker).

I have heard that you had pretty good leadership qualities. Is that true?

Presumably so. [Laughs] That's what they said. Well, I managed the Crawfords from 1927 'til 1930. And I played center field all the time. I was the field manager and captain and everything.

You were instrumental in signing Josh Gibson.

I signed him. I brought Josh Gibson into the semi-pro picture. Each year there was a man that lived on the north side of Pittsburgh and he picked the all-star team from the sandlot teams of black players and I was picked. Two of us from the Crawfords were picked on that team. Nineteen twenty-seven was the first year. Neal Harris — that was the left fielder — and I was picked to play with this all-star team.

We played a white team on the north side of Pittsburgh and this kid was playing third base. Now you can believe this — Josh Gibson — I ain't never seen nor heard of him. I noticed him. First thing, he was such a fine-looking specimen for a young man. He was so adequately built for baseball and I noticed his movements in the beginning of the game. He made several plays at third base and the thing I noticed about him was his coolness. He threw out runners; he'd let them run a little while, then he'd cock his arm and throw and he could really throw the ball. I said, "We could use this kid."

As the game progressed, he had a couple of hits but in about the seventh inning he hit a ball out of sight, up over a mountain. They didn't even think about going where that ball went. [Laughs] And I told Neal, I said, "Look, this boy would make us just about what we need to be." I didn't know he was a catcher, but it was a funny thing. Our catcher was the weakest hitter on our team at that time.

I asked him would he like to play for a real baseball team and he said, "Yeah," so I said, "You come up Tuesday evening and you'll be playing for the Pittsburgh Craw-fords." And he showed up. Somebody had seen him play with a company team — ele-vator drivers from Gimbel Brothers — and they said he was catching that day when we saw him and he looked good. So I asked him and he said, "Well, that's what I am — a catcher." [Laughs] I said, "You'd never think it by looking at you play third base. From here on, you'll be the catcher for the Crawfords." He was a hit right off the bat. He was only 16. He was really built; he wasn't nothing but muscle.

I saw him hit plenty long ones but they tell me hit one out of Yankee Stadium. They say he hit one over the center field wall in Forbes Field. [It was 457 feet to the wall.] He was playing with the Grays then.

Don't let anybody fool you. There's a whole lot of people that say they discovered him but that's the way he was discovered. He was something and he was a fine man, too; he was a clean-living kid when we had him with the Crawfords. Perfect. You give him an ice cream cone and he was satisfied.

What kind of money did you guys make in those days?

Making money? Very seldom did we make any money. When we established ourselves as a strong semi-pro team, we were able to book out-of-town games, like mining towns, and these were the games that we were paid. But, in general, we had a hard time giving the kids any money because you had a big crowd but you didn't have much financing. You couldn't charge at the gate when the Crawfords played in a community field. You couldn't charge to go into the field, all you could do was pass the hat.

The first one will knock you out. The first game we played with the Crawfords — I brought four other guys from Edgar Thompson with me, we had grew up together through all these teams I played with — and we played a game before about 3,000 people it looked like and we took up, I think it was $13. [Laughs] That's the truth.

And then we went to this new field where the Crawfords really established themselves. That was up on Bedford Avenue. We played there twice a week and we took in sometimes $30–35. By the time you paid umpires and bought baseballs, you didn't have much left. We'd divide it up with the players but it was very little. We played because we loved it.

That's the way it stayed with the Craw-fords all the time. The more popular we became, the more attractive games we booked out of town and quite naturally we were making a little bit more than we were before. But until Gus Greenlee took the team, we didn't have no real income from baseball. When Gus Greenlee took the team, he told me — I think it was two weeks after he took the team — he was gonna put us all on contract. And he said, "You either have to play baseball or keep your job, whatever one of 'em you want to do."

I'll tell you what he paid me: $80 a month. That's what our salary was. That was '30, I think.

Didn't Satchel Paige join the Crawfords somewhere around then?

Yeah, he joined us during the 1930s.

We had played the Grays — they finally gave us a game. We were so popular, we were defeating all the teams they were defeating, so [Grays owner Cum] Posey finally gave us a game. We played them at Forbes Field and we almost won that game. They had won 42 straight games the night we played and they beat us, 3–2. Oscar Owens pitched for the Grays and Harry Kincannon pitched for the Crawfords.

We didn't get Satchel 'til the beginning of '31. We beat the Grays the first game that Satchel pitched, but he didn't pitch the whole game. Harry Kincannon — the boy that almost beat the Grays the year before — he started and they got a couple runs off of him. Three, I think, in two innings, then they brought this big skinny guy in. Nobody knew Satchel around here. As a matter of fact, we didn't know him. They brought him in and he pitched a shutout for the rest of the game.

I guess a lot of guys got to know him.

Oh, you better believe it! In a hurry! [Laughs] He wasn't throwing anything but fastballs. His changeup was a fastball. I didn't see him afterwards pitching, but what I saw was enough.

Was he the best pitcher you saw?

Oh, I would just about say that.

That big boy Harry Kincannon was a great ballplayer. He pitched against the major league all-stars after Gus took 'em. I wasn't with the team any longer and I didn't see the game, but they tell me that these players from the National and American leagues marveled at Harry Kincannon's

ability to throw his curveball with a 3-and-2 count and he made some of them look bad.

We had a couple more who were good. One of the boys that I think would've been one of the greatest of all pitchers — he died early, he had meningitis — was Gilbert Hill. You probably never heard of him. A righthander. A fastball and a curveball pitcher with the Crawfords. He died in '28; he was very young. It was sad. He was one of the finest young men I ever knew. He never played in the Negro National League. He was great.

Josh was the best hitter, but who was the best player you saw?

The best player? You've never heard of this guy, either. We had a boy playing second base; his name was Charlie Hughes and I played a lot of baseball with him because he came up through all those teams I told you I played with. He played second base. He was the greatest ground-ball player I've ever seen. Fielding.

The Crawfords, with all of our efforts to try to keep our diamond right, there was a ridge that ran across second base and everytime it would rain it would make this gully across there and they had a hard time taking it away. There was nobody to keep the field; it was just a sandlot field.

I saw this boy pick balls out of that gutter. I asked him one day, I said, "Charlie, how on earth do you come up with those ground balls that hop into your face?" [Laughs] And he said, "Well, I'll tell you. I watch the ball until it goes into my glove." I'll tell you, he was a marvel. He was just a natural. Some guys just naturally have it.

I believe in all my heart that the '29 and '30 Crawfords — before Gus took 'em — all of those boys would've played in the minors and several of 'em would've been major league stars *if* they had've had the opportunity. You know, they didn't have any training or anything; they just *grew* into baseball.

Is there one game that stands out?

As far as I'm concerned, the game that we played the Grays the first time. None of us had ever been inside of Forbes Field. All my life I had been peeping through holes that I had cut in the fence and I never dreamed that I'd be playing in Forbes Field. When I walked out on the field that day it was like going to another world. [Laughs] I looked up at those stands in center field, that was a thrill!

And to play against the Grays! All my life I had looked forward to playing against the Homestead Grays 'cause I saw 'em when I was 14 years old and they were an established team then. That was one of the greatest thrills I had. Oscar Owens pitched a no-hit game until the seventh inning and I got the first hit off him — a line drive to right center. I'll never forget it. And when I got my hit, three other guys followed with hits. We should've won the game. The last out was a line drive to left center that Vic Harris made a great catch on off of Charlie Hughes. We would've won the game if that ball had went through. [Laughs] That was one of the greatest thrills I ever had.

How big were you?

I weighed around 170, average playing weight. I weigh about 158 now and I'm 90 years old. [Laughs]

I've been told you were pretty quick in the field.

That's what they said. You know why? Because I loved it. I loved to chase fly balls on a baseball diamond.

Did you steal many bases?

No, I didn't, but I could steal 'em. The Crawfords when I managed, we only had a couple of boys on there that we let run. One, he'd run anyhow, whether you let him or not. [Laughs] I had trouble with him. And he could run. If he went to first base, invariably he would steal. And he'd make it. Neal Harris — he played left field. That was Vic Harris's brother. You know, we had two on our team that was related to Vic — his two brothers. Neal Harris played left field and Bill Harris played third base and first base for the Crawfords at the same

time their brother was playing left field for the Grays.

Neal was the best hitter of all of 'em. I was taking batting averages out of one of the scorebooks a couple of months ago and Neal Harris was batting around .450. He was a natural hitter; he hit line drives all the time. He hit the ball to right field very hard. You could put a hit-and-run on with him anytime.

What was your average?

Oh, around .290. I hit about one or two home runs a year. I hit some tremendous ones, though. I remember one I hit in Bluefield, Virginia, the first time I went on a road trip with the Monarchs. We never took a road trip before. The first game the first time up I hit a ball over the left field fence. It was a tremendous drive and from that time on — we played two games there — anytime I came up with anybody on they walked me. [Laughs] I'll never forget that one. That was a tremendous home run. I didn't blame 'em for walking me after they looked at that. [Laughs]

Do you have any regrets from your baseball career?

No. I got a lot of satisfaction out of seeing the happiness of the people, particularly when we were coming up with the Crawfords. Those were hard times and people didn't have much money and to see them happy just made me happy.

Would you do it again?

I believe I would.

What did you do when you left the Crawfords?

When I quit the Crawfords I wanted to get away from it because it broke my heart to have to quit at that time. Baseball was in my blood. I stayed out of it for three or four years 'til a man from Hazlewood told me he had a bunch of kids playing. He asked me would I come and manage the team for him. They were at the bottom of the league and I told him, "I'm out of baseball. I got a family and I don't want to be away from my family. If you'll agree to take my family, provide a car and bring my wife and kids when they want to come, I'll consider taking the job." So he agreed to do that, so I took it. In one year we came from the cellar to playing in the playoffs. [Laughs] I played center field for 'em. I was young — not real young but young. Early 30s. It's in your blood; you know what I'm talking about. I did that two years.

I got into it real good again with really the first integrated baseball team in the Pittsburgh area — sandlots or semi-pro. Terrace Village decided to get a baseball team and I heard about it so I went over just to listen to what they was doing and one of the guys that was forming this thing,

he saw me in the back of the room and he suggested that they try to get me to manage the team. I accepted. I really wanted to get back into that thing.

We came from nowhere to be one of the best sandlot teams in the Pittsburgh area. In two years, we played Dormont for the championship and they were the best semi-pro team around here. We had some great boys. As a matter of fact, we had five or six of 'em signed. The Giants took two of our outfielders.

It sounds as if you had a great time in baseball.

I did. I liked every bit of it.

HAROLD C. "HOOKS" TINKER, SR.
Born 1905, Pittsburgh, PA
Ht. 5' 10"   Wt. 170   Batted and Threw R

Year	Team, league	Pos	G	AB	R	H	2B	3B	HR	RBI	SB	BA
1928	Pittsburgh Crawfords, ind.	OF-Mgr										
1929		OF-Mgr										
1930		OF-Mgr										
1931		OF										

Al Fennar

Beck's Buddy

NEGRO LEAGUE DEBUT: 1931

All of the teams in Negro baseball did not belong to leagues, especially in the early days, but even though there were no league affiliations, these were Major League–caliber teams. They played tough barnstorming schedules against each other and against league-affiliated clubs.

This was the way it was well into the 1930s, and times were tough. Al Fennar began his professional career during the Depression playing for these barnstorming teams. He played only four years of professional ball, but he played for *seven* teams: Lincoln Giants, Harlem Stars, New York Black Yankees, Brooklyn Royal Giants, Atlantic City Bacharach Giants, Cuban Stars and Pennsylvania Red Caps. (Technically, the first three named were basically the same club with different names.) He switched teams so often because of the economy of the time. With no contractual obligations he went where the money was best, and there was always demand for a good infielder.

With marriage came other responsibilities, so from the mid–'30s to the late '40s he played semi-pro, then coached youth baseball.

The Harlem Stars were your first team. Is that right?

When I was in high school. I was 18 or 19, somewhere in there.

Actually, it was the Lincoln Giants that I played with. They were the ones that scouted me. I was playing in New Jersey in what we called a preliminary game to the big game. That day, the Lincoln Giants were going to play our home team; that was in West New York, New Jersey.

I was playing with a team that played in the preliminary game and unknown to me — I had no idea — the Lincoln Giants were sitting around watching me play. I was playing third base. The infield at this particular field was what we call a skin diamond — no grass. They got ahold of me and they said, "Listen. If you can play third

base on this field, you can play third base on any field." They gave me information on how to keep in touch with them, which I did. I was still in high school, so they said, "When you graduate, then you get in touch with us."

A very interesting thing started right there because, when I went with them — I hate to mention years because a lot of times you find out that it wasn't correct, but I will say that I think it was 1932 — the Lincoln Giants became the Black Yankees.

I had played a few games with the Harlem Stars. When I was playing with them, I was playing shortstop and here comes this guy up at bat, looked like a bulldog. Looked like Hack Wilson, but bigger than Hack Wilson. Number Four on his back. I moved back as deep as I could play in the infield and the third baseman was a man named Marcelle — Oliver Marcelle, you remember him? He said to me, "Get back!"

Now, I'm a rookie, right? Earlier than a rookie, really. He said, "Get back!" I said, "What's the matter with him? Don't he see that I'm back already?" He said again, "Get back!" so I move back and now I'm on the outfield grass. He looked over there again; he said, "*Get Back!!* That's Beck!"

That batter was a man named John Beckwith. Ever hear of him? He was devastating. He was awful! Beckwith hit the ball — I was way out, I was back — Beckwith hit the ball and I jumped and the ball hit in the glove and took the glove and everything and headed for left field.

That was one of the best things ever happened to me, although I didn't know it at the time because Beck and I became very good friends. What a great ballplayer he was.

I'm gonna tell you something and you can quote me: The Baseball Hall of Fame is *not* a true hall of fame until John Beckwith gets in there. He belongs! It's not a hall of fame without him. He played various positions — shortstop, he did a little catching, he played everywhere. All they wanted was to get his stick in there.

Although we became very good friends and he managed me, I never mentioned this to Beck or anyone. I believe that, being a rookie, he said, "Oh, they've got a fresh kid out there. Let's see what he can do." I believe he hit that ball to me intentionally! [Laughs] "I'm gonna try this kid out."

He and I became great friends and that's why I say that incident was a wonderful thing for me. I think he respected me after that. I visited him at the Harlem hospital and took him fruit and everything and went to his funeral.

I'm gonna tell you a story that I haven't told anybody. Nobody knows this but you. We went to this game and he was the manager, he was in his civilian clothes, he didn't put a uniform on. He was sitting there with a friend talking and the ballplayers, as they were getting dressed to play ball, were talking about boxing. Somebody mentioned Sam Langford. Beckwith was a man of few words, but we had a very good rapport. He said to me, "You hear that guy they're talking about? He made me into a ballplayer." What do you gather from that? I gather that when he was a young man he was interested in boxing and somehow he got in the ring with Sam Langford and Langford changed his mind about it. [Laughs] That's a true story.

He was a great guy. He was one of the greatest hitters that I ever saw. He could mash a baseball something awful. Nobody ever took the glove off my hand but him.

Did they give him a hit or you an error?

Well, I thought it was an error but that was a hit. Oh, yeah. I was mad at myself. I said, "That guy hit the ball to me — right at me — and there he is on first base!"

Who was the best pitcher you faced?

Oh, there were a lot of those guys. You know, I've gotta tell you, they all look alike. One guy may be a little faster or have a little more stuff, but it'll just take you a minute or two and you figure it out.

The black teams always batted against the fastest guy within a hundred-mile radius. I know guys made a living pitching against black teams — call him and say, "Hey, we're playing so-and-so Thursday night. Can you come down?" So they would pitch against us. The regular pitcher, he didn't want to go in there. I've been told that. I had guys tell me, "I ain't pitching against you guys tonight," so they got somebody else from out of town.

I'm going back a long way. They were semi-pro teams but they were great. A lot of 'em could've beaten the pro teams in those days.

How long were you with the Black Yankees?

I didn't play with them very long. I was a rookie and a rookie at that time got a half a share, so a couple of months into the season I was offered a chance to go with the

Brooklyn Royal Giants. If I go with them, I get a full share, so that's what I did.

I want to make a point here. No white paper is going to accentuate it, but the point is that they would help you. If you could better yourself, they would help you. In other words, you're gonna leave their team, go to another team — they would help you do that; they would be in your corner. So they probably got me the opportunity to go with the Brooklyn Royal Giants, where I got a full share. In fact, I signed for $150 a month. That was a lot of money back in 1932 or '33 or somewhere in there.

That era was not a stable era. We had the war and I played in a war plant then and the economy was terrrible — the Depression. I went where the money was. If I could make a little more money, I'd go. See, I was in my early 20s and I didn't get married until I was 25 and that changed things again. At that point — getting married — I played semi-pro around home but I still played with and against some of the same teams.

I learned my baseball in New York and New Jersey. I had a wonderful coach. You might know of him because he's in the Basketball Hall of Fame; he's one of the first people who went in there. His name is Dave Tobey. He was my coach in high school.

I went to a good high school — the best in the country. They still keep in touch with me and in 1997 we're going to celebrate their 100th year and I'm invited to go to that. DeWitt Clinton High School in New York City.

Back then, New York was probably the number one source of professional ballplayers.

Yes, it was. They come from Australia now. [Laughs] In those years, they came from New York, New Jersey.

Back when you played, travel was difficult. How far afield did you guys go?

I played with the New York teams from Canada to Florida. The whole East Coast.

The furthest west I played was Pittsburgh.

Did you encounter problems in traveling?

Well, you got flat tires in those days, and you had narrow roads and bad roads. I remember one time, we had a Pierce Arrow — remember them? — and we had a running board and on the running board we had a cage and the bags were stuck in this cage and some were on top of the car. That was the uniform bags. Somebody sideswiped us and there were bags all over the place.

Roads were not good. What are highways now weren't even in existence then.

Were there decent accommodations?

That was covered. We never had any problems. Many of the fellas talk about the problems they had getting food and staying in the South; we didn't have any problems. We had an advance man to take care of everything.

Where did you spring train?

We spring trained in New York. The season started in March — that was spring training. The regular season started in April.

We used to meet around 11 o'clock in the morning — that's the heat of the day, the best part of the day from 11 to about one — and we'd get our spring training in there.

How many players were carried on the roster?

About 15 or 16. Don't forget, a pitcher pitched nine innings those days. Like today, they're lucky to get five out of one, but when you handed a guy the ball he knew he was going nine innings.

Let me tell you something. I'm going back now to when I was playing. Some *idiot* they interviewed about professional baseball, they said to him, "There are some great black ballplayers. How come none of them are in the big leagues?" And he said, "They're not good enough."

So we got together the next time we played. "Did you hear what that guy said?" "Yeah." So we went out and beat that team, 32-to-nothing. Yet we weren't allowed to play on a white team.

I played with a team in Patterson [New Jersey]. It was a black team and we played every Sunday. We used to play all the big teams at Henchcliff Stadium. There were a couple of white fellas who were very good ballplayers and they said, "We want to play with you guys." We said, "Come on." [Laughs] They were good hitters, good ballplayers. One was a catcher, one was an outfielder. We didn't have any color line.

How many years did you play altogether?

I played from 1931 or '32 up to 1947, and then I managed and coached Little League and Babe Ruth and semi-pro for 17 years after that in my hometown of Englewood, New Jersey.

We — my Mrs. and I — moved to Florida since I retired. She passed away a few years ago, but we moved here in 1987. Baseball is the reason for that. Ray Dandridge lived here and he was always after me. I told him the Mrs. and I were looking in Florida for a place to live. He said, "Why don't you come down here with me? Ain't nobody down here but me and my dog." So he talked me into coming down here and I'm still here. If I was younger I don't think I'd like it, but at my age it's great. I'm 85. I try to stay in shape.

Do you have any regrets from your baseball days?

No. If you can arrange it and I could get a chance to do it over again, don't change a thing. Let it go exactly the way it was.

You know, there's so much BS written about black people, but these people in baseball at that time were the finest people that you would ever want to be associated with and I would *gladly* do it over again. They were great athletes and they were wonderful people.

Remember we had the reunion in Kansas City? I came back from Kansas City and I had my family laughing. I said I never got so many hugs in all my life from *men!* I said, "I don't mind hugs from women, but these were men!" [Laughs] I had to get used to that.

Let me tell you what that's all about. We had a little group — you know how groups get together — and we started talking. This guy was saying, "Well, I started in 1947," or '49 or '50 or '55 or something like that. So after they all got through talking, I said, "Gee, it's nice to be around you young guys." They said, "When did you start, Al?" I said, "I started in 1931." They all grabbed me and started hugging me. "Man, if it wasn't for you we wouldn't be here talking like we are now." I got a lot of hugs. It was great.

When we left, you know what we told 'em? "When you gonna do this again?"

ALBERTUS A. "CLEFFIE" FENNAR
Born 5-12-11, Wilmington, NC
Ht. 5' 8"   Wt. 170   Batted and Threw R

Year	Team, league	Pos	G	AB	R	H	2B	3B	HR	RBI	SB	BA
1931	Lincoln Giants, ind.	SS-3B										
	Harlem Stars, ind.	SS-3B										
1932	N. Y. Black Yankees, ind.	SS										
	Brooklyn Royal Giants, ind.	INF										
1933	Brooklyn Royal Giants, NNL	INF										
1934	Atlantic City Bacarach Giants, NNL	SS-3B										
	Cuban Stars, ind.	INF										
	Pennsylvania Red Caps, ind.	INF										

Rodolfo Fernandez

Cuban Hall of Fame

Negro League Debut: 1932

Rodolfo "Rudy" Fernandez was born in Havana, Cuba, in 1911, and played more baseball there than anywhere else, but in 15 years as a professional pitcher, the righthander worked for teams in no fewer than *eight* countries: Cuba, the United States, Canada, Mexico, Nicaragua, Panama, Puerto Rico, and the Dominican Republic.

He played in this country for both the Cuban Stars and the New York Cubans in the 1930s. Unfortunately, there are no records to show what kind of pitcher Fernandez may have been, but to give an idea, here are a few facts that are known today:

1. The New York Giants were National League champions in 1936 and 1937. In an exhibition game in the winter of '37 in Cuba, Fernandez tossed a four-hitter and shut them out, 4–0.

2. In another exhibition game in Cuba, this time in the winter of '42, he shut out the NL champion Brooklyn Dodgers, 3–0.

3. In 1935 in Puerto Rico, he beat the Cincinnati Reds, 2–1.

4. He's a member of the Cuban Baseball Hall of Fame.

After his playing days, Rudy Fernandez became a coach and manager in Latin America, but made his home in New York City, where he still lives today in retirement. He played with or against some of the outstanding players of baseball history in every country that had a professional league in those days.

Rodolfo Fernandez: I started with Almendares baseball club in Habana. I played, I think, ten season with Almendares. Also, I play in the Mexican League, play in Provincial League in Canada — Sherbrooke — long time ago, around '44 or '45. I play in Venezuela, I play in Puerto Rico, play in Dominica Republica. I manage in Panama and Nicaragua — coach and manager. After that, I retire playing. I work at the baseball for a long, long time. I telling you, too many years ago. I don't remember exactly.

You were with the New York Cubans for a few years.

Yeah, I play with the New York Cubans. I play couple of seasons. Before, I play with the other team named Cuban Stars. But the Cuban Stars don't play in the Negro league; they play independent baseball. In 1935, play for New York Cubans. Decade of the '40, I play about five or six year because before, you know, we don't make money and we playing everywhere. Sometime play Mexico, play Venezuela. We play in the summer in Maracaibo and the Nicaragua Central League. We call it winter — we play in Puerto Rico, Dominica Republica. After that I retire. I pitch more than 15 year. We need to play around the year because we no

make the money. My best salary—
$400. Maracaibo in 1938.

*Your brother, Jose, played for the
New York Cubans and he was your
manager there.*

No, my brother don't play for the
New York Cubans. My brother play
and manage the Cuban Stars. After
that, he manage for the New York
Cubans.

*His son, Pepe, played in the Negro
leagues.*

He play for not too many years.
He played only two or three years.

*You had three really great exhibi-
tion games against major league
teams.*

The New York Giants—I remember the manager for that team. Bill
Terry. Remember Bill Terry? I beat
them, 4-nothing, in Cuba. The
other team, the Brooklyn Dodgers,
Durocher manage that year—3-
nothing.

In Puerto Rico the Cincinnati
Reds one year make spring training
there. I was there when the Cuban
All-Stars play in Puerto Rico for a
couple of week. I remember we play
three game with the Cincinnati Red.
We beat 'em, because the first game Martin
Dihigo pitch. Manuel Garcia—we call him
"Cocaina," nickname, you know—pitch
the second game. And the last game, I beat
Cincinnati, 2-1. Around '35 or '36.

I don't remember exactly because we
traveled too much because no have a
record. We have a record from the memory.
From the colored league we got nothing.

*Records or not, you had a reputation for
being a good pitcher. You're in the Cuban
Hall of Fame.*

Right. I was elected the Cuban Hall of
Fame about ten year [ago]. In Miami.

I pitch good ball in Cuba and everywhere because you need to play ball. You
no have the time for nothing. You play
around the year. I remember one year I
play in three different countries.

Rololfo Fernandez (courtesy of Rodolfo Fernandez).

The winter ball start playing right now.
The Venezuelan League, it start play. I
finish, then play in Puerto Rico and
Domenica Republica. The next year
because they start the season in October
and finish around February, play in the
Caribbean Series. And I play in Cuba in
1936 to '37 and '37 I play in Domenica
Republica. Satchel Paige, he pitch for us in
Domenica Republica. Call it Ciudad Trujillo. It's the name of the city when Trujillo
was president.

Do you know who was catching? Josh
Gibson. And in the outfield Cool Papa Bell.
You read something about him?

When I finish that year in Domenica
Republica, I going to Venezuela. I start in
Cuba, go to Domenica Republica, end in
Venezuela. I play over there I think about

*Rodolfo Fernandez (courtesy of the Negro Leagues Base-
ball Players Association; artist Ron Lewis).*

two or three months, then back to Cuba
and play in Cuba again.

We don't make money. Everybody in the
colored league, you don't have a room for
sleep. Sleep all the time in the bus. Pretty
rough. We used to wear only one uniform.

Right now, it's very easy for everybody.
Got everything. Somebody told me I born
too early. I said, "No. I happy to be born
early because I stay living now." Eighty-
four now. I very happy.

*Who were the best players you played with
or against?*

Oh, no. Too many, too many. I remember when the Giants play in Cuba, you
know who play right field? Mel Ott! He in
the Hall of Fame. And when I pitch to

Brooklyn, they have a strong team.
Pee Wee Reese play shortstop and
Billy Herman play second base and
the outfield, Joey Medwick and
Dixie Walker. Oh, too many, too
many!

Josh Gibson — oh, tremendous
hitter, man. He's a low ball hitter.
Oh, yeah. If Gibson play in the big
league, I think he make a record for
home run. Everybody say so.

And Cool Papa Bell. One of the
fastest men in baseball. A good
ballplayer.

Right now, everybody have a
chance to play. Before, too many
people don't play in the big league.
Too many people don't make a con-
sideration about the baseball we
play. Too many now — I don't call it
big league ballplayer because too
many teams. Before only eight team
in the National League and eight
team in the American League. Too
tough. I remember it. I saw Baby
Ruth and too many good ballplayers.
You had DiMaggio, Leo Durocher.
The first time I come into the country in U.S. in 1933 — I been 21 years
[old], I born in 1911 — I saw Lefty
Grove. Too many good ballplayers. I
remember Charlie Dressen manage
for Cincinnati when they make exhibition
games in Puerto Rico.

*Who was the best pitcher? You mentioned
Satchel Paige and Martin Dihigo.*

Well, they different because Satchel
weren't the best pitcher in the colored
league. Dihigo, he play in different position. He could pitch, too. Dihigo I think
the number one Cuban ballplayer. I no
compare right now because every year
everybody different. But Dihigo, he a
strong guy. Play good outfield, pitch —
everything he make easy. He's the most
wonderful baseball player I saw in my
life — Martin Dihigo.

Josh Gibson — he's a power hitter. I
don't know if you hear something about

Buck Leonard — play first base. Very good ballplayer. Gentleman. I remember when Buck Leonard and Josh Gibson play for the Homestead Gray. They got a good 1-2, one of best in the league. I pitch against them.

I around baseball for 45 year. And now I take it easy. When I finish play ball, I work in the hospital. I need to work. I got no money. Sometime I talk to too many about the salary we make. Three year straight we play ball in Puerto Rico for $8 a week. When Cincinnati make spring training over there where condition better, we make $15 a week. [Laughs] Believe it or not.

Does one game stand out?

One year I pitch a one-hitter in Cuban League — only 27 hitters because in the first inning somebody make a hit. He tried to go to second base and the catcher throw a *perfect* throw to make him out. My catcher that year — Mike Guerra. Remember him? He was a pretty good friend. He passed away a long time in Miami. He was my catcher. Only 27 men. I retire 24 men in a row, only one hit.

Sometimes I lose a couple of games, too, but everywhere I pitch I pitching good ball. Cuban League — a pretty good league, it's a strong league.

Do you think we'll get more Cuban players in this country?

I think too many good ballplayer in Cuba, but the government no give a chance to come here. Many ballplayer from Puerto Rico, from Venezuela, and from Dominica Republica, but right now I think about 14 or 15 from Cuban family, from Florida. Like [Tino] Martinez, play first base for Seattle [now with New York]. I think he born in Tampa. Canseco, Palmeiro, Rene Arocha. The government don't give a chance to come here to play. Everything, you work for the government, that's all. That guy [Castro], I don't like to talk about him.

The last time I was in Cuba in 1960 — 35 years ago. Everybody in my family has passed away. I lose about five sisters, my brother Jose. I have a niece about 74 year [old]. I don't go no more to Cuba. They give me the chance to go, I don't go. It's a different life now.

How long have you lived in New York?

Oh — 1944. You know, when I play ball I moving. Sometime, my wife, she stays home. I go to Puerto Rico, to Venezuela, but all the time back to New York. New York City. But before 1944, I play in the Negro league. I play in 1935, 1934. After that, I play in Puerto Rico, manage in Venezuela and everywhere. I was in Panama, too, and Nicaragua. I traveled.

Did you enjoy playing baseball?

Oh, sure, sure. I still like baseball. You know, I think the playoff is too long. The World Series may be coming in snow. [Laughs]

RODOLFO "RUDY" FERNANDEZ
Born 6-27-11, Guanabacoa, Havana, Cuba
Ht. 6' 1"   Wt. 190   Batted and Threw R

Year	Team, league
1932	Cuban Stars, ind.
1933	
1934	
1935	New York Cubans, NNL
1936	Cuban Stars, ind.
1939	New York Cubans, NNL
1943	

Fernandez played winter ball in Latin America, including a dozen seasons in his native Cuba. He was credited with a 4-5 record in 1937 with Ciudad Trujillo in the Dominican Republic; 8 wins in 1931-32 and 7-4 in 1939-40 with Almendares in the Cuban League; and 4-5, 4.52 in 1942 in the Mexican League. He remained an active player through 1947. Further records are not available.

Burnis "Wild Bill" Wright
The Complete Ballplayer

NEGRO LEAGUE DEBUT: 1932

The "complete" ballplayer — one who can literally do it all — is rare. "Complete" means a ballplayer who has the five tools — hitting, hitting with power, running, fielding, and throwing — to an extraordinary degree. Five *outstanding* tools.

Look down through the history of baseball. Who were the truly "complete" ballplayers — those outstanding in everything? Ty Cobb? No (his arm). Babe Ruth? No (his speed). Lou Gehrig? No (glove and speed). Joe DiMaggio? No (speed again). Ted Williams? No (glove, arm, speed). Mickey Mantle was probably one, but he was hurt. Willie Mays was the most complete ballplayer of the last 40 years, maybe of all-time in the major leagues. Barry Bonds and Ken Griffey, Jr., are, so far. And of all the men who have ever played major league baseball, that's about it.

But maybe the best never played in the major leagues because of his color. His name is Burnis "Wild Bill" Wright. His Negro leagues career ran from 1932 to 1945, and he played on through 1956 in Mexico.

Bill Wright was called "The Black Joe DiMaggio," and that was pretty flattering — to Joltin' Joe. Wright was bigger, stronger, and faster than DiMaggio. He had a better arm and was a better baserunner.

He batted a league-leading .488 for the Baltimore Elite Giants in 1939. Four eighty-eight is good for Little League, but this was against pitchers such as Satchel Paige, Hilton Smith, Leon Day, and Theolic Smith. Twice Wright led the Mexican League in batting and in 1943 won the Triple Crown. Among the players he beat were Hall of Famers Josh Gibson and Ray Dandridge.

He could circle the bases in 13.2 seconds. He led in stolen bases or was among the leaders annually. His range in the outfield dictated that he play center field, but he had a right-field arm so he played there, as well.

Look at his career stats. His Negro leagues batting average was .361, his Mexican League average was .336 and he played there until well into his forties. He appeared in seven Negro league All-Star games and batted .318. In 27 exhibition games versus major league pitching, he batted .371. This was against the likes of Bob Feller, Dizzy Dean, Bobo Newsom, Larry French, Ewell Blackwell, and Max Lanier.

Bill Wright is in the Mexican Baseball Hall of Fame and the local Aguascalientes Hall of Fame. He needs to be in one more: Cooperstown.

Do you belong in the Hall of Fame?

I think so, sure. I should be in if they're gonna put anyone in. I should be in there.

You began as a pitcher. Is that how you got your nickname?

Yeah. I was a pretty good hitter, you know. I was young when I started out. I was 15 when I started in training with the Nashville Elite Giants. See, that was in April and I was gonna be 16 in June. I quit pitchin' 'cause they needed outfielders. I was a good outfielder; I mean, I believe I was as good an outfielder as anyone they had on the team. When I was a kid that's all we did was play baseball.

When did you learn to switch hit?

I started that as a kid, too. See, I was one of the better ballplayers — hitters — so when I hit against righthanders, I had to bat righthanded. When they pitched a lefthander, they made me bat lefthanded. I become a switch hitter there. They made me do it because I could hit better than anyone else as a kid, around 11 or 12 years old.

You were always with the Elite Giants.

Yeah, I didn't play with any other team in the States.

Is there any game that stands out?

Well, you have so many. I played so long, you know, you never think about anything. Like some guys buy the newspaper to see what happened and what it says about them. No, I wasn't that kind of a ballplayer.

In 1939, you batted .488.

I could drag — drag bunt — and I was fast. Really fast. So that's what kept me up in the batting average all the time. When I hit, the first baseman had to play in — he

Burnis "Wild Bill" Wright (courtesy of Bill Wright).

couldn't play too far back and I could pull the ball. I was strictly a pull hitter, so I'd hit the ball by him. It's easy if you learn how. I had a good teacher in baseball — an old guy, Joe Truett; he's one of the oldest ballplayers. That guy could just foul those balls, foul those balls. He taught me how to do everything I knew about baseball.

They called you "The Black Joe DiMaggio," but you could outrun him and outthrow him.

Yeah, I could outrun him easy. [Laughs] I could run rings around him.

1939 Baltimore Elite Giants—winter team
Back row (L. to R.): Pepper Bassett, John Terry, Wild Bill Wright, Bill Hoskins, unidentified, Green (secretary), unidentified, unidentified, Lonnie Summers, Jim West, Mitchell. Front Row (L. to R.): Marlin Carter, Hoss Walker, Bill Harvey, Lefty Glover, Jake Dunn, Terris McDuffie. Kneeling in front: Bat boy (courtesy of Bill Wright).

Who were some of the best pitchers you faced?

I faced Leon Day, I faced Satchel Paige, I faced Hilton Smith. There's so many good pitchers we had in those days. Satch was the best, naturally. He hit 95 to a hundred, you know. When he wanted to throw, he could *throw*. He was amazing. He barnstormed all over—North Dakota, South Dakota, Oklahoma. When we played the major leaguers in Los Angeles and all—exhibition games—in September and October, we'd say, "That guy can hit low pitchin', Satch." He'd say, "I'm gonna find out if he can hit low pitches." And he'd throw him right down where he could hit it and he couldn't hit it. He was *blazin'!*

In those exhibition games against major league pitchers, you batted .371. Some people write it off as just exhibitions, but those guys didn't want you to get hits off of them.

No, they didn't wanna get beat. No. You know, that kinda looked bad for us to beat 'em. Bob Feller, you know, he pitched years

and years on the coast in L.A.—three to five innings—and he never could beat us.

They had a pitcher out there about five years and he finally beat us one game and he quit pitchin'. His name was Larry French. He pitched out there one day, I think it was just before Christmas; he said, "I don't give a damn if you guys are drunk or what, I don't care. I beat you, so I'm quitting!" [Laughs]

You went to Mexico to play. Why?

They were just after me 'bout goin' down, goin' down. There was only three games a week and we didn't travel any. When we traveled, it was by plane or by train. Better travelin' conditions; we didn't have to ride [a bus] too much.

You wouldn't believe this. We played in Cleveland—night game. We left Cleveland between 11 and 12 at night. We had a four-team doubleheader in New York at Yankee Stadium [the next day] and we had to play the first game. Now you know how we traveled. It's around 500 miles. [Laughs] We had to be there at 1:00, so we rode all night long. All we did was pass by and throw the bags in the hotel and kept on goin' to the ballpark.

You must have spent a lot of nights on a bus.

Yeah. A little less than the Grays. The Grays, we went trippin' with them once. We went out with the Grays and we played Chambersburg, Harrisburg, and all through there, you know, and make the same amount of money, but with the Grays you spend it all on gasoline and driving. So we quit. We didn't ride too much out that way.

Did the Grays have better financial backing?

No, they didn't have any better backin'. That wasn't it. The thing about it, they traveled so much. Our secretary said, "Why travel so much when you make the same amount of money around here?" You know, we played Red Bank and over that way. That's when I first seen Pete Gray, the one-armed ballplayer. 'Member him? I think it was in Red Bank. I don't know how he could do it. He could catch that ball and throw that glove up and throw. He had a *good* arm. He could *throw* it.

You came back to Baltimore from Mexico and then returned in 1946. What did the Pasquel brothers offer to get you back down there?

It was about the same [as the U.S.]. We could have a little more money, but it's just like I said, it was much easier in baseball. We didn't have to travel so much. We played Mexico City Friday, Saturday, and Sunday and the other cities we only played Saturday and Sunday, doubleheader on Sunday, so we didn't have to travel too much. We practiced durin' the week.

In 1943, you won the Triple Crown down there.

That was the year Dandridge had me by about three points in the battin' average. We was talkin' that night. He said, "You can be the home run leader and I'm gonna take the battin' average." So I just said,

"We'll see Sunday." I had to at least get two hits more than him, so the first time I dragged a bunt and got on. [Laughs] He missed. Next time up, he got a base hit, so that put us even. So he got two and I got three. He got 2-for-5 and I got 3-for-4, so I beat him out. By two points or somethin' like that.

It was good baseball down there. They had better Mexican ballplayers than they do now. I don't know why we don't have many Mexican ballplayers in the major leagues.

Why did you decide to stay in Mexico?

I was livin' in Los Angeles, you know, and Los Angeles got a little rough so I decided to stay here. It's [L.A.] real bad now—*real* bad—so I'm glad I decided to stay here. This was a small city where I'm livin'. It only had 75,000 when I first came here—1953. Now we have almost a million 'cause we have a lot of industry now. We have that Nissan and it's growin' big and big and big here in Aguascalientes.

Do you still have your restaurant?

I retired a long time ago. My kids have it now. My wife is Hawaiian.

In 1950, Rufus Lewis was knocked out with a bat by Lorenzo Cabrera. You saved Lewis's life.

I had—what do you call that thing you get in your eye?—a sty-like, you know. I was playin' the outfield and I couldn't look up—it hurt—so I came out of the ballgame. When the time for me to come up to bat, the guy that went in for me, it was time for him to hit.

So we were sittin' there on the bench and a boy of the name Grisham—Bob Grisham, a big pitcher—say, "How could he hit with that little bat?" I says, "That's the bat he hit with, it's a 34 but good wood." So he didn't get the good wood on it; he made a pop fly out in the outfield, almost fell for a Texas Leaguer and we was talkin' about it.

Cabrera come to bat [the next inning]. We said to Lewis to pitch in on him 'cause he hit to right field. He could hit to right field a long ways, he could hit home runs to right field. So we was tryin' to pitch in on him. I said throw him a curveball but throw the curveball inside, be sure you throw it right at him and be sure to make it break inside corner. So he threw the curveball but it didn't break so the ball went all the way back to the stands. I reckon it brushed him but we said it didn't even hit him. The umpire said it brushed his uniform. So he was walkin' down to first base with the bat in his hand. He's on a little bit of the infield on the grass side, so when he got even with Lewis he made a dash for Lewis. When he hit him [with the bat], he knocked him down. By that time, me and Grisham was on top of him. He had his bat up in the air to hit him when he was layin' on the ground. If he got him on the ground, he would have killed him.

He won the [batting] championship that year and he was kinda headstrong. Some guys can't take it. It didn't hit him; I know it didn't hit him. It might have brushed his uniform 'cause the ball went all the way back to the backstop and that was about eight or ten yards back to the grandstand. He wasn't throwin' at him because you had a man on first base and we were down two runs. You couldn't throw at nobody in that situation. He was tryin' to pitch in on him, keep him from hittin' the ball — try to make him hit into a double play.

He had did that the day before. He had run into a little shortstop and we had to take him offa the shortstop — Mexican boy, maybe about 165 pounds and Cabrera weighed over 200. We had to take him off the boy. He was runnin' out there, gonna jump on that little young kid. So that Sunday he did it.

We're friends. We speak. He thanked me for comin' in and stoppin' him, you know, 'cause he'da been in jail right now as far as

Pasquel was concerned, 'cause he said he'da put him in jail for life. He's a coach for the Jalisco ball team. He's way up in his 60s.

You're in the Mexican Baseball Hall of Fame.

I got in there in 19-, I think it was 82. Late, *real* late. I think that [the fight] had a lot to do with it, you know. We have one here in Aguascalientes, too. A little hall of fame.

Who was the best player you saw?

I think Martin Dihigo was the best player because he could hit, he could pitch, he could play first base, he could play outfield, he could play second base. He was a tremendous ballplayer. He was Cuban. I seen him play everything but catch; I never seen him catch. Big guy, too —'bout 6-foot-5. He could throw. He could bring it about 92; he could throw that ball. He was a good ballplayer.

You were a big man, too, about 6-4, 200-something.

210 or somewhere along there.

Do you have any regrets from your career?

No, I didn't have any regrets at all. The only regrets I have, I should have had a higher salary.

What was your top salary?

Seven hundred. The owners look at the grandstand and not too many people and they had a lotta exhibition games. The owners had a pretty tough time, you know, tryin' to keep that team together. Thomas T. Wilson — he was a great guy in baseball. He was the owner that bought the Elite Giants.

Did you enjoy your baseball career?

I really did. I really enjoyed it.

Would you do it again?

I would. If I had to I'd do it all over again. As a kid comin' up I'd have to try it over again.

BURNIS "WILD BILL" WRIGHT
Born 6-6-14, Milan, TN Died 8-3-96, Aquascalientes, Mexico
Ht. 6' 4"   Wt. 220   Batted B Threw R

Year	Team, league	Pos	G	AB	R	H	2B	3B	HR	RBI	SB	BA
1932	Nashville Elite Giants, NSL	OF	12	40		12	1	1	0		2	.300
1933	Nashville Elite Giants, NNL	OF	21	78		19	2	2	0		0	.244
1934		OF	12	50		6	0	1	3		2	.120
1935	Columbus Elite Giants, NNL	OF	21	82		20	1	0	2		4	.244 (.288)
1936	Washington Elite Giants, NNL	OF	21	74		25	2	5	1		2	.338 (.365)
1937		OF	31	100		41	4	2	7			.410
1938	Baltimore Elite Giants, NNL	OF	35	174	73	55	11	10	7	27	19	.316 (.235)
1939		OF	27	99		40	1	3	3		2	.404 (.488)*
1942		OF	44	167		54	14	2	1		2	.323
1944		OF	2	8		5	0	0	2		0	.625
1945		OF	44	165	34	62	11	8	5	52	17	.301 (.382)

The statistics for Wright are among the most confusing of all the Negro leagues players. Different sources give highly varying numbers; the batting averages shown above are from two different sources and neither may actually be correct.

Record in Mexico.

Year	Team, league	Pos	G	AB	R	H	2B	3B	HR	RBI	SB	BA
1940	Mex. City, Santa Rosa, Mex	OF	87	350	94	126	30*	10	8	67	29	.360
1941	Mexico City, Mex	OF	100	387	98	151	25	9	17	85	26*	.390*
1943		OF	88	352	65	129	25	5	13*	70*	21	.366*
1944		OF	87	334	59	112	24	7	10	60	14	.335
1946		OF	85	316	47	95	11	8	5	52	17	.301
1947		OF	79	249	36	76	10	4	3	38	13	.305
1948	Monterrey. Mex	OF	68	258	47	86	16	3	0	32	12	.333
1949	Torreon, Mexico City, Mex	OF	74	293	48	81	14	3	7	43	3	.276
1950	Mexico City, Mex	OF	63	248	32	75	10	1	2	31	5	.302
1951	Mex. City, Nuevo Laredo, Mex	OF	30	104	23	38	10	2	2	25	2	.365
1952	Orizaba, MxSE	OF		129		43						.333
1955	Aquascalientes, MxC	OF	68	250	49	75	12	3	3	40	6	.300
1956		OF	79	297	48	102	8	3	8	45	7	.343

Record in Puerto Rico.

Year	Team, league	Pos	G	AB	R	H	2B	3B	HR	RBI	SB	BA
1941–42	San Juan, PRWL	OF		157		44			4	27		.280

Buck Leonard
Hall of Fame

NEGRO LEAGUE DEBUT: 1933

Buck Leonard could play baseball. As a batter he was compared to Lou Gehrig, as a fielder to George Sisler and Hal Chase. From the mid–1930s to the mid–1940s, it has been estimated that he *averaged* 34 home runs a year. Those who observed him throughout his career say he hit more than 500.

The complete records are not available today and it's a loss. It's a loss, too, that he never played in the major leagues where he belonged, but he was a victim of his times.

What is known of his record, though, shows that Buck Leonard was superb. He played only semi-pro ball until he was 26 or his legend today would be even larger than it is, but once he began playing professionally — a career that lasted until he was 48 years old — he was awesome. The partial records show a Negro leagues batting average of .340, a Mexican leagues average of .323 (compiled from the ages of 43 to 47), a Negro leagues All-Star average of .317 in 12 games with a record three home runs, a .433 playoff average, a .320 Negro World Series average, and an exhibition average of .382 versus white major league barnstorming teams. In 1953, at the age of 45, he played ten games for Portsmouth, Virginia, in the Piedmont League and batted .333 (11-for-33)!

Leonard played 17 years for the Washington, D.C.–based Homestead Grays as well as several years for other teams. He led various leagues in home runs at least three times and in average at least twice. Several times his slugging average exceeded .700.

Leonard was called "The Black Lou Gehrig," a nickname equally flattering to Gehrig, and he teamed on the Grays with Josh Gibson, "The Black Babe Ruth," to form the most feared 1-2 punch in the history of Negro leagues baseball as the Grays dominated the Negro National League, winning nine straight league championships from 1937 through 1945. The Grays won again in 1948, after Gibson's death, and the 40-year-old Leonard may have won the Triple Crown that year. He led in home runs and average, but RBI records were not kept accurately.

Buck Leonard and his slugging teammate Gibson were elected to the Hall of Fame in 1972.

You didn't begin your professional baseball career until you were 26 years old. Why?

I was workin' at the railroad shop and playin' ball every time I got a chance. I got cut off at the railroad shop and I started playin' [professional] ball. I lost my job. I enjoyed playin' baseball. I was playin' baseball in the evenin's when I got off from work. Semi-pro.

Whom did you sign your first pro contract with?

The Baltimore Black Sox. In 1934 is

when the Homestead Grays got me. I was 27 years old and I was there 17 years.

Do you know how many home runs you hit?

No, I don't know. I can't keep up with 'em.

It's been estimated that you averaged 34 or 35 a year for a seven- or eight-year period.

That's just about right. The pitchin' was weak then.

An awful lot of fellows were facing that same pitching and not hitting 35 home runs a year, so don't diminish your ability.

[Hearty laugh] That's right.

Speaking of pitching, who was the best pitcher you saw?

Satchel Paige. He was in that same league I was in for about three years. He pitched for the Pittsburgh team — the Crawfords. My team, we had Raymond Brown. He was a pretty good pitcher. Connie Johnson was in the colored leagues.

Who was the best player?

Josh Gibson was a good catcher. He caught for us for nine years. He said he hit 70 [home runs] one year.

How long were your seasons?

We started playin' about the spring and played on. We traveled all over the country. We went to the West Coast to play exhibition baseball games.

You played a few years down in Mexico.

We only played Tuesday, Thursday, Saturday, and Sunday. We had about half the time off. They only allowed three [U.S. players] on each team — black players and white players. The best ball was played over here. Mexico only had three [U.S.] players on each team; all the others were Mexican players. I played 17 years in the United States and five years in Mexico.

Clark Griffith approached you and Gibson in 1939 about playing for him. What happened?

We didn't ever know what happened. He

Buck Leonard (courtesy of Buck Leonard).

asked us would we like to play in the major leagues and we told him yeah. He asked us if we thought we could make the major leagues and we told him we were tryin'. He told us we would hear from him and we didn't ever hear from him again.

[Later] Bill Veeck asked me to try out with a team. I told him, "No, I can't try out with a team. I'm too old now." I was in my 40s.

Were you approached when Jackie Robinson was signed?

No. I was too old then. I was about 40 or 42 or 43.

In the exhibitions against the white teams, what kind of pitching were you facing?

It was first-line major league pitchers. We were throwin' mediocre pitchers at them. If we were playin' a good team — a

Homestead Grays, 1946
(L.-R.): Sam Bankhead (.358 for the season), Josh Gibson (.379), Buck Leonard (.322), Dave
Hoskins (.260), Jerry Benjamin (.296). Gibson died in January 1947 (author's collection).

good major league team — we'd pitch a
good pitcher but against ordinary teams
we'd just use ordinary pitchers.

We always could get baseball players
who could hit. We found out that players
that could hit could take care of major
league baseball. We always carried players
that could hit.

How much money were you making?

$80 a month to start. The highest I *ever*
got was a thousand dollars a month. I was
about 44, 45 years old then.

*The Grays dominated Negro baseball in
the '30s and '40s.*

We had good hitters. That's what we dominated with — good hitters. We always found
good hitters. That's what we advocated.

*How do you think players like you and
Gibson and Paige would have fared in the
major leagues?*

We could have made it. Yeah, we could
have made it.

Would you be a ballplayer again?

I reckon so. I liked it.

WALTER FENNER "BUCK" LEONARD
Born 9-8-07, Rocky Mount, NC
Ht. 5' 10"   Wt. 185   Batted and Threw L

Year	Team, league	Pos	G	AB	R	H	2B	3B	HR	RBI	SB	BA
1933	Brooklyn Royal Giants, NNL	1B										
1934	Homestead Grays, NNL	1B	9	35		14	1	0	2		0	.400
1935		1B	35	151		51	14	2	2		0	.338
1936		1B	5	21		5	1	0	3		0	.238
1937		1B	14	54		18	1	0	2		0	.333
1938		1B	18	58		20		0	4		0	.345

Year	Team, league	Pos	G	AB	R	H	2B	3B	HR	RBI	SB	BA
1939		1B	25	69		22	2	0	4		0	.319
1940		1B	52	175		67	15	3	8*		2	.383
1941		1B	37	116		37	4	5	6		2	.319
1942		1B	20	79		14	4	0	0		3	.177
1943		1B		187		56	11	11	3		0	.299
1944		1B	48	161	32	51	11	6	7	30	1	.317
1945		1B	40	144	29	54	9	4	6	25	1	.375
1946		1B	37	118	28	38	5	4	5	37	2	.322
1947		1B	31	105	31	43	11		7		1	.410
1948		1B	47	157		62			13*			.395*
1949	Homestead Grays, NAL	1B										
1950		1B										
1953	Portsmouth, PiedL	1B	10	33	5	11	2	0	0	4	1	.333

Record in Latin America.

Year	Team, league	Pos	G	AB	R	H	2B	3B	HR	RBI	SB	BA
1936-37	Marianao, CubWL	1B		171	26	52	3	1	1	19	4	.304
1940-41	Mayaquez, PRWL	1B		118	45	46	17*	0	8*			.390
1948-49	Marianao, CubWL	1B	30	65	9	15	4	0	2	18	0	.231
1951	Torreon, MexL	1B	83	273	64	88	19	1	14	64	5	.322
1952		1B	86	295	50	96	15	1	8	71	12	.325
1953		1B	58	190	39	63	20	2	5	38	4	.332
1955	Durango, CMexL	1B	62	218	46	68	14	3	13	60		.312

Josh Johnson

From Catching to College

NEGRO LEAGUE DEBUT: 1934

Fifty and sixty years ago, a college-educated baseball player was a rarity. Indeed, many never even finished high school. And once a player reached the top there was little chance for college — no time, no incentive. So Josh Johnson was definitely a different breed.

After graduating high school in 1931, he entered semi-pro ball and within three years was with the great Homestead Grays. A catcher, he was successful with several teams, but eventually rejoined the Grays in 1940. That year, Hall of Fame catcher Josh Gibson was lured to Mexico to play. In his stead, Johnson responded by batting .429 in league games.

Before this, though, there had been the desire to go to college — he wanted to be a teacher — so in 1937, six years after high school, he entered Cheyney Teachers' College, carried a full load of classes, and graduated in four years. Then he earned his master's degree at Penn State in one year. All the while, he played a full season of baseball every summer.

After serving in World War II, he spent the rest of his working life in education. It was baseball's loss.

I played semi-pro after high school. The Grays brought me up for a look-see in 1934 and sent me back. I played semi-pro in Pittsburgh. That's my home.

Josh Gibson at that time was with the Crawfords. Gus Greenlee had just about decimated the Grays. He took the good ballplayers, all but Buck [Leonard]. He didn't take Buck but he took Josh Gibson and several other players and put them on his team, the Pittsburgh Crawfords.

Back in '34 I was playing with a team called the Pittsburgh Giants, a semi-pro team; it served as a little farm team — a feeder team for the Grays and Crawfords. Both the Grays' catchers got hurt in '34. Satchel Paige pitched that same day — the Fourth of July. He pitched a no-hitter against the Grays.

The Grays needed a catcher so they came down on the lots and got me and I finished out the season with them. I caught the second game that day.

In '35 they formed a team down in Cincinnati. They sent me down to the Pittsburgh Giants again and then they shifted me over to the Cincinnati Tigers — me and Jelly Taylor, Neil Robinson, and a few other guys. We formed the nucleus of the Cincinnati Tigers ballclub.

It was an independent team then. We stayed there for three years, but later it became a member of the Negro American League and Double Duty Radcliffe came down and managed it. In the American League we finished third behind Kansas City and the American Giants. We had a young ballclub. I was there '35, '36, and '37. In '38 all the players went to Memphis but me. I went over to the New York Black Yankees in '38.

I played there in '38, and in '39 I was over playing with the Brooklyn Royal Giants. In '40

I rejoined the Grays. That was the year that Josh Gibson and several other major leaguers went down to Mexico and played for the Pasquel brothers. They were passing out a lot of pesos. They raided the team and took Gibson and that left a vacancy; they knew where I was so they called me and had me rejoin them.

I had good years with the Black Yankees and Brooklyn. I went over to Brooklyn because Fats Jenkins was manager and he and I were good friends. We were teammates on the Black Yankees. He got the Brooklyn job and asked me to come go with him, so I did. It's pretty much like these guys are doing today with St. Louis and Oakland. LaRussa's taking his boys and Jenkins took me. Jenkins was the old New York Renaissance basketball player, too. He was the captain of the Rens. He played left field for the Black Yankees.

My last full year was with the Grays [1941]. I came out to Illinois to teach school and coach athletics down here in Madison, near the St. Louis area. The Black Yankees and Birmingham came through there on Decoration Day in '42 and played a doubleheader over in old Sportsman's Park in St. Louis. I was just over the river in Illinois and I went over the night before and visited the guys.

I walked in the hotel and they said, "Hey, where in the heck you been? We been lookin' for you." I said, "I've been over there across the river teaching school." That was the last day of school — graduation day — and they said, "You lookin' for a job?" and I said, "Yeah. I'm going back East." So they said, "Put your stuff on the bus, come on over tomorrow, and we'll get you in the second game of the doubleheader." So I did. I hadn't had a ball in my hands except around the schoolhouse.

I caught the second game of the doubleheader and threw my stuff on the bus. We barnstormed from St. Louis all the way back East to Philadelphia, through Indiana, Ohio, and on back in to Philadelphia. When we got to Philly, I got off the bus.

There was a request there for candidates to get in the war effort in the navy yard in Philadelphia. That was my line of work, industrial arts — sheet metal, shop work, that kind of stuff. My sister said, "You ought to try this."

I told the manager — his name was Tex Burnett — I said, "Tex, I can continue with you but I don't want to get drafted. I can go down there and get in the ship-building program and play on weekends." That lasted about six weeks and I got drafted anyway. [Laughs] That's the way my luck was running. I was drafted in August. I was in four years. I went to OCS when I went in; I was a second lieutenant but I'm a major now. Retired. I stayed in the reserves.

You were still a young man when you ended your playing days.

Yeah. I was 28. I was 32, going on 33, when I got out. I returned to teaching and coaching.

I worked up to principal and then I joined the state school superintendent's staff as an assistant. I worked at the state level for about 15 years. I retired in '78 from the education office and I was appointed by the governor to the state board of elections and I served on that for ten years. I served 'til '88 and then I retired. All I do now is go around to Negro League reunions and card shows and stuff like that.

Talk about the conditions during your playing days.

When we came along, we started out getting paid by passing the hat and dividing the money up after expenses. As we moved along, the first contract I got I agreed to $60 a month and room and board.

In small towns there weren't any black hotels and you had to either sleep in the bus or someone would take you to their home. Even when you came to St. Louis you couldn't stay in a good hotel. In Chicago they had some pretty good black hotels. As I recall, Birmingham, Montgomery, Atlanta, Indianapolis — there were

Josh Johnson (courtesy of Josh Johnson).

black hotels. You couldn't stay in a white hotel anywhere back then.

There were the segregation laws and signs were up at drinking fountains and restrooms. There was quite a difference in maintenance between the white restrooms and the black. It didn't say "Black"; it said "Colored Men" and "Colored Women."

And you had to go around to the rear to get served a meal. If there was a colored entrance, it was on one side of the counter and the white was on the other side. If a white man was with you, he couldn't eat on your side. It was that way in the service. A white buddy and I thought, since we were on the post, we could eat together. We went to the restaurant and this young lady came over and she said, "I'm sorry, but I can't serve him." And he said, "Why not?" He got very indignant. She said, "You have to go to the other side of the counter."

Our transportation — we didn't ride on Pullman coaches. In the early days when Rube Foster formed this league, he started out riding his men on trains but most of the owners couldn't continue that. They had cars — limousines that funeral directors turned in and they would be purchased by the baseball owners. They all had jump seats in them like taxi cabs and we'd put a board between those seats and put an extra man on there. There was only about 15 men on a squad and that wasn't because there weren't enough players. They just didn't have enough money and room to carry them.

The Grays and the Crawfords around Pittsburgh pretty much had the pick of the crop. The overflow — the good youngsters they had coming out of school and off the sandlots — they put them on one team. That was the Pittsburgh Giants. We'd pick up some of the surplus bookings the Grays and Crawfords got. If they had a couple of spare players that weren't going to play in that next game, they'd send them down to the little team to work with us — keep them in shape like they do in the majors now. It was a rough way of doing what they do now — shuttle players between St. Louis and Louisville. It was the same thing but it wasn't called that.

We'd play towns like Erie, Fairmont, West Virginia, and all those places. Those bookings were done on a guarantee. You'd get a rain guarantee and also with the Grays or Crawfords, they agreed to pay a certain amount of money. That money the manager would take and split a portion of it among the players. We did hat-passing back on a lower level.

Who were the best players you saw?

I'd have to say by position because you

Josh Johnson (courtesy of Josh Johnson).

can't compare a pitcher with an everyday man.

[Martin] Dihigo I remember when I first came up. He could do almost anything. I didn't play against [Oscar] Charleston; he was managing then.

When I came up in '34, Smokey Joe Williams had come out of retirement. Cum Posey, the owner of the Grays, had brought him out of retirement and would dress him out and he'd go with the team just to make spot appearances. He was the Satchel Paige of his day. Before Satchel it was all Smokey Joe Williams. He was the best thing going.

All of us kids on the lots down in semi-pro, we wanted to be like Smokey even though we weren't pitching. We wanted to emulate Smokey Joe Williams; his name was a household word. He had a lot of fans throughout the area where we traveled. He had been a fixture with the Grays.

So he traveled around with us and I had a chance to catch him when I came up. It was exciting for me. Here I was, trying to emulate him on the lots and now I'm sitting in the dugout with him. He's telling me about the different batters. If he knew he was going to pitch that day, he'd call me and say, "Come on, kid, let's sit down here and go to school," meaning he was going to teach me something about the hitters. We'd sit there and he'd tell me about this one and that one.

He would tell me, to protect me and to help me retain confidence, he said, "You go ahead and call your game. If I don't agree with it, I won't toe the rubber," meaning he won't get on the mound. When I'd give a signal and he'd toe the rubber, I'd know that's the one he wanted. In effect, he was calling the game. [Laughs] What he was doing, he was trying to protect me from the hecklers in the stands. I knew what he was doing and I felt good about it. He didn't shake his head; he said, "I won't shake you off," because if the hecklers in the stands or the armchair managers saw that, they'd say, "Aw, that kid doesn't know anything." Word gets out: "They've got a know-nothing catcher." [Laughs] That helped me over a lot of humps.

How did he compare with Satchel?

I saw Satch pitch in his prime and he would throw aspirin tablets. He could throw. They compared Smokey Joe with Walter Johnson and Christy Mathewson. Smokey Joe was in his prime when they were pitching. It's like they compared Dizzy and Satch — both could fire the ball. And Bobby Feller.

But Satch was good. There's no way about it. His strong suit was control and a blazing fastball. His curveball was a change of pace, more or less, by comparison.

Back then — in the '20s, '30s, and '40s — every town in western Pennsylvania and

Ohio and Kentucky and they tell me Illinois had a ballclub — town team. They'd go out and load up their lineups when he was going to come through. We'd play a guy here one night and the next day he's over in the next county playing for them. They were proud of their teams and a lot of times the whole town would close up; everybody would converge on the ballpark.

And, oddly enough, soccer was that way in western Pennsylvania then, too. They had a lot of people from Europe in the steel mills and coal mines and all the industries and they brought their values and customs with them and soccer was their national game. The young kids played it but you'd find older guys playing soccer, too.

Would you be a ballplayer again?

If I was coming along now? Well, I played all three — basketball, football, and baseball — and I liked them all. I liked football, although I didn't earn any money doing it. [Laughs] I didn't earn much playing baseball. I liked them equally well.

What was your top salary?

I got $345 a month. That was just at the beginning of the war. Some of the guys who played during the war tell me they made better than that, and they got more meal money.

For meal money, first we got 50 cents, then 75, and then I got a dollar-and-a-half with the Grays. Buck Leonard told me, "Before you came with us, we wasn't getting but a dollar." [Laughs] We could eat on a dollar then; I tell the kids when I go around to these schools today, they can't even get a malt and a hamburger now.

I always had a desire to go to college and I finished high school in '31. It was six years before I got a chance to go to college. Once I got a chance, I went on and put in five years straight. I had my schooling in before I went to the ship yards. I'd just gotten my master's that year before — in '41. I went to Penn State and did a whole year. I got out in May and came out here to Illinois that fall and taught a year. After that I got drafted. Forty-two was the year the Black

Yankees and Birmingham came through St. Louis and I rejoined them.

There were no student loans, no scholarship money available. I saved what I got. I had to work on the campus, do odd jobs and things like that, and I'd leave campus every year with a bill and I had to come back, pay up that, and start a new one next year.

I was motivated by my coaches in high school and by the people around me — my environment, more or less. I knew playing ball wasn't going to get me anywhere. I could see my teammates in the winter; they were bell-hopping around hotels, they were working in the train stations red-capping, some were even working on the WPA following the city maintenance crews. Those were honest jobs — nothing wrong with the jobs — but you can't make any money doing that. You've got to have something else; when you look down the road, that's not going to take you too far. And I knew that baseball wasn't going to take me that far — or any other sport. I saw it then.

We were all hoping back then — a lot of us were — that the big leagues would open up and that the situation and conditions wouldn't exist forever. We were told by a lot of forward-thinking adults at that time, "You guys just keep on playing and do your best, because you never know who's watching. Sooner or later, they're going to pick guys like you." That was the one thing that kept me in school.

Back then, a lot of guys — Billy Yancey and a lot of players out of New York — were going down in the Dominican Republic, playing down in South America and those places. They had to do that, they had to play the year around to make ends meet.

One day I went down to the Black Yankees office — we had to convene there to get on the bus — and there was this guy in the main office talking to the owner, trying to line up ballplayers to go down to play in the winter league in Venezuela. I walked in and I heard them talking baseball so I slowed down to see what was going on. They wanted a catcher, so I started toward the door and Jenkins, my manager, said, "Where you going, Johnny?" He called me Johnny.

"I'm going and talk to the man, see if I can get on." I figured I could lay out of school one year and go down there and play, make four or five hundred bucks, and come back. Man, that's almost a semester's fee. If I stayed all winter, I might be lucky and make a whole year's worth. I wouldn't have to wash dishes, sweep, haul out ashes, and all that kind of stuff. [Laughs] I could spend more time studying and taking it easy. Or so I thought.

He said, "I'll tell you what. If you take one more step toward that office, I'll take this fungo and wear you out as long as I can keep up with you." He was a little guy, too. [Laughs] I had a lot of respect for him — that's why I played for him. He said, "You don't need to go down there. We're all proud of you in school and you should stay in school and finish." I had two more years to go. He said, "We'll send you a box score paper and send you what the guys are doing and you can read all about it. We'll tell you about it when we come back." You know, they sent me that stuff — they sent me those clippings from down there.

Before they left, we had an all-star team in New York — barnstorming — and at the end of that season the guys passed the hat among themselves. They did it while I was in the shower. When I came out, they had about a $190 in a hat and the manager and the owner kicked in some money. They gave it to me to help me back in school. That's what they thought about education.

Some of those guys were off the farm — I could see where they didn't have a chance to go [to college]. Some of them hadn't even been to grade school. All they knew was baseball and that's all they were going to do until they got to where they couldn't do it. They realized what was down the road for them and they didn't want to see me mess up. I always appreciated that and I think about it a lot.

JOSHUA "BRUTE" JOHNSON

Born 1-24-13, Evergreen, AL

Ht. 6' 1"   Wt. 195   Batted and Threw R

Year	Team, league	Pos	G	AB	R	H	2B	3B	HR	RBI	SB	BA
1934	Homestead Grays, NNL	C										
1935	Homestead Grays, NNL	C										
	Cincinnati Tigers, ind.	C										
1936	Cincinnati Tigers, ind.	C										.289
1937	Cincinnati Tigers, NAL	C										
1938	N. Y. Black Yankees, NNL	C										
	Homestead Grays, NNL	C										
1939	Brooklyn Royal Giants, ind.	C										
	Homestead Grays, NNL	C										
1940	Homestead Grays, NNL	C										.429
1941	Homestead Grays, NNL	C										
1942	Homestead Grays, NNL	C										
	N. Y. Black Yankees, NNL	C										

Edsall Walker

"Big"

NEGRO LEAGUE DEBUT: 1934

He was a lefthanded pitcher with a 100 mph fastball. He joined the Homestead Grays in 1936 with the nickname "The Catskill Wild Man," a commentary on his control. And he would warn a batter that he might throw at him. With that combination, it took a pretty strong heart to dig in too deeply when Edsall Walker was on the mound.

One of the top pitchers in the Negro leagues during his decade there, he was one of three Walkers on the Grays. He was the biggest, so he became known as "Big." He teamed with righthander Raymond Brown to head a formidable rotation which also included Roy Partlow and Roy Welmaker at various times. To complement his spot as starter, he was also the Grays' top relief pitcher. The Negro leagues' records are incomplete or non-existent, but in 40- to 60-game league schedules Big Walker had individual seasonal marks of 10–5, 8–1, and 8-3 for years that statistics are available.

Even with these records and even considering the fact that the Grays won nine consecutive pennants, Walker never received the acclaim he should have, nor did many of the other team members. Instead, the ink was used on some of the greatest ballplayers in history: Josh Gibson, Buck Leonard, and Cool Papa Bell — legends all.

But having teammates such as Edsall Walker did a whole lot to ensure that those three were kept in the limelight. They couldn't have done it without help, and Big was there when they needed him.

You joined the Grays in 1936. How did they acquire you?

I was playin' here in Albany with a team here and on the team was an old guy that used to be in the Negro League named Scrappy Brown out of Baltimore or somewhere down that way. They had a bar down near the station and he was down there and See Posey, the secretary of the Grays, come in town and Scrappy seen him, so Scrappy say, "What you doin' in town, See?" See say, "I'm lookin' for ballplayers." Scrappy say, "You ain't gotta look no further. I got one for you."

We had a game that night up at Bleaker Stadium, so he brought See up there and See wanted to take me away, so I asked him, I said, "What do you pay?" He say, "I'll give you $150 a month." I said, "That's no money. I make more'n that here," and I wasn't makin' 15 cents. [Laughs] But, anyhow, we argued, then he says, "Tell you what. You come on with me and we'll straighten it out 'fore we get to the office," so I said okay.

So I left with them that night for Springfield, Ohio; that's where I met the team and that's how I got with the team. And I got $200.

You had a heck of a nickname. They called you "The Catskill Wild Man." Was that because you didn't know where the ball was going sometimes?

Edsall "Big" Walker (courtesy of Edsall Walker).

Most of the time. [Laughs] I could throw hard but I couldn't throw straight. I could throw a hundred [mph] or a little better.

You were arguably one of the best left-handers in the league.

We had four or five, I guess. There was three on the Grays at one time: me, [Roy] Welmaker, and a guy named Roy Partlow.

Add Raymond Brown from the right side and that pitching staff is a good reason why the Grays won so many games.

Oh, boy, I'm telling you! We won 48 straight one time.

How was your breaking pitch?

I could throw a curve. I would slice it kinda three-quarter, you know. I started outside so when it got to 'em it'd be low and inside. I could get anybody out with that pitch.

You were better against righthanded hitters than lefthanded. That's very unusual. Why?

On accounta that pitch. I'd wrap 'em up with it. I never seen nobody else do it.

Do you know how many games you won?

Impossible. The records weren't kept. In fact, you see, I was their number one reliever. I was the only one that did any relievin'. I was number two starter. I'll tell you what. If it was a big game and we only had one, I pitched it. I beat Satchel in Washington before 30,000, 6-to-1.

I coulda pitched more, but, you see, Ray Brown was the boss's son-in-law. It helps. So after a while, Brown wasn't doin' so good, so the boss say, "Any time you want a well-pitched game, pitch Walker," so most of the single big games I pitched. If I didn't, I was in the bullpen to relieve Brown.

You had another pitcher there named Walker.

Had *two* others named Walker. [Laughs] I was named Edsall; they called me "Big" Walker. I was around 5-11, 215. Then we had another one named R. T., and that was his name, and then we had another one named George. He was the smallest one of the three. He was the one called "Little" Walker. "Big," "Little," and R. T.

The Grays traveled all over the country.

Oh, man, it was fun and it was *tough.* One year we traveled 36,000 miles and played every day it didn't rain. And if we was around New York or some big city, we used to play three games — two in the city and then go out on the outskirts and play the third game. Two day games and a night game. Once I pitched five games in eight days. [Laughs] Let me explain it to you. I started three and I relieved in two.

I figured I was gettin' pretty good pay. I didn't know what the rest was gettin'. I heard later that Josh was gettin' a thousand dollars a month. Buck, he had to be gettin' that much, too. In the end, I was gettin' around $500 a month.

It was fun playin' with those two behind you. Oh, man! In 1938, I lost one ballgame all year.

Was that the year that you had a bet with Brown over who would lose the fewest games?

Right. He lost two. He lost two to the same team the same day. We were playin' Baltimore. He lost the first one. He got mad and he asked Vic Harris — he was the manager then — could he pitch the second game. He pitched the second game and lost that one, too.

We never kept records of wins and that's the only time I kept records of losses. We'd bet but there wasn't money in it.

You made the All-Star team in '38. Do you remember that game?

Don't ask me 'bout that. I don't even wanna talk about it. I'm telling you, it was bad news. I was the startin' pitcher and my catcher was a guy named Biz Mackey and he was a man that had his confidence in the high hard one and my best pitch was a low fastball. Keep it low. And every time I look up, he had that one finger up for that high hard one and I couldn't get it up there. I had to take a lot off a pitch to get it up there and, doggone, they scored three runs off of me in three innings and I could beat 'em blindfolded. None of the western teams *ever* beat me a game.

Your World Series record was outstanding.

Don't you know I never started one. I relieved. I think my ERA was point seven or somethin' like that.

Bringing a man throwing 100 mph out of the bullpen must have been pretty unsettling.

Oh, I'm telling you! And then, on top of that, I was mean. I would tell 'em they better get out the way and if they didn't I would throw one close to their head. I got so I had control but I never told them that. I would let 'em know I would throw at 'em but I didn't throw *behind 'em*. I never tried to hit 'em and I never threw at a rookie that didn't know what the game was all about. I wouldn't hit 'em. I knew who to throw at and where to throw.

Now you take Mule Suttles. He was a tough man up there, but don't you know he hated to see me pitch and I would get him out *any* kinda way because the first pitch I'd throw at him was at his feet because he had bad feet and I'd throw the first pitch right down in the dirt at his feet. Then he'd look at me and I'd tell him, "Get out the way there!" From then on, I didn't have any trouble with him.

Willie Wells was another one. One day — it was right after the '38 All-Star game — he rode with us from New York to Buffalo and he cussed me the *whole* trip. "You big hard-throwin' so-and-so, we can't beat you but you go out there and let them suckers beat you!" So I say, "Hey, Willie, I'm gonna pitch to you one of these days." "Aw, I ain't thinkin' about you. I got a helmet." That was about the first helmet we ever seen, you know.

So, sure enough, when we got to Buffalo, Vic give me the ball. When Willie come up to the plate, I say, "Hey, Willie! Here I am!" And the first pitch, I hit him right in the shoulder blade. I knew what I was doin', see, 'cause I threw my overhand curve — sliced it up there — and didn't have too much on it. From then on, he would stay six feet from the plate. Finally, about the fourth innin', he figured I had forgot and he *eeeased* up to the plate and when he did, I dusted him again to let him know I hadn't forgot. He put that in his book — *Dandy, Day, and the Devil*. I'm in it. He put that in there.

Who was the best ballplayer you saw?

Best ballplayer I saw? It's hard. It's hard.

You see, Mule Suttles, he wasn't that good a ballplayer. He was a hard hitter; I ain't gonna say he was a good hitter but he was a hard hitter. I don't know what his average was.

The best hitter I ever seen, I guess, was Boojum Wilson. Yeah, man. From the left

side. He could get up in the middle of the night and tear Satchel up. He was a *ball*player.

We had another guy there was a damn good outfielder — Jerry Benjamin. See, we had a team that nobody got any ink but Buck, Josh, Cool Papa Bell. Here's a team with three Hall of Famers on it; who else was gonna get any ink? They would advertise 'em and that's all they would write about.

Who was the best pitcher?

I would have to go along with [Leon] Day. See, Day was like me but they didn't know it. Day would dust you in a minute, too. Oh, he'd ease that ball up close to you, but he wouldn't talk about it and he wouldn't do it as bad as I would, but he would dust you in a minute.

And don't you know what? Me and Day never hooked up. All them years, never hooked up. [Laughs] I'll tell you the reason why. I think it was '37. We played Newark in Newark and Day and Brown hooked up and Day beat Brown. Me and a guy named [Terris] McDuffie hooked up and I beat McDuffie and that was our regular routine, oh, two or three years. I'd always get the second game and I'd always get McDuffie. Brown said, "I can beat Day," but he never did. So, finally, after 'bout three years, Vic told Brown, say, "You can't beat Day." So he say, "From now on, Walker gonna pitch against Day."

So we met up in Columbus, Ohio, one day, so Vic said, "If Day warms up, you warm up." So Day started warmin' up, so I got up. They sit Day down, I sit down. They got Day up, I got up. And that's the closest we *ever* come to pitchin' against each other. And don't you know, we were the best buddies you ever wanna see. He was my man.

Listen to this, we had another man — played right field for us, Dave Hoskins. Now he wouldn't pitch for us. He might pitch an exhibition game, you know, when we didn't wanna waste a good pitcher. He went to Cleveland [Indians] and pitched for the Cleveland team.

It's too bad Day didn't get in the Hall of Fame when he should have.

You right, but you know what? That's the biggest joke, I think, in the world. The whites are bad enough, but the blacks are worse yet. I was surprised this year that they didn't put Buck O'Neil in. He wasn't that good a ballplayer.

Hey. I got a letter this year from out in Memphis from a guy — he's sendin' out letters wantin' everybody to vote on who was the best man to go into the Hall of Fame and I put down Bill Wright.

From what I've heard, he was a fantastic ballplayer.

Oh, man, yeah. Yes, he was. But, see, he was a man in the shadow of Cool Papa Bell and that's somethin'. In fact, they had Cool Papa Bell, Satchel, Buck Leonard, Josh. He had plenty of competition against him but he was a hell of a ballplayer.

Name a few Negro leagues players who belong in the Hall.

Oh, man! Let's see. Boojum Wilson, Turkey Stearnes.

What about Smoky Joe Williams?

I don't know 'bout him. Never seen him. Yes, I seen him, too, because he used to come through Albany here with the old Brooklyn Royal Giants, I think, but I never seen him in his prime or nothin'.

How about Verdell Mathis, lefthanded pitcher with Memphis?

Yeah. I beat him, too. All them guys down there. And Kansas City when they had — who the heck did they have playin' outfield? Two heavy hitters. I always get in arguments about these two when everybody told me Jackie Robinson was the first to go into the majors. I say these two went with St. Louis before Jackie was with Brooklyn. Willard Brown was one. He had a tryout in '44, '45.

Buck Leonard, your first baseman, was a terrific ballplayer.

This man was just like a father to me. The finest man I ever met. He took me over when I got with the Grays and Vic Harris, the manager — he was playin' left field sometime and Vic wouldn't even come in to the pitchin' mound if somethin' wasn't

goin' right. Buck would come over there and do the talkin' to me. Vic'd stay out there in the field.

Harris was a very successful manager. He knew what he was doing.

Oh, yeah! Hey, let me tell you what. He was a hell of a ballplayer, too, now.

He should be considered for the Hall of Fame off his playing and managing.

I think so, too. Mo Harris was his brother. An umpire.

You were still a young man when you left the Grays.

No, I wasn't. [Laughs]

I thought you were 31 or 32.

When I left? Heck, no. I left in '45. I was 35. You see, in '45 in spring trainin', we played a team and some guy got a base hit off me and I was just tossin' the ball up there. So he come back up there with his chest stuck out so I figured I would show him somethin' and I tried to blaze one by him and my arm went. In '45 I couldn't pitch. Four, five innings was the most I could pitch. After '45 they wanted to send me to the New York Black Yankees but instead of goin' there I just retired and come on home. It was time.

You played with a few other teams.

I played with Philadelphia in 1941. They sent me to Philly the whole year. They got that mixed up in most of the records. They claim I played with the Black Yankees. I never played with the Black Yankees. I guess the Grays traded me to the Black Yankees in '42 but I never went with 'em. I stayed in the shipyard the whole year. I worked every day in the shipyard but when any Negro league team came to Baltimore to play, if it was an exhibition game they'd get me to pitch it for 'em. So I pitched for Philly, I pitched for the Grays, I pitched for Newark — all these guys came for an exhibition game. I pitched as long as I could. I didn't have no practice or nothin' like that, so I told 'em, I say, "I'll pitch as far as I can go."

So you earned a few extra dollars that way.

What kinda extra dollars? I didn't get paid. Heck, no. [Laughs]

Is there one game that stands out?

[Laughs] Well, there's so many of 'em. I'll tell you a game. I pitched one game. We played Chattanooga. In fact, Chattanooga is the team that I threw my arm out against. Before that, we were playin' Chattanooga in Washington and they advertised this left-hander to pitch against the Grays. Had his name *all* over the paper and everything. I started for the Grays and the second innin' they got two runs. For the rest of the game, didn't nobody see first base. So they said, "You was advertisin' the wrong pitcher." We won, 3– or 4–2.

As hard as you threw, did you strike out many?

Would you believe, I wasn't a strikeout pitcher. I'd only try to strike out a man in certain situations. If they had somebody in scorin' position, then I would try to strike the man out. Or maybe Buck or somebody say, "You gotta strike this man out." Okay, then I'd do that. But my main idea when I went out there was just to win the game. Save yourself.

You were a good hitter.

Oh, I never told you that? I was their number one pinch hitter. I hit a ball outta the Polo Grounds. I got plenty of home runs. If the crowd didn't know any better, if I hit one somebody'd say, "Who hit it?"

They'd say, "Josh." [Laughs] I could hit.

I never did nothin' up there but pitch. See, Partlow came there and they was payin' Partlow more'n they was payin' me and I didn't know it. One day, Partlow come to me and said, "Looky here. Is my pay right?" So I looked at it and I say, "Yeah." Now this is his first year and he's gettin' more than me.

We was in New York City, too, and I went straight to See. I say, "What kinda crap is this?" He said, "What you talkin' about?" I said, "Partlow's gettin' more'n me and he's just a first-year man." "Yeah, but he's playin' the outfield." I said, "The more he plays the outfield, the more I gotta pitch." And I told him I wasn't leavin' New York unless they straightened that thing out. I bet you they straightened it out before I left there.

Do you have any regrets from your baseball career?

Not a one. I had a lotta fun and I-wouldn't change it for nothin' in the world. I'd do it right over again tomorrow.

But then, I don't know if I could stay there for the simple reason that I got a mind of my own. If they're gonna try to make me change my style of pitchin' and all this crap I'd tell 'em to go chase theirself. Just like the DH; if I pitch, I wanna hit.

EDSALL "BIG" or "THE CATSKILL WILD MAN" WALKER
Born 9-15-13, Catskill, NY Died 2-19-97, Albany, NY
Ht. 5' 11" Wt. 215 Batted R Threw L

Year	Team, league	G	IP	W	L	Pct	H	BB	SO	SHO	ERA
1934	Zulu Cannibal Giants, ind.										
1935	Albany Black Giants, ind.										
1936	Homestead Grays, NNL										
1937											
1938				8	1	.889					
1939											
1940				10	3	.769					
1941	Philadelphia Stars, NNL										
1942	see note below										
1943	Homestead Grays, NNL			8	3	.727					
1944				4	3	.571					
1945											

In 1942, Walker worked in the shipyards in Baltimore for the World War II effort. During the year, he pitched for traveling teams when they had games in Baltimore. For the season, he pitched for the Homestead Grays, Philadelphia Stars, and Newark Eagles.

Red Moore
Defensive Whiz

NEGRO LEAGUE DEBUT: 1935

When talk turns to the top fielding first basemen, a few names always come up. Some say Hal Chase was the best, others claim it was George Sisler. Then there were Elbie Fletcher and, more recently, Wes Parker and Don Mattingly.

Those who saw the Negro leagues may tell you that Buck Leonard was the best all-around first baseman who ever played the game, but still others say the best glove belonged to Showboat Thomas.

But *the* best fielding first baseman of all time may well have been James "Red" Moore, whose relatively short career prevented him from gaining the fame that would have been his had he played longer or, better, been allowed to play in the major leagues.

Effa Manley, the legendary owner of the Newark Eagles, recognized Moore's ability. When he joined the Eagles in 1936, the infield consisted of Mule Suttles at first, Dick Seay at second, Willie Wells at short, and Ray Dandridge at third.

Suttles is one of the great sluggers of baseball history but was relatively immobile in the field. When Moore joined Newark, Mrs. Manley had Suttles shifted to the outfield so Moore could play first base. Had Gold Gloves been given, it's likely the Eagles would have taken the award at all four infield positions.

I went to [Booker T.] Washington High School. I was playin' locally around Atlanta around '31, '32, '33 with local teams. They had a team here called the Atlanta Black Crackers and some of the older players saw me back in '33. At that time, they weren't affiliated with no league; they was just playin' barnstorm baseball, goin' from city to city, so when I got outta high school in '33 I played with them and traveled with them, playin' teams in different little places — in Florida, up in Tennessee, and other places. I was 16 then.

Your reputation developed quickly as an outstanding fielder.

That was my greatest fame. I wasn't a home run hitter; I was kind of a spray hitter. My greatest part of playing was my fieldin'. I was a real good first baseman and a pretty good ground ball man. You couldn't get 'em too low; you could throw 'em high, but I could pick 'em up pretty good on them bad diamonds we had back then. A lotta times we didn't get to play on a field like Ponce de Leon [Park, in Atlanta] often and when we traveled around there'd be high school fields and open fields in different cities we'd go in. There wasn't no park or nothin', but they'd have chairs around and people would have to pay to see us play.

In 1934, I started out with the Crackers

*Red Moore (courtesy of the Negro Leagues Baseball Play-
ers Association; artist Ron Lewis).*

down there with the North team.
She saw me playin'—I was playin'
with the South team—and she
asked me if I'd play with her and I
told her I would.

So, what happened, they was supposed to pick me up to take me to
spring trainin' and she didn't contact me, so, in the meantime, a team
from Schenectady, New York—the
Schenectady Black Sox—came
through and I went to Miami to
train with them in 1936. Then we
barnstormed back to New York and
I went to Schenectady and they
played in a little ol' league up there
goin' to Canada.

That was May. In the first part of
June, she learned where I was at so
she called me up and got in touch
with me and she sent a man to Schenectady and got me and brought
me to Newark. I was with Newark in
'36 and '37.

Monte Irvin was on that team and
Leon Day, he was pitchin'. And Willie
Wells was the shortstop. And Mule
Suttles, big first baseman. William
Bell, the manager, moved Mule Sut-
tles to the outfield and put me on first
base for defensive purposes.

Now, in '38, Atlanta had a good
team and when I came home, this
fella—he owned a theatre, he was a Jew—
had took over the Black Crackers. So I came
back home in '37 and they found out I was
home, so I talked with him and what he
done, he gave me a little ol' job at the theatre, two or three hours in the evenin'—a
little subsistence, you know, to kinda help
me live a little bit.

So I stayed with the Black Crackers there
in 1938. I signed with him and I made more
with him 'cause I was at home—didn't
have to pay no expenses and everything—
so I done a lot better with him. But in 1939,
he sold the team to a black fella, Mr.
Harden, who owned a fillin' station down
on Auburn Avenue.

and then I went to the Macon Peaches.
They had a team down in Macon. In '35,
somebody else saw me. At that time, a contract wasn't valid—it wasn't binding. You
could sign for X amount of dollars—you
wouldn't make too much; we were playin'
mostly for the love of the game anyway
back then. So, anyway, in '35 I went to the
Chattanooga Choo-Choos. They wasn't
doin' too good—wasn't makin' no
money—so I come back to Atlanta and I
played the season with Atlanta.

We were playin' the North and South
All-Star game down in Jacksonville,
Florida, and it so happened that Mrs. Man-
ley, who owned the Newark Eagles, was

James "Red" Moore, in Atlanta Braves uniform for old-timers game (courtesy of James Moore).

In '39, we were supposed to have gone to Indianapolis as the ABCs. Somethin' happened. We played some exhibition games for them up around Kentucky and so forth, but when the season opened — our season didn't open in April like the rest of the leagues; our season didn't open until May — somethin' happened and he lost the franchise and the park, so that's when our team disbanded.

So what happened, Tom Wilson, who owned the Baltimore Elite Giants — they'd seen me play in the Negro National League — got three or four of our players.

They got shortstop [Pee Wee] Butts, catcher [Bill] Cooper, pitcher Bullet Dixon, and myself. [Joe] Greene went to the Kansas City Monarchs.

So, anyway, I went to Baltimore. They got rid of their first baseman, a boy named [Jim] West — he went to the [Philadelphia] Stars. On that team we had Campanella. I was just a little older than him. We was roommates. Campy and I was pretty tight. We had some good ballplayers on Baltimore. Junior Gilliam came on later, after I had left. I stayed with them until 1940.

I played winter baseball in Los Angeles, California, in a winter league out there. Black teams and white teams would play in that league. Major league all-star teams. Commissioner Landis would let them play for about four to six weeks after the season was over. That's when I got a chance to really play against white major league players.

Evidently we musta done real good 'cause Commissioner Landis stopped 'em from playin' us. The public, they liked to see the competition, but the commissioner, he didn't have that attitude after he found out that we were drawin' real good crowds and we were beatin' 'em a lot. When Satchel Paige and Bob Feller and them would meet up in all-star games we'd win some and they'd win some but out there in the league we would kinda overpower 'em, so he stopped 'em from playin' us back in 1940.

I met Jackie Robinson; he was in school out there. He and Kenny Washington — that was the tandem out there playin' football. Jackie Robinson was a four-letter man: football, baseball, track, and basketball.

I registered for the draft in 1940 — October 16. I was in California. I wasn't a native of California so in January of '41, when the winter baseball season was over in Los Angeles — January 15 — I left from out there and then I went to Baltimore 'cause I had a girl there. I wasn't married at the time.

We went to spring trainin' in April of 1941. I came back from Florida, back to Baltimore, gettin' ready to open up our season around the first of May. My mind went to thinkin' — I had never been in any kinda organization; I had never been in no boy scouts or nothin', so they said if you have a railroad job or worked for the post office or some other government job, you won't have to go to no army, so I just called my daddy up. He worked for the Southern Railroad. At that time, the good workers, they looked out for their next of kin. If he had a son, they'd let him start workin' on the recommendation of his dad. So Dad told 'em 'bout me and so he told me to come on home, he had a job for me.

So in '41, in the latter part of June, I went to work for the railroad. I didn't work too long out there — six weeks. Some fella at Colonial Stores out here where I retired from had a ball team. He heard about me, he had seen me play around and he looked me up and he found me out here where I'm residin' now — in the same neighborhood. He come out and say, "Hey, Red, we got the boss to hire you. You'll have to do a little work, but you'll play ball."

That was a good openin' for me. I went with 'em and got on the team — made me captain of the team. I had to work, too. I went in the service from there in 1942, come out in '45.

Then I played ball on the weekends in '46, '47, and '48 for the Black Crackers. I was 30 years old when I came out of the army. I had married in '41 on the sixth of December. Pearl Harbor was bombed on the seventh and war was declared on the eighth. I'll never forget those three days.

Going back through your career, do any games stand out?

There was a triple play that was made. We was playin' a four-team doubleheader in Yankee Stadium. I was playin' with Baltimore back in '39. My best thing was my fieldin'. That's what really was my forte.

They gave me a day at Ponce de Leon in 1938. Earl Mann was there — gave me some gifts. They took up some money for me. That was somethin' that was outstandin' for me.

I made the East-West All-Star team in 1938 playin' with Atlanta, but I had fractured my ankle and I wasn't able to play in the game. I played in three North-South games in Florida.

Who was the best player you came across?

We had so many good ballplayers. A lot of people ask me 'bout Jackie Robinson. Was he the best player? I tell 'em no, he wasn't the best ballplayer but as he progressed through the Brooklyn chain he got to be great in order to make the Hall of Fame. They picked him out because of his cultural background. He was born in Cairo, Georgia, but he was raised out in California and was fortunate to be around white personnel practically all his life — goin' to school and playin' games and like that. He was better qualified to open up the way for our black boys.

We had some more college fellas playin' in the Negro leagues, but they wasn't too many of us and I don't think we had none of his caliber who had been in the type of culture that he was. I don't recall none durin' my time — up to '48 — that had been around and done anything in white schools — you know, been involved in that culture. He was best qualified because I believe that Branch Rickey had to indoctrinate him into the system and what he was goin' through.

They got a picture out, *The Soul of the Game*, which depicts a little history of it. They had the premiere here and they had me down there with Blair Underwood — he's the one playin' Jackie Robinson. We were talkin' and he said he wished they'd've had me there when they was makin' the picture. I could give them little tidbits. It was based on those three stars — Robinson, Satchel Paige, and Josh Gibson — because, see, when I was playin' back in the '30s and '40s, Josh Gibson was one of the greatest catchers that was playin' in that day and Satchel Paige was one of the greatest pitchers.

We had a fella I was playin' with on the team named Willie Wells, a great shortstop. Dandridge — Ray Dandridge — was a *whale* of a third baseman. He played for Minneapolis in the Triple-A league for a long time and he was an old man. Lennie Pearson — I think he was over in there, too. Luke Easter — he played with the Homestead Grays before he went to the Cleveland Indians.

We had a bunch of players that I believe could have gone in if they had've had the chance, so just pickin' out one, I'd have to pick out position-wise, you know what I mean?

Cool Papa Bell was an outstandin' outfielder. He could run that ball 'til it gets small as a pea. He could run. He was a fast, fast, *fast* man. And then we had Judy Johnson, another great third baseman. When I came up, I saw him play some. I didn't play against him too much because he was goin' out. But Dandridge, I was with him. He was on the team with me. Both of 'em are in the Hall of Fame.

Wild Bill Wright — I was on the same team with him in Baltimore. Wild Bill and [Henry] Kimbro. That Wild Bill was a big man, he could run, and he was a good switch hitter. He could do it all. He was a great player. I've seen him the last two or three years and he's kinda in bad health now. His legs — somethin's wrong with his ankles and everything. He's in a wheelchair.

Double Duty Radcliffe — he was a good one. Pitched and catch. He was a legend. [Laughs]

Who was better — Satchel or Day?

Both of 'em were good, I tell you. Satchel had been there when I got there and Day was just comin' on and both of 'em, in their day, would've made it if they had the opportunity.

If you had to win a game, who would you want to pitch?

Well, they're righthanders. We had some good lefthanders, too. It's a toss-up 'cause when Day pitched against Satchel, it would be 2–1 or 1–2, 1–nothin', or somethin' like that, so it was just the breaks of the game that somebody was beat when they played against each other. I'd have both of 'em on my same all-star team. [Laughs]

Who was the toughest pitcher on you?

Most lefthanders was pretty bad. I learned how to hit 'em in time. They had an ol' big boy named [Roy] Partlow, left-hander for the Grays. He was tough.

Satch was rough against me when I first went up against him. He struck me out three times in a game. I was young — 'bout 18, 19 years old — and ol' Josh was catchin' and Josh would be talkin' to you: "Hey, young boy. You can hit a fastball, can't you? He gonna throw you a fastball." And he'd throw you one. He'd tell you where he's gonna throw it. [Laughs] The first he throwed to me was inside — pretty close — and I had to get out. I said, "Unh-unh. He's bad to throw it at me." Satch had good control but I didn't know all that then the first time. Everything worked out pretty good; I got a couple hits later on.

What was your salary?

The highest I ever got was $250 a month. That's all I got, just before I went in the service. Meal money, the most I ever got was a dollar-and-a-half a day. I was thinkin' about it — you could feed your kids, feed your family off of two dollars a week. A nickel for this, a nickel for that. People don't understand. They get more eatin' money [today] than we made in a month. If they play in a World Series, they make more money than some of the players would make in years and years and years and *years*. The owners were gettin' all the money but now they got it to where the ballplayers is gettin' their fair share, too. Some of 'em are bein' overpaid, but that's all right. Let 'em get it while they can.

I just thank God that I'm able to enjoy some of the benefits from my baseball career. I go out and sign autographs and stuff like that, make a little speech and all. I thank God for lettin' me live as long as I have 'cause so many of our players didn't have a long life.

Any regrets?

That's what I've been asked a lotta times. One of the sports writers for the *Atlanta Constitution* 'bout ten years ago wrote me and he asked me did I have any regrets. I

said no. We mostly played for the love of the game. We just *loved* to play, you understand.

I don't have no regrets. I played out there against those white teams out in California in 1940 and I had played against some up in New York state. We used to play against white boys up there, too. They'd have some major league ballplayers intermixed with them then. People'd come out and see us play.

I said in my heart and mind, eventually we'll make it. Things will open up down the road a piece and I didn't think I'd be one of the ones to be in it, but I said, well, I'm here openin' the way for somebody else. It was in my mind.

Josh and Satch was kinda upset when Jackie Robinson was picked over them. Everywhere you went, you heard about Josh and Satchel Paige. It upset Josh pretty much; he didn't live long after Jackie Robinson was picked by Branch Rickey to go to Montreal and then back to Brooklyn.

As you pointed out, talent was not the reason Robinson was chosen. If that was the only criterion, someone like Josh or Satch or Buck Leonard would have been the one.

Yeah. Buck was a whale of a first base-man. Buck was a little old then, though. He's in a wheelchair himself now. He's had some strokes. He's close to 90.

Would you go back and play again?

Relive my life? I think I'd do the same identical thing; only thing I'd do, I'd stay in school before I played. That's the only thing I'd do different. When I was comin' along, we blacks — not many of us — didn't finish college much, but I had an opportunity but I didn't know how important education was. We had doctors and school teachers and things of that nature, but most of us boys worked at the post office and such and you didn't need but a high school education for that.

I think right now, the way I look at it, I had a good time so I ain't gonna regret it none. I got a chance to travel a lot. I think I covered about 40-some states. I've been everywhere; I've done everything.

JAMES "RED" MOORE
Born 11-18-16, Atlanta, GA
Ht. 5' 10"   Wt. 165   Batted and Threw L

Year	Team, league	Pos	G	AB	R	H	2B	3B	HR	RBI	SB	BA
1935	Chat. Choo Choos, ind.	1B										
	Atlanta Black Crackers, ind.	1B										
1936	Mohawk Giants, ind.	1B										
	Newark Eagles, NNL	1B										
1937	Newark Eagles, NNL	1B										.280
1938	Atl. Black Crackers, NAL	1B										.331
1939	Indianapolis ABCs, NAL	1B										
	Baltimore Elite Giants, NNL	1B										
1940	Baltimore Elite Giants, NNL	1B										.238
	Newark Eagles, NNL	1B										
1941-45						military service						
1946	Atl. Black Crackers, ind.	1B										
1947		1B										
1948		1B										

Henry Kimbro
Not So Evil

NEGRO LEAGUE DEBUT: 1937

"Marquis Grissom. That was me. That was just the way I played, 'cept I batted left." Those were the first words I heard Henry Kimbro say as I entered the Negro League Baseball Shop in Nashville.

Maybe so, maybe not. Henry Kimbro hit for a higher average than Marquis Grissom does, and maybe he had a better arm and more power.

Henry Kimbro was so good in center field that Wild Bill Wright was moved to right field, and Wright was a great center fielder himself and a great ballplayer. But Kimbro was also a great ballplayer. His lifetime Negro leagues batting average was in the .320 range, and he was the league's leading hitter in 1939. At various times, he also led in doubles, runs, and stolen bases, and was second one year in home runs. Several years he was among the top ten hitters, and he played in six All-Star games.

Described by many as "evil" or "bad," he explains why he feels he was called that. His education ended after elementary school and he did not have the opportunity to learn all he wanted to. Because of this, he felt he was unable to adequately express himself, so, rather than show this inability, he would keep to himself. His words on paper do not sufficiently illustrate how deeply he feels about this, but in hearing and watching him tell it, it's obvious how much he wanted an education.

He made sure the same thing did not happen to his children. He put all three — two daughters and a son — through college.

You were nearly 25 years old when you began playing professionally. What had you been doing up to that point?

Oh, let's see. Was I 25 years old? Yeah, it was along in there somewhere. I had been working at a service station and playing baseball in the summertime at the city parks. First started out amateur. I'd go in the park and we'd choose up and play side by side.

All over town, you got north Nashville, east Nashville, south Nashville, west Nashville — all parts of town had parks at that time. Headley Park, Napier Park, Edge Hill Park. Every part of Nashville had a park. We played sandlot. Every community had a team and we'd play from one park to another all in the summertime.

Tom Wilson is the one that got the team together here in Nashville; he had a little semi-pro team in south Nashville. I played a little bit with him — his team — and he was trying to get me to go away from home but I wouldn't leave home at that particular time. During the baseball season I played a little bit around here in Nashville and played with his team a little bit. This guy in Chicago that managed the Chicago American Giants — Jim Taylor — he got in touch with me after the baseball season and he was getting a team together to travel, going south to play everywhere. He asked me did I want to go. I had never been no place, so I said, "Yeah, I'll go."

Their team left Chicago and come on down here through Nashville and I joined 'em and went with 'em. We played in Birmingham, Atlanta — all the cities — in the fall of the year. Then after I played with that team, the next year Tom Wilson got me to go with the Elite Giants. He moved the team to Columbus, Ohio, and put the team in the league and I went with him. That's when I first started professional baseball. Now what year it was I done forgot. [It was 1937.]

But anyway, we went to Columbus, Ohio, and played there that season, whatever year that was. The next year, he moved the team from Columbus, Ohio, to Washington, D.C., and we played there that baseball season, and the next baseball season he moved the team again! To Baltimore. That was it. The Baltimore Elite Giants played right there 'til the league disbanded. I played with him every year, with the exception of one year. I think that was '41. He sold me to the New York Black Yankees and I played over there for one season and the next season I was right back in Baltimore again. He bought my contract from the Black Yankees and right back to Baltimore I went. That's where I finished up at.

Were you always a leadoff hitter?

Tex [Burnett, Black Yankees manager] tried to make a fourth-place hitter out of me when I was over at New York but I didn't like that so well. I was so used to taking pitches.

I just was used to being leadoff man. I had done that all along — playing 'round here in Nashville and then when I went down with Jim Taylor — all down through Birmingham and Memphis and New Orleans. I hit leadoff all my whole baseball

Henry Kimbro (courtesy of Henry Kimbro).

career and when I went over to the Black Yankees, Tex moved me down from leadoff man, had me hit in fourth place there for a while. I said, "Oh, *brother!*" I always liked to wait on that one pitch.

You were fast. Were you a base stealer?

Yeah, I was real fast on my feet. I don't know how many bases I stole. I really don't know, but I sure did run and I mean I could run, too. I was real fast and had a strong arm and I had a good eye at the plate. I was so strong I didn't cock my leg and swing like you see a lot of hitters. I didn't do that; I just stayed right in and that ball'd get up there and [flicks wrists] and just like that. Just that simple. I was strong as a bull.

How many home runs did you hit?

I don't have no idea. I didn't ever hit a lot of home runs. I didn't believe in that home run business. I liked to shoot that ball through that infield. I'd hit that ball between third base and shortstop — that was my spot. I could hit that ball through there so hard and so sharp. I got all my base hits right through there somehow. I don't know how. I very seldom pulled the ball.

I went to New York and Tex started me pulling the ball — hitting the ball over the fence and all that kind of stuff. I didn't like to hit in no fourth place. I done pretty good at it but I didn't like it and when I went back to Baltimore the following year I went right back to leadoff 'cause [manager] Felton Snow put me right back to hitting leadoff like I was used to hitting and *liked* to hit. I liked to shoot that ball through that infield.

Is there one game that stands out in your memory?

We played in Philadelphia. I'll never forget that one. Forty-fourth and Parkside — that's where the Philadelphia Stars were home team. They had a lefthander pitching. I never will forget that. I hit two home runs that day off that lefthanded pitcher. I don't remember his name but he was a pretty fair ol' pitcher. Both home runs went to center field, right over in the tennis court. I hit both of the balls in that tennis court. I sure felt good that day, too. [Laughs] That second home run I hit — ooh brother! We beat Philadelphia Stars a doubleheader that day. That was on a Sunday.

One more ball that I hit — this here was really disgusting. We was playing the Homestead Grays on a tour — where we travel playing each other — and we went to Detroit. I don't know if it was Raymond Brown but it was one of them good pitchers pitching that day, one of their ace pitchers. I hit that ball *out* of Briggs Stadium! *Out* of Briggs Stadium. You know what size Briggs Stadium is — it's a mile high. I hit the ball out of the park over the right field roof.

The next morning I picked up the newspaper and you know who hit that ball out of the park? [Bill] Hoskins, my left fielder. I was really disgusted but I never did say anything about it. I just let it go. I didn't attempt to call the sportswriter. There

hadn't but one ball been hit out of there before I hit that — by that lefthand hitter used to be with the Boston Red Sox, Ted Williams. That was the onliest ball had been hit out of there at that particular time. I went back to that stadium since then and looked at that distance and I don't know how I got that ball up there 'cause I didn't ever hit the ball to that side of the field. I always hit the ball to the left side of the field.

Who was the best player you saw?

I got to go along, I guess, with Cool Papa Bell. He was an outfielder and he was so fast. He was really fast. You couldn't mess around; he could hit that ball to the infield and if you didn't play it perfect you wouldn't get him. He was just that fast. He didn't look like he could run that fast. He'd hit the ball leaning like and then he hit it running. He didn't look like he was running fast when you'd see him run, but man, he'd be flying! I don't know how he could run like that. Don't bobble the ball. I was fast but I wasn't fast as Cool Papa. No. Wasn't nobody fast as him. And steal bases? He would steal bases.

We had some good hitters in our league. You take guys like Hook-Leg Dandridge, Willie Wells. They wasn't home run hitters but they'd run you crazy. Like I hit — balls through that infield. Most times, people don't pay no attention to people unless they are fence-busters, you know — home run hitters.

Who was the best pitcher?

We had some good pitchers. You take Bill Byrd — he was one of our pitchers. Raymond Brown. That ol' big boy we had from up here outside of Lebanon, Tennessee — Bob Griffith. He was good, too.

Who was the toughest one on you?

What was his name — used to play with the Black Yankees? He was a lefthander. He was hard for me to hit. I didn't have no trouble out of [Luis] Tiant [Sr.]. Neck Stanley, that's his name! I had trouble out of him because Neck Stanley would throw at you, throw behind you, and all that kind of stuff. He was a little dangerous and he had that move to first base. I still think that was illegal, though. He'd swing up and swing that leg and when he'd come back around, if you was off that base he'd throw it to first base. If you was on the base, he'd throw the ball on to the catcher. He'd raise his leg and he did it slow. I don't know how he did it. He balanced himself up there some kind of way.

Tiant'd really bring that ball up there to you and if you're off base, when he grunted he'd throw to first base. He was good. He was pitching for Havana Cuban Stars, Fred McCreary was umpiring, Goose Curry was the hitter. Tiant went up and come down and grunted and throwed that ball and Goose Curry swung and said, "Jesus Christ! Man, how'd I miss it?!" Fred McCreary told him, "I oughtta call you out. That man throwed to first base." [Laughs] Tiant throwed to first base and Goose *swung.* He had a way of swinging and spinning and he'd sit down on the ground.

Do you and Bill Wright belong in the Hall of Fame?

No, I won't say that. Bill Wright might, but not me 'cause I wasn't a home run hitter. If I had hit the ball over the fence, with my other capabilities it would've been terrible. I did it getting hits and stealing bases and with my strong arm and playing in the outfield.

I had a bad way with ground balls 'cause I come up in these parks around here and these rocks and ditches and things, but that fly ball now, I could run that fly ball crazy. I could catch the balls that almost seemed impossible to catch. I've caught balls that just don't seem possible.

I started out my first year when I went to Columbus, Ohio. I played left field. Bill Wright come up playing center field. The next year when we went to Washington,

Henry Kimbro (courtesy of the Negro Leagues Baseball Players Association; artist Ron Lewis).

they moved me to center field. I never will forget that. That center field in Washington was just like a lawn. You had plenty of room to run and I could just lay my head back and run and catch them balls that seemed unplayable. Unbelievable catches. I had good hands and a strong arm and I was fast.

Talk about the travel.

We had the same problems, just like everybody else had. Traveling conditions wasn't exactly good. We played a [Sunday] doubleheader in New Orleans and the next game was on Tuesday night in Baltimore. We got there that morning about one or two o'clock, somewhere along in there. In the meantime, we had to ride, eat, and everything. We'd stop in the grocery store and eat — buy food. You couldn't go in no restaurant or nothing. People wouldn't let you in a restaurant, so we'd stop and buy cold cuts in the store, put it in the bus, ride that night, eat, get to where we were going the next day.

If we were going to Baltimore or Philadelphia or places like that — New York — they had hotels. The Woodside Hotel in New York. But the other places where we didn't have places to stay, we'd get on that bus and let that seat back. They bought a 40-something-thousand dollar bus.

Why do some say you were evil?

When I was a boy I lived out in the county. The railroad — the Tennessee Central Railroad — came all around town and across the railroad [track] was the line for the city. When I finished my grade school, I couldn't go to high school right across the railroad — the city high school. The school I was supposed to go to was at least eight or ten miles [away]. Cameron Junior High and High School was right across the railroad. I couldn't go to that school because that was inside the city.

That had its effect on me. I couldn't say the things that I wanted to say because I didn't go to school to learn to do that. It just tore me all to pieces. I been around guys and hear 'em talk and they talk-talk-talk so nice and everything and I couldn't do it and that just tore me all to pieces. So I didn't talk too much. Somebody come and want to talk to me about something or other, and if he don't watch himself I'd be gone. I think that's where this "evilness" come from.

There was so much I wanted to do and some things I couldn't do. That hurts you. It hurts real bad. There was sometimes things I wanted to say or talk about and I couldn't do it because I couldn't express myself the way I wanted to. People started calling me "bad man" and "evil" and all that kind of stuff and it just followed me all

around my whole baseball time and after that.

I've been told if somebody messed up, you'd let him know about it.

[Laughs] In a way. In a way. I had my way of doing things and getting around people.

What did you do when you left baseball?

I come back here in Nashville from Baltimore and I had bought a brand-new De-Soto when I come back from Cuba in 1942, or somewhere in there. A brand-new pea-gray DeSoto and when the league ended I drove that car to Nashville and a guy — Bill Martin — had a taxi cab company here and I put it on his taxi stand. It was a four-door. I drove it about two years and then I bought the company from him. I run that taxi cab company and run a [service] station right there at 12th and Joe Johnson for 22 years. Had the filling station and taxi cab company right on that corner there — Bill's Cab Company — for 22 years. That's where I retired from.

I run from 13 to 15 cabs. When I had the heart attack I had 15 cabs. I didn't retire then. I kept on working. After I got over that heart attack, I come back and kept on working, then I had a stroke. I kept right on working after that. The doc told me there was too much stress and strain, said I ought to get away from there. I kept working and had *another* stroke. That's when I retired. I should've retired on the first one. I sold the company.

Would you be a ballplayer again?

You mean if I could go back? Yeah. I loved to play baseball. I loved to play the game.

Any regrets?

No. No regrets, 'cause I took things as they come and went on and did the best I could. That's all you can do.

I don't see how I hit that ball out of Briggs Stadium! I was't that type of hitter. I still don't know how I ever hit a ball out of that stadium.

HENRY ALLEN "JUMBO" KIMBRO
Born 2-19-12, Nashville, TN
Ht. 5' 8"   Wt. 175   Batted and Threw L

Year	Team, league	Pos	G	AB	R	H	2B	3B	HR	RBI	SB	BA
1937	Colubus Elite Giants NNL	OF										.276
1938	Wash. Elite Giants, MNL	OF										.318
1939	Baltimore Elite Giants, NNL	OF										.310*
1940		OF										.269
1941	N. Y. Black Yankees, NNL	OF										.247
1942	Baltimore Elite Giants, NNL	OF										.288
1943		OF										.333
1944		OF									*	.329
1945		OF		*								.291
1946		OF			*							.371
1947		OF			*		*					.353
1948		OF										.314
1949	Baltimore Elite Giants, NAL	OF										.352
1950		OF										.370
1951		OF										.366*
1952	Birm. Black Barons, NAL	OF										
1953		OF										

* Kimbro is acknowledged as leading the league in these categories in the years marked, but the actual numbers are in dispute. He also led the Cuban League with a .346 average in 1947-48, and in stolen bases with 18 in 1939-40.

Lyman Bostock, Sr.

First Generation

NEGRO LEAGUE DEBUT: 1938

The name Lyman Bostock should be familiar to fans of recent baseball history. In the late 1970s, Lyman Bostock was one of the better hitters in the major leagues, first for the Minnesota Twins and then for the California Angels. How great he may have been we'll never know; he died of a gunshot wound shortly before the end of the 1978 season, leaving behind a career .311 batting average for his four years. He was only 27.

This ill-fated young man was Lyman Bostock, Jr. Forty years earlier, Lyman Bostock, Sr., was breaking in and he, too, was a heck of a ballplayer. The elder Bostock was a good-fielding first baseman who played in the 1941 East-West All-Star game, going 1-for-2 with a run and an RBI.

He was batting over .300 in '42 when he was drafted into World War II, and it was 1946 before he returned to the Negro leagues. By 1949 he was batting well over .300 again, but he realized that the Negro leagues were nearing their end so he went to Canada, along with the likes of Leon Day, Willie Wells, Bubba Hyde, Barney Brown, and many other stars of black baseball, to play in the ManDak League. After four seasons there, he retired.

You were born in Birmingham. How did you get to Brooklyn to start playing baseball?

My brother was living in New York. I had aunts there. I played with all the [semi-pro] teams. I went with the big teams — I didn't mess with the little ones — to try to stay in condition. I was nothin' but a young fella — 18 years old — when I went up to the Black Yankees [for a tryout]. I went to the Black Yankees first. I played around on the Polo Grounds, on the lots with the youngsters playin' semi-pro baseball, but I knew I was better than that.

I went up to Yonkers to spring training up there and they didn't treat me so well — the older fellas. I was the youngest thing there. [Laughs] They didn't want us [young

players] and they think they're jeopardizin' themselves. I was catchin' around with 'em and they'd say, "Catch the ball!" I happened to drop a ball. "Catch the ball!" I had a guy with me — he was a big, tall, gangly fella like Satchel Paige but every time he didn't know where it was goin'. Anyway, at the end of the practice that day, a guy asked about me — Roy Williams — "What about Bostock?" "He ain't got enough experience." Made him mad as hell. He said, "How in the hell is gonna get experience if you don't let him play?" [Laughs]

So I moved on to the Brooklyn Royal Giants. They were around the corner from them. I went and asked 'em if they would give me a tryout and they said they would

and they did. They needed a shortstop and I was playin' shortstop
then. I went to trainin' with those
guys and they had a catcher named
Joe Lewis, from Virginia, and he
brought a guy from Virginia there, a
shortstop. I hit from the left side; he
hit from the right side.

Aw, they drilled us. Man they
drilled us! I would field — stretched
out left and right, in and out. At the
bat, a guy named Lefty Starks was
pitchin'. Lefty Starks was a veteran
ballplayer, a lefthanded pitcher. He
was tryin' me, to see how I hit, and
Lefty threw the ball and it kinda
curved, but I was right on the ball.
At the end of the day, the guy say —
he called me "Layman" — he said,
"Which one will you pick between
the two shortstops?" He said, "I'd
take Layman. We couldn't suck him
in on the curveballs." "You reckon
that he know what he's doin'?"

See, I could get my bat on most
anything and I would hit the ball to
left field most of the time, but
[John] Beckwith, the manager — he
was a great ballplayer, good hitter,
too, strong — he says, "Layman, put
your bat on your shoulder." See, I was hittin' late but I hit the ball. "Keep your bat
on your shoulder." I put my bat on my
shoulder, couldn't move no way but forward. I started wailin' that ball to right
field and *all* fields.

I didn't play in the outset. I had to sit
and watch, so a game one day we was over
to Jersey and we had a pretty good first
baseman and I could play first base, too,
but he couldn't hit. [Laughs] So we needed
a first baseman that day. I hit the ball so
they let me play there and I beat that guy
out. He was a great basketball player for the
Renaissance. Zack Clayton. He was a professional referee [later].

That's how I started playin' with the
Brooklyn Royal Giants. I played there a
year. I had to come home; my daddy was

*Lyman Bostock, Sr. (courtesy of the Negro Leagues Base-
ball Players Association; artist Ron Lewis).*

sick. I left there and came to Birmingham.
Pipe shop teams were there playin' ball —
good ball and good teams in Birmingham — and they gave me a job 'cause I
could play ball. I knew I wasn't gonna stay
there; I just stopped there. We worked
three or four days a week. I stayed in condition and the manager of another pipe
shop said, "Bostock, why don't you come
over here with us? We work all the time
every day." And they sure did! [Laughs]

He showed me around the place, bought
me my dinner and everything. He was
dealin' with pipe from a half a inch up to —
you seen these great big ol' sewer pipes? I
went there and examined that place and I
didn't see nothin' but smoke. [Laughs] You
couldn't see. Everybody was black.
[Laughs] I said, "Unh-unh. That's not the

place for me." I went over stayin' in shape with the Engel Iron Works. They made parts for ships.

Jim Taylor, he heard about me. He said, "If a man's talked about in his hometown, he's doin' somethin', but if he's not talked about in town, he's not doin' nothin'." So he came out there and saw me and I hit a home run. I was playin' first base and Jim Taylor, he say, "Bostock"—he acted like he been knowin' me 40 years—"how'd you like to play for the Birmingham Black Barons?" I said, "I don't mind." "Come out Saturday." And I joined 'em.

That Sunday we was playin' Kansas City Monarchs and they had a guy, he could pitch. Hilton Smith. He could pitch! He had a good curve, one of the best curveballs you'd want to see. He was tough. I got a couple hits off of him that day. I was a tough youngster, too. [Laughs] Yeah.

The ex–first baseman there was old [Fred] McBride—he was 35 years old; 'course, he was done anyway. They put McBride off in Tulsa, Oklahoma. We had to go through there and that's where they dropped him off after I linked up with them. And I went on from there.

You made the All-Star team.

In '41. That was exciting. Satchel Paige was pitchin' on that, you know. We had 51,000 people there in Comiskey Park. [Henry] McHenry was pitchin' on the other side, for the East, and I got a hit off of him. I came to play, I'll tell you that, when I was playin'.

You were drafted and spent four years in the service.

Yes, I did. That was really somethin'. After, I came back to Birmingham. Man, you talkin' 'bout tough! I had got great big, so when I came back from overseas I was almost musclebound. I had to take my leg and put it up on the curbstone—pick it up—'cause I couldn't step up there. I was in bad shape. Everybody's sittin' down durin' the season and I'm runnin', tryin' to get in shape.

'Course, I knew to be effective I really had to work at it and get that weight down. You think you're swingin' and hit the ball two hops to the pitcher. The guy's throwin' gumdrops—we called 'em—and I couldn't hit them. It took me three years to get in shape. You know, when I got in shape, that I wore 'em out. [Laughs] Took me all that time to get that weight off. I was a young man at that, too. I came out from overseas when I was about 26 years old, 27. But I was musclebound. I'd run, run, run myself crazy, but I finally got back in shape.

After the Birmingham Black Barons, I played with the Chicago American Giants in '47. They traded me to Chicago. Forty-eight I went to New York Cubans and I came back to Chicago in 1949. Nineteen fifty the league was breakin' up. It was the end of the line and I knew it, so Willie Wells suggested that I go to Canada to play ball, so I went to Canada where the pickin's was better. I went with the Winnipeg Buffaloes and we got every ballplayer that played in the [Negro] National and American league that we could and we brought a brand of baseball there that, of course, they'd never seen. Sorta made things look good 'round in Canada. That was a tough league up there.

I was with the Winnipeg Buffaloes a couple of years, then I left there and went to the Carman Cardinals and stayed there a couple of years. We had a team outta Minot, North Dakota, in that league and we had a team—Brandon—in the league. And we had the Elmwood Giants that wasn't far away from Winnipeg—'bout four or five miles. Maybe not that much. We got guys that played in South America and everywhere—Mexico—and got 'em to come to the league.

Leon Day and me, we played on the same team. Leon pitched the longest game I ever played in my life. We played 17 innings and he pitched 17 innings and we beat Brandon for the championship, 1–nothin'. And it was *cold*. Those guys had two or three sweatshirts on. I couldn't play with that many on. They would have beaten us but I leaned backward and caught a ball goin' down that line. It would've went for a home run down there. There wasn't but three hits and I got one of 'em. We got two and the other guys got one. They put Willie Wells out the game. [Laughs] They threw him out.

Who was the best player?

That's hard to say. There's a whole lotta *best* players. Pee Wee Butts, shortstsop at Baltimore Elite Giants. Junior Gilliam. Junior wasn't nothin' but a youngster but he learned to play. I saw him playin' in Nashville and I say, "Who that little poor boy hunchin' the ball to first base?" [Laughs] But, boy, I'm tellin' you! He went along playin' second base on the side of Pee Wee Butts — boy, that was a combination! They tried to buy both at one time.

Who was the best pitcher?

[Laughs] I won't name *one* pitcher. I'll name *some* pitchers. Gentry Jessup, Hilton Smith, Gene Smith. They had some tough lefties, some real go-getters. Verdell Mathis, Memphis Red Sox.

What kind of money did you make?

We wasn't makin' no money. The best I ever pried 'em out of was 'bout five or six hundred a month.

What was your meal money?

That's how I left Birmingham. [Laughs] I came in a great big out-of- shape fella and we wasn't gettin' but two dollars a day for eatin' money. I called a meetin' on [Black Barons' owner] Tom Hayes. He was from Memphis, Tennessee. To make sure they got the message, we came before him. He said, "I understand you're havin' a meetin' down here." I spoke 'cause them guys wanted to stay at home and I didn't give a hoot where I played, so I said, to make sure he got the message, I said, "Mr. Hayes, the cost of livin' is up. In the face of the economic situation, I think we would like for you to give us a dollar [more] come May

Lyman Bostock, Sr.

the twelfth." The season starts in May. I say, "As of now, we're not askin' that, but when that time come, we expect to get three dollars. We have to play in them doubleheaders and hard games on Sundays. We need that."

Hayes said, "Ah, I see Bostock is your spokesman." Nobody said nothin'. I got the message. I was traded to Chicago. [Laughs] He later said, "Bostock will cost me money."

I played four years in Canada. I had given up playin' but I got a call from Rochester, Minnesota. A guy said he'd been lookin' at me and I went to Rochester. I had been playin' around with the kids on shop teams — helpin' them out. I went there and the guys was throwin' those gumdrops and I couldn't hit 'em. They wanted to send me to the Mayo Clinic because of a separation in my wrist, but I said, "No. Send me home." [Laughs]

I came home and passed the examination for the U.S. Post Office. I worked there about 28 years and one month. I was an artist all along the line. I made all kind of furnishings. I made tables, lamps, centerpieces, inlaid table tops, headboards, cornices. I've got some unfinished work I'm gonna have to do 'fore I die. [Laughs]

You know, when we was growin' up , things was crude, tough. Things was hard, didn't have no bats. I made some crude bats. I make bats for baseball memorabilia now. I sell 'em now. I made that big bat they had in Kansas City.

Your son was a heck of a ballplayer.

He called me once 'bout his hittin'. I'll digress a little bit.

Mule Miles lived in San Antone, Texas. He was strong and he could hit. Miles got in a slump, wasn't hittin' the ball, and Jim Taylor — on the team we called him "Uncle Jim" — was a great manager. We was playin' in Chicago then; he said, "Miles, stop lookin' at that goddamn fence! Every time you look at the fence you hit the ball two hops to the pitcher." [Laughs]

You see, we had to play 10-11 games out there in the East. We played the Bushwicks. They had old major leaguers all the time. We played 11 games and Miles hit 11 home runs! [Laughs]

I wanted to tell my son the same thing. I told him just to hit the way they was pitchin' it. And he did and he went on. You know he wanted to give his salary back one year 'cause he wasn't doin' with the Angels what he thought he oughtta be doin'. He was in a slump. He could play.

Would you play baseball again?

Would I!?! If I had that opportunity, man, what are you talkin' about! [Laughs] For the kind of money these guys are playin' for and some of them really need a lotta tutorin'. Some of these guys have got a lot of talent but they just need a little more trainin'. Would I play again? Man!

LYMAN WESLEY BOSTOCK, SR.
Born 5-11-18, Birmingham, AL
Ht. 6' 1"   Wt. 215   Batted L Threw R

Year	Team, league	Pos	G	AB	R	H	2B	3B	HR	RBI	SB	BA
1938	Brooklyn Royal Giants, ind.	1B										
1939												
1940	Birm. Black Barons, NAL	1B										
1941		1B										
1942		1B										
1942-45						military service						
1946	Birm. Black Barons, NAL	1B										.265
1947	Chi. American Giants, NAL	1B-OF										
1948	New York Cubans, NNL	1B										
1949	Chi. American Giants, NAL	1B										.336
1950	Winnipeg, MnDkL	1B-OF										
1951		1B-OF										
1952	Carman, MnDkL	1B-OF										
1953		1B-OF										
1954		1B-OF										

Bostock played part of the 1949 season with Guaymas in the Mexican League. Statistics are unavailable.

Max Manning

"Dr. Cyclops"

NEGRO LEAGUE DEBUT: 1938

Max Manning undoubtedly struck fear in the hearts of batters. First, he was very tall — 6' 4". Second, some hitters may have worried over whether he could see them because he wore very thick glasses. Teammate Jimmy Hill called him "Dr. Cyclops" because he had just seen the movie of that name and Manning was the first player he had ever seen with glasses. (The other players called him "Milio," a contraction of Maximillian.)

One former opponent said he had no one great pitch but he was a great pitcher, and the records available today bear this out. In the 60- to 80-game schedules his team, the Newark Eagles, played, Manning was credited with various seasonal records of 15–1, 15–6, 11–6, and 10–4. One reference gives him a 68–32 career Negro leagues mark, but it is only partial. It's likely he actually won well more than 100 games in his nine years in the Negro leagues.

He joined the Eagles in 1938, spent 1942–46 in the army, and then rejoined the Eagles through 1949 (the team was in Houston the last year). Through those years, he teamed with several other pitchers to give Newark a rotation other teams feared to face. One man said, "There was never a break with the Eagles. Every game they put a great pitcher out there." Joining Manning in the Eagles' rotation at one time or another were pitchers such as Leon Day, Terris McDuffie, Jimmy Hill, Lenial Hooker, and Rufus Lewis.

When a shoulder injury finally ended his career, Manning returned to college and became a teacher. He was as successful at that as he was at baseball.

Is it true you were offered an organized ball contract after high school?

That's right. Nineteen thirty-seven. A guy named Max Bishop — he used to play for the Philadelphia Athletics — became a scout for the Detroit Tigers. I got a letter from him and he sent me a scouting form — how you bat, how you throw, your weight and height and so forth and so on. He said in the letter he wanted to be able to see me at spring training. This was in the fall of '37. My father brought me up against the wall and said, "Look. Let me tell you something. You've got to face real life here. You've got about as much chance of playing ball for the Detroit Tigers as a snowball in hell." [Laughs] He went on to explain all these different kinds of things about prejudice and the whole racial thing. He said, "You've seen pictures of ballplayers and you don't see any there your color, do you?"

Did Bishop know your race?

No, he didn't. In those days, scouts didn't travel around as much and I was playing on an all-white team and I was the only black on the team. My name — Max

Max Manning (courtesy of Max Manning).

Manning — wasn't what you'd call a traditional Afro-American name.

Can you imagine what Commissioner Landis would have done if you had showed up at spring training?

[Laughs] Yeah. Like with my first tryout I was supposed to go to. It was with the Philadelphia Stars pretty much around the same time. I went up there and I had my shoes tied together around my neck and that old bag. [Laughs] I know I was a sight.

You were born in Rome, Georgia. When did you leave there?

We must've left there almost immediately because what I remember the most in terms of my real youngish days was Vicksburg, Mississippi. My father was the head schoolmaster there, a place called the

Vicksburg Industrial School. Most of the real early days, the memories have to do with Vicksburg.

There are real shadowy memories I have of Atlanta, but not Rome, because my paternal grandfather lived in Atlanta. I remember the Grady Hospital; I remember the ambulance going down the street. [Laughs] It's the things that attract kids.

My father decided we would move to Philadelphia and we stayed there for about a year perhaps, then we moved to Pleasantville [New Jersey]. At Philadelphia, he worked at Wanamaker's, then he got a teaching job in Pleasantville and we moved here. That's where I've spent the major portion of my life. I guess when I got here I was about 6 or 7 years old.

What problems did you face, both in the deep South and then in the North?

You know, it's strange. It's like another world. At least in Mississippi you lived in another world and I think that the only time that I saw white people really was when we went to the store. They had a store called Piggly Wiggly and that was when we saw white people. Nothing ever seemed to grab me in terms of what was really going on. I just didn't seem to be aware of anything really, except that everybody that I knew was the same color that I am.

My mind was not shaped in any one way or another and pretty much the same thing was true when we moved to Philadelphia. The same thing was taking place because we lived in a section where there were all blacks. It was one of those things where nothing becomes delineated because your mind isn't grasping what's really going on and, believe it or not, it was a long time before it really grabbed me. [Laughs]

In fact, even in Pleasantville there was segregation. We had all black schools and when you went to the movies you had to go upstairs and sit on the left and things like that. Sometimes you get accustomed to a certain lifestyle. You don't know anything different and then all of a sudden something comes up and this stuff gets pointed

out to you. Then you begin to realize what the hell is going on.

How did the Eagles come to sign you?

I went to college one year — I went to a college called Lincoln University in Chester, Pennsylvania. I went in the fall of '37 and I came out in June, but while I was there I met Monte Irvin and we became friends. The owner of the Eagles came out to Lincoln University and he signed us both right out there.

You joined the Eagles at the age of 18 and joined a pitching staff that had some talent. How much of a chance did you get?

I got a *big* one. [Laughs] I started right out.

One of the most wonderful things, I think, about my life is that, when I was in high school, I had a coach — his name was Ty Helfrich and he had played in the old Federal League and he was a baseball *fanatic*. He was really into baseball and he knew it, so in my first experience in playing ball with a uniform on he was very impressed with me and he taught me a lot of things about my position and fielding it and doing a lot of things and the fundamentals of baseball because he knew them.

Then my next stop was under John Henry Lloyd. At the time, I didn't know who John Henry Lloyd was. In fact, I didn't know anything about the Negro leagues even, and the person that told me first about the Negro leagues was Ty Helfrich. He said to me, "You probably won't get a chance to play in the majors, but you can make a pretty good living playing in the Negro leagues," and he went on to tell me about them, how he had played against them and the House of David and all those different clubs. He said that they do pretty good and not only that, they have a chance to go to other countries and play.

He said, "Take care of yourself." He always said that. He caught me one time. I liked track, well, the field portion of track; I liked to high jump and I liked to throw the discus and the javelin. He caught me one day out there on the field with a discus

1946 Newark Eagles, Negro League World Series Winners, 4 games to 3, over the K.C. Monarchs (author's collection).

in my hand and I've never seen a person as angry as this man was when he saw me with that discus. He practically snatched it out of my hand and he told me, "Don't you ever pick that pie plate up again!" [Laughs]

You were a big boy. You should have been able to throw that thing a long way.

I could, and the javelin, too. And I high-jumped pretty good, too.

He said, "If you want to play another sport, try basketball because you'll be running a lot and your legs will be in shape," because a pitcher actually pitches off his legs. He said, "I'll see to it that you get on the team." [Laughs] He was the athletic director and he was also the baseball coach. He talked to the basketball coach and I don't know how he put it to him, but he must've told him, "I've got somebody that you're *going* to put on your team." [Laughs]

It just so happened I turned out to be a pretty good basketball player so I did play varsity ball in high school and also played out at Lincoln University.

When someone asks me, "What was the most memorable game that you ever pitched?" I guess they expect me to say like pitching against the Bob Feller All-Stars or some other memorable thing, and I say, "The game that I really remember as being the most memorable game was the first game that I pitched for the Newark Eagles."

I remember, we were on our way north from Miami — we had trained in Miami — and we stop and play different games on the way north. We stopped in Winston-Salem, North Carolina, and they handed me the ball there and I pitched against the Homestead Grays. You know they're going to give me a baptism of fire here, but the thing about it is that I struck out the first five guys and that included anybody that was up there — Josh and Buck and everybody.

Two of the greatest hitters who ever played.

That's right. And I beat them. That's what started me off as being in the rotation. *That* was my most memorable game because I said to myself, "I made it," because I figured that was my test. I made the team and I think that anytime you make a team, it should be memorable.

We always seemed to have a good staff of pitchers, all the way down to 1946 even. We had people who could throw the ball and we had hitters, too. We had it all.

You entered the service in 1942.

I was drafted. Never picked up a ball [in the service]. Picked up a whole lot of other things, but there was no baseball. I went in the army in September of 1942 and I came out in January of 1946.

The experience must have agreed with you because when you returned you had one of the greatest seasons anyone ever had.

That's right. I think that one of the things that did it was the fact that I put on about ten pounds and that helped. It was solid [army] food, at least in the beginning 'til we got to rations — K rations and C rations and all that sort of stuff.

The whole team, not just you, had a fantastic 1946.

Nineteen forty-six was probably my best year in baseball, in terms of things that I did and accomplishments that I managed to do. It began with the season I had with the Newark Eagles. I was the champion pitcher that year; I won 15 and lost one. I lost the first game [Laughs] and I said, "Oh, Lord, it's going to be a bad season for me. That damn army ..." and so on. Then I won 15 straight.

Then the next thing that happened, I was picked for the East-West game, which is our all-star game, and then in the fall of that year I went on a tour with Bob Feller's All-Stars with Satchel Paige. And then it was my first year in Cuba. Everything happened that year. [Laughs] It was a good money year.

I went down there [Cuba] for four winters. I met Carl Erskine and we became friends and we'd stand on the sidelines and

talk. There was one hitter I used to have a *lot* of trouble with and he seemed to have no trouble with him at all, so I said, "What do you throw this guy to get him out?" He told me it was a straight change and he showed me how to throw it. I picked it up real quick and I began to use it right away and I began to get him out. [Laughs] It became a part of my repertoire after that.

How was your overall experience in Latin America?

I'll tell you. You know how it is when the sun comes up after night? That's pretty much what it was like. I'm saying in terms of being somebody, when you went to Latin America, you were somebody and you were treated as somebody and the newspapers treated you as somebody and the people treated you as somebody. You had the best accommodations of all. When I was in Cuba, I lived in the *best* part of Cuba. I had my wife down there the first year and the next year I took my wife and my newborn son. He learned to walk down there. It has some real nice memories for me.

They had a beautiful stadium down there called Grand Stadium. We had a trainer and I said, "What's a trainer?" [Laughs] It was just a marvelous experience and everywhere I went in Latin America it was the same thing. One of the things I think that did drive the black ballplayers was that they all wanted to go through that window and get down there because everybody would come back talking about it, so you played *harder* in order to get there. You had a goal that you wanted to achieve: to get to Latin America. Bill Wright never came back and Bonnie Serrell practically lives there now.

Sometime in the late '40s, the New York Giants contacted you.

What happened there was when I came out of Ruppert Stadium, somebody handed me a note and said to call this number. It had Alex Pompez [New York Cubans owner] on it and it gave me a number. I thought, "I wonder what he wants with me?" There was a pay phone right across the street from the stadium, so I went over and dropped in a dime — at the time — and I called him. He said to me, "How would you like to play for the Giants?"

So, me with my sense of loyalty, I said to him, "Who you need to talk to is Mrs. Manley because she has my contract." I don't know how he was planning to do this or what was supposed to happen, but after I told him that, he didn't say anything. He said, "We'll see," or something along those lines. I was pretty sure that he was going to call her and try to make some kind of deal, which he may have done and she might have said, "Name the price."

One of the things is that Mrs. Manley wanted to keep her team pretty solid and she didn't want to give me up without adequate compensation and so she declined the offer. He might have suspected that. At that time, we weren't what you would call bosom buddies; we weren't that close. I had just had a big-time argument with her about salary and I held out. She was a little upset with me but she finally paid me what I wanted and she had the nerve to tell me, "I don't think you're worth it but I'll give it to you," or something like that. I know her; if she felt I wasn't worth it she wouldn't have given it to me. I know that. [Laughs]

At any rate, I never heard any more about it.

You pitched on.

Yes, I did. The problem was that in the spring of 1948 I suffered a shoulder separation. I didn't know what the heck was wrong with my arm. It was the year after I held out, too. What happened was that I played winter ball and I held out and I thought I was in good enough shape because I had pitched winter ball and I didn't figure I needed a whole lot. They kind of rushed me a little bit in terms of the rotation.

I remember; I pitched in Wilmington, Delaware, and we played the Philly Stars, I think. Biz Mackey was the manager and he told me, "You go down to the bullpen. Hooker's gonna start this game and if we need you we'll bring you in and give you a little workout." It just so happened that Hooker lasted about one inning and I went in and pitched from the second inning, I think it was, 'til the ninth. And I wasn't in condition and something went wrong. [Laughs]

The next thing I knew, I was in pain and from that point on I learned how to pitch all over again. I was pitching with pain, I'll tell you that. I kept pitching for Newark and I learned how to spot pitch — throw slow, slower, and then slower — and I managed to win ballgames.

I went to Canada and I played up there with Sherbrook and I played with Brandon. I can remember sitting on the bench up there in Sherbrook and at that time they didn't have Tylenol and Excedrin and all these pain relievers. The only thing they had at that time was aspirin. I remember sitting on that bench, inning after inning, popping aspirin, trying to reduce the pain. You don't realize what you go through after 'cause I didn't know how to do anything else but play ball.

My shoulder would swell right at that joint and it would just puff up. I guess if I'd have used ice it might have been better, but at that time the only thing they knew was liniment and heat — just the opposite of what I needed.

I went to Mexico after that and I played down in Torreon. My wife wrote me and said, "Look, fella, I don't want you to be a baseball bum." They had this thing that was called the G.I. Bill of Rights and she said it would be expiring that fall and she said,"You get your butt home here because they're going to pay all your expenses; they'll buy your books, they're going to pay your tuition, they're going to do everything. I'm going out here to the college and talk to this lady and tell her you're coming and you be here." She was in college then. I'm glad she did. I'm forever indebted to her, so what I did was I went to management and I told them, "I gotta go." I have a piece here now that I cut out of the paper in Mexico. It says, "El Grand Max Se Va."

I came home and went to school for four years, graduated, and taught for 28 years. I taught sixth grade most of the time. It was a wonderful experience. I enjoyed most of it.

You saw a lot of players. Who was the best?

The best player I ever saw. That's a goodie, a real goodie. I just got through talking to a person and I said to him, "You know, one of the things I think that is a problem, public-wise, is knowledge of how many real good baseball players there were in the Negro leagues. Try to pick an all-star team and you're going to wind up with maybe three guys at first base and you'll get to second base and you've got pretty much the same thing." I mean, you go around the diamond and you're going to find that you're two or three deep in each one of people that you think rate as all-time all-star people — just those that you've seen, let alone those you haven't seen play.

Judy Johnson and Ray Dandridge and Felton Snow. That's just third base. At shortstop, look what you've got. At second base, you've got Sammy T. Hughes, you've got Bonnie Serrell, and you've got Dick Seay. Piper Davis. You've got so many great infielders.

I'm still trying to answer your question. The best ballplayer — I don't know. I'll have to exclude pitchers. I probably would say Ray Dandridge.

The thing about Ray Dandridge was the fact that he was an exceptional fielder and he hit for the average, as was Willie Wells, too. That's what makes it so difficult. Those two people are very comparable as infielders, but they played different positions. The only way that you can really sort of settle it, I guess, is to say, "Flip a coin," but I would still pick Ray Dandridge. Willie Wells was great and he was very, very close in my mind to Dandridge, but I think Dandridge brought something to a game. Willie Wells was a more relaxed-like individual; Dandridge would bring fire to the game, and exuberance and excitement.

Willie would do the job but he didn't bring the same thing to the game that Dandridge did. He'd fire you up.

One of the problems I have with the literature of Negro leagues baseball is that most of it centers only on the players people have heard of — Josh, Satchel, and a few others.

I have a problem with that because you get Negro league household names and everybody talks about Satchel and Josh and Cool Papa Bell and so forth and so on — and justifiably so — but what it does, it limits the perspective that people have about the Negro leagues. You know, "There were a few good players here and there," but that's not true.

I've left out Cuban ballplayers, like Dihigo and Silvio Garcia, Avelino Galizares, Francsico Coimbre, and Pedro Pages. You can get a lot of good ones there. And the Mexican players. It limits the perspective that people have about the quality of play. Now we're beginning to call our leagues the Negro major leagues.

Who was the best pitcher? This may be tougher than the best player.

I don't think so. A lot of people may disagree, but I would say Satchel Paige. The thing that made Satchel Paige the top pitcher — and Leon was one of the closest friends that I've ever had in baseball — there was something about Satchel that was different. Leon had a better curveball and he was a better fielder and, of course, he could hit the ball and I think that this accents him quite a bit, but in the mind, the phenomenon of Satchel was that Satchel had a minuscule curveball and a great fastball and was one of the best pinpoint control masters of all-time. He could throw the ball anyplace he wanted to throw it anytime he wanted to throw it there.

A lot of people used to talk about his "be-ball" and when he mentioned it, people would always think that he meant the insect, but he said his "be-ball" was that the ball that would "be" where he wanted it to be. [Laughs] And that was true and that was the secret of Satchel's success, because with that little tiny curveball he had, he could make it look like it was four feet because of where he placed it — where he put it. He could throw it anywhere he wanted to throw it.

But I would also say this: Leon was great. Just like we talked about Wells and Dandridge — you have a thing there that's very similar, but I would edge my buddy out.

The other thing, which I guess a lot of people think about, if you had one game that you wanted to win, you might pick Leon because of all the *other* things he could do — the fact that he could run, he could bunt, he could field, and he could also pitch. He gave you another dimension in a game where you would look up and you had nine hitters in the lineup and you had another infielder. You have that dimension going for Leon in terms of, "I have one game to win. Who do I want to pitch?" Okay — Leon. He was a complete ballplayer.

One of the greatest injustices of recent times was his Hall of Fame election at a point where he could neither enjoy it nor benefit from it.

I was in the hospital with him when he was elected. Outwardly, it seemed as though everybody was more worried about him going in than he was. It seemed to me that he could have gone in sooner, especially if you know a guy's on his last legs. There's very little empathy or understanding that goes into something. I figure this: a guy's either eligible or he isn't. If he is, other considerations shouldn't be there. They say, "He's going to go in, but he won't go in 'til next year." You look at other considerations. This guy is walking around, he's healthy, he's got another five or six years, so we'll put Leon in because it doesn't seem like he's going to last too long. If

he's going to go in the next year, why wait?

The other thing is that he needed the money. It was really a travesty, as far as I was concerned. Because he was my friend, I knew his financial condition and I knew his physical condition and I knew that if he'd've gotten a year of pay for being a Hall of Famer, I think it would've made gobs of difference in bills and things that had to be paid and all those things.

There are other men like him, both black and white, who deserve some recognition before it's too late.

You are certainly right. I feel the same way about them.

Would you go back and be a ballplayer again?

I certainly would. I think, really, some of the most gratifying years of my life was playing baseball. I think teaching ranks up there, but I think that the memories that come to my mind in terms of the friendships and the fun we used to have, the traveling and the busses, telling jokes and singing and doing all those different kinds of things in the bus, the ribbing and the funny things that we did — they're memories that can never be erased from my mind and couldn't have been gotten any other way. It was a very unique experience.

I talk to a lot of people and I say, "You know, it's a strange thing about my life. If I had my life to live all over again, I would want to live it the same way. I wouldn't change a thing. I'd want to do it the *same* way, even in the army because I still do things I learned there. And the places that I saw, the places that I went — I went to France, to Germany, to Manila, Japan. I would never have gotten there.

And my family. To me, that is one of the things that makes me not want to change anything that happened in my life.

MAXIMILLIAN "MILIO" or "DR. CYCLOPS" MANNING
Born 11-18-18, Rome, GA
Ht. 6' 4"   Wt. 185   Batted L Threw R

Year	Team, league	G	IP	W	L	Pct	H	BB	SO	SHO	ERA
1938	Newark Eagles, NNL										
1939				11	6	.647					
1940				5	4	.556					
1941				6	4	.600					
1942		16	91	7	7	.500	55	15	24	1	
1943–45						military service					
1946	Newark Eagles, NAL			15	1	.938					
1947		23	169	15	6	.714	113		104	0	
1948		16		10	4	.714	95	35	73		
1949	Houston Eagles, NAL	16	94	8	4	.667	87	16	28	1	
1951	Sherbrooke-Branford, ProvL										

Manning also played several winters in Latin American countries.

Art Pennington

Superman

NEGRO LEAGUE DEBUT: 1939

Art Pennington was a switch hitter who batted .300 everywhere he played. In the Negro leagues, he batted .336; in the Mexican League, he batted an even .300; and in the minor leagues he batted .322. And he was one of the most versatile players to ever wear a glove. The only position he didn't play in a 20-year professional career was catcher.

It would seem that with his versatility and performance — and age (he was only 23 when Jackie Robinson was signed by Brooklyn) — he would be a prime candidate for organized ball, but he was playing in Mexico at that time and not too eager to return to the States, having both better conditions and more money south of the border.

Maybe it was a case of wrong place, wrong time because, on the strength of his impressive record, Art Pennington looks as if he would have made it in Major League Baseball.

When did you become a switch hitter?

I become a switch hitter when I was a young kid. My dad was quite a ballplayer and he saw I was havin' trouble hittin' 'em from the left side — lefthand pitchers — so he told me to switch. That made the difference.

When did you get the nickname "Superman"?

I was about 10 or 11, somethin' like that. My mother give me that name. I think we was goin' out fishin' or somewhere and there was a flat. We didn't have no jack, so I told her that I'd pick the wheel off high enough for 'em to put some bricks up under it so we could take the tire off and put a spare on. She thought I was gonna hurt my back, but I lifted it, I'd say, about five or six inches so we could put some bricks under it and change the tire. Mom said, "My little superman." She kept callin'

me Superman. The ballplayers as I went along, they heard the name. My mom would call me Super or Superman. That's where it began.

I bet the other kids didn't bother you much if you were going around picking up cars.

No, they didn't bother me much in school. [Laughs] I was built pretty good in them days.

How did you come to join the Chicago American Giants?

There were two teams before I went with the American Giants. I went to Happy Foreman's team. That was the Zulu Clowns, with them grass skirts on. We had a good team. They'd have the guys hit a fly ball but it wasn't a ball. People'd be lookin' at it and I'd run and jump in the outfield and come up with a ball in my glove and the people thought I'd caught it. That was the first team and I was very young then. Then next I went with the West Indian Royals out of Miami, Florida, and we had a good team there.

The American Giants was playin' the Memphis Red Sox in Memphis. My aunt sent me five dollars to come from Hot Springs to Memphis, so I got a tryout with the American Giants and they hired me right then. I beat out one of the old veteran shortstops. They had a grudge on me then; they didn't like it at all.

From then on I was with the American Giants 'til I jumped to Mexico and played there in that winter and summer league down there with all them major leaguers. Mickey Owen, Max Lanier, Sal Maglie, Fred Martin, and all them guys jumped outta the majors down there 'cause they was makin' more money. The Pasquel brothers was the head of the whole league.

In Monterrey they had another rich guy. We was in New Orleans playin' a game and they come in, got three of us. They asked me what's the best three we had on the American Giants that would go for a thousand [dollars] apiece. At that time, I don't think we was makin' over $400, so I said, "What you need?" He said, "We definitely want you and we want a second baseman and we want a lefthand pitcher." So I said, "I'll get 'em for you. I'll have 'em in the room and you can talk with 'em."

So I got Lefty McKinnis, one of our ace pitchers, and Jesse Douglas. He was a firecracker second baseman. So he hired us and we all drove to Mexico and we played on the Monterrey team. They didn't want all of us together, so they separated us on different teams. Too many Americans on one team. I think it was four or three [allowed]. See, they had some Cubans, too, and they could have four or five foreigners. They had me and two Americans on that Monterrey team and the rest was Cubans and Mexicans and Santo Domingans.

They let me go to Puebla and I finished down there with Sal Maglie, used to pitch for the [New York] Giants. 'Fore I went

there, I hit a homer off of Sal Maglie. My wife was in the hospital; I told her to listen on the radio. I said, "It's the Fourth of July. I'm gonna hit you a home run today." [Laughs] Sal Maglie, he threw me his curveball and I hit him over that Fourth of July sign in Puebla. [Laughs] She told me she heard all about it on the radio.

I went right from summer to winter ball and I was gonna stay in Mexico. I was gonna live there 'cause I married a Spanish girl down there. My mother and dad, they had a fit to think I would live in Mexico and not come back to the United States but I just told 'em, I said, "The things the way it is in the United States" — it was so prejudiced — "Mexico is freedom. They don't think about no color." This Spanish girl I married down there was white so I tried to explain to 'em but my mother didn't see it, so I stayed down there, I think, three or four years playin' winter and summer ball, then she got so that I come back to the United States.

We caught a train all the way from Laredo, Mexico, to Little Rock. On the train they wanted my wife to sit up in the white part, said we couldn't sit together on the train. I told 'em she'll never move. I had my baseball bat in my luggage. [Laughs] I said, "Don't bother me. We are married and she's not goin' anyplace. She's gonna sit right here."

We got to Little Rock. My dad was supposed to meet me there. When we got there, they wouldn't let her in the colored waitin' room and we couldn't go in the white waitin' room, so we had to stand outside and wait 'til my dad and mother drove from Hot Springs to pick us up. My dad saw my wife. [Laughs] He was nervous, he was an old Southerner. He said, "Get in the car. Let's go. Hurry." [Laughs]

My wife couldn't speak no English. That's what helped us a lot. Then when we went to Cuba in '47 — Havana, Cuba — and played there, I hit the first grand slam in that winter league. We left Havana and we flew back and I don't like to fly too much.

Art Pennington (courtesy of Art Pennington).

We got in Miami — a layover or somethin' like that — and the sightseein' bus from the airport was drivin' us around. My Spanish wife, she didn't speak no English at all, so when she got on the bus she sit right behind the bus driver and I went and sit right with her because it didn't bother me; we all come on that airplane from Cuba. I was takin' a nod 'cause I got a headache in that hot weather flyin' from Cuba, so when I woke up the guy had us at the police station.

Here come a policeman, tappin' me on the shoulder. "Wake up, Unca." I said, "My name's Art Pennington. I'm no Unca." He said, "Where you comin' from?" "Havana, Cuba." And we talked and he asked my wife somethin'. I said, "You got to speak Spanish. She don't understand nothin' you say." He said, "You're supposed to sit in the back." I said, "I'll tell you what. Tell him to take us back to the airport. I wanna make a complaint. I'm a professional baseball player. I'm gonna make a complaint about it because we didn't ask for this. We were supposed to be flyin' straight through and you all stopped us for some trouble and had a layover here." So, anyway, the guy took us back to the airport. I made a complaint and we stayed at the airport and finally we got outta there and went on. It was a lotta problems in them days, but it didn't bother me too much.

Many fellows have said that Mexico was so much better for the ballplayers.

Oh, my goodness. When I left the United States, I never had so much freedom in all my life because you could eat anywhere and they got the finest restaurants, the beautifulest women — all colors, don't make no difference — and they're crazy about athletes. They got dance halls and I used to love to dance. I just told my mother, I said, "Mom, you should see this country. It's beautiful. Mexico City and Monterrey and Acapulco. Everybody swimmin' together."

I couldn't believe it and that's why I didn't wanna come back but she got me back and liked to got me in trouble down in Hot Springs and I told her, I said, "See! That's what I told you about me comin' back. It's gonna be a problem because you know I'm not gonna back off of these people about my wife."

Yeah, they wanted my wife and I not to stay together in Hot Springs. I went down and talked to the sheriff and chief, told 'em my granddaddy was white. He was white and married my grandmother, had 13 kids in Hot Springs, and I asked 'em, "How is it so bad now? I got my wife — she's white — and you all givin' me problems?" So the sheriff told me, "Forget it, Art. Just go 'head and enjoy yourself. don't pay 'em no mind." So they didn't bother me no more but every time we'd go somewhere they'd be lookin'. I went to the colored clubs and things and they were nervous, too, because it was segregated in them days. She was a beautiful, beautiful woman; she almost could've been a movie star. Her name's Anita — a beautiful redhead. She was strictly a ball fan. That's how I met her. We had two girls.

How was the barnstorming through the South?

Oh, it was bad. The whites would book the Kansas City Monarchs, with Satchel Paige, and American Giants. It was a drawin' card. They would book us all the way down to Mississippi, all them little farm towns, and Montgomery, Alabama. That's one place. They had a big watermelon contest out there. All the blacks would sit on one side and the whites on the other side. I just couldn't believe it. They had this watermelon contest and they had, oh, I imagine it was six or seven black people and who eat the watermelon the fastest got ten or twenty dollars. I looked at them people eatin' that watermelon. One guy eat the rinds and everything. It was just embarrassin'.

It was tough. We played in Mississippi and the guy booked the game, he was good. He booked us down there, he was nice; we couldn't stay in the hotel, couldn't get in no restaurant to eat. He went and got us fried chicken, then we had to sit outside the school and eat it. Then we took our showers in the school and that was it.

We came through one town in Mississippi and some of the guys didn't know what's what and we was thirsty and went to a park. They jumped off the bus and went to get some cool water. [Laughs] Some white fella come up there and said, "Hey! Read that sign there!" It said, "White." When you're thirsty, you're not gonna read no signs.

My mother and all her sisters is white. Oh, man, you couldn't even tell the difference. I got a picture sittin' right here now. But that's the way it was then. That's what I told 'em down there, I said, "I can't believe my granddaddy had 13 kids here — mixed — and you bother me on my wife and we stayed in the same house my granddaddy had his kids?!"

I'll say one thing. I don't care how bad it was in the South in them days, they had a lotta respect for baseball players. Any athlete — they had a lotta respect for 'em. We played in one place down in, I think it was Waco, Texas, or somethin' like that, and one guy was callin' us niggers and things and the guy that booked us down there told a couple of cops to go get him. Shoot, they put him outta the ballpark. They said, "We're not gonna tolerate that." He said, "We get these guys down here. You all enjoy seein' 'em and you gonna call 'em all kinds of names?"

We never had no problems. They fed us, we just couldn't eat in restaurants and go in no clubs or nothin' like that, but, see, I didn't take my wife with me at them places. Unh-unh.

We drew a lotta people. When I was with those Clowns, those Zulu Clowns, oh, my stars, the people thought we was real Africans. [Laughs] We had them Zulu skirts on, our face all painted, and some guys had the bones on their hair. Man, they would hit that ball and run and that skirt would fly! [Laughs] Yeah, that was a lotta

fun. That was great. They don't have that no more since they had this integration and took all the best of all the black teams. They don't have the barnstormin' and the sandlot teams.

How did you avoid World War II?

I didn't wanna go to the army in the first place and when they drafted me, I was in Hot Springs, Arkansas. I told 'em, I said, "I don't want to go to the army. What I got to fight for? I can't eat in no place, can't go no place. Why do I wanna fight? I don't know nothin' 'bout no Japs. They ain't did nothin' to me." So they got hot at me then. One of the guys said, "Onliest way that you won't go to the penitentiary is you gonna go out there and work on that rubber plant for the government." And I said, "Well, I'll go out there and work." I was just gonna work for the winter until baseball season.

They put me in some shoes with tie things on 'em and it was real hot and my feet got hot. I stayed out there for about a couple weeks and I got tired of that and I quit. Next thing, they wanted me to report. When they said report, I went to Chicago. The big boy that owned the team, J. B. Martin — he was a multimillionaire — he said, "Don't worry about it. We'll make 'em transfer you to Chicago." So they sent me down to the draft board in Chicago and they sent 'em a letter down there and that was all to it. He got three or four ballplayers outta the army. That's how I missed it.

I'da been dead by now, 'cause they'da killed me sure as the world 'cause I was very stubborn in them days. I was young and I just didn't realize life — why people were so mixed up about things and some people could have freedom and do what they wanted and others, they had to take the back seat. I just never did like it.

My mother and dad would say, "Yes, sir," and "No, sir," to people down there and Momma would get mad at me because she'd introduce me to some of her white friends and I would say just, "Yes" or "No," and Momma'd get mad. I'd say, "Momma, I've been raised in Chicago. I been there

Art Pennington (L.) and Bill Cash, 1952 (?), Culiacán, Mexico (courtesy of Art Pennington).

practically all my days. I'm not workin' for 'em; I'm a professional baseball player and I just can't do it."

It's a lot better for everybody now. We didn't make the money. These guys makin' millions of dollars and can't do nothin'. I wish I could've come along and made some of that money.

What was your top salary?

In the United States? $600. In Mexico I made $5,000. That was a lotta money in them days. My parents, I think they was workin' for $15 every two weeks at a hotel, so I bought a taxi cab stand and put 'em in a restaurant and had my mom and dad quit and run that and that's how we got on our feet.

I made $3,500 but it wasn't but one season in Santo Domingo. They give me $3,500 a month down there but that's only four-and-a-half months. In Cuba, I only made a thousand. See, I didn't make the money that Mickey Owen and them made. They paid them for their name. I out-hit all of them guys. Mickey Owen didn't hit nothin' in Mexico. Danny Gardella and [George] Hausmann and all that bunch. I think Mickey Owen made $25,000. They got paid for the names.

But I enjoyed it. I did all right, so I don't have no regrets. I don't have no regrets at all. I'm just sorry that when they took Jackie Robinson, everybody in the black leagues, they didn't think Jackie was gonna make it because he wasn't that good in our leagues. We had so many better than Jackie Robinson. He fooled us all. I told 'em after, when they come and interviewed me, I told 'em, I said, "Sure. Jackie wasn't the best player. He wasn't even in the big ten hittin'. I was in that big ten in hittin'. But I'll tell you one thing. They picked the best man. No doubt about it. They picked the best man. They couldn't've picked a better man than Jackie Robinson." He was well-educated, he was a college graduate, he was a lieutenant in the army.

Nobody would've took that. I remember, they put a black cat on the field in St. Louis — throwed it out there when he was gettin' ready to bat — and Jackie walked over and picked that black cat up and patted him and give him to one of the guards. See, now, if it had been me or some of them other guys, they're liable to throw that black cat up in the stands. That would've been bad for everything. They picked the best man and Jackie proved it. I don't think nobody could've did a better job than Jackie. He's a heck of a ballplayer to take all that.

That's why he died so young. He took all that and his hair was all white in no time and that kid of his give him a lot of problems, too. He was a heart-breaker for his dad, but I think his daughter's still livin'.

You played everywhere but catcher.

Yeah, I didn't catch. I could throw so hard, Jim Taylor from the American Giants would save some of his pitchers when we got quite a few runs or if we have enough runs, he'd call me in from the outfield or first base, whatever, and have me to throw the last couple or three innin's. And I could fire that ball. [Laughs]

I enjoyed just throwin', but I played every position on the field — first, second, third, outfield. I didn't play catcher. In the outfield I played center, sometimes left and right, but the guys when I first started, all of 'em would call me a hot dog 'cause I was young and when the guys would pitch, I'd tell 'em, "Throw it and duck!" 'cause I could hit. And the onliest man made a fool outta me was Satchel Paige. I told him to throw it and duck, that sucker struck me out three times in Detroit in front of 44,000. [Laughs] Jim Taylor said, "Don't let that bother you. He's struck out a-many." I couldn't believe it! I couldn't catch up with that fastball. He was somethin', I'm tellin' you. That guy could throw that ball. He was the best pitcher I ever seen in my *life!*

Dizzy Dean, when I hit the home run off him, he could throw but they had excuses that Dizzy Dean had hurt his arm. They always got excuses. One guy walked up to me after I hit the home run; after the game, he said, "I don't believe you could've hit Dizzy when his arm was all right." I said, "Well, he's throwin' mighty hard now. If he threw any harder I couldn't see the ball." [Laughs]

Him and his brother Paul was with the Cardinals and he would barnstorm against us and then Satchel would take an all-star team out to California and play Bob Feller's all-star team. Bob would tell Satchel, "I don't need but one run." And Satchel would say, "If you don't need but one run, I need two." [Laughs] And we'd get two runs for him and that was all.

Are there games that stand out?

Well, let me see. I was in Barranquilla, Columbia, and I hit 5-for-5. I won a bike over there. In 'Frisco, I hit the second home run outta that ballpark. [Joe] DiMaggio hit the first one; I hit the second one. That was a thousand dollar bond. Seals Stadium. Abe Saperstein had trouble tryin' to get me the money. They said the money was for the [Pacific Coast] League players and Saperstein said, "Then take the sign off."

And then the next one is one of the longest hit in Comiskey Park. That upper deck on that corner, I hit a line drive that hit that corner. It was goin' outta the ballpark but it hit that corner and bounced back. That was a good one.

I hit quite a few home runs in Caracas, Venezuela. Then I hit a grand slam to open a ballpark in Culiacán, Mexico. They got my name on the ballpark down there. I got $500 for hittin' a grand slam in Cuba, and a radio. They had all the major leaguers down there and they put in the paper, "Who's gonna hit that first home run in this park?" We had a big banquet and I raised my hand, I said, "I'll hit the first one." [Laughs] Them guys looked at me and when I hit that grand slam to win that game that night, two or three of the guys wouldn't even speak to me. I told 'em, I said, "I'll hit 'em outta any ballpark. It don't bother me one bit. You guys got the names, sure, but we got the ballplayers. That black league is strong as anything that ever moved." And we had some strong players.

Mule Suttles was strong. He was a tough ballplayer. And that Cool Papa Bell, I thought I could outrun him. I was young and when we played his team, Taylor would have us get out and run the 100-yard dash. We would run, but all at once ol' Cool Papa would walk on by me. And I could fly in them days.

I stole some bases. Onliest thing I did when I was playin', I would always slide and come up at the same time. I would always stay close to the base —first base— and I would limp, you know, like somethin' was wrong with my leg, and they didn't pay too much attention to me 'cause I never got off too far. Then, all at once, I'm gone! [Laughs] That's the way I always did.

Would you play baseball again?

I sure would. I sure would. You know, I really miss it. I miss it more than playin' in the major leagues. I had so much fun playin' in different towns and runnin' around with all them different pretty gals. You can imagine. In them days, they had washtubs full of pop in the South they called Nehi. I remember all them good things.

And then they'd have barbecue and we'd eat good. Oh, yes, I'd do that again. I really enjoyed the life.

ARTHUR DAVID "SUPERMAN" PENNINGTON
Born 5-18-23, Memphis, TN
Ht. 5' 11"   Wt. 185   Batted B Threw R

Year	Team, league	Pos	G	AB	R	H	2B	3B	HR	RBI	SB	BA
1940	Chi. American Giants, NAL	1B-OF										
1941		1B-OF										
1942		OF		65		12	3	1	1		0	.185
1943		OF		62		12	1	3	2		1	.194
1944		OF	46	157	35	47	6	3	4	37	4	.299
1945		OF	68*	234	48	84	16*	1	5	24	15	.359
1946		OF										
1949	Chi. American Giants, NAL	OF	57	201	39	70						.348
	Portland, PCL	OF	20	53	7	11	1	0	0	2	1	.208
	Salem, WIntL	OF	18	65	15	20	3	0	2	16	3	.308
1950	Chi. American Giants, NAL	OF	43	146	40	54	10	2	6	28	14	.370
1851		OF										
1952	Keokuk, III	OF	116	427	126	149	17	10	20	89	24	.349
1953	Keokuk, Cedar Rapids, III	OF	64	225	45	74	13	1	4	31	10	.329
1954	Cedar Rapids, III	OF	119	423	88	146	22	6	16	79	11	.345

Year	Team, league	Pos	G	AB	R	H	2B	3B	HR	RBI	SB	BA
1955	St. Petersburg, FSL	OF	128	419	94	142	26	7	8	93	12	.339
1956	Modesto, CalL	OF-1B	108	359	62	92	18	5	10	65	14	.256

Record in Latin America.

Year	Team, league	Pos	G	AB	R	H	2B	3B	HR	RBI	SB	BA
1946	Monterrey-Vera Cruz-Puebla, MexL	1B-OF	80	290	40	91	14	3	5	48	8	.314
1947	Puebla, MexL	1B-OF	123	437	86	127	10	10	5	50	6	.291
1947-48	Leones, CubWL			77	6	18	3	1	9	10	1	.234
1948	Puebla, MexL	1B-OF	84	276	48	83	18	8	4	42	12	.301
1953	Cibaenas, DRSL	OF		48	12	11				12	1	.229

Frazier Robinson

Satchel's Catcher

NEGRO LEAGUE DEBUT: 1939

Everyone who ever batted against him says Satchel Paige was the greatest. Frazier Robinson agrees. From his position, he could see those batters struggle. Part of their struggle, though, was due to Robinson. As Satchel's catcher, he was calling for those pitches they couldn't hit.

A professional ballplayer for more than a decade, he also was Leon Day's catcher later in his career. Robinson was noted for his hustle and had an excellent arm, and twice in his Negro leagues career he was on championship teams. At one time or another, he caught some of the greatest pitchers of all time. In addition to Paige and Day, there were Booker McDaniels, Bill Byrd, Joe Black, Jim LaMarque, and Connie Johnson. A man who can handle pitchers such as those is an asset to any team, yet Robinson also contributed a batting average in the .280s. He more than earned his salary through the years.

Frazier Robinson's younger brother, Norman, was also a long-time Negro leagues star. A very fast outfielder, he was the regular center fielder for the Birmingham Black Barons when young Willie Mays joined the team, but it took a broken leg before Mays could replace him in center. Slowed slightly after the injury, Norman Robinson moved to left field.

You and your brother started playing professionally together with Satchel Paige's All-Stars. How did you come to join his team?

They sent for me and my brother from Kansas City. The team was owned by J. R. Wilkinson, and they sent for him [Norman] and they had to have a catcher and they sent for me. I was in Texas playin'. They had an old league down there called TOLA—Texas, Louisiana, Oklahoma—League and we were playin' down there. It didn't ever get up off the ground.

You were Satchel's catcher. Was he as good as they say?

[Laughs] Yes, he was. When I first started catchin' him he had caught cold in

his arm down in South America and he was throwin' the ball underhanded. We worked with him and his arm come around and we were gettin' ready to play Grover Cleveland Alexander's House of David that Sunday in Oklahoma City. I noticed him out there throwin' the ball pretty good, so he come in and told me I better be ready today and I told him, I said, "Man, I can catch what you been throwin' with a work glove," 'cause he'd been throwin' underhanded, you know. [Laughs] And the first pitch, he knocked that mitt and mask off. I called for a fastball 'cause he'd been throwin' the ball underhanded and he threw it too hard. He knocked the mitt *and* mask off! I said, "I'll be ready from now on." [Laughs] "He'll

Frazier Robinson (courtesy of Frazier Robinson).

went from there to Canada — Winnipeg, Canada — and stayed up there four years. The ManDak League. North Dakota was in that league. Most of the ballplayers from Negro leagues was up there. That's the only way they could get to play and make a little money.

Me and Leon Day was teammates and roommates up there. When he passed, I had gone in the hospital myself. He passed about a week after they enshrined him in the Hall of Fame.

It's a whole lot of players ought to be in [the Hall of Fame] and it'll be a long time before they get that straightened out. It's a good thing to be in and know that you were able to make it, but, then again, if you don't make it you just don't make it. There's a whole lot of things you'd like to have you can't have.

Were you a teammate of Bill Wright in Baltimore?

No. My brother was a teammate of Bill Wright. Bill Wright went to Mexico before I came to the Elites. He left around '41 or '42. He liked it down there. I think he should be in the Hall of Fame 'cause he was an outstandin' player. Played outfield and hit the ball good. One of them lifetime .300 hitters, you know.

How good a hitter were you?

I hit around .285. A couple of years I hit .340 or somethin' like that, but when you're catchin' it take a whole lot out of you.

I understand that you had a good arm.

Yeah, I had a good arm. I think I threw Cool Papa [Bell] about twice. The only way I threw him out, he would telegraph when he was gonna steal. I knowed when he was goin'. If he'd take a big lead he wasn't goin' nowhere, but the minute he stood on that base — didn't take no lead — you better hurry up and get rid of that ball. [Laughs] And he could run! A lot of times he'd be thrown out but he knew how to slide. He'd

never do that no more." He straightened me up that day.

That was 1939. I caught him 'til 1940, then I went to Baltimore to a team a guy was tryin' to get in the league. I went up there but I didn't stay up there too long 'cause they called me and made me come back to Kansas City. They had me under contract, you know. I went up there because my brother was up there — Norman — but they made me come back to Kansas City, so I stayed with 'em 'til 1942, when we beat the Grays in the World Series four straight. Then I was called in the service.

I was in the service from 1943 to '45. I come out in 1945 and then I got my release from Kansas City and went to Baltimore Elite Giants and I stayed there 'til '50. I trick the second baseman or the shortstop. You couldn't hold that ball a split second. When the pitcher got it to you, you had to be throwin' it.

Was he the fastest man you saw?

Yes, he was. Now [Minnie] Minoso was fast, but there was one boy I seen — played on the Grays, same team Cool was on — that could beat him to first base but after first base couldn't nobody beat him. That was a boy called [David] Whatley. He played right field for the Grays for a while. He could beat him to first base but Jesse Owens couldn't beat him after he left first base. [Laughs] And he was a pretty fair hitter. He didn't hit the long ball but he could get on that base — bunt and drag the ball. He'd run over you if you get in his way. [Laughs]

Your brother Norman was pretty fast, too.

He was. He'd run that 100-yard in 9.5 [seconds]. He was playin' center field and he broke his leg in 1947 and then they were scoutin' [Willie] Mays and they asked him to move to left field and let Mays play center after he broke his leg. He was a lifetime .300 hitter. I didn't see where he lost too much speed. I thought he always kinda kept that in mind 'bout him breakin' his leg. He broke a small bone in his left leg, I think.

He broke his in '47; I broke mine in '48. I broke it in the later part of the season. We won the pennant that year and won the championship. It was durin' 'bout the last week of the season and then I was out of the championship games. I broke my leg in Des Moines, Iowa, slidin' into third base. They had those upraised bases and my foot went under the base and popped. That was my ankle. We came back okay. We was in Canada together on the same team for a couple of years.

Of those two pitchers you talked about, who was better?

You mean between Satchel and Day? I'd have to class Satchel as good as anybody ever pitched because he could pitch three or four days a week. He could get the ball

up there about 98 miles an hour and then he could throw it in the strike zone. He'd throw strikes. Now, to me, this is good 'cause he had good control and you wouldn't have to be jumpin' around catchin' him 'cause he threw the ball where you asked for it.

Now, Day had good control, too, but Day was a pitcher that would keep you honest. If you hit him one time, he might hit you the next time you come up there. [Laughs] This is his claim to success — that he made those hitters *beg* him not to hit 'em. [Laughs] I know — I caught him in Winnipeg, Canada. The first year we got up there we won the championship. A game went 17 innings and I caught him and we beat the team — Brandon — 1-to-nothin'. He went all the way. I was kind of tired that night [after the game] but we were glad to win it. But he's that type of pitcher — one of them gutty little guys. He could pitch and play any position you put him — outfield, infield. He couldn't catch but he could play all the rest of the positions.

Which of those two did you enjoy catching more?

I enjoyed catchin' 'em both, but if I had to pick one that I wanted to catch and be rested the rest of the night, I'd pick Satchel. [Laughs] His control was so great.

See, Satchel studied hitters. This was his life. He studied hitters *all* the time and if he seen you hit the ball a long ways off another pitcher, you never would hit him. He knowed where your power was and how to slow the ball up on you and how to do everything. This made him a great pitcher. He pitched against [Dizzy] Dean and all the rest of 'em.

Mr. Wilkinson that owned the Monarchs put him under contract and sent him out with the All-Star team and we barnstormed with the Israelite House of David on the West Coast. Both Satchel and House of David was drawin' cards. We packed 'em in everywhere we went. Satchel would pitch maybe two or three times a week. They may send for him to come someplace else and pitch but he had to come right back to that team.

I remember in 1942 he pitched in Detroit against a team that won everything that year. They asked us to play 'em and he pitched against them. He pitched a no-hitter that Sunday and we had to play that Monday night in Toledo—play the Toledo Mud Hens. They was a Triple-A team. We went over there and he pitched the first four innings and when he come out the score was tied, 1-1, but we beat 'em. We brought in a pitcher called [David] Barnhill. He was with the Clowns but Wilkinson had got him and told him he wanted him to follow Satchel. He went in there and they didn't get nothin' off of him.

He looked like 'bout half of the height Satchel was. When he come in, they said, "Yes! We can get our runs now off of this little guy!" [Laughs] And the first pitch he threw I called a fastball and he threw a fastball and they said, "Who is this—Satchel with his legs cut off?" [Laughs] He could throw it! He went up there in Triple-A and stayed up there. He was up there where [Ray] Dandridge was.

How was the barnstorming?

Sometimes we'd have to play two and three games a day. [Laughs] A lot of times we wouldn't have time to change our uniforms, but then again that didn't happen but a couple of seasons. We played in Reno, Nevada, and Spokane, Washington, and all up and down the West Coast. The House of David had a good team, too. We had decent hotels to stay in, and [decent] food.

Did you barnstorm through the South?

Only when we were breakin' spring trainin'. The first year I went with Satchel, we trained in New Orleans. We played our way all the way from New Orleans back to Kansas City and then we picked up the House of David and went on to the West Coast.

They had some good teams out there. San Jose had a good team. We played there and they'd beat everything. They told us, "If you guys lose tonight, it's no use you all

stayin' for tomorrow." We had two games. We beat 'em, 6-to-5, that night and the next night we played. A boy called [Jack] Matchett come in and he pitched seven innings and he had 'em blanked, 3–nothin'. Satchel had to pitch or they wasn't gonna pay him and Satchel was standin' around, wouldn't put on his uniform. He say he owed 52 speed citations in California and there was a bunch of highway patrolmen standin' there lookin' at the game. He didn't know whether they were gonna pick him up or not. The man that was runnin' the team was Wilkinson's brother, Lee Wilkinson; he told him to go ahead. If they picked him up, he'd get him out.

So he come in, wasn't warmed, and they tied the runs on him right quick. He said, "Time!" and he threw to third base, shortstop, second base, threw to first base, and he say, "I'm ready now." We went 14 innings and the score was tied, 3–3. We had a boy playin' right field called [Leandy] Young. He hit the ball over the fence, so we beat 'em both games.

We played other pretty good teams out there. San Francisco Seals had a pretty good team. I enjoyed playin' out there. We seen more than if we'd've been playin' there in the league. We played in Kansas City. Chicago, Memphis, Birmingham, the Clowns, and teams like that was in the league.

Did you play against Verdell Mathis?

Yeah. He was a good pitcher—good left-hander. He played for Memphis. One of the best pitchers.

Who were the best players?

You had so many. You had just about anybody that you would pick could play in the major leagues. They might have to polish up a little, but they could play. You couldn't play on these teams I'm talkin' about. They wouldn't carry you; they'd send you home. You had to play your position.

You had this boy [Bonnie] Serrell—he went to Mexico, too—he was one of the best second basemen you could find anywhere. Jesse Williams, he played short-stop for the Monarchs. They were one of the best combinations anywhere you could find. Banks and Baker wouldn't compare with 'em.

These guys could play. You had Buck O'Neil, Josh Gibson, Buck Leonard — all these guys. [Gene] Benson, a boy named Marvin Williams, you had Howard Easterling. I could sit here for the next two hours and call you ballplayers I know could've played up there.

There's people now — due to the fact that we couldn't play all our games in major league ballparks — that say it's not top-rank baseball. Just like when I was in Baltimore. Baltimore never did have a championship team 'til we played there. We used to play the Triple-A team after our season was over. We'd have 18–20 games we'd play with them and with some of the major leagues — Washington Senators and teams like that — and we'd beat them people so bad people said they wasn't comin' out there to see us. This is just a brand of baseball that you played and had to play it. If you loafed, you went home. It was not that you was gonna loaf and get by with it. These small salaries they paid you, you earned it.

Now, I think they killed baseball when these scouts go out and get a boy that can pitch or somethin' like that, they pay him before he ever makes it. If you give somebody two million dollars, or one million, to sign it just takes away some of the hustle. You give a kid that much money to sign, he got it made. He don't care whether he make it or not.

When we played, you had to hustle to stay on that team. They've taken the joy out of baseball and they've made it a business. We played it for the love and sport that was in the game. These people now play it for the money that's in it.

How much were you paid?

Highest I got paid in the United States was $500 a month. A lot of times I did most of the catchin'. In our league, that was a pretty good salary for them to pay. We played a lotta times in crowds big as major leagues had, but some people pocketed the money and there's nothin' you could do 'bout it because this was your job and you couldn't beat it. You had to take what they offered you.

What about meal money?

We got about two dollars a day. Then you could eat on it, but now look at major league ballplayers — they get as much money to eat on as a lotta guys' salary was. More.

They're takin' all the sport out of baseball. They pay [Barry] Bonds all that money. No one player is worth that much money. You have people that can throw that money around, but just like [George] Steinbrenner, the Yankee owner; he can get just about any player that he go after. It hasn't did him any good.

What did you do when you left baseball?

I went to California and I started workin' for the L.A. city school board. I went out there in 1966. I lived in L.A. for 23 years and then I moved down here after L.A. got so bad. It got to be the dope capital of the world and it was 'bout time for me to get away from there. This is my wife's home. My home is Oklahoma. That's where I grew up.

When I left Oklahoma I came to Akron, Ohio, and I played baseball there and then I went to Texas and went to playin'. Let's see, I lost 'bout seven years. I should've been already up there. And when I did get a chance to go up there, when I went to Satchel over there, I was throwin' out those runners and hittin' the ball. They say, "This is the man we been lookin' for all along." [Laughs]

Satchel and I become lifelong friends. When I quit playin', he *begged* me, he said, "Don't quit. You're quittin' too early." Then he'd went to St. Louis Browns and I said, "My legs is gone."

When he went to Cleveland, he was 41, I think. He would always jive 'bout his age. When I really knowed his age, his wife showed it to me. He had passed and I went to the funeral; I was honorary pallbearer. I flew from California, me and my son and a boy called Archie Ware, played first base for the Cleveland Buckeyes, and we went to his funeral, so I asked her — there was two newsmen sittin' there and they was talkin' to her and talkin' to me, too, 'cause they knew I caught him — and I asked her, "How old was Satchel when he died?" "He was 75; I have his obituary right there." He made people think that he was older than what he was. He said a goat eat up the Bible or somethin' like that. [Laughs]

He left [major league] baseball before he was eligible to get his pension and Bill Veeck got Atlanta to pick him up and keep him for six weeks, then he could be eligible to get his pension. When that happened, I picked him up at Chavez [Ravine] and that's when I talked to [Hank] Aaron that day. He was kinda slumpin'. I picked

Satchel up and brought him home 'cause he always liked to stay with me when he got close around. He told me about what was happenin'. If anybody deserved it, he did.

All of you guys deserve a pension. It was no fault of yours that you weren't able to play in the majors where you could qualify for one.

I heard that they were workin' on that. They spoke of that in a meetin' in Kansas City, that they was tryin' to get us some kinda pension from the major leagues.

Do you have any regrets from your baseball days?

No, I don't have any regrets because if I had to do it over I'd do it again because I loved the game. I played for the love of the game. If I wasn't gonna get paid, I would've played anyway. I don't have no regrets. It was just fun playin'. Like O'Neil, I wasn't 20 years too soon.

HENRY FRAZIER ROBINSON
Born 5-30-16, Birmingham, AL
Ht. 5' 11"   Wt. 178   Batted and Threw R

Year	Team, league	Pos	G	AB	R	H	2B	3B	HR	RBI	SB	BA
1939	Satchel Paige's All-Stars	C										
1942	K. C. Monarchs, NAL	C										
1943	Baltimore Greys, ind.	C										
	K. C. Monarchs, NAL	C										.294
	N. Y. Black Yankees, NNL	C										
	Balt. Elite Giants, NNL	C										
1943-45					military service							
1946	Balt. Elite Giants, NNL	C										
1947		C										.286
1948		C										
1949	Balt. Elite Giants, NAL	C										
1950		C										.225

Mahlon Duckett

The Youngest Regular

NEGRO LEAGUE DEBUT: 1940

How many 17-year-olds have stepped into the starting lineup of a major league team and stayed there?

Kids such as Mel Ott, Bob Feller, and Jimmie Foxx made it to the major leagues at the age of 17, but none stayed in the lineup on a regular basis for the first year or two. Robin Yount was 18. Al Kaline and a few others were regulars at 19, but only *one* man (or boy, if you will) ever joined a major league team at the age of 17, became an everyday player, and stayed there.

He is Mahlon Duckett. He joined the Philadelphia Stars of the Negro National League in 1940 when he was only 17 and spent his entire 11-year career as a regular player.

Of course, to hold down a starting position for that long he had to be good and some say he was the best second baseman they ever saw. For five years, he teamed with Frank Austin to give the Stars one of the top double play combinations in baseball history.

His talent was widely recognized. After the 1950 season with the Homestead Grays, his only year not spent with Philadelphia, he was signed by the New York Giants. Unfortunately, he came down with rheumatic fever then and had to leave baseball, his career ending at the age of only 28. Too bad; he had a lot of good years left.

You came to the Stars at 17 from semi-pro ball.

Actually, when I came up in 1940, they didn't have any Negro minor leagues. Now they get a lot of kids out of school, but they didn't do it in those days. The major leagues had minor league teams but they didn't have nowhere *near* as many as they have today.

The way Negro ballplayers was drafted, I guess you'd say, into the league was upon recommendations from other teams, like they had a lot of great semi-pro teams, not only black but white, because of the fact the money wasn't there in those days. The

major leagues, they wasn't makin' any money, either; they was only makin' like $6-, 7,000, so there was a lot of good ballplayers that had jobs and played on semi-pro teams. They had a lot of great semi-pro teams, black and white. That's how they got the ballplayers for the Negro leagues.

Like I was playing in the pretty strong Main Line League in the Philadlephia area and I was recommended by a fella who had played Negro baseball. He was the manager of what they called Norristown, Pennsylvania. He recommended me for a tryout. Actually, I never played high school

Mahlon Duckett (courtesy of Mahlon Duckett).

baseball because I went to Overbrook High in Philadelphia here and we had a national scholastic championship track team and I ran track. That took all our time because we ran both indoors and outdoors in those days. I had a little publicity for my track ability and a lot of people in this area knew me and I got a tryout.

Fortunately, the first couple of games I played I did pretty good. I signed a contract within a week. But we didn't have any minor league teams. We had a lot of teams *we* used to say were minor league teams, especially through the South, like Florida, they had a league, and North Carolina. They called it the Negro Southern League.

That was mostly around North Carolina and Georgia. A lot of ballplayers came from that league, so indirectly you could say it was a minor league.

You mentioned track. You had a reputation for being very quick; were you a base stealer?

In the Negro leagues, the stats wasn't kept accurately. And we wasn't out there playin' for stats or anything like that, we was just out there to play to win. I stole quite a few bases but the records wasn't kept.

First of all, we didn't have coaches or anything like that. All we had was the manager. The manager may coach third base and our first base coach was one of the ballplayers that wasn't playin' that day, but we didn't have a lot of plays we put on. The ballplayers would get together. I usually hit number one or number two in the lineup and if I was on first base I would have plays with the fella that came behind me in batting. I'd give him a signal I wanted to steal or whatever. We made up our own plays.

But as far as base stealing and all that, the records wasn't kept. They talk about Cool Papa Bell—he *was* fast, but we had a lot of fast ballplayers in our league. Even Cool, they couldn't say how many bases he stole. We played a lot of games in small towns throughout the South where, if we didn't send it to the Northern papers, they'd never know about it.

All these books we have today—first of all, they're just goin' by what they heard and I haven't seen one book that was really accurate yet. Lot of people heard about certain ballplayers and if they had a name, they'd build 'em up. Just like in my case, after the war years, say in '47, '48, '49, '50—I had terrific years but you wouldn't see it in a book. But I have newspaper clippings, 'cause when Doby went up in 1947, when Doby was a second baseman and I was a second baseman, everybody just knew I was goin' to the All-Star Game in Chicago. In fact, I thought so up until the last week and then it came through that Branch Rickey was lookin' at Junior

Gilliam. He played second base with Baltimore and at the last minute they said let's take him to the All-Star Game. He was young, too. I can't take anything away from Gilliam; he was a heck of a ballplayer, we all know that.

But that's how they did things in our league, you know, 'cause I think at the time of the All-Star Game I was hittin' like .360. I thought that was fantastic 'cause I never hit no .360. [Laughs] I think I ended up that year with like .320 or something like that. But, see, you never see that in a book. They get on certain fellows like Josh, Satchel. Well, they have to get on Josh Gibson 'cause he was the greatest. Greatest hitter.

But there was so *many* great ballplayers in the Negro leagues that should have much more recognition than they did. I'm not speakin' of me, now, but I'm just sayin' when they talk about the Hall of Fame, there's so many names that I could submit that I thought would be qualified.

Weren't you offered a contract by the New York Giants?

I signed with the Giants. Then an unfortunate thing happened to me; see, I was supposed to go to Phoenix—their training camp, that was 1951, the same year Willie was out there—and I came up with rheumatic fever. That ended my career. I was on bed rest for a year but my heart recovered and I never had any problem with it. Still don't. But I was laid up for a year and they said I'd never play baseball again.

I've heard you were an outstanding fielder at second base.

That's what they said, yeah. [Laughs]

Who was the best shortstop you played alongside?

I'd say Frank Austin. He was a Panamanian. We had Pee Wee Butts, who was with Baltimore at the time; I thought he was the best fielding shortstop. I had played with Pee Wee on All-Star games.

They said I was a pretty good fielder. I made a lot of double plays—me and Frank Austin. He [later] played with Portland [PCL].

1944 Philadelphia Stars
Back row (L. to R.): Stanley Glenn, Garrel Hartman, Bill Ricks, Henry Miller, Marvin Williams, Edward Bolden (owner), Ed Stone, Goose Curry (manager), Jim West, Hubert Glenn, Spoony Palm, Oscar Charleston (coach). Front row (L. to R.): Frank Austin, Charles Boone, Mahlon Duckett, Barney Brown, Ulysses Mahoney, Gene Benson, Bill Cash (courtesy of Stanley Glenn).

You said Josh Gibson was the best hitter. Who was the best all-around ballplayer?

Durin' my career, I was fortunate enough to either play with or against about seven of the Negro Hall of Famers; you know, the fellows who went from the Negro leagues. As far as the greatest hitter, Josh Gibson, by far, as far as I'm concerned. I played with the Homestead Grays a year and Buck Leonard was great, too. He was still playin' like somebody who was 21 years old. Buck was great.

There's just so many of 'em, it's really hard to say. Harry Simpson was with our team — Suitcase Simpson. He came from Philadelphia. We had Gene Benson, who was a great outfielder, and the Cubans, I thought they had some great ballplayers. They had a center fielder named [Lazaro] Salazar. Of course, Martin Dihigo, he could do everything. I played against him, but I saw him when he was a little older and he was still great then.

Take like Oscar Charleston — now he was old when I played against him and *with*

him 'cause he was our manager and he played some of the games. I can just imagine what he would've been like in his day. When he was managin' our team I know he was at least 50 and he was hittin' the ball outta the ballpark. He was just a great ballplayer.

Then you take a fellow that was just inducted in the Hall of Fame — Leon Day. Great pitcher and he could do everything. He could play second base, he could play outfield, and he could hit the ball and he could run. He was just an all-around ballplayer.

I'm speaking mostly of the fellas in the eastern league 'cause I was Negro National League and out West, Kansas City always had a nice team. They speak of Satchel Paige; well they had a fellow that came in and relieved Satchel practically every day — Hilton Smith. I would rather face Satchel eight days a week than face Hilton six, that's how great Hilton was, but he never got the recognition because he came behind Satchel. Any black ballplayer can verify that. I'm not just sayin' that because I had trouble hittin' him; he was great. To me, that's a name they *all* should put up for the Hall of Fame.

Then you have fellas like Willard Brown, who played outfield. I could go on and on about some of the great outstanding ballplayers they had. You figure this way, each team was only carryin' about 15 ballplayers and all these leagues — the Southern League, they had leagues out on the coast — so when you get the greatest black ballplayers from all over the country, there's some outstanding ballplayers. They was tough!

Each team only carried about 15 ballplayers and we had six teams in the East and six teams in the West, which wasn't that many ballplayers, so the ballplayers that was in our league, they had to be good to keep their jobs.

In our league, we had no rules, no laws or anything. We had to face pitchers that we knew was gonna throw at our heads — we had no helmets — and we had spitball pitchers, we had pitchers that would cut the ball. All that wasn't even outlawed in our league. We complained to the umpire. Like me, if I complained, he'd say, "Hey, you young so-and-so, you'd better get up here and try to get a base hit." That's the way it was, but they didn't have to contend with that in the major leagues.

Plus the fact, in the major leagues, they had coaches for everything. In our league, when you came in the league, you played on your natural ability. We had no one to teach us. Like when I came in the league at the age of 17, just about all the ballplayers, they were mean and that was their liveli-hood. They all had families and they didn't want anyone to take their jobs. They wouldn't tell us anything. You just went out there and I tried to learn as I went along. I did have one fellow — Dick Seay, who was a great second baseman at the time, he was playin' with Newark Eagles — and he took a likin' to me and he told me some of the things about second base, what

to watch out for because those fellows would try to hurt you. I wasn't used to all that stuff. They'd spike you and all that kind of stuff. But it didn't take you too long to learn the ropes.

But we had no one whatsoever to teach us anything or tell us anything. You just played on your natural ability and, like I said, I played in Negro baseball 11 years and as I went along, I picked up different things. That wasn't only me. That's the way any fellow that came in the league had to do it that way.

You mentioned traveling through the South. How was that?

Terrible. Terrible with capital T. It was a problem for me at first because I was born and raised in Philadelphia and we had a lit-tle segregation here but nothing like they had down there in the '40s. In the '40s it was terrible. They had the Klan down there, they had lynchin's and so forth. That was the only thing — my mother, she was a little leery. She was always afraid when we went below Washington. Well, I had to do it, you know, when we went to places like Alabama and Mississippi, Louisiana, and so forth.

They didn't have any hotels for us to stay in because the smaller towns in the South, they didn't have black hotels. Now, in Birmingham they had a couple and Atlanta and towns like that, but *if* we were lucky enough for some of the blacks to take us in — different houses — that was all well and good but so many nights we just slept in the bus. And we had to sleep in the bus because we didn't have a place to sleep and then there wasn't any place to eat. We played night games and they had curfews down there on the blacks and durin' the game they all had to be in and *after* the game we couldn't go to any white store to get anything. If we did, we had to go to the back and they would give us like loaves of bread and lunch meat.

But it was pretty rough. It was a rough life. Just sitting here talkin' about it now, I can realize what we really went through, but we were young and we knew the conditions of the South and what we had to face. Plus the fans, they didn't treat us right. It was really something. Now I think about a lot of things that happened that were really scary but at the time it didn't seem that bad.

I went to a white school. It was integrated, but it was mostly white. I lived in a mostly white neighborhood here in Philadelphia at the time and I just couldn't get used to it. I wasn't ready for it. But it didn't take me too long to go by their rules.

Other than the racial situation, do you have any regrets from your career?

As I look back on it, I regret the fact that I really didn't get a chance to play in organized baseball. At the time we was playin', we didn't even give that a thought until Jackie went up and then most of us had been in the league so long.

Another thing, the major leagues had a quota at that time; they was only takin' X amount of ballplayers, *if* they took any. The two New York [National League] teams — the Dodgers and the Giants — they did the most, but they had a quota, too. That's the reason Ray Dandridge never made it because they came out and said, "Well, we have four." I think they had, at the time, Mays and Irvin and Hank Thompson, they had Noble catchin' and that was it. The Dodgers, they had their quota; they had Jackie and Newcombe and Joe Black and Junior Gilliam.

I don't know. I was hurt, I can say that, because it was rumored two or three times that I was scouted, but then it was always some excuse. Not only me, but other ballplayers, too.

Another thing, before they signed Jackie, it was war years and Major League Baseball

was on a decline. We would play in the Polo Grounds or Yankee Stadium on a Sunday and we would have 40- to 50,000 people. You know how Brooklyn Dodgers was; they was only drawin' like 8- or 10,000. Here in Philadelphia, they had the Philadelphia Athletics and the Philadelphia Phillies and we would play Monday nights and fill the stands and the major league teams would have 10,000 or so on a Sunday. They knew if they was gonna take a black ballplayer and put him in the white leagues, the fans was gonna come to see him. That was one of the main reasons I think they did it.

Would you go back to 1940 and be a ballplayer again?

In the Negro leagues? If the situation was like it was then, I'd say yes. I'd do it, sure. I don't regret none of the days I played. In fact, it was an experience I couldn't buy for a million dollars.

What about if you were a young man today — would you try to be a ballplayer?

If I were a young fellow today, yeah, I'd rather be a baseball player than anything else. A lot of the fellas — most of the black players around the Philadelphia area — are mostly goin' for basketball now. I would prefer baseball, not only because I played it but I think it's a better sport and you live longer and make just as much money. And it's more fun.

Today, you have to think about the education, too. If you don't have that education you're in bad shape. We try to talk to the kids in this area. You *always* have your education and it's only a small percentage that do go in the pros.

I've always been a person that believed in athletics and if I were young, I would prefer baseball.

MAHLON NEWTON DUCKETT
Born 12-20-22, Philadelphia, PA
Ht. 5' 10"   Wt. 170 Batted and Threw R

Year	Team, league	Pos	G	AB	R	H	2B	3B	HR	RBI	SB	BA
1940	Philadelphia Stars, NNL	3B										.234
1941		SS										.146
1942		SS										.117

Year	Team, league	Pos	G	AB	R	H	2B	3B	HR	RBI	SB	BA
1943		SS										
1944		SS–2B										.233
1945		2B										.277
1946		2B										.209
1947		2B										.216
1948		2B										.268
1949	Philadelphia Stars, NAL	2B										
	Homestead Grays, ind.	2B										
1950	Homestead Grays, ind.	2B										

Frank Duncan, Jr.

Second Generation

NEGRO LEAGUE DEBUT: 1940

It's not unusual for a boy growing up to want to do what his dad does. Frank Duncan's dad, also named Frank, played professional baseball and was especially good at it. Most observers consider him to be one of the best catchers in Negro leagues history.

Young Frank followed in his father's footsteps, but he made his mark as a pitcher. He began with his dad's team, the Kansas City Monarchs, in 1940 as a utility player, but in 1941 the Duncans made up the first father-son battery in professional baseball history.

Military service separated them in 1942 and during his time in the army, Frank, Jr., signed with the Baltimore Elite Giants. Along the way, he played with and against some of the greatest players ever to play baseball.

You signed originally with the Monarchs, your dad's team.

I was just a utility player. I wasn't among the first-stringers but I could play all positions and I could spell any of 'em for a rest period, like two or three or four days. I was gettin' ready to go in the army and then when I went in the army I was lucky enough to be in a camp that made all the athletes stationed permanently, which was Aberdeen, Maryland, about 30 miles out of Baltimore. Then I started pitchin' on the camp team there.

They got the Baltimore Elite Giants to come down and play us an exhibition game. I was playin' shortstop for the camp team. They came and we had an overflow crowd, but we didn't have but two pitchers 'cause we didn't play but once a week. Both of 'em came up lame, so, in the meantime, I'd always been messin' around pitchin' battin' practice and stuff, so our C.O. told

me that I was gonna have to try. So I did. I stayed out there the full nine innings and they beat me, 2-to-1.

We were in the showers in the barracks after the game and Roy Campanella came up to me; he says, "Your camp is only 30 miles from us. There's six teams in the league. The Homestead Grays are playin' outta Washington, D.C.; that's only 75 miles from your camp. To the north of us would be the Philadelphia Stars, which is 90 miles from the camp; the Newark Eagles, and the two teams outta New York City." See, the New York Black Yankees were usin' Yankee Stadium when the Yankees were on the road, the Cubans were usin' the Polo Grounds when the Giants were on the road.

I stayed in that one camp three years and five months and played with them all the time that I was there. The night games I could make 'cause we were off at 5:00. I'd get on a train or sometimes Campanella would come down to camp and get me. And I had my weekends off automatically. We'd usually play a Saturday night game and a Sunday doubleheader.

With the Monarchs, you and your dad appeared as the battery.

Yeah, but that was a more or less experimental thing. It wasn't that I was a regular member of the Monarchs pitchin' staff. It was just one or two ballgames we did that and the newspapers made a big thing out of it. I was just playin' out the time 'til I went in the army.

When I got out of the army, I didn't go back to the Monarchs. I stayed out east with Baltimore; that's 'cause those guys had become all my good friends. I knew Campanella's dad. His name was John; he was an old Italian huckster out of Philadelphia. I knew all his sisters. See, Campanella's mother was black but his father was Italian. We were real close, he and I.

Do you know any of your seasonal records?

Forty-five was the first year that I started pitchin' regularly and I think I went about 13-and-3. Forty-four I must've been about 9-and-4. And then the rest of the seasons that I was there, they were pretty weak in the bullpen and we had a slew of starting pitchers and they always want a hard thrower to close out a ballgame and I guess I might've been the hardest thrower there. They asked me would it matter to me if I relegated myself to the bullpen for the betterment of the team, and if they ever did run short of starters, you know, I could always be ready. So that's what I did the rest of the time.

Eventually you played minor league ball.

I played minor league ball in San Angelo, Texas, in the Texas League and I played a season over in Mexico. I did a little stint with Chicago—the Chicago American Giants.

Frank Duncan, Jr. (courtesy of Frank Duncan).

Was there one important game?

One game we were tied up with the Homestead Grays. See, the season was in halves. The first half ended on the Fourth of July and whoever was out front was declared the winner of that particular half. Then, the latter part, if there was two different teams that won the first half and the second half, then they'd have to play off for the championshp. The Homestead Grays won the first and we won the second half. This was in '45. The Grays, they had Josh Gibson, Buck Leonard, Cool Papa Bell, and Jud Wilson, Sam Bankhead. Jud Wilson was playin' third base, Sam Bankhead was playin' shortstop, Buck Leonard was playin' first base, Cool Papa Bell was in left field, Jerry Benjamin was in center field, and Raymond Brown was in right field.

I pitched against the Grays, I guess, for three solid years and I'm very proud to say that Josh Gibson and Buck Leonard never cleared the fences on me. Andy Porter, he was a pitcher on our team; Bill Wright was the right fielder on our team; as I told you, Campanella was the catcher, and they will attest to that.

Buck Leonard came to me in spring trainin' in '46 — we were just finishin' spring trainin'. Buck came up in the hotel room in Asheville, North Carolina, and told me that their manager — Vic Harris, an ex-great outfielder — was tryin' to swing a trade for me. They sent Buck to talk to me; he knew how close I felt to Campanella and those guys. He asked me, if the trade did go through, would I agree to it. I said, "Yeah. Sure. I wouldn't have no choice." He said, "They sent me to tell you. They're in the process of gettin' it together now. We just wanted to make sure if it was complete, you would agree to come." But, you know, they never did agree. I don't know what the stalemate was. I really didn't wanna go; I didn't say that I didn't wanna go, but I would much rather have stayed.

Who was the best ballplayer you saw?

All around? It would be a toss-up, I would say, between Campanella and Bill Wright. Bill was a *heck* of an outfielder and could run like the wind and was a switch hitter and a distance hitter from each side. He was a heck of a ballplayer. See, I'm talkin' about who are outstandin' at the bat and outstandin' with the glove on their hand. Campanella was *truly* that. He was a heck of a receiver, could throw like a *bullet*, and a dangerous, *dangerous* hitter. He'd hit outta there often as Josh or anybody else.

Who was the best pure hitter?

Everyday hitter? Well, I have to put Bill Wright in that category and I'd have to put Josh there. You know, Josh was hittin' when he wasn't hittin' home runs. He would still hit singles and doubles. I'd have to put Josh, Bill Wright, Kimbro. We had a center fielder name of Henry Kimbro. He could hit.

Who was the best pitcher?

You must mean after Satchel. There was Hilton Smith with the Monarchs, there was Bill Byrd with us — with Baltimore, there was Jonas Gaines with Baltimore, Andy Porter with Baltimore, and there was Neck Stanley with the Black Yankees — spitball pitcher, lefthander, he was good, too. You know, Don Newcombe was over there with Newark. The Newark Eagles — they had three guys over there, man, I think these three pitchers went two or three months and a relief pitcher didn't get off the bench, and that was Leon Day, Rufus Lewis, and Max Manning.

That Satchel was a character. I went on a barnstormin' tour with him one time. We were out in Wyomin', I believe it was. He was drivin' — four of us were in his car — and he drove like Mario Andretti. So the police pulled him over and Satchel told us, "Don't say nothin'; just keep quiet. Let me talk." So the guy walked up to the window and says, "Say, don't you guys know we have old folks and kids in this area, like anywhere else in the country? You're drivin' like maniacs." So Satchel says, "I guess we didn't realize." He says, "Where you goin'?" Satchel says, "We're on our way to Phoenix." "What you goin' there for?" "We play baseball." He said, "Damn it, I *knew* your face looked familiar. You're Satchel Paige." He said, "Yes, sir." He said, "Mr. Paige, it sure is nice meetin' you. It's gonna cost you $25." He got the book out and started writin' a ticket. So Satchel reached in his pocket and handed him a $50 bill and started the car. He said, "Wait a minute! Here's your change." Satchel said, "Keep it. I'm comin' back through here the same way next week."

Then Satchel got outta the car and was walkin' down the side of the road with the guy, arm around him. We say, "Uh-oh, Satchel got him now." So when Satchel came back to the car, he got in the car and showed us the $50 bill. The guy give it back to him. That guy was a character.

In his later years, he could still get you

out. There was a lotta pitchers couldn't throw hard as he could then. He always threw effortless. No strainin'. And the main thing about it, he was such a beautiful guy, such a *nice* guy. You can't overemphasize his popularity. Sometimes I believe it embarrassed him. Everybody liked him. Never, never tried to act bigger than nobody else. Great guy. He and I were great friends.

What kind of money was being paid then?

It would start with $3-, 350 a month and it would work up to $7-, 800 a month. 'Course, you know, Satchel was makin' *triple* that. Josh was makin' a thousand or so.

Any regrets from your baseball career?

No, other than my bad luck. I got hurt — hurt my arm — and had to cut it short. I was 24, 25 years old.

Did you enjoy your career?

Oh, very much so. You know, to see the country and see the Latin countries and I got a year, year-and-a-half in the minor leagues. Oh, I enjoyed it.

Would you do it again?

Oh, would I?! I'd *crawl*; I'd crawl on my stomach to be able to!

FRANK DUNCAN, III
(also known as Frank Duncan, Jr.)
Born 10-10-20,
Ht. 5' 10"   Wt. 178   Batted and Threw R

Year	Team, league	G	IP	W	L	Pct	H	BB	SO	SHO	ERA
1940	Kansas City Monarchs, NAL			utility player, did not pitch							
1941											
1942-45				military service							
1942	Baltimore Elite Giants, NAL										
1943											
1944				9	4	.692					
1945				13	3	.813					
1946											
1947											
1956	San Angelo, TxL										

Duncan played in the Mexican League in 1957.

Wilmer "Red" Fields

Triple Threat

NEGRO LEAGUE DEBUT: 1940

Wilmer Fields must have been a heck of a ballplayer. He joined the Homestead Grays at the age of 17, won 13 games at 18 and 15 at 19. World War II occupied his time for the next three years, but following his return in 1946 he put up a record of 72–17 over the next five seasons. His total Negro leagues record was 102–26!

And along the way, the Grays began using his bat more often. He played third base and outfield after his return from the service, in addition to pitching.

Numerous contract offers from major league teams came, but he was content with what he was doing and refused them. He did, however, join Triple-A Toronto for one year (1952) as an outfielder, batting .299.

Once the Grays disbanded, Fields went to Canada to play with Branford in the ManDak League. In four seasons there, he won 38 and lost 7 and batted .392, being named the MVP three times. He also earned MVP honors in Puerto Rico and Venezuela.

Total records are not known, but Fields probably won around 200 games along the way in the many countries in which he played, and his cumulative batting average must have been in the .340–.350 range at least. In the history of baseball, very few players have had the ability to excel on the mound, in the field, and at the plate to the extent he did. Three come to mind: Martin Dihigo, Leon Day, and Babe Ruth. All three are in the Hall of Fame.

Today, Wilmer Fields is president of the Negro Leagues Baseball Players Association. It's an organization that has misused the former players over the years and it's in a sorry state now, but Fields and others are working to correct the situation.

Were you a pitcher who could hit or a hitter who could pitch?

I'll give you an answer like this and you make the decision. I started out in '39 with the Homestead Grays at the age of 17 as a pitcher. From '39 through '41 — three years — I pitched and after that I went in the service and stayed in there three years. I came out in '46 and I started pitching and playing third base and playing the outfield. I played these positions pretty good because there were five major league clubs wanting me to play three different positions.

When Jackie went up, I was supposed to go up two months after he went up. A guy came on the field at Yankee Stadium and asked me did I want to go and I told him no. That's the first major league offer I had — in '46. The Brooklyn Dodgers wanted me as a pitcher to go to Montreal with Jackie. I think they were trying to find a roommate for him.

I had four others — one with the New

York Yankees to play third base and I turned them down, too, and sent their money back. Then I had one with the Washington Senators. I knew Clark Griffith, who owned the Senators, wasn't going to give me any money. Then in '51, I had a contract offer with the Philadelphia Athletics to play the outfield. The last one I had was with the Detroit Tigers in '55 to play the outfield and I figured I was doing all right playing summer baseball and winter baseball.

I played 12 years in Latin American countries. During that tour of duty, I picked up five MVP's and I won six batting titles. My best record was in 1948 with the Homestead Grays, when I had 16-and-1 pitching and I hit over .400 that same year. I hit over .400 three times. There were a few people before that could pitch and hit, but nobody did what I did.

You led the Grays to the World Series in 1948.

We played the World Series in New Orleans with Birmingham Black Barons. We played down there and this reporter from Pittsburgh asked where I was. I didn't go down with them; I came through Virginia and picked up my family 'cause my wife was from New Orleans and I drove down there from here.

The Series was supposed to be on Sunday, so I got in there on Saturday. I drove a 1947 Chevrolet 27 hours without stopping, but we had to stop because I couldn't go on any further. We were going through the state of Mississippi. I told my wife, "I'm sorry I have to stop, but I've got to." It was five o'clock in the morning in Mississippi and during those years you had to be really careful down there stopping on the road. I said, "Just give me a half hour," so I got down on the grass on the side of the road and went to sleep for a half an hour and I got up and came on in to New Orleans.

Wilmer Fields (courtesy of Wilmer Fields).

It was on a Saturday when I got there. I went on to the ballpark and Vic Harris, he handed me the ball. I was in such bad shape I was shaking. My ball didn't run or move like other people's balls move, but that day I was in such bad shape it was moving — just like a slider. Even Artie Wilson came up, said, "Fields, I didn't know you could pitch like that." I said, "I didn't know, either." [Laughs]

We beat 'em real bad that day. That was the first game — on a Sunday — and I won the fifth game, also, in Birmingham.

I'm real proud of my record but very little recognition I'm getting.

Do you think you should be in the Hall of Fame?

If the rest of the black ballplayers are in, I should be. Yes, they were outstanding players in their positions, but I played three positions. One year I played shortstop in Mayaguez, Puerto Rico. The shortstop got hurt; I moved from pitching and third base to shortstop until they could get somebody. The guy broke his ankle.

The guys who played more than one position and pitched, you can count 'em on one hand. I mean, those that did something. See, any time you play over ten years in Latin American countries in winter time, somebody gave you respect. You had to do something here in the States in order for them to notice you so that you could play winter baseball.

I always stayed in shape. I pitched Saturday and win and Sunday I came back. The manager would come, say, "Fields, can you pitch the last three or four innings?" I'd go out there and shut 'em out the last three or four innings. We played three games on weekends and sometimes we won three games. Saturday at two, Sunday morning at ten and in the afternoon at two or Sunday night.

What were your pitches?

Fastball was my main pitch, and I had a slider, which they called a curveball. We didn't know anything about the slider. Then I developed a knuckleball and that's what I went to sometime. You know, you throw your knuckleball and sometime it's good — it's working for you; sometime it's not. When it was working, I wouldn't care — it didn't make any difference who came to the plate. It was a good one.

I threw one one time up in Canada. This guy was batting lefthanded and he swung at the ball and the ball went through his legs. [Laughs]

You were an All-Star in '48. How many other appearances did you make?

I didn't make but the one, but I should've made it the three years — '46, '47, and '48.

Let me tell you how that was. If you were a young ballplayer, the owners of the ballplayers look over you and take old ballplayers. I wouldn't've went in 1948 if it hadn't been for Sam Bankhead. Sam Bankhead went to See Posey and told him, "Are you crazy, man?" That's what he told him. I was 8-and-none or 8–1, something like that.

I'll tell you who beat me the ballgame in 1948. Johnny Vander Meer. He pitched those two no-hitters in succession. He beat me, 2–1. I think he allowed three hits and I allowed four; he struck out ten and I struck out 11.

Who was the best pitcher you saw?

Satchel. I hit Satchel out in Puerto Rico and the people there gave me $125 through the chicken wire. He came in in the sixth inning to save a ballgame for Santurce. Santurce and San Juan are twin cities. The two batters before me, he struck 'em out. They had played in the majors. They came past me and I said, "Oh, you'll get him next time."

I was the next batter and I know how Satchel pitches. The first pitch, he threw it past me. If you didn't hit the first pitch — this is the way he pitched — he threw the next pitch to the *same* spot. He threw it to the same spot and I hit it. That was my second home run that game. I hit him out.

What got to me, after he threw the first pitch past me he hollered up there, "Aw, you can't hit nothin'!" And the stands are real close around and everybody heard that. When I hit him out, I went to first base and I went to second and he followed me all the way around the bases, staring at me. When I got between second and third, I said, "Old man, go back home!" [Laughs]

He still followed as I came on around the bases. I crossed home plate and people started handing me money through the chicken wire. I picked up $125 extra.

In Latin American countries they paid you for what you could do. I was the highest paid American in Latin American countries at one time. Now, when I first went down there, no, but after I built the reputation I had, I know I was the highest paid ballplayer. I was paid as high as $2,200 a month and all expenses. That was in 1952.

Who was the best hitter?

I'll tell you who I had trouble with. One of them was Willard Brown. He could hit that ball. Bill Wright — he couldn't touch Willard Brown. He wasn't no Willard

Brown. No. He couldn't touch Willard Brown. Very few could with that bat. I played against Brown quite a few years and one year I got a chance to play with him on a team. He was batting four and I was hitting five. I had an outstanding year that year in Maracaibo, Venezuela.

Have you heard the name [Terris] McDuffie? McDuffie was pitching against us and I was hitting McDuffie good. I mean, I was killing him down there in Maracaibo. He'd tell Ray Brown, my roomie, he'd say, "You watch tonight. I'm gonna get him out." If McDuffie couldn't get you out one way, he'd try to get you out another. So Ray Brown came and *told* me this and I said, "Well, he ain't gonna pitch me inside. He's going outside."

And that night, first time up I tripled up against the center field wall. The next time up, I hit one out; the next time up I singled to left field. Now McDuffie doesn't tell anybody what I'm getting ready to tell you. When the season was over, my wife and I and the baby were in bed and he came up to the door and he called my wife to the door. She was awake at the time. And he told her, he said, "That's all right. Let your husband sleep. I just want to tell you — you tell your husband he can hit that ball." McDuffie didn't tell anybody that. He wasn't that type of person. He never congratulated anybody for doing anything in life. He said, "Tell him he can hit that ball." And I used to wear his butt out.

He was a good pitcher. I have to give him credit. He had the stuff to throw, too — fastball, slider, curveball, knew how to pitch. When he was 48, he was still pitching in Maracaibo. He had a record of 11-and-1 down there. He was tough.

Does one game stand out?

At the end of the year we played a Caribbean Series. We played in four different countries, like Venezuela, Panama, Mexico, Cuba. We played one year in Puerto Rico — San Juan. Cuba had all the good ballplayers — they had played in the majors and all around.

The team I played on, we didn't win the championship in Puerto Rico but the team that won it was able to pick up a ballplayer from another team, so they picked me up. It was Caguas who picked me up. The first night we played — we were playing 'em and McDuffie was pitching and that night he had us, 1-nothing, in the ninth. The first batter got on base some kind of way and they asked me to pinch hit against McDuffie.

The first two pitches he threw right past me. Threw it right past me. He went like a fool and threw me a changeup and I hit him across that fence about 400 feet. We beat 'em, 2-to-1. That same night, they gave me $100 through the chicken wire.

So the next night I pitched against Cuba and I was throwing hard and my slider and all was moving and I gave 'em three hits. That's the best ballgame I've ever pitched. They had all the major league ballplayers — Hector Rodriguez, [Willie] Miranda. They had everything. That's one of the best ballgames I've ever been involved in.

I've been blessed in ballgames. It was very easy for me to write my book. Very, very easy. I was sitting up there at work one night and I said, "I don't know what might happen to me. I'm gonna write something for my family in case somebody wants to know my history," so I set down and started writing. I used to write two or three or four pages in about an hour, hour-and-a-half.

When I finished, I went to a printer to get it printed and when I took it to the lady, she looked at me, said, "You ought to show this to a publisher." I said, "Lady, I don't know any publishers." She gave me two and I came home.

Then I contacted John Holway, who wrote four or five books, and he gave me three more. So out of that five, I contacted three and within a week all three of 'em wanted to publish the book. I went with Meckler in Connecticut. I have another one in manuscript form.

Every day I wish, as I talk to people, and talking to different ones, especially those like lawyers and counselors and CPA people, I wish I had had a little more education. You see, I just finished the second year in college.

Edsall Walker said you could go in white restaurants and buy takeout food because you were light complected.

[Laughs] We were traveling through Mississippi and we needed some gas for the bus. We stopped at a general store and everybody was asleep except Josh and I. We were sitting up front. Josh looked at me and said, "Chinky"—that was my nickname—"I'm hungry. You think you can go in there and get me a couple of sandwiches?" I looked at him. He said, "Here. Put on my hat."

His head's bigger than mine, so I put on his hat and it came down on my ears. [Laughs] I went in there and there was a bar there and about 13 men sitting at the bar. I told the manager I wanted a couple of sandwiches — ham and cheese or something like that. He started fixing the sandwiches.

I looked up and here come R.T. [pitcher Robert Walker] walking through the door. He came through the door and said, "Hey, Chinky! Get me a couple of sandwiches!"

The manager looked at me and looked at him. He said, "You with him?" I said, "Yeah, I'm with him." He said, "Get out of here!" [Laughs]

What about the traveling conditions?

We traveled by bus and we traveled 4- or 500 miles to play one ballgame. And when traveling, we'd sing, play cards all the way. We had a good time. No fights occurred on the team while I was there. We had a good relationship. We had like a family feeling that stayed with us all the time — helping each other. When one didn't have something to wear, the other would help him, like sanitaries or shirts or something like that.

The only thing they hated was to lose. [Laughs] The Homestead Grays, you know, won nine out of ten and 11 out of 12 pennants. When they were playing one of the

league games and they would lose, they'd get on the bus like somebody had died. [Laughs] It was something.

What racial problems did you encounter?

I did all right but I'll tell you about one incident in Florida. I was down there in spring training with Toronto. They was a Triple-A club in the International League. Jack Kent Cooke was the owner; he's the owner of the [NFL's Washington] Redskins now.

One day I came in to practice in spring training and I was one of the last ones that came in the door to the locker room and there wasn't a chair. When I was playing in the black leagues, we used to call each other "Horse" — Horse this and Horse that — so the clubhouse man was there and I said, "Horse, get me a chair." He looked at me and said, "Who you callin' Horse?!" Then our equipment manager said, "Get the ballplayer a chair." He didn't get a chair. He went outside, went out the door.

I was the last one coming out of the clubhouse and I looked over and he was setting on a Model-T Ford with a shotgun across his lap. Don't ask me why I kept walking. He saw I wasn't paying him no mind. I was about 25 or 30 yards away from him. There were some wires I had to go under and some blackbirds were setting on 'em. Man, he blasted away and knocked one of the blackbirds off of there and it fell down in front of me. I just kept walking and I went on out to the field and it never bothered me until after the manager told me to take my hitting practice.

Evidently it affected me a whole lot because I went up there and took three swings and I went on out to the outfield. When I got out there I started thinking about it. I didn't tell anybody; I didn't even tell my wife. She was from New Orleans and she knew how it was down there. I never told anybody for a long time 'cause if I told my wife, she'd say, "Let's go home."

Would you go back and do this again?

Yeah. You know, when I was a young boy, like 8 years old, here in Manassas,

Virginia, we had dusty roads. There wasn't pavement. I used to read about Lou Gehrig and Bill Dickey and all these ballplayers and I used to wonder and I'd say, "Why ain't there some black ballplayers in the majors?" But there never were any. I used to read black papers — the *Afro* — about black ballplayers playing here in Griffith Stadium. I kept up with them the whole time.

Like I say, when I was 8 and younger I used to get on my knees and pray to God to give me the ability to play professional black baseball.

Even in our high school, we might play two ballgames the whole year — I mean, against other teams. But I had three older brothers that I used to compete against every day playing baseball and I tried to play as good as they were playing. This developed my skills to play baseball. Being able to catch the ball, hit the ball, and everything. It was through my brothers that I developed the skills I had.

I would do the same thing, but if you were talking about today and them coming up and say, "Look, we'll give a million dollars for signing. We'll give you so much a year." I could see where I could accomplish this for my family. I'd have to take that. But back then, the major league salary for a beginner was $4,500 a year.

What was your top salary?

It was in the Dominican Republic — $2,200 a month and all expenses. My best salary here was $1,000 a month. That was good money. I didn't make any thousand dollars with the Homestead Grays. They took me for granted. They knew I wasn't going to say no.

I pitched in Griffith Stadium on a Sunday. New York Cubans beat me. That was the only game I lost in Griffith Stadium the whole time I pitched. They beat me, 5–2. On Monday night we were playing in Baltimore. About the fifth inning, Vic Harris said, "Can you come in and try to hold this for us?" It was a league game. I came in and stopped them. That's Monday night.

Then Wednesday night we played in Forbes Field in Pittsburgh. We played the Baltimore Elite Giants again. Man, I went to the ballpark with no idea I was pitching. I was sitting in the dugout there and Vic came up and handed me the ball. I looked at it. Vic Harris said, "You know what it's for, don't you?" [Laughs] I went out there and beat 'em again. I went nine innings that night.

I felt good. Like I said, I was in shape. In Puerto Rico I went 11 innings on a Saturday — we played at 2 P.M. — and beat Mayaguez, 4–nothing. In fact, I tripled in that game to beat Mayaguez for San Juan. That was Saturday. On Sunday, I went the last three or four innings to hold the lead that we had.

But they would pay you extra money in Latin American countries. If I pitched a good ballgame, they'd give me $50.

You're the president of the Negro Leagues Baseball Players Association.

The association was started in 1990 and the members took over in 1994. In taking over, we had a meeting in Baltimore and they came to me and asked me — the media was there — they came to me and said, "Fields, why can't you be president?" I said, "Look, I don't *want* to be president. I want to help as much as I can, but I don't want to be president." Then they asked me, "Why not?" Wilmer Harris said, "Why not?" I said, "Wait a minute. Let everybody leave the room except the ballplayers." They left and I said, "Here's the best way to do this. Send a form to all of the ballplayers for them to pick a choice to be president of the association."

So four months later, we had the results back. They gave me 67 percent of the votes. I couldn't turn my back on these people. These men are 76 years old — that's the average age. I'm working every day — almost — on projects, trying to get something started. Things look like they're going to materialize for us.

All during those years from 1948 up until the late '80s, nobody contacted us for anything. Not one thing — having reunions, autograph sessions, nothing. Nobody contacted us. If a person came to us — we wouldn't care if it was Joe Blow — and wanted a conversation, we were ready to talk to him at length. We were ready to talk to a wall — anybody about anything at any

time. It was a sad picture, to tell you the truth.

Do you have any regrets from your baseball days?

Not one. Thank God, no. I asked the Lord for something and He gave it to me. I'm thankful.

WILMER LEON "RED" "CHINKY" FIELDS
Born 8-2-22, Manassas, VA
Ht. 6' 3"   Wt. 215   Batted and Threw R

Year	Team, league	G	IP	W	L	Pct	H	BB	SO	SHO	ERA
1940	Homestead Grays, NNL			2	1	.667					
1941				13	5	.722					
1942				15	3	.833					
1943-45						military service					
1946	Homestead Grays, NNL			16	1	.941					
1947				14	7	.667					
1948				13	5	.722					
1949				17	2	.895					
1950				12	2	.857					
1951	Branford, MnDkL			11	2	.846					
1952	Toronto, IntL										
1953	Branford, MnDkL			10	2	.833					
1954				9	3	.750					
1955				8	0	1.000					
1956	Fort Wayne			6	1	.833					
1957				5	0	1.000					

Record in Latin America.

Year	Team, league	G	IP	W	L	Pct	H	BB	SO	SHO	ERA
1947-48	Mayaquez, PRWL		136	6	6	.500		73	87		4.57
1948-49				10	4	.714					
1949-50				8	7	.533					
1953	Oriente, DRSL	11	67	2	2	.500					3.90
1958	Mex. City-Monterrey, MexL	1		0	0	.000					

Batting record.

Year	Team, league	Pos	G	AB	R	H	2B	3B	HR	RBI	SB	BA
1940	Homestead Grays, NNL	P	1	2	0	1	0	0	0	0	0	.500
1941		P										
1942		P-3B	1	4		1	0	0	0		0	.250
1943-45					military service							
1946	Homestead Grays, NNL	P-OF-3B	12	30	6	7	1	2	0	3	0	.233
1947		P-3B	14	49	4	14	2	0	0		0	.286
1948		P-OF	47	148		46						.311
1949		P-OF										
1950		P-OF										
1951	Branford, MnDkL	P-OF										.382
1952	Toronto, IntL	OF-P	51	167	24	48	10	1	2	13		.287
1953	Branford, MnDkL	P-OF										.381
1954		P-OF										.379
1955		OF-P										.425
1956	Fort Wayne	OF-P										.432
1957		OF-P										.387

Record in Latin America.

Year	Team, league	Pos	G	AB	R	H	2B	3B	HR	RBI	SB	BA
1947-48	Mayaquez, PRWL	OF-P		184		58			5	41	0	.315
1948-49		P-OF-3B		325		108			11	88*	1	.332
1949-50		P-3B-OF		279		91			6		0	.326
1950-51		OF		279		90						.323
1951-52	Caracas, VenL	OF		207	48*	72	21*	2	8	45*	2	.348*
1953	Oriente, DRSL	OF-P		107	15	42			0	19	2	.393
1958	Mex. City-Monterrey, MexL	3B	25	88	10	33	2	0	7	35	0	.375

Chester Gray

Jackie's Roomie

NEGRO LEAGUE DEBUT: 1940

The Kansas City Monarchs of the 1940s are generally regarded as having one of the most outstanding pitching staffs ever assembled in baseball. In the war year of 1945, a lot of the talent was in the military service but the Monarchs still had a staff any team, war or not, would like. Numbered among their pitchers that year were Satchel Paige, Hilton Smith, Booker McDaniels, Theolic Smith, Lefty Jim LaMarque, and Jack Matchett. Paige, of course, is in the Hall of Fame; and there are several reasons to believe that the others on that list should be also, with the exception of Matchett, who nonetheless had individual season records of 6–0, 8–2, and 5–3 and won two games in the 1942 World Series.

This great staff had to have a catcher, and two men shared the duties. Although five receivers appeared behind the plate for the Monarchs in 1945, the bulk of the catching was done by Frank Duncan, the manager, who was then 44 years old, and Chester Gray, a veteran in his only season with Kansas City. Gray, who played in the outfield when not catching, batted a solid .292 that year.

Also in his only season with Kansas City — indeed in his only season in the Negro leagues — was a shortstop, a young college-educated World War II veteran named Jackie Robinson. The rookie Robinson roomed with the veteran Gray.

Both men went elsewhere in 1946 — Robinson to Montreal on his way to Brooklyn and the Hall of Fame, and Gray to retirement. He played with the Toledo Cubs of the United States League in 1944. This league was the idea of Branch Rickey to try to develop Negro league players for possible futures in organized ball, and several of the teams were run by whites, such as the Cubs' Hank Rigney. Previously, Rigney had been an officer of some Negro league teams. The USL was a short-lived venture, but it did produce a couple of future major league players, most notably Dave Pope.

Chester Gray left baseball after 1945, but he had a career to remember. He caught Satchel Paige and Hilton Smith, and he batted against Leon Day and Bill Byrd. Anyone would remember that.

How did you become a professional baseball player?

I started out down South — Tennessee — and then after I got about 18 or 19 I went up to Mounds, Illinois, and started playing with the team up there. A guy named Adack Johnson was the owner of the team and had a nightclub and stuff like that. I started playing with him, then in 1940 we went to Jacksonville for spring training. After that — '42 — we merged with the Black Yankees in New York. I guess I was about 26 or 27 then.

You were a catcher. Did you play other positions?

I played outfield, too. I could run a little.

How big were you?

I weighed 165 pounds, about 5-6½, I guess. I'd hit some triples and every once in a while I might get lucky and hit a home run. I'd hit doubles and triples.

Who was the best pitcher you batted against?

There was quite a few of 'em that was good. Byrd with Baltimore, he was good. And then Barney Brown with the Philadelphia Stars, he was good, and Leon Day with the Newark Eagles, he was *real* good.

Who was the best one you caught?

Satchel Paige. Satchel and Hilton Smith — both of them was good pitcehrs. We had about, oh, about five or six good pitchers on our team. Lefty LaMarque, Booker McDaniels, Jack Matchett — they was all real good.

You were Jackie Robinson's last roommate in the Negro leagues.

I was his roommate when he went to Brooklyn to see Branch Rickey. He [Jackie] was a nice guy, a quiet guy, carried on a whole lot of foolishness. Didn't drink or smoke. Didn't anybody know exactly how good he was. Rickey figured he would be the one could stand that stuff that they was gonna put on him.

You started playing in the South and then barnstormed through there for several years. How was that?

To me, I didn't think it was too bad. We didn't run into too much trouble 'cause we always had a place to stay. We always stayed in the colored hotels. We ate at the colored restaurants. It wasn't bad for me.

What kind of money were you making?

Three hundred dollars a month. We'd get two dollars a day eating money. In New York, we ate at a place on 7th Avenue, a Greek restaurant.

Chester Gray (courtesy of Chester Gray).

Who was the best player you saw?

Oh, there was a *lot* of 'em. Willie Wells was good; he was a *good* player. And then Josh Gibson, he was all right but the thing about him, he wasn't too hot on them high flies. Pop-ups.

Was he the best hitter?

I don't know. He was good, but Mule Suttles was a good hitter, too. I played against him in Wiliamsport. He was old then.

Any regrets?

I'm just sorry I couldn't make it to the major leagues after they started drafting 'em. I think Jackie and I was close together, 'cause when I was in Kansas City I think I was 30 or 31, if I'm not mistaken. I think I was a little older than him, not too much older than he was.

I played all my games here in the States; I didn't go to Puerto Rico and Mexico like a lot of the other guys did. Guys talk about a lot of the times they was down in Puerto Rico and places like that, the plane they was riding going from one place to the other, they had to hold ropes and one guy fell out of the airplane. [Laughs] They said they had to dodge them mountains and things with them little ol' planes.

The eighth of next month [January 1996] I'll be 82, and this year was the first I ever been on an airplane. Went to the Meadowlands and then went to Kansas City in October.

I started out in Toledo with a guy named Hank Rigney. I don't know what [league] that was; we would just go out and make trips for 15 and 20 and 23 days like down through Texas, Arkansas, Louisiana, and places like that. Rigney caused me to go to Kansas City.

Kansas City had another boy there that caught named [Chico] Renfroe and Sammie Haynes. When I went, Sammie, he had went to the doctor to have his eyes operated on, and Renfroe, he come up with a sore arm so I would catch sometimes and then I would play outfield.

Is there one game that stands out?

We played the Chicago American Giants. I hit a triple that night then later on they put me out of the game 'cause I bumped the umpire. [Laughs]

How was the umpiring?

There was some nice umpires in the leagues. They kept a *lot* of control. Like now, the way things are in the major leagues now, you throw close to players they want to start a fight. We didn't get into nothin' like that. If you crowd the plate, they gonna throw up under your chin, try to get you off of the plate. Like it is now in the major leagues, you throw close to one of 'em, they wanna come out and start a fight.

How many umpires would you have for a game?

We'd have two — one behind the plate and one down around first base. We didn't have no three or four like they do in the major leagues.

If you were a young man today, would you be a baseball player?

I would. With the money they makin' now?! [Laughs] The money they get now, a lot of 'em ain't worth that much.

How about if you went back to when you started, would you be a baseball player again?

Yes, I would. I enjoyed it very much. Only thing our trouble was at the time, we was riding buses. It was all right, but, you know, a lot of times you might make one of them 6- or 700-mile trips. We played the ninth of September in Detroit, then we left and went back to Kansas City and played in Kansas City and left out next day for Oklahoma City. While we're traveling, a lot of times we'd be sittin' up playing cards, especially in the daytime. Duncan, our manager, he drove some and then we had another guy named [Dozier] Hood; he was a bus driver, too.

When I was on the team in Mounds, on our way from Texas to Mounds, I was driving and I kind of dozed off and we went off the side of the road. [Laughs]

But that was the only problem — the buses. I'd sure do it again.

CHESLEY "CHESTER" GRAY
Born 1-8-14, Tennessee Died 4-18-96, Ann Arbor, MI
Ht. 5' 6"   Wt. 155   Batted and Threw R

Year	Team, league	Pos	G	AB	R	H	2B	3B	HR	RBI	SB	BA
1940	St. Louis Stars, ind.	C										
1942	N.Y. Black Yankees, NNL	C-OF	12			2						.167
1943	Harrisburg-St.L. Stars, ind.	C-OF										
1944	Toledo Cubs, USL	C										
1945	Kansas City Monarchs	C-OF										.292

Connie Johnson

Wanderlust

NEGRO LEAGUE DEBUT: 1940

Clifford "Connie" Johnson was 28 years old when he joined St. Hyacinthe (Quebec) of the Provincial League in 1951, but he had been pitching professionally for a dozen years by that time.

As a boy he wanted to travel, to see the country, so in 1939, at the age of 16, he joined the Toledo Crawfords. He saw professional baseball as a means to see the places he had heard about, and it worked. When the Crawfords folded after his first season, he went to the legendary Kansas City Monarchs. Except for time out for World War II, he stayed with the Monarchs through 1950.

In 1951 at St. Hyacinthe, he won 15 games with a 3.24 ERA and led the league with 172 strikeouts. Off that record, the Chicago White Sox purchased him and sent him to Colorado Springs of the Western League in '52. He started 30 games that year and hurled 248 innings (8¼ innings per start), posting an 18–9 record with a 3.38 ERA. Again, he led the league in K's and his 233 set a new league record.

He began 1953 in the American Association with a mediocre Charleston squad. The Chisox called him up at mid-season and he went 4–4, 3.54, the rest of the way as a 30-year-old rookie. But the next spring they shipped him to Toronto [International League] against the wishes of White Sox skipper Paul Richards. He was 17–8 there, but in 1955 he once again found himself in Toronto. By mid-season he was 12–2, 3.05, and new White Sox manager Marty Marion needed help.

The Sox were in the thick of things in the fight for the flag, but their pitching was faltering. Bob Keegan, a 16-game winner in 1954, suffered a knee injury and could not contribute, and former Rookie of the Year Harry Byrd, picked up on waivers from Baltimore, was ineffective, so Johnson was called up and inserted in the rotation. He went 7–4, 3.45, in 16 starts, and one of his wins put the Sox into first place. They finished third, though, five games out; it was their closest finish in 35 years. Johnson's 19 wins for the season (major and minor) were the third-most in professional ball that year.

Nineteen fifty-six began with Johnson as the forgotten man on the Chisox staff. More than a month into the season, he had pitched only 12 innings in five games. Richards, his first major league manager, was directing the fortunes of the Baltimore Orioles at this time and a big trade was consummated between the two clubs. On May 21, Chicago sent George Kell, Bob Nieman, and Mike Fornieles to Baltimore in exchange for Jim Wilson and Dave Philley.

Richards, one of the best judges of pitching talent in the game's history, said to the White Sox, "You're getting our best pitcher in Wilson, a proven starter. Fornieles is still unproven; how about throwing in another arm? Maybe someone not in your plans, someone like Johnson."

So, after a short deliberation, three days later (May 24) Johnson was included in the deal as a throw-in. He spent the rest of '56 as the Orioles' ace, leading them in ERA (3.42), strikeouts (130), and complete games (9) and finishing second in wins (9) despite joining them nearly six weeks into the season.

Then, in 1957, he became one of the top pitchers in the American League. He went 14–11, 3.20, and ranked high in nearly every pitching statistic: wins (seventh), complete games (fourth), shutouts (fourth), innings (fourth), ERA (ninth), fewest hits per game (seventh), fewest bases on balls per game (sixth), strikeouts (third), strikeouts per game (second), and opponent's lowest on-base percentage (fourth).

Age caught up with him in 1958, but for his five big league seasons of which only three were full, he won 40 and lost 39 with an ERA of 3.44. His effectiveness is underlined by the fact that the latter figure was a full one-half run below the league ERA for the same period.

From the standpoint of his major league performance, it's apparent that Connie Johnson came along at least a decade too early, but he doesn't think so. To him, the time he played was the right time for him.

You were born in Stone Mountain, Georgia. How did you get from there to the Toledo Crawfords?

Yeah, I was born 14 miles from Atlanta. I was born there December the 27th, 1922. I left about 5 years old and went to Atlanta and I went to school in Atlanta 'til I was in about the sixth or seventh grade, and then I went back to Stone Mountain to start school there, and then I quit in the eighth grade.

Then I started playing ball with a tennis ball. I didn't play no hard ball—I just played with a tennis ball. I was kinda afraid of a hard ball, you know. We all just played tennis ball.

There was other guys played hard ball—the guys that had a little team in the town. I wasn't thinkin' about playing any hard ball. The only time I played hard ball was in school one day—we were playing the city team. It was kind of a recreation day—the school team was playing the city team. We didn't think about *beatin'* 'em, but we played 'em. The largest guy there got hurt and I'm the next biggest guy there [Laughs] and they look at me, "Come on." "I ain't playin' no hard ball! Unh-unh!" They say, "Come on." I say, "I ain't never played no hard ball. I ain't *never* played no hard ball!"

They kept on beggin' me and callin' me sissy and things like that. I said, "Okay, I'll go play. I'll go out there in the outfield. If the ball comes there, I ain't gonna catch it—I'm gonna let it fall and I'll pick it up and I'll throw it." I could throw.

So what happened, I went out there. First doggone inning, two men was on and one was out. Man was on first and second. That ball was hit out there to me. I started runnin' and I say, well, if I get close to it I might throw one of them guys out goin' home. I happened to look up and saw it—it's awful close. For some reason, my arm just reached out and I caught it! And the man was caught goin' to second; I throwed it back to first and I got him and doubled him off.

Oh, man, then I got to run! The girls try to kiss you and I'm bashful, too. I'm flyin'!

When I come up, two times I come up and looked at the ball—I wouldn't swing. "Come on, swing at the ball!" See, I was scared of a hard ball. So the last time I went up—man, they were leadin' us by one run. "Come on, Johnson, swing at the ball! Swing at the ball!"

So I say if he hits me it can't hurt me too bad. And he throwed the ball low and I hit it and the last time we saw it was going over the trees! Then they want me to play with the city team.

So I did play with the city team. I was playin' center field. I went down to Lithonia

[Georgia] once and I was catchin' everything they hit out there and the people were hollerin' in the stands, "Don't hit it to center field! Hit it on the ground anywhere!" And I hit pretty good, too.

The big team from Atlanta — the Black Crackers — came there to play us one Saturday. Boy named Sammy Haynes and all of 'em came. So they want me to pitch.

I tell you how they found out I could pitch. One day we was out there — you know, we'd scrap up and get a team and play 'til dark. So I told 'em, "Lemme pitch." The catcher said, "Aw, you can't pitch. You can't even throw a curveball!" I said, "Yes, I can!"

So I reared up and throwed to him and he reached up to get it and it hit him on his knee. He grabbed his knee and said, "Man, what was that?" I said, "Curveball." He said, "Can you throw it again?" I throwed it and it hit him on the knee again. He said, "You pitch!"

So I got out there and started pitchin' and I struck out so many they stopped playin' ball and started gettin' in a line to see how many I could strike out. [Laughs]

Connie Johnson (courtesy of Connie Johnson).

So when the guys [Black Crackers] come, they want me to pitch. I had never pitched a game. I pitched four innings and it was rainin' hard and a guy named Sammy Haynes, who once played with the Monarchs, he come out; he said, "Johnson, don't throw that ball," it was wet, "you're throwing it too hard. You'll hurt your arm. You *can* be a pitcher." So after four innings I stopped throwing the ball.

The next weekend — I had never been to a professional ballgame — the Toledo Crawfords and the Kansas City Monarchs came down to play in Atlanta — Atlanta Stadium. For some reason, I went up there. I was lookin' at 'em. I saw them guys — "Boy, look

at them guys catch that ball and throw it," I thought. So the guys I was with said, "Hey, Johnson, you ought to be with them!" See, I was bashful. I said, "Aw, man." Well, I went on home that day.

I intended to see four places — that was New Orleans, California, Chicago, and New York. I wanted to see them four and then I'd come on back home. I even prayed to see 'em.

So I'm settin' out there workin' with my father, using a four-pound hammer, just thinkin' of going over the hill, kind of run away. I hated to go and I looked at my father and I thought, "I hate to go without tellin' him." Somethin' told me to hold it — you know, like somebody just help me out.

I looked up and I saw a black car — a black LaSalle. I thought, "That's somebody come to get me to play ball." He'd stopped up at the blacksmith shop and they sent him out there to see my daddy. I said, "Here I am." I walked over there.

They said, "We want you to play ball with us." "Well, if you want me to play, I'll play with you." That was the Toledo Crawfords — didn't have no pitchers but I didn't know that, didn't know I was going to pitch. So I said, "Okay." "Do you have a glove?" I said, "Yeah." "Do you have spikes?" I said, "Yeah."

So I got into the car and went on home and got my stuff and went on up there. Now, what I'm tryin' to find out — how much to charge 'em after the game. I don't want to charge 'em too much and I didn't want to charge 'em not enough. That's what I'm worried about.

The guys up there are lookin' at me, talkin' to me and I'm a bashful kid — I ain't never been nowhere. They say, "Hey, you carry Abe?" I say, "Abe? No, I don't carry no Abe." I didn't know what Abe was. They mean a knife — they thought everybody in Georgia carried a knife. [Laughs]

I am six-foot-three weighing 160-somethin'. They give me a uniform — a 48. You shoulda seen that uniform on me! Sleeves just hangin' everywhere. I had to double it around me. The cap bill was the longest cap bill I ever seen in my life. When I walked out on the field the people started laughin' — they thought I was a clown. But I didn't pay 'em no mind — all I wanted was to get that money.

He said, "Go warm up." "Okay." I thought he meant just throw. The guy took me to the pitchin' mound; he said, "You warm up here — you're pitchin' today." I said, "I ain't never pitched a whole game in my life!" He said, "Well, that's what we gotcha for."

So I warmed up. They got on their knees cryin' when they saw me walk out on that mound with that big hat and the pants fallin' off and all. I didn't look like nothin'.

A boy name of Spoon Carter come out and showed me how to get on the mound. See, I was gettin' on the mound like somebody was on base. I didn't know how to get on the mound.

About the fourth inning they stopped laughin'. [Laughs] I just struck out everybody. I know one guy up there said, "Who's that throwin' that? Smoky Joe Williams?" After that, the guy came and said, "We're goin' to take you out of the game. It's not that you're not doin' good — you might hurt your arm."

I'm tryin' to see Joe Greene on the Monarchs team. I used to throw to him when he came home. I wanted to see him so I could find out how much to charge. I couldn't see him. I got my clothes on and was ready to go. A guy come in, "You want somethin' to eat?" He kept after me so I said, "Okay." I thought they were tryin' to pay me off in chicken, so I ate a whole chicken.

Jesse Owens, the runner, owned half the Toledo Crawfords, said, "Hey, we want you to go with us." "Go to where?" He said, "Play ball. You played the best team in the league — the Kansas City Monarchs — struck out all of 'em, just about. We want you to go with us." I said, "Are you kiddin'?" He said, "No." I said, "Well, you have to ask my mother." So they went down there and asked my mother. She said, "I know you want to go." She said to them, "You goin' to take care of him?" It was Oscar Charleston, one of the greatest ballplayers ever. He said, "Yeah, I'll take care of him."

So that's the way it started.

What was your record with Toledo?

I really don't remember. I was just pitchin'.

One thing about it — I wanted to go away from home. I'm tryin' to find out where I'm goin' to leave these guys, but I don't know where. Then one night I'm sittin' there thinkin' about the places I've been — Memphis and all those. I was in

Connie Johnson with Baltimore Orioles, 1957 (courtesy of Connie Johnson).

Chicago. I was thinkin' about all the places I wanted to go. I woke one of the guys, I said, "Hey." He said, "What's wrong?" "I want to ask you a question." He said, "Man, it's four o'clock in the morning!" [Laughs] I asked him, "Do we ever go to New Orleans?" "Yeah." I said, "What about New York?" "Yeah, we go to New York, too." I said, "California?" He said, "No, we don't go out to California."

I stopped and started thinkin'. "Hell, this is what I want." [Laughs] I wrote my mother a letter that night, tell her I'm all right and this is exactly what I wanted — to travel. I was travelin' with the team and didn't have to pay nothin'. I loved to travel.

At night I used to get in the bus in Texas and be ridin' and look at the moon in Texas — the prettiest and the biggest moon I ever seen in my life. I loved the scenery. I just loved it.

After a year with Toledo, you joined the Monarchs.

The Crawfords went out of business.

I was good but they had some good pitchers there [at Kansas City]. They had Satchel, they had Hilton Smith, which was just as good as Satchel. Then they had [Booker] McDaniels; we had about nine. Dizzy Dean came there once. We played him once barnstormin'. He said, "Man, if I had this pitchin' staff here, I'd win a pennant anywhere!" [Laughs] We had eight or nine of the best pitchers you'd ever want to see — you could put any of us out there!

One year, I won 11 straight. I hurt my arm and I came back and won 11 straight. The twelfth one the umpire took away. I struck Monte Irvin out and he gave him two more strikes and he got a single and that won the game. I came out of the army in '46 and hurt my arm a little while later, so that was about '47 or '48.

[I was in the army] three years. It didn't bother me — I got stronger. I was young when I went there. I played in the army. I struck out 15 or 16 — that was a fair game. The first sergeant said, "You did all right, but you gotta strike out 18 or 19 or 20 for a good game." [Laughs] One time I struck out 24. The other three popped up.

How did you get your nickname?

There was a singin' duet — sisters — and one of 'em was named Connie and I liked her singin'. That year I just called everybody Connie. I did that when I was young. I might get a name and call everybody that name all the time. It might be Willie or Timmy, but this time it was Connie, so they called me that.

How did you join the white leagues?

I'll tell you what happened. I went down to Panama — Chet Brewer got me to play

down there — and there was a white guy there that played up in Canada at St. Hyacinthe. He said, "I think you can play up in Canada with me. I'm going to talk with them about gettin' you up there." I wish I could remember his name; he's dead now. I said, "Okay." "You can make some money up there," he said. "Some good money."

Hamilton! His name was [Tom] Hamilton. So we called to see what they'd give me. So I tried to get some money from the Monarchs. They didn't want to give me nothin', so I told 'em they [St. Hyacinthe] wanted to buy me, and he wrote a *nasty* letter to the man and said he wasn't goin' to sell me and things like that.

Before then, my arm had been hurt. John O'Neil was the manager; I went to him one day, I said, "Look, I'm quittin'." He said, "No, don't never quit. Let 'em fire you." So I started runnin' and went to a chiropractor in Laredo, Texas, and he helped me out. When I come back, he told me to run all the time. So I just started runnin', runnin', and runnin'.

When my arm came back, I didn't have the speed but I had control. I had won six games and then seven straight and the guys used to laugh at me 'cause I'd run — make fun of me. One day, up in Memphis, I looked around and the whole team was followin' me! [Laughs] I said, "What you runnin' for?" They said, "Oh, shut up." Every pitcher there was runnin'. They figured if it helped me they was goin' to run some, too.

But about Canada, the owner said he wasn't goin' to sell me. At the time, players were goin' to Mexico. That was an outlaw league — you go down there, your team got nothin' for you. So I told him — I wrote a letter, said I was goin' to Mexico next month. Before I could turn around, he called me to tell me he'd sold me. [Laughs] See, if I'd gone to Mexico he couldn't have got a nickel for me. I wasn't goin' to Mexico. I never even thought about it.

So I went up there. A guy named [Bill] Cash, a catcher, was up there and they

[White Sox scouts] was lookin' at him. I throwed a two-hitter that day and hit a home run. Next time, I throwed a one-hitter. They said, "We don't want Cash, we want Johnson." They got me and I didn't even know it! I got a letter from Chicago, said they just bought me. The guy gave it to me; I said, "Okay." "Hey, wait a minute! ain't you glad?" he said. "You ain't got no expression or nothin'." I said, "Yeah, they bought me. That's all I can say." [The White Sox also purchased Cash.]

They sent me to Colorado Springs. I broke that lefthander's record there — struck out so many. What was his name? Shantz! Bobby Shantz. He had the record out there and I broke his strikeout record. From there I went to spring training with 'em just to throw battin' practice and they kept me. Then I got wild and they sent me down.

The next year I was at Toronto and I was 12 and 2 up there the next year and they brought me up. Marty Marion was managing in Chicago then. I stayed with 'em then.

Paul Richards had gone to Baltimore and he made a deal for me. The deal was for a couple of other guys but Richards wanted me and I was sort of throwed in. Marty Marion just throwed me in the deal. In Baltimore they said, "We was really after you but we had to make this trade with them others and they got 'em to throw you in."

I had a good record in Chicago. When I come up I was 7 and 4. And I didn't pitch when I was supposed to pitch. But I ended up pretty good.

With Baltimore the year after the trade I was 14 and somethin'. We had a bad team. We lost 25 games by one run. We had guys would hit the ball up against the wall when nobody's on base. Get the bases loaded, they can't get it out of the infield! A lot of them games I hit 'em in. I had to start hittin' 'cause they wasn't hittin'.

In spring training I told 'em to throw me nothin' but curveballs. I went down to Cuba that year and beat 'em down there. One guy lost seven games and he lost 'em all to me. He said, "Why do they keep pitchin' me against you?" I hit his curveball — I used to couldn't hit it.

You were well into your 30s by then. What did you do when you left the Orioles after 1958?

I went to the Pacific Coast League — out there at Vancouver. I had a pretty good year — 8 and 4 — but they sent me a letter and said they was goin' to try to use nothin' but young ballplayers and was goin' to send the older ones down. I told 'em I was goin' home.

Some guys tried to get me to go to Japan. I said, "No, I'm through." I was gettin' tired. Anytime I walk in and it's hard to put on the uniform — tiresome — I know it's time to stop.

I left baseball and went to Kansas City and I was a bread salesman there with a bakery. They let me go down to Mexico and play for a little while, but that team — Pueblo — didn't have no money. They gave me $600 to come down there but I got down there and he didn't have no money — couldn't buy no socks and hats. [Laughs]

I went to one game, but I knew it was time to go home. I wasn't goin' over them mountains no more. We'd drive over the mountains and the driver'd be turnin' around talkin' and it'd be so foggy you couldn't see ten feet and there was curves and such. So I come home and didn't look back.

You played for more than 20 years. Who were the best players you saw?

Oh, there was a lot of 'em. The best hitter I'd say was Josh Gibson. No, the *best* hitter was Oscar Charleston. He managed the first team I played for. Oscar Charleston was about 50 then — and he walked up to the base with the score tied up and they'd walk him. I'd never seen nothin' like that.

He put his foot up in front of the base and he'd act like a kid — he wasn't — and he'd say, "Hey! Somebody get on! Let ol' Charleston hit!" And somebody'd get on and he'd get his bat and walk up there — hit the ball out of the ballpark. He could hit.

Hollis Thurston, first man who ever won 20 games for a bottom team, was from St. Louis — not the Cardinals, but the other one, the Browns; he asked me one day — he was coachin' — he said, "You know Oscar Charleston? I've seen Babe Ruth and [Jimmie] Foxx and all of 'em — that's the greatest hitter I ever seen. We barnstormed with him one year and he hit home runs every night! I ain't never seen nobody hit like that!"

I've seen him spit at two balls and then hit one out! At 50 years old! I said, "*What did he do when he was young!?*"

Then I met a guy down in Texas when I had my bad tooth and I went to him. He said, "You're a ballplayer, ain't you?" I said, "Yeah." "You ever heard of Oscar Charleston?" I said, "Yeah, he was my first manager." He said, "I played with him! That was the doggonedest man I ever seen in my life! I ain't never met nobody in my life like Oscar Charleston!" [Laughs]

There was nothin' that he couldn't do! I seen him play, at 50 years old, every position in a game. At every position he was great! He was all around the best. And I didn't see him play baseball — he was just managin' and would play sometimes.

Now the best hitter that was still playin' — oh, he was a first baseman, he's in the Hall of Fame. Leonard! Buck Leonard!

Now Buck Leonard was somethin' like Lou Gehrig. Josh Gibson's home runs overshadowed him, but just a natural hitter — probably the best natural hitter you'd want to see. One day I was throwin' *hard* and he just fouled the ball — tippin' the ball off. He come to me, he said, "Man, you're *throwin'* that ball today!" I said, "Maybe, but I ain't gettin' none by you!" [Laughs]

Then you got some more ballplayers like Bonnie Serrell. He loved to go to Mexico — he could speak that stuff just like the Mexicans could. He played Triple-A. He played fancy but that's the only way he could play. Just like Goose Tatum — you know, basketball. If Goose Tatum didn't clown he couldn't play. You might as well take him out if he couldn't clown.

Bonnie Serrell was like this — he wasn't clownin' but he'd get the ball and throw it over his shoulder and behind him and all like that and make double plays. This guy used to be with Brooklyn saw this and jumped up and said, "Lord, have mercy! I can't have this! This would kill me all year!"

Then Hank Thompson was a *great* ballplayer, but when he killed this guy, ooh, he just went down. Started drinkin'. But Hank Thompson could have been one of the greatest second basemen if he hadn't did that. He maked bad hops look good.

Who was the best pitcher you saw?

Well, the pitcher was Hilton Smith. Hilton Smith. You ever heard of Hilton Smith? If I had to get a pitcher to put out there and say, "Get this man out," I'd send Hilton Smith.

Was he better than Satchel?

He was better than anybody I ever seen. If you put him and Bob Feller out on the mound and go up in the stands, you couldn't tell who was pitchin'. They pitched that much alike and looked that much alike in a uniform. Bob Feller had a great curveball but Hilton's was a little better.

And he could hit as good as anybody on the team. Bully Brown and all of 'em! He was a hitter! Three hits wasn't nothin' for him. He tried to play the outfield, but he couldn't — he was *so* slow. If he wasn't so slow you could put him on first base. He was a great hitter — I mean a *great* hitter! Four-for-four, 3-for-3 — you don't ever get him out all day.

When I first saw him, I was up there in Fort Wayne, Indiana. We played 'em up there and I said, "Who's this ol' big-eared boy — this country boy?" A man said, "Country boy? Man, that's Hilton Smith!" I went up to bat and I found out who he was! Boy, he throwed me three knee-high and I walked away. I couldn't hardly see 'em. [Laughs]

A lot of people say he should be in the Hall of Fame.

That's right — he should. If anybody should be there, it's Hilton Smith. O'Neil's on that panel [Veterans Committee], so he'll make it. He's got to make it one day. 'Course, I could name a lot of great players, but them's the ones I pick out first.

Is there one game that stands out as your best game?

One of the best I think I pitched was at Indianapolis, Indiana. My arm used to get so strong I had to put alcohol on it to weaken it. That's how strong my arm would get. So I put some alcohol on it. It was not too cold but it was not a warm night. But nobody would warm me up!

Frank Duncan said, "I ain't gonna warm him up!" Some other guys said they wasn't gonna warm me up, "He's throwin' too hard!" And the catcher, Jim "JJ" Greene, said, "I've got to catch tonight — you know I ain't gonna warm him up." You know how I got warmed up? I had to go out there and walk three men and had three balls on the next hitter to warm up. That's the only way I could warm up! I got three balls then I struck him out. I struck out about 20 in a row. [Laughs]

They got one hit off me that night and why they got a hit — they hadn't been hittin' me — the second baseman was in, just standin' up there, and the ball blooped right over his head. I struck out 22 or 23. The regular hitters wouldn't hit — they'd send the pitchers up to bat.

One game — I come out of the army — and we was playin' up in Belleville, Illinois, right out of St. Louis. They got lights but they ain't lights like these big stadiums. I was just out of the army and I was throwin' hard and Piper Davis was managin' the [Birmingham] Black Barons. He come over and he said to our manager, "Now I know you want this money tonight, don't you? Look, if that man pitch out here we will *not* play!"

First man up went back to the bench. Davis said, "We will *not* play!" The first man said he didn't see the ball. "You know, we're *not* goin' to walk up here in this light with the man throwin' like he doin'." So I had to get out and they let Jimmy LaMarque pitch.

Two times they did that to me, 'cause when I came out of the army I was throwin'

bullets. I never throwed the ball in the majors hard like I did with the Monarchs. I had none of the speed but I had control. I still struck out a lot but I could've been higher if I throwed like I did then.

A guy used to coach for Cleveland saw me pitch before then. He used to tell 'em, "Hell, he ain't throwin' nothin' like I first saw him." What was his name? Coached third base for Cleveland. [Tony] Cuccinello. Cuccinello said, "I saw him when he was pitchin'. Unh-unh — he ain't throwin' *nothin'* like he used to throw!"

They had a team over in Brooklyn of all major league ballplayers — had played in the major leagues — but were workin' over there. Bushwick. Nobody was beatin' Bushwick. Me and Satchel beat 'em twice. No black team could go in there and beat Bushwick. They played with dead balls — put 'em in the icebox and you couldn't hit 'em far. [Laughs] Me and Satchel struck out a million of 'em.

Did you save souvenirs from your career?

Only thing I saved was one thing. I throwed the others away. When I came back up to Chicago, there was a coach there — I forget his name now, used to be a catcher. He'd take some balls and drawed pictures of different things — elephants and me and things like that and how I won the game. I got seven of 'em — I won seven and I got the balls from the seven I won. He coated 'em with somethin' slick 'cause they're not gettin' old or nothin' like that.

Here's the number one ball. He got on here, "Johnson struck out five, gave seven hits in first '55 start for the White Sox." On the other side it got, "Man, our boy can hit, too." He got me up there with the bat. "A very bad game for A's at Kansas City as Connie beat the A's. Connie get his kicks with two hits as Dropo, Kell, and Carrasquel hit homers." Then he got the box score down here. That's the number one ball.

Number two, it said, "Chicago, 12,000 paid. Davy Crockett, hell no, Connie Johnson, Injun." We played the Indians; he got a Indian up here sayin', "Me loosem 12 brave warriors. New Indian hunter — Connie Johnson." [Laughs] Then it says, "C. J. struck out 12, allowed six hits, to beat Early Wynn in Chicago. Great job." Then it got the box score. They're in color — red and blue.

The third one, it says, "New York, 18,000. Rivera drove in one, Dropo two with home run as Sox and Johnson beat Yankees in New York." He got a picture of Casey Stengel lookin' crazy. "Casey has the shakes as Johnson stops New York." [Laughs] Then it says, "Great job, Connie. Sox first again in fight for flag. Turley loses."

These are all I kept. I gave all the gloves and everything away when I was through with the game. When Baltimore invited us back up there for that reunion, I got a uniform. I kept it.

If you went back to being a kid in Stone Mountain, would you be a ballplayer again — do it the same way?

The same way. People ask me, "Didn't you come along too soon?" I say, "Unh-unh." Like O'Neil say, I come along at the

right time. I wouldn't want to be comin' along now — see, the things they're doin' now with dope and them things.

Back in those days I learned somethin'. The change and learnin' from older people cut off in '45 when the women went in the factories. There was nobody home and the kids didn't learn — there wasn't nothin' handed down to 'em. They don't know things, but they can't help it. Things used to come down from older people all the way down, but it stopped in '45. The first ones who went in the factories, they left their kids. And it's the same for generations since then.

Today everybody's *got* to work, and I'll tell you why you have to work. When the men went in the army and the women went in the factory, both of 'em's makin' too much money so they had to raise the prices. What hurt was the family that didn't have nobody workin' but one. He got hurt because the other people was makin' so much money they had to raise the prices. People had too much. And the prices shot up.

CLIFFORD "CONNIE" JOHNSON, JR.
Born 12-27-22, Stone Mountain, GA
Ht. 6' 4"   Wt. 200   Batted and Threw R

Year	Team, league	G	IP	W	L	Pct	H	BB	SO	SHO	ERA
1940	Toledo Crawfords, NAL										
1941	K. C. Monarchs, NAL	4		2	2	.500				0	
1942		3		3	0	1.000					
1943-45						military service					
1946	K. C. Monarchs, NAL	13	85	9	3	.750				1	
1947		3	10	1	1	.500	5				
1948		7	33	2	2	.500	42	18	19		
1949											
1950		14	112	11	2	.846	98	23	70		2.17
1951	St. Hyacinthe, ProvL	38	250	15	14	.517	225	112	172*		3.24
1952	Colorado Springs, WestL	30	248	18	9	.667	215	103	233*		3.38
1953	Charleston, AA	15	102	6	6	.500	92	50	86		3.62
	Chicago, AL	14	61	4	4	.500	55	38	44	1	3.54
1954	Toronto, IntL	34	201	17	8	.680	187	86	145		3.72
1955	Toronto, IntL	16	121	12	2	.857	107	40	86		3.05
	Chicago, AL	17	99	7	4	.636	95	52	72	2	3.45
1956	Chi.-Balt., AL	31	196	9	11	.450	176	69	136	2	3.44
1957	Baltimore, AL	35	242	14	11	.560	212	66	177	3	3.20
1958		26	118	6	9	.400	116	32	68	0	3.89
1959	Vancouver, PCL	48	111	8	4	.667	109	35	61	0	3.16
1960		1	1	0	1	.000	6	0	0	0	27.00

Record in Latin America.

Year	Team, league	G	IP	W	L	Pct	H	BB	SO	SHO	ERA
1954-55 Marianao, CubWL		31	175	13	11	.542	175	84	128*		3.45
1961	Puebla, MexL	3		1	0	1.000					

Verdell Mathis

The Best Lefty in the League

NEGRO LEAGUE DEBUT: 1940

Steve Carlton's 1972 record of 27 wins for a last-place Phillies team that won only 59 games is pointed to as one of the greatest individual seasons ever by a pitcher. Others look at Ned Garver's 20 wins for the 1951 Browns, a team that lost 102 games (52 wins) and say it's the best.

But how about Verdell "Lefty" Mathis in 1945? The Memphis Red Sox of the six-team Negro American League finished dead last with a record of 17–61, 40½ games behind the world champion Cleveland Buckeyes and 17½ in back of the fifth-place Cincinnati Clowns. The Red Sox were terrible that year, but their ace, Lefty Mathis, put together a season that stands with any pitcher's at any time in any league. Although Negro league records are difficult to find, research indicates that Lefty had a 10–11 record that year for Memphis. Without him, the Red Sox were 7–50. He had nearly 60 percent of the club's wins!

That wasn't Mathis's only good season. Indeed, he was acclaimed as the top southpaw in the NAL in the 1940s and is one of the few pitchers to have a winning career record against Satchel Paige. And he shares with Paige the distinction of being the only pitchers in Negro leagues history with two All-Star game victories. Although the records are incomplete, Memphis appears to have managed a .500 record only once during the decade Mathis pitched for them, yet he held his own with the rest of the league and justified the accolades bestowed upon him.

By the time the Dodgers signed Jackie Robinson, Verdell Mathis was past 30. A couple of major league teams expressed interest, but he knew it was too late. And that's a shame.

One of the criteria given for Hall of Fame election is for a man to be the best at his position. Lefty Mathis was, for a decade.

When did you first play professional baseball?

My professional baseball first year was 1940. Nineteen thirty-seven — that was a semi-pro team I was with.

The Memphis Red Sox did not want to sign you and Reuben Jones talked Dr. B. B. Martin, the owner, into it.

I met up with him [Jones] in 1937. We had a semi-pro team from Memphis and he had a semi-pro team from Texas, and we met up out in North and South Dakota and Ioway and Minnesota and we played against each other for the whole season — barnstormin'. [Jones was associated with Negro league baseball from 1918 through 1949 as a player and manager.]

I was a pitcher and I played a little outfield. I wanted to be an outfielder. I didn't want to be a pitcher, but the only

123

Verdell Mathis, above and opposite (courtesy of Verdell Mathis).

way I could get to play in the Negro league was I had to pitch, so I went ahead and pitched, but I played outfield just a few games.

You were a good hitter.

A pretty good hitter. That's why I liked to play, for the hits.

During the time you played with Memphis, the team was rarely very good, yet you had the reputation of being the best left-hander in the Negro American League.

Well, yes. We had a pretty fair team. I stayed in shape pretty good; I didn't do no runnin' around or anything like that. I just

stayed in shape and did my best and I come out okay.

You were an All-Star three times.

They didn't want to take me to the [1941] All-Star game anyway, so the first year I went, they let me pinch run. I was disgusted at that. So later on, there was a manager that managed the Birmingham Black Barons; he said he was gonna take me to the All-Star game regardless, and he did. It was 1943; he took me but I didn't have no idea in the world I was gonna start the game. I went and I started the game in 1943 and I was the winnin' pitcher for that game and he carried me the next year. In 1944 I started the game for that year and I won that game. I won two in a row.

In the meantime, the Sunday before the first game I had a confrontation with Satchel Paige. I beat him that Sunday. It was Satchel Paige Day in Chicago—Wrigley Field. I beat him, 2-to-1. I went on from there to the two All-Star games.

How many times did you pitch against him?

I pitched against him about five or six times. You see, you have to be special—in special games—to pitch against him. You didn't pitch regular. This game was his day in Wrigley Field in 1943; that was the first game that I beat him. Then another game I pitched against him in his home town, Kansas City, and that score come up 2-to-1. 'Course, he beat me down in New Orleans and he beat me in Texas, and so, as a whole, we wound up 2–2.

I thought you beat him 1–0 in extra innings once.

Yeah, I did. Three wins.

Not many guys beat Satchel more than he beat them.

That's right. You can say that again!

As a hitter, they never got you out in the All-Star games: 3-for-3.

That's right! I could hit pretty good. No doubt about it!

You had a great pickoff move. You got Jackie Robinson several times.

I had a good one. I caught him, oh, three or four times.

There was a team in the league—this team was out East, the New York Cubans, and the Cubans had a lefthand pitcher by the name of Tiant. It was Tiant's father, used to pitch for Boston. His father was on the team—the New York Cubans—and that's where I got that pickoff move. I used to watch him and, boy, he had some *terrible* move. I practiced that move during the winter when I was off from playin' ball. I practiced that move by myself and I got it *just* like he had it.

You had elbow surgery.

I had elbow surgery in '49 and I didn't go back to pitchin'. I set out half of the season of '50 and I went to playin' outfield pretty regular then. I played 'til '56, barnstormin' with Campanella and Jackie Robinson and those fellas.

Who was the best player you saw?

Oh, boy, that's a tough one. The best player—he wasn't talked about very much. His name was Willie Wells, Sr. He played shortstop for the Newark Eagles. That's the one I thought was the best and a lotta others said that he was good.

Who was the best pitcher?

Well, we just talked about him. [Laughs] Satchel. He beat everybody.

With all those countries [he pitched in] the year 'round, he pitched, pitched, pitched, pitched and right today don't *any*body know how many games that we played, how many that we won, because there was no records, you understand? You only guess, you get an idea, but we never knowed how many games that we would play a year because we only had a scorecard. Well, after the season somebody'd do away with the scorecard, so there was no record kept. There are really untold records of the black leagues today. Not a thing.

They've found *just* a little bit. They've searched back and the game that I pitched against Satchel in Chicago on his day, there was a black newspaper in Chicago called the *Chicago Defender* and a man went searchin' to find something on my record and he ran across that old *Chicago Defender*, which is out of business now — been out for a while — and he's got in his possession the game that we played in 1943. That's how I know it was 1943 that we played that game. He got that paper preserved.

Was that your best game?

Yeah, that game against Satchel and those two All-Star games.

Were you ever contacted by the white leagues?

Yeah, but they contacted me too late. The Dodgers did and the St. Louis Cardinals did.

Any regrets?

No, I don't have no regrets because that was the way it was then and I don't think you could have done anything about it. We just went ahead and played to the best of our ability and enjoyed it. Another thing, we played the game *not* for the money because there was very little of that. We just played it for the love of that game and did our best.

My top salary was $600 a month my last three years. I started at a hundred-and-fifty and we were gettin' two dollars a day to eat off of. You could do it.

Do you belong in the Hall of Fame?

They're tryin' to work that up to gettin' me there. They take their time 'bout that.

VERDELL "LEFTY" MATHIS
Born 11-18-14, Crawfordsville, AR
Ht. 5' 11" Wt. 150 Batted and Threw L

Year	Team, league	G	IP	W	L	Pct	H	BB	SO	SHO	ERA
1940	Memphis, NAL	4	24	2	2	.500	15	2	16	0	
1941		5	19	1	2	.333	22	4	12	0	
1942		14	74	7	5	.583	37	8	20	2	
1943	Mem.,NAL; Phi., NNL	18	102	7	5	.563	88	12	31	1	
1944	Memphis, NAL	21	130	9	9	.500	130	35	86	1	3.46
1945		25	168	10	11	.476	162	32	85		2.79
1946			35	2	6	.250	22	2	6	1	
1947		15	75	5	5	.500	77		38	1	
1948		31	153	9	12	.429	196	48	82		4.75
1949		23	155	9	11	.450	166		70	0	

Mathis played into the 1950s with Memphis as an outfielder, first baseman, and pitcher, but records are unavailable. A good hitter, he was credited with batting averages of .310, .261, .200, .276, and .263 from 1944-48, when he often played in the field when not pitching.

Piper Davis

Willie's "Father"

NEGRO LEAGUE DEBUT: 1942

Top teams have always been strong up the middle, particularly around second base. A top keystone combination is all-important to a team's success.

One of the best middle infield duos of all time played together for five years, but due to the versatility of one, only had one season as the second base/shortstop combination.

On two occasions in his career, Lorenzo "Piper" Davis played all nine positions in a game. In 1948, he left his preferred and probably best position of first base to move to his original position of second base for the Birmingham Black Barons. Because first base was his best position does not in any way mean that he was not a superb second sacker as well. Veteran observers say he may have turned the double play nearly as well as Bill Mazeroski and had the range in his younger days of Bobby Knoop. In fact, even though he was his team's everyday first baseman, Davis played second in the annual Negro leagues All-Star game, where he teamed up with the Black Barons' shortstop, Artie Wilson, to give the Negro American League an impenetrable middle defense. And Davis had a .385 All-Star batting average to go along with his superior glove.

But 1948 was the only year these two spent an entire season together up the middle. What a year it was, though! Each man played every game as they led the league in double plays. Wilson led the Negro AL in batting (.402) and hits, while Davis batted .353 and led the league in RBIs (69 in 76 games). They combined to lead the Black Barons to the championship.

Later, Piper Davis played "white folks" ball and I was fortunate enough to see him play when he was in the Pacific Coast League in the mid–1950s. He was 33 years old when he left the Negro leagues and his best days were behind him, but still, in nine years in organized ball, he batted nearly .280. Most of his time was spent in the Open classification PCL, the strongest "minor" league there ever was. His average for his Negro, Mexican, and winter league years, when he was young and at his peak, was an estimated .350.

Davis did not even have a chance at "white folks" ball until he was 30, when the St. Louis Browns offered contracts to Hank Thompson, Willard Brown, and him. Thompson and Brown signed, but St. Louis told Davis he would be sent to Toledo (International League), so he declined their offer.

Three years later (1950), he became the first black to join the Boston Red Sox organization. The purchase price was divided: $7,500 up front (of which Black Barons' owner Tom Hayes got $6,000 and Davis $1,500) and an additional $7,500 if Davis was still Red Sox property on May 15, 1950. Hayes and Davis were to split this second payment, 50-50. This was the most ever paid for a Negro league ballplayer up to that time, and this included such stars as Larry Doby, Roy Campanella, Don Newcombe, and several others.

Sent to Scranton of the Eastern League, on the morning of May 15 he was leading the team in home runs, RBIs, and batting average and was tied for the lead in
stolen bases. He was counting on the money coming, but, instead, a phone call came.
For what was termed "economical reasons," he was released. He later learned the
reason was his age, but anyone who knows the history of the Red Sox with minori-
ties knows there were other reasons as well.

He went home to Birmingham and then played some in the Mexican League.
Soon after, a call came from Brick Laws, owner of the Oakland Oaks of the PCL and
a man who was always interested in acquiring a good ballplayer, regardless of his
age. Davis spent the next six seasons on the coast.

He and Wilson were reunited briefly in Oakland, but it was 1952, his first full
season on the coast, when Davis really made his presence known.

San Francisco Seals pitcher Bill Boemler had a reputation as a head-hunter and
had spoken out against breaking the color barrier — a bad combination. Boemler
had hit Davis and Oaks' teammate Ray Noble with pitches earlier in the season and
on July 27 had knocked Davis down twice with pitches in a game in Oakland. Davis
eventually reached the San Francisco southpaw for a double and a few minutes later
was rounding third and heading for home as Boemler covered the plate.

Davis crashed into Boemler, setting off one of the most serious fights ever wit-
nessed in a ballpark. Both benches cleared and the melee spread even into the stands
as fisticuffs broke out among the fans. Later, "The Group of 19," a gang of Seals fans,
threatened to get Davis and Noble the next time the Oaks played across the Bay. There
was considerable tension for a while, but fortunately nothing came of it.

Piper Davis also played basketball for the Harlem Globetrotters to further
underscore what a fine athlete he was, but his greatest contribution to sports came
in 1948 when, as Birmingham's manager, he signed a young shortstop still in high
school to his first professional baseball contract. Because of the kid's arm and speed,
Davis moved him to center field. The boy was Willie Mays, who once said Davis
was "like a father to me."

And like a father he was. Birmingham's top pitcher, Jimmy Newberry, had a
serious drinking problem. After games, Davis would keep the teenaged Mays away
from Newberry, as well as from anyone else who might adversely influence the young
man.

After his playing days, Piper Davis returned to the Globetrotters for a while
and eventually scouted for several teams for nearly a decade.

---

*How did you come to play with the Globe-
trotters?*

There's a story behind that. I was playin'
city league [base]ball around here.
Winfield Welch, the manager of the Birmingham Black Barons, was also the manager
of the Harlem Globetrotters. In the city
league, we could practice with the pro club
until our season started, then we couldn't
anymore, you know, so about a day or two
ahead — maybe more — they offered me a
contract. The Barons did. The Globetrotters
were runnin' the Barons. When I got ready

to sign my contract, that's when I found it
out.

Bob's Savoy Cafe had a basketball team.
I had the pen in my hand fixin' to sign for a
certain figure — I can't remember how
much it was, but, anyway, I tell 'em all the
time the Lord was in the plan — when Bob
Williams, the owner of the cafe, came by.
He said, "Well, that boy can play basketball." I said, "Yeah. I played one year of
college."

[Abe] Saperstein was runnin' the ballclub for Tom Hayes in Memphis, and Tom

Piper Davis (courtesy of Lorento Davis).

Hayes was afraid of transportation and everything — you know, durin' the war — so he called up Abe and said, "Abe, this boy can play basketball, too. Bob says he was his best player." He said, "Give him another $50 on the month and tell him he gotta try out with the Globetrotters." That's how I got with the Globetrotters.

How long did you play with them?

'Bout five or six years. My last year I was manager of the second team. They had two teams that year. The mornin' for the cut-down for the Globetrotters, Abe says, "Shame to send all this talent home." Welch said, "Don't send 'em." He said, "What do you mean?" "Have another club." He said, "That means transportation and somebody to run it and all like that."

'Course, I had done some secretarial work for Welch. That was my top subject in high school and college. Welch said, "You just start workin' on the schedule. I'll get somebody to run it." And walkin' back to his house, he said, "Won't you take 'em?" And I said, "Yeah, I'll take 'em." That's how I got to be manager of the second club.

But it got too hard on my legs. At the end of the season, when the season was over with, I came and told Abe that was my last year. 'Course, I had had a couple of offers to go down to Puerto Rico and Venezuela. I started goin' down there and playin' winter ball.

Later you became the first black signed by the Boston Red Sox.

They was workin' here with Birmingham and they saw me play. They paid me that year [1949] to play the *next* year. If I'm under contract May fifteenth, I would've got another $7,500, I believe, but that mornin' when they were supposed to pay me another $7,500 — I'm leadin' the club in hittin', RBIs, home runs, and tied for stolen bases — and the minor leaguers go out and practice in the mornin' so I went out that mornin' — the fifteenth — and went downtown afterwards and was messin' around, then I came back to the house where I was stayin' — I was stayin' with one of the bellhops at the hotel where the team stayed, you know — and the lady said, "Where you been? They been callin' for you all mornin'."

So I called Boston and he told me, "Well, I got to let you go." I said, "For what, man?" He says, "Economical reasons." I said, "Shoot," and hung up. And I had to pay my own fare back home.

I came back to Birmingham and wasn't there long before I got a call from the coast. Artie Wilson was out there and a couple of ballplayers and I went to the same team he went to but they had called him up. They called him up to the Giants and I went to Oakland.

You ended your Coast League career with Los Angeles.

We won the pennant that year. The next year I went to spring training with the Cubs.

You know, every player has to go before the man in spring trainin'. He'll tell you what you did, discuss what you did last year, and tell you where you're goin' this year. So, came my day to [go] up there, I went up and talked with him and he say, "Come on in, Pipe. What we want you to do is go down to Fort Worth and help the manager, Lou Klein — help him with our young ballplayers." That's what I was supposed to have done. So I went down there and when I got there, the write-up was in the paper about the players and everything and Lou Klein was the manager and Harry Perkowski was the pitchin' coach. Not a *word* about me. Nobody tell me nothin' to do, so I would go out and help the infielders, you know. The next year, they sent me out a little ol' contract and I sent it back, told 'em I'd had enough. I was pretty old then — 40, 41 years old.

You always hustled.

Thank you. There's one thing about it — that's what I told ballplayers: *Play* when you're on the field. Give it all you got. Don't put on no show or add nothin' to get a laugh or nothin' like that. Just play baseball. That's the way I taught Willie. Play every day you're out there. That's what you're gettin' paid for — to play.

You were Willie's first manager.

I played with Willie's dad when I was young. Willie Mays's daddy's nickname was "Cat." I was manager of the [Black Barons]. Willie was in high school and school was about over then, see. They say, "Cat got a boy can play baseball." I say, "Yeah?"

I saw him in Atlanta once. A fella 'round here would take the better-lookin' ballplayers and go off and play Saturday and Sunday and come back home. And he was still in high school then. I said, "Don't you know if they catch you out here playin' baseball for money, you can't play no ball in high school next year?" He say, "I don't care!"

And I told him, I say, "If your daddy let you play, have him to call me." And his daddy called me, say, "If he wants to play, let him play." So when we came back here that Sunday — had 'bout a couple more weeks to go in school, see — I signed him. So he played, then he went on the road with us.

How good was he?

Oh, he was a pretty good prospect. I had been in baseball a *long* time and when I saw him play, number one was the arm and number two was the speed. You can handle the rest in teachin'. If he got plenty of sense, too, you can help him out. He was 'bout 17. Yeah, he was 17 'cause I was 17 when I started.

Who was the best player you saw in your career?

That's hard for me to say. I couldn't tell you exactly who was the best player that I've seen. I saw some good ones. We had one boy here — Herman Bell, a catcher. He played here in the city league. He wasn't a good hitter for a catcher, that's why he didn't make it too long.

Several off the Black Barons that I had played in, as we say, white folks ball. Bill Powell, myself, Artie Wilson, Ed Steele — oh, I can't remember all of 'em. Jimmy Newberry — he was one of the better pitchers, one of the *best* pitchers playin' in that league.

Who was the best pitcher?

Oh, that's hard for me to say. Feller was pretty rough! Satchel was the tops! Then Kansas City had two or three, at least two. I can't think of the names right now. Clowns had one or two. Most all the teams had one or two ballplayers that could've played in the white folks league. Homestead Grays had three or four, just like we had. At least four, I know, or five ballplayers off the Black Barons played in the white folks league.

Any regrets?

No, no. I don't have any regrets. See, what I did, I went into Negro ball, as I told you, to educate my two kids. My wife's a beautician. She works a little bit right now.

I went down to Alabama State in Montgomery. There's a story behind that. See, I was born in Piper, Alabama — coal mines. I was in school all the way through the ninth grade, but my last two years at Piper, they added on a subject each year. I wasn't a dummy and math was my top subject. I had four uncles livin' in Fairfield. You know, Birmingham was flush with steel mills. I went up there and I was supposed to go in the tenth grade. Went up there that mornin' and I went in with the tenth grade class and when they handed out the book assignments, I told the lady, "I done had that." They handed out the math and that was my top subject; I said, "I done had that, too."

She said, "Wait a minute. Come on here, let's go to the office." And we went to the office. She say, "He done had two of these subjects already." He said, "What? Where's the card?" And she showed him my card and he kinda put up a frown, said, "Aw, go on. Put him in the eleventh." Just like that.

Shoulda been valedictorian my [senior] year in high school, but they gave it to a girl who had stayed out and had a baby. She turned out to be a school teacher.

I had a part scholarship to Alabama State and my daddy was a coal miner, down in Piper. My daddy had to borrow the rest, so I quit. Went to work, started playin' ball. Don't regret a thing.

LORENZO "PIPER" DAVIS
Born 7-3-17, Piper, AL   Died 5-22-97, Birmingham, AL
Ht. 6' 3"   Wt. 186   Batted and Threw R

Year	Team, league	Pos	G	AB	R	H	2B	3B	HR	RBI	SB	BA
1942	Birm. Black Barons, NAL	INF	2	4	0	0	0	0	0		0	.000
1943		SS		57		22	9	1	1		1	.386
1944		2B	64	253	40	38	3	3	2		1	.150
1945		1B	58	211	36	66	10	7	3	33	7	.313
1946		2B	4	11		3	0	1	0		0	.273
1947		1B	56	228	52	82	1		2			.360
1948		2B	76	295	63	104	19	8	1	69*	6	.353
1949		2B	82	299	63	113						.378
1950	Birm. Black Barons, NAL	2B-1B	42	149	36	57	10	2	3	28	4	.383
	Scranton, EL	2B-SS	15	63	6	21	4	0	3	10	0	.333
1951	Ottawa, IntL	2B-1B	78	278	18	73	10	3	3	32	7	.263
	Oakland,PCL	2B-OF	79	289	38	77	16	1	4	35	5	.266
1952	Oakland, PCL	2B-3B-OF	122	399	57	122	24	6	8	44	1	.306
1953		2B-1B-OF	174	670	90	193	39	8	13	97	1	.288
1954		2B-OF	120	365	40	105	19	2	9	59	3	.288
1955	Oakland-S.F., PCL	3B-OF	126	369	39	90	19	1	6	41	1	.244
1956	Los Angeles, PCL	3B-OF	64	152	19	48	9	0	6	24	1	.316
1957	Los Angeles, PCL	PH	2	2	0	1	0	0	0	0	0	.500
	Ft. Worth, TxL	1B-3B-OF	87	219	11	47	10	2	2	20	0	.215
1958	Ft. Worth, TxL	1B-3B-OF	82	220	23	62	9	1	2	36	3	.282

Record in Latin America.

Year	Team, league	Pos	G	AB	R	H	2B	3B	HR	RBI	SB	BA
1947-48	Caguas, PRWL	INF		188		57	5	4	10	49	4	.303
1948-49		INF						8	66			
1949-50	Ponce, PRWL	INF		304	52	89	14	8	3	59		.293
1950	Jalisco, MexL	1B	30	116	29	33	4	3	6	15	6	.284
1951-52	Caguas-Guayana, PRWL	INF										

Willie Grace
A Pennant for Cleveland

NEGRO LEAGUE DEBUT: 1942

The Cleveland Indians finally were a good team again in the late 1990s after more than four decades of undeniable mediocrity. Earlier, from 1920 to 1948, the team suffered through a similar run of unimpressive finishes.

That 28-year dry spell was mainly in the era of segregated baseball, and it's probably no coincidence that in 1948, when the Indians were the world champions, the only two African-American ballplayers in the American League were key members of the team.

Cleveland, though, was never a city known for baseball success, black or white. During the same period, the city was represented, at one time or another, by no fewer than 12 teams in four different Negro leagues, and the results pretty much mirrored the success of the Indians.

Cleveland's first entry in the Negro major leagues was the Tate Stars in 1922, and the club finished last in the eight-team Negro National League. The city tried again in 1924 with the Browns, who also finished eighth. In 1926, the Elites tried their hand and were a simply awful club: eighth, with a 7–41 record (shades of the Spiders). In 1927, the Hornets gave it a go, but once again the city was represented by an eighth-place club. Finally, in 1928, a Cleveland NNL club escaped the cellar; the Tigers climbed all the way up to seventh.

There was no Negro major league ball played in Cleveland again until 1931, when the Cubs finished third out of six teams then in the NNL. The next year, the Cubs were in the Negro Southern League, but fell to fourth (of 11). Also in 1932, the Stars played in the short-lived East-West League, finishing sixth out of ten. In 1933, the Giants, in the NNL again, failed to finish first, but the final standings are not available. In 1934, the Red Sox were sixth out of eight.

The city switched to the Negro American League in 1939, and the Bears were middle-of-the-pack clubs both that year and the next. The Buckeyes moved from Cincinnati to Cleveland during the 1942 season and were out of the running, as was the franchise in both 1943 and 1944, finishing each year around .500.

Finally, in 1945, the long-suffering fans were rewarded with a good — no, make that a great — team. The Buckeyes had a 53–16 record, and their .768 percentage is one of the best on record for any major league baseball team. They finished 14 games ahead of runner-up Birmingham, the defending NAL champion, and then swept the Homestead Grays, the defending world champs, in the World Series.

It was an apparent easy race for the Buckeyes, but there was one major problem. Lloyd "Ducky" Davenport, the team's leading hitter at .345, jumped the club following the All-Star break and finished out the season in Mexico. (Davenport should have been nicknamed "Jumper"; he played for 12 Negro league teams and 4 Mexican teams in 15 years.)

With Davenport's departure someone had to emerge, and switch-hitting outfielder Willie Grace came forth. He led the club into the World Series, where he batted .313 in the four-game victory over the Grays. To illustrate how Grace influenced the club, at the time of Davenport's departure, their lead was 3½ games; in the second half they pulled away to their eventual 14-game margin.

The club returned to the World Series in 1947 as Grace batted .301 for the season, but this time they fell to the New York Cubans in five games.

And the Buckeyes' success was over. In '48, they dropped to third (of six), moved to Louisville in '49 and finished last, then returned to Cleveland for 1950 where their last gasp was hardly even that. The club finished the first half in the cellar of the NAL East (five teams) with a 3–37 record, lost the first two games of the second half, and folded.

Willie Grace continued to play well, though. In 1948, he had his finest year — .322 — and in 1950 batted a combined .273 for the hapless Buckeyes and the Houston Eagles, whom he joined after the Buckeyes dropped out.

Although Cleveland was finished as a Negro leagues city, Grace, then 32 years old, put in one more season. In 1951, he joined Erie in the Middle Atlantic League in so-called organized ball. He went out with a bang: .299. With one fewer at-bat, he'd have batted an even .300.

The doctor's always tellin' me, "You know one thing that's amazin' about you: You 'bout as healthy as anybody I know of at your age." I'm 77 years old. I got every tooth I ever had. The only thing wrong with me, all the years I got glaucoma and cataracts in my eyes. They've operated on 'em four or five times in the last eight or nine years. That's the biggest thing got me tied down. I even talk to the girls sometimes. [Laughs] That's about all it is, a conversation.

You're from Memphis. How did you get to Erie?

Word gets around 'bout ballplayers and I was managin' a ballclub down in Mississippi when the man come to see me about playing ball. That was in 1942.

I was supposed to be gettin' ready to go in the army, but one of my best friends broke that up for me for a while. We had been down to Camp Shelby and was accepted. At that time, you had 21 days or somethin' like that before you had to leave to go in the service, and he and I went up to a place we frequented all the time and I didn't even know the guy had a gun. I'd carried him by my house and given him a white shirt to put on to go out and then he

got to arguin' with some young girl in there, so I was tryin' to stop him and he wouldn't, so I kinda hit him — knocked him down — and told him, "If you gotta fight, let's go outside — me and you — and fight."

And when I walked out that door, I heard the people fallin' off stools and everything and I looked around and I looked right down a gun barrel. He shot me two times, once in the leg and once in the hand. My hand is the one that saved me. That's stupid as hell, throwin' your hand up tryin' to stop a bullet, but it saved my life. It just wasn't my day.

They picked me up and carried me to the hospital. When it got ready for my time to go back to Camp Shelby, they re-deferred me. They set my time back, you know, and they said they would get in touch with me later. So, by that time, when I got called back again, I had moved to Erie playin' ball. They called me again and I went down to Pittsburgh and was examined down there and that's the first time I'd seen what you call Mormons — the Mormon people. I guess they had 35 or 40 down there. It was a community of 'em. They had long whiskers sorta like the

House of David baseball team and I thought that's what they were when I first got in there.

I came on back and about ten days later they wrote, "You have been classified 1B 'til a later date." So I went on and played ball and never heard from the army no more 'til the season was over with in 1945, after everybody'd been doin' everything. I come home one day and this card was there. I say, "Oh, my gosh! The war is over with and everything, now I got to go in the army!" I looked at the thing, says, "You have been classified 1A 'til a later date," and I haven't heard from the army no more from that day to this.

One day, just before this happened—went down to Camp Shelby—another friend of mine, we was walkin' up town one day and at that time they was lettin' you volunteer. We was walkin' right in front of the post office and he said—his name was Grover Hunt—"Let's go on in and volunteer." I say, "Okay," but I got up top of the steps, I say, "I'm gonna wait a while. I ain't gonna do it," and he went on in and about two weeks he were *gone*. The last time I saw him, we was playin' in Chicago one day and he was at the ballpark. He say, "You really tricked me!"

How did you come to sign with the Buckeyes?

There had been three or four guys down there to see me 'bout playing with them. A guy from Kansas City had come down to see me. Dizzy Dismukes was the secretary of Kansas City—he had been there, and a guy called Uncle Jim Taylor. They was actually comin' to see two of us there. There was another good ballplayer there, probably one of the best lefthanded hitters I ever saw in my life—his name was James Bell. They came there to see both of us but Bell had already gone to the service. I was still there, so we talked. I had told Mr.

Willie Grace (courtesy of Willie Grace).

[Ernie] Wright—he owned the Buckeyes at that time; they trained at New Orleans that year—when I made up my mind I would join the ballclub, then I came here [to Erie]. The guy who knowed I was here and he was up from Pittsburgh, there with the Homestead Grays, but I had told Mr. Wright I was gonna play ball for him, so that's how I went on and joined and stayed with the Buckeyes.

You got better every year.

What make me feel real good about that now is that—you know, you never think how good you were 'til the ballplayers that you played ball against say somethin' good—and two or three of these guys was interviewed with me have told me these things. A guy told me the other night something I had never heard before. He said he was talkin' to Buck O'Neil—he did the commentary on this thing they run on TV and he was with Kansas City at that time. He said the guy asked him, he said,

"Well, I'm goin' to the Buckeyes to interview Willie Grace. What kind of a hitter was he?" He said, "You're probably goin' to interview one of the best hitters in the game." And then he said, "Some other guy told me, he said, 'This guy Willie Grace, he used to come down to spring training and wouldn't even take no spring training,'" because the company I was workin' for I never did leave 'til they had been in spring training two weeks. I was workin' at the Hammermill Paper Company at that time. He said, "Snow would be knee-deep, he'd come down and start hittin' the ball right on you."

This other boy, Connie Johnson, he's tellin' me once, he was sittin' there tellin' Ted Williams what kinda hitter I was. He said, "I know I got a good curveball and I can get anybody out with it, but I couldn't get Willie Grace out with it." Those kinda things, you know, and the guy that they just put in the Hall of Fame, Leon Day, a pitcher they put in there 'bout two or three days before he died and he and I were good friends. Last time I saw him we were in Cleveland together and he said, "I still don't know how to get you out." Things like that, you know, makes me feel good that your peers respect you.

Everything [awards] they ever gave away in Cleveland I won and we had some good ballplayers on the ballclub. Why I won is because the ballplayers on the ballclub voted for me. If you're out there playin' ball and you got 20 guys on the team and it's four or five guys in the running and about 16 out the 20's on there vote for you, that you deserved the honors two or three times in a row. It must be tellin' that you're doin' all right.

Another kid told me the other day; we were down to Cleveland, he was there, he's some kinda director of a youth movement in Chicago named Jesse Williams and he told me the same thing. He said, "I used to enjoy sittin' there watchin' you play right field out there all the time." He was about 18 years old then and he said, "How I

admired you. Now I'm 70 years old and you're still here and I admire you." Well, that makes you feel good that you musta been doin' somethin' right, you know.

You had a heck of a good arm.

Yeah. Well, I was a pitcher. I hurt my arm once. Even then, I could hit. One day I was pickin' up the ball in the outfield, wasn't hurt on the mound. I was out in the outfield shaggin' fly balls and I was just gonna roll the ball back to the infield. I picked the ball up and a guy say, "He's goin' to second! He's goin' to second!" He's just clownin' 'round and I hauled off and threw the ball in on a fly to second base. I went right down on the ground and rolled all around on the ground because it's hurtin' so bad. They thought I was kiddin', but that was the end of my pitching career. Then I started playing the outfield because they still wanted me to play on the sake of my hittin', so I just moved into right field and started playin'.

But I pitched two or three games after that happened. The last game I pitched was a no-hitter against the Atlanta Black Crackers in Dayton, Ohio. I didn't even know I was pitchin' a no-hitter. Some guy was sittin' in the stands behind our dugout. He had never seen me pitch and I was walkin' in from the mound and he says, "What the hell you gonna do out there?" and I didn't know what he was talkin' about. I went on down and set down in the dugout and the manager came out 'cause they were givin' a night for another pitcher. Well, he had pitched that Sunday in Chicago at the All-Star game — Theolic Smith — and they was gonna have a night for him on a Monday night but he wasn't gonna pitch that night because he just had pitched that Sunday — three innings in the All-Star game. So the manager said, "Who's gonna pitch it?" I said, "Well, I'll pitch it." So I got the ball and pitched.

He didn't wanna take me out in the seventh inning. I said, "What's the matter?" He say, "You pitchin' a no-hitter." I said, "A no-hitter!" I didn't even know I was pitchin' a no-hitter. [Laughs] But he went on takin' me out because the fans had come to the ballpark to honor the other guy, you know, so Theolic come in and pitched the last two innings. He said, "Now you got me in a mess. I got to go out here and pitch!" He went out there and he got 'em out and we pitched a combined no-hitter. That was in 1944.

The Buckeyes were the world champions in 1945.

We played a ballclub, the Homestead Grays. Me and [Sam] Jethroe was talkin' about it; he couldn't understand what I was saying. I said, "Sam, can't you understand what I'm saying?" I said, "On that ball-club — not even the Yankees nor no other ballclub you know of, had four guys in the Hall of Fame on the team at the same time." He said, "Oh, no. There's plenty of teams got four guys in the Hall of Fame." I said, "Sure it is, but do you know any team that had four Hall of Fame ballplayers play-ing on the team at the same day?" The Homestead Grays had Buck Leonard, they had Cool Papa Bell, they had Josh Gibson, and they had Judy Johnson. One's a third baseman, one's a catcher, one's a first base-man, and one's a center fielder. I said, "You can't think of no other team that had those same type of guys on the same ballclub. Four everyday players."

Wilmer Fields was on the Grays. I said, "We were tellin' the world what a great ballclub you had." I said, "'Cause we beat you, but we was still tellin' the world that's the greatest thing that ever happened to me as a ballplayer was beatin' a team like this." We swept 'em, four straight. Out of the five or six runs we made durin' the four-game series, I think I drove in three or four of 'em.

You look back and when the other fellas tell you how good you were, it makes you feel like, well, you musta been good because those kinda guys are givin' you their recognition and everything. I 'mem-ber one day we's settin' there and we was goin' down to Cooperstown and a couple guys were sittin' there and there was a Cuban ballplayer sittin' there — I can't think of his name right now but he was playin' with the New York Cubans and another guy named Joe Scott from the Memphis Red Sox. When I got on the bus — it made me feel good, my kids was with me — he said, "That was the greatest curveball hitter in the world right there."

You hit a home run in that World Series.

I was the onliest one hit the home run in the World Series. The pitcher for the Grays, his name was "Green," but they used an assumed name. His name was [Johnny] Wright and he had been in the navy and he carried his right name in the navy, but he was gettin' out on the weekends on a pass and he would come in and pitch for the Grays.

The second game, I set that one up with somethin' I never did do and I shocked everybody. A man was on third base and I laid a bunt down right in front of home plate and I was runnin' and Archie Ware scored the run.

You played both All-Star games in 1946 and went 4-for-8.

I was the only one guy; I played both of the All-Star games and I got hits in both games. That's what I was tellin' you about Leon Day. He was pitchin' for Newark and he opened up that All-Star game in Chicago before 'bout 50,000 people. That's the biggest crowd that had ever been in the White Sox ballpark. First time up, I singled off him. Later, he said, "See. You're doin' the same thing all over again."

We got to be good friends over the years. I was at Cooperstown when they was enshrining Leon Day and Mike Schmidt and [Richie] Ashburn. I was standin' up there and this lady kept pulling on me and they was fixin' to take a picture of her and I 'membered seein' her but I don't see that well no more and she said, "Willie, I want you to take this picture with me." Now out of all the ballplayers that she's known in the [Negro] National League and everything — the league he played in — she wanted me next to her on the side and I don't hardly remember her but it made me feel good, so I asked the boy who was there and he said, "That's Leon Day's wife."

In 1947, the Buckeyes were probably a better team than in 1945, but the New York Cubans beat you in the World Series.

You know, that's a funny thing to me. I don't know how these kinda things happen. It reminds me of when I played in my last year with Erie here in the Middle Atlantic League. We set a minor league record that year—'51. We beat Niagara Falls in the Middle Atlantic League, which was [Class] A ball at that time. We beat 'em 13 straight over the season and at that time we were playin' split seasons. We met 'em in the playoff; the team beat us four straight! [Laughs] We just couldn't fathom what could happen because the same pitchers, they beat two of our best pitchers. Later, at Washington, D.C., a pitcher we had, a boy named Dean Stone, he was the winnin' pitcher in the [major league] All-Star game.

You were 32 years old when you played for Erie. You batted .299 and you stole 12 bases. Your age was against you, but did you have a chance to go on and play further after that?

Yes. I was in Washington Senators chain—that's why I played here with Erie, but I know what that was for. That was a cover-up. You see, Washington didn't want no blacks on their ballclub. Boston [Red Sox] didn't, although Boston was the first team to look at black ballplayers—Jethroe and Jackie and those guys—but they didn't want none on the team. Boston was the *last* team to take a black player and they'd taken Pumpsie Green. The press was givin' 'em the devil.

The same thing was happenin' in Washington, so they signed myself and another boy named [Maurice] Peatross—he was from Pittsburgh—and another boy, Hill I think was his name. That's what they had in their system, so when the press started gettin' on 'em they'd say, "We're not that way. We got blacks in our system."

The guy that was managin' the ballclub

was Pete Appleton; he had pitched in the major leagues. They wanted me to go out to Texas that next year and I said, "No. I'm not goin'. I'm out of it," because I'd been playin' ball ever since I was 13 or 14 years old and I wanted to kinda settle down. I had met a girl here that I had got married to and I wasn't about to go 'way no more. I was just gonna stay home.

I finished out that year and Washington gave me a little piece of money under the table—that's what they always called it. They put you down for one salary but they was payin' you more money than that salary really said. At that time, I was gettin' $327 a month, but actually I was gettin' $675 a month. They did that in the majors and everywhere. If you were in a league at that time, you couldn't get but a certain salary.

What kind of money did you make with the Buckeyes?

The major league salaries when I was playin' ball was only like $5- to 7,000 a year. I was makin' $600 a month here with the Buckeyes. There was two or three other ballplayers makin' a heck of a lot more than I was, guys like Buck Leonard and Josh Gibson. All those guys were makin' around $900 a month. Sam [Jethroe] found that out and he told 'em, when Brooklyn signed him; he found he was makin' more money [in the Negro leagues].

I would've played baseball for nothing, which I did for a long time, but I told the owner, "I'm not gonna leave my job out here where I'm working to go to spring training and stay down there a month without pay." What he did, he fixed me up in a way that I got my money through spring training, which would come out to $600 a month. That was good pay!

But, you see, so many ballplayers had different things in their contracts. Sam was makin' as much money as I was, Theolic Smith was makin' probably more money 'cause he's our best pitcher, and Archie Ware's up in that category. It's what you could get. My biggest weapon was that I was working. Hell, I was only makin', at that time, only about 65 cents an hour at Hammermill, but you could work as long as you wanted to work because it was durin' the war and everybody was workin' what we called "victory shifts" and overtime and everything like that. Sam got his because he coulda stayed in Cuba; he'd go down to Cuba or Venezuela and play ball every winter. You had those things as weapons to hold over their heads, a little leverage to go with.

Who was the best player you saw?

My feelin' on this is that, "How good was this guy, how much better was he over other guys over a ten-year period." I don't think no ballplayer was better than Stan Musial was from the '40s to the mid '50s. He probably played ball as good as anybody in the world. And Mickey Mantle, if he don't get hurt, coulda been.

But, like [Leo] Durocher said, Willie Mays was probably the greatest ballplayer that ever lived for one reason: anything you name on the field, he did it better than anybody else. He hit for average, he hit for distance. I think Mays coulda stole 50 or 60 bases every year if he'da wanted to. This 30-30 club, this is a joke. Mays, Bonds, or any of those guys coulda done it. This big boy with Oakland did [Jose Canseco] it — 40-40. What the heck you think guys like Mantle and Mays and those — they coulda been in the 50-50 club, but you're not gonna take your power hitters like that and tell 'em to steal a base because they could slide into a base and be out for the rest of the season.

But when you go right down to it, over the years for 20 years, day-in and day-out, Willie Mays was probably the best ballplayer. He could throw with anybody, he could run with anybody, hit with anybody. You'll find some outfielders as good on goin' left or right. They can't come in. That's Mantle's biggest fault; hit the line drive straight at Mantle, it would mess him up. It would mess up a *whole* lot of center fielders, hittin' the ball straight at 'em. But

goin' to the right or left, they'll catch anything hit out there. They'll catch a raindrop if it's falling out there.

That's why I say Mays was just a little bit more outstanding. As great as DiMaggio was, DiMaggio didn't have the arm like Mays had. Some players could hit as well, had as much power, fielded as well — but *none* of 'em could do it all as well.

A guy we was talkin' about the other day was a great hitter — he won a batting championship — and I said this guy had to be a great hitter to do this because the man couldn't run. I could carry a piano on my back and be as fast as he could run and he was an All-Star catcher — Ernie Lombardi. The guy couldn't run a lick, but he won a batting championship at .345 or something like that. You know everything this guy got was a hit; he didn't steal no hits. He didn't lay no bunts down and outrun 'em. All his hits had to be good clean hits, so that shows you what kinda hitter he must had to be.

Who was the best pitcher?

When you're talkin' pitchers, there's no way you can get around namin' Satchel or Martin Dihigo. My theory on that is Martin Dihigo or Satchel Paige. Now there was a lotta great pitchers I saw pitch ball in the majors — I never hit against 'em. I'm talkin' 'bout the guys that I did hit against. I watched Sandy Koufax and I did hit against Robin Roberts and those kinda guys — and Jim Konstanty — they all was great pitchers, but when you look at a guy — talkin' about Satchel is like talkin' 'bout Mays. This man wasn't a human bein'; I don't know what he was. He would pitch over here all summer, then go to South America and pitch all winter.

We was all sittin' around the hotel there in Cleveland talkin' 'bout it. I say, "Has anybody ever really drove him off the mound?" And two or three of the guys said, "No, I can't remember it." It never happened while he was in the majors, in the four or five years he was in the majors.

He throwed as hard as anybody I ever seen and he knew exactly where the ball was going. A lot of fastball pitchers like that was wild — up and down, up and down, up and down — but not Satchel. Sometime he'd tell you, "I know what you can't hit and I can throw it there as long as the wind blows."

I 'member one day we beat him in Kansas City, 1-nothing, in the first ballgame and we thought we was through with him, you know. We ain't got to worry 'bout him no more, we got two more games with Kansas City. We got up and went to Wichita, Kansas, to play 'em the next night and they was takin' infield practice and we didn't see nobody on the sideline warmin' up, so we look up and here's somebody workin' out at third base. Satchel was over there at third base fieldin' grounders. Somebody say, "Oh, no!" Somebody say, "What do you mean, 'Oh, no'?" He say, "He gonna pitch. Every time you see Satchel go to third base and monkey around with throwin' the ball up and down the infield, he gonna pitch." And so help me, he did! Before the game started — five or six minutes — he went over and started warmin' up. And in about the fourth inning they got a run. He drove the run in! They throwed him out at first base, but he came by the dugout and say, "Fellas, that's all." And we didn't get no runs. The man just did this day-in and day-out and you never hear him cry about, "My arm is sore, my arm is tired," or nothing like that. He just did it.

Someone told me they thought he pitched about 400 innings a year for 25 or 30 years.

That's exactly what I'm saying. We would play our 90-game schedule over here, but we'd play more because the only games that counted in the standings we had to play 'em in a league park. A lot of times we'd be down south and if they had a ballpark there, we'd play ball in that ballpark. Say we went to Greenville, Mississippi, to play Memphis a game on a Monday night. They had no kinda league there — they had a good ballpark but it's not in a league; well, that game's not gonna count in the schedule. And he's still taking his turn of pitching.

'Bout 1935, Satchel Paige had his All-Stars and Dizzy Dean had his and they went out and played and I think Satchel's team beat 'em 'bout four straight out there and Dizzy Dean made a remark then, he said, "If we'da had Satchel Paige, we could go fishin' the fifteenth of August." That's just what kinda man he was.

There wasn't no swelled head. He wouldn't hardly monkey around with the older ballplayers; he always hung around with the youngsters. He said, "They don't know nobody like you old-timers do. I like to be around with the kids." He'd come down and take 'em into Kansas City. He had a little Jeep; he'd come out and pick up four or five of the young guys, carry 'em out to his place out there, sit around, entertain 'em all day. He was just one hell of a nice guy.

He was crazy 'bout pitching the line for pennies. We'd be in front of the hotel some time stayin' up and somebody got some change rattlin' in their pocket. They'd draw a line and he would do that *all* day. [Laughs] And wasn't gonna win no more than 15 or 20 cents, but that's just what he wanted to do. It was a lot of fun to it. He was a character.

In there one game that stands out in your memory?

I would say that first ballgame against the Homestead Grays in the [1945] World Series. That's the day I hit the home run. They told me not too many balls been hit over that fence at League Park because the fence went all the way to the top of the grandstand. I didn't even think the ball was going out of the ballpark myself and I was runnin' around the bases and the guy said, "It's out." I said, "What you mean, it's out?" He said, "Ball's over that fence." I looked back and I couldn't believe it myself because I had tried to do it so many times in battin' practice. I could never hit that ball over the top of that fence in battin' practice and nobody else could. That's the one game I like, I believe, because it all happened when it had to happen.

Would you have liked to play in so-called organized ball earlier?

Well, you know, really, I don't know because when I was coming along I'd watch the [white] teams come into Memphis and play and I never did see that those boys did anything that we couldn't do.

I was talkin' to a guy and I was tellin' him 'bout they was interviewin' Rod Carew on ESPN and I said, "I don't understand those people. They had to belittle 'em [blacks] on the way they made the major leagues." *Sports Illustrated* interviewed me here and I said, "Hey, I was playing ball with the best ballplayers in the world," the ballplayers I played with and against. The ballplayers that left our league, like Banks and all those kinda guys, I said, "We must had to be the best ballplayers in the world."

We never thought of Jackie Robinson bein' a great ballplayer. We never thought of Ernie Banks bein' a great ballplayer. When he got to the majors, he was great. Roy Campanella was considered to be maybe the fourth or fifth best catcher in our league. Dave Hoskins — we couldn't give him away to nobody here when we were with the Buckeyes and we look and he win all those games with the Cleveland Indians. I'm basin' it on this: I was playin' ball with the best ballplayers in the world and I got those kinda guys that's in the major leagues now to prove it.

The Rookie of the Year in the National League was a Negro leagues graduate year after year in the early years of the award.

Last night I was layin' in bed tryin' to think. Sam was Rookie of the Year in 1950, [Don] Newcombe was '49, Jackie was '47. Junior Gilliam was '53. [Mays won in 1951 and Joe Black won in 1952; the only non–Negro leagues graduate to be named top NL rookie in the first seven years of the award was Alvin Dark in 1948. In 1954, Banks was second and Henry Aaron was fourth in the voting.]

Now there was a ballplayer we didn't hardly know we had him on the ballclub! He came to spring training with us and we called him "the little quiet boy." He was sittin' over there and we carried him through the spring training and he used to like to sit in my seat or Jethroe's seat because sometime on the bus we'd let the bus driver take a nap and me or Jethroe would drive the bus. And this little kid come over and he would sit there on my seat. Nice enjoyable kid — didn't say too much — and when we got back and we broke camp, we had to let him go. He went right on to Baltimore because the guy that owned the team in Baltimore was from Nashville and Junior Gilliam was from Nashville and they picked him up and kept him.

Once we went into Baltimore to play a series and the [Brooklyn] scout was there. He was gonna take us to dinner, me and George Jefferson. He said, "I want to get this kid. I want to get some reports on him." And while we're sittin' around eatin', I said, "Who you talkin' about?" "Junior Gilliam." I said, "Who in the hell is Junior Gilliam?" He said, "What do you mean? He played ball with you on your team!" I said, "Junior Gilliam? We ain't got nobody on the team named Junior Gilliam."

And George said, "Oh, that little kid from Nashville, Tennessee, playin' infield?" He say. "Yeah, pretty good ballplayer in the infield." I said, "Well, hell, I didn't hardly know him. He's a nice little kid and everything." And the guy said, "Yeah, we just got him. We're gonna send him to Montreal." And then he was in the majors.

I kinda felt like I and Buck and Josh and a lot of the other guys was 34, 35 years old. Let's be frank now; they didn't even want a white boy in the major leagues if he's 28, 29 years old. They didn't want him; he's too old.

A scout from the White Sox they sent down and talked to me in Memphis and [Leon] Kellman — he was a boy from Panama — and we was sittin' there talkin'. Then Washington's farm team was here in Erie and they come talk to me and I said I'd think about it. He said, "We'll slip a piece of money under the table." I played that one year and they wanted me to go out in Texas in the Texas League, but I was about ready to quit because I had proven my point that I could play in [Class] A ball and could play baseball.

They [white ball] can't say they trained these ballplayers because Miss [Effa] Manley, they way I got it, she told Cleveland, "I'll sell you Larry Doby but you ain't gonna send him out to no farm team." They said, "We was wantin' to send him down to brush him up." She said, "He's better'n anybody you got on your ballclub now. He's not goin' to no farm team." She told the New York Giants the same thing about Monte Irvin at the same time so they couldn't get no credit for developin' them.

When Willie Mays came to the Giants, he went hitless the first 12 or 14 times. He spent a little time with Minneapolis. [Leo] Durocher said, "I got the best center fielder in baseball." Mays never looked back. And Satchel never went to no minors. Banks never went to no minors. We thought of Banks as just an ordinary ballplayer, a little skinny kid playin' for the Monarchs. The first thing we know, we look up and here he is hittin' home runs over everybody in Chicago in the Cubs' ballpark.

Some guys are going to hit anywhere, guys like Musial and Williams and Leonard and Gibson and Doby.

That's the point I'm talkin' 'bout. Those guys could hit! Athletes are born. Hitters is born. Nobody gonna make no hitter outta nobody. You may improve some guy's average a little — five or ten points. When I first seen Stan Musial, there's no way in the world I think this man can hit. I remember back in 1933 or '34, the Athletics had a guy — Al Simmons. The guy stood like a girl in the batter's box! Connie Mack said, "Don't nobody touch him! He's hittin' .380 like that. I don't want nobody improvin' on it." That just goes to show you, some guys are *born* ballplayers.

Harvey Kuenn said it and everybody knows what kinda hitter Harvey Kuenn was. He said, "Hitters are born. You can say all this 'bout the batting coach and everybody, but hitters are born." And he was one guy could hit himself. We used to wonder — guys like Marvin Williams, all them kinda guys, they'd come to the plate and you couldn't get 'em out! You'd throw everything!

The pitcher I was talkin' 'bout a while ago — I told Sam, "He's from your hometown, too. He's the onliest pitcher I've seen that reminds me of [Greg] Maddux so much. He pitched with us and I bet you can't think of who he is." He sat there thinking and thinking, and I said, "Theolic Smith." He said, "You know, you're right." When you was playin' there with him, you had to be on your toes because he got the ball and he was ready to pitch and there was no 3–2, 3–1, 3–2, 3–1. Mostly he's like Satchel; you may got 2–2, but that was it. It could happen some time, but with Theolic most of the count was 1–1, 2–1 like it is with Maddux. I think when Maddux walks a guy, I think it's mostly because he might near *wants* to walk him. "If he ain't gonna hit my pitch, I'm not gonna give him his pitch." But I think when he wants to get that ball over the plate, he can throw that ball mighty near where he want to throw it.

[Smith] couldn't throw hard as Paige, but he could throw hard enough, and he was a smart pitcher. That's what it is. I think Maddux is smarter; he's a magician out there on that mound. He's always thinking. I think when you hand Maddux that ball, that's his ballgame. He know where he's going with it. And that's the way Theolic was. We'd look at Theolic, he'd come in and if he got the guy out, he'd say, "That wasn't me. The guy got his own self out. He swung at a bad pitch."

And he wasn't no crybaby. If you missed the ball, when you'd get to the dugout he'd be the first guy to say, "Hey, man, you was *trying.* Let's get the next one." He wouldn't sit there and cry, "That ball oughtta been caught!" and this and that. He'd just look at you and sometime, to help a guy, he'd say, "Hey, we make mistakes out on the mound like this guy made 'em out there somewhere."

I don't think I'd wanna go through life without a mistake because if I did I would never know I had made a mistake. [Laughs]

Like some guy said, "How the hell do you remember, you so damn old." I said, "Well, I got pretty good memories of things that happened." It was a good way to go.

WILLIAM "WILLIE" GRACE
Born 6-30-18, Memphis, TN
Ht. 6' 0"   Wt. 170   Batted B Threw L

Year	Team, league	Pos	G	AB	R	H	2B	3B	HR	RBI	SB	BA
1942	Cinc.-Clev, NAL	OF										
1943	Cleveland, NAL	OF										
1944		OF	56	177	27	42	7	0	1		3	.237
1945		OF	32	112	14	26	5	0	0	13	1	.232
1946		OF	59	226		69			1		3	.305
1947		OF		256	39	77						.301
1948		OF	78	307	42	99	15	3	0	45	5	.322
1949	Louisville, NAL	OF	76	244	22	54						.221
1950	Clev.-Hous., NAL	OF	55	198	20	54	6	4	0	21	4	.273
1951	Erie, MAL	OF	120	488	86	146	14	5	2	53	12	.299

Bill Cash

A Star in Philadelphia

NEGRO LEAGUE DEBUT: 1943

Bill "Ready" Cash was born in Georgia in 1919 and grew up in Philadelphia, where he played semi-pro ball until he was 24 years old, when he joined the Philadlephia Stars of the Negro National League. He played with the Stars into the 1950 season (it was a member of the Negro American League the last two years). In 1948 and 1949, he made the All-Star team, and in '49 he caught the entire game for the East squad in their 4–0 victory and doubled in four at-bats.

Nineteen fifty was his last year of Negro league ball, but he actually spent most of that season playing for the Mexico City Red Devils. He spent 1951 with Granby of the Provincial League and then joined the Chicago White Sox system for one season (1952), where he was plagued by injuries. After a season with Brandon in the ManDak League, he spent a few years playing in the Dominican Summer League (he had played winter ball in Latin America for years).

When he left baseball, he returned to his job as a machinist for Westinghouse and became active in community work, for which he received several awards. He was elected to the Delaware County Black Baseball Hall of Fame and the Bob Douglas Hall of Fame for his contributions to baseball.

Most of the country was deprived of seeing many great players due to the color barrier, but considering Bill Cash's ability to communicate and his love for the game, the sport also lost a potential outstanding coach and manager.

You were 24 years old when you began playing for the Stars. Where had you been before that?

I had been playing semi-pro ball. In 1940, I played with the Bacharach Giants and they went out of existence after about a month-and-a-half. Then I joined the Meteors, a semi-pro team in Philadelphia. I played with 'em in '40 and '41 and I was with Webster McDonald in '42. We had a semi-pro team that played in Hilldale Park, over in Darby, and we won the semi-pro championship of Philadelphia and vicinity. After that, I got with Philadelphia in '43.

They asked me to come to what they called spring training. We spring trained at Parkside; 'course, you know the war was going on and they didn't do a lot of traveling, so we spring trained in Philadelphia. Their catcher went in the army and I thought they're gonna have three or four different catchers there, but I was the only one there all during spring training. That's when I started playing with the Stars.

You were an All-Star twice.

In '48 I was in the All-Star game and I didn't get a chance to catch but I think I had a time at bat, and in '49 I caught the whole game. 'Course, they had Hack Barker there. I was supposed to catch half the game; he was supposed to catch the second half. Since we were 4-to-1 underdogs and we were leading the West, 4-nothing, he told the manager, "Let him catch the whole game." So I caught the whole game in '49.

Who was the best player you saw?

When I played they had so many good ballplayers in our league. I think the best ballplayer I've seen play is Josh Gibson. He was the greatest hitter that ever lived. Boy, I wish the people of today could have seen him play.

I was in Caracas, Venezuela, playing with Vargas. Sam Bankhead was the manager. We were in a hotel playing pinochle—Sam Bankhead, myself, Hilton Smith, and Henry Miller—and a guy came in and said, "Bankhead! Telegram!" That was the twenty-first day of January, 1947. Josh died. He died on the twentieth. He [Bankhead] went out that night, got drunk, came in and tore up everything in his room. They had to send him home.

You know Clark Griffith, he wanted to buy Josh Gibson and Buck Leonard because they [the Homestead Grays] played in Griffith Stadium. The Senators played on a Sunday afternoon; they'd have 2,000 people in the stands. Homestead Grays would come in that night and fill the park— 35,000. He was scared because of the other [American] League members. Just like at Pittsburgh. Pittsburgh wanted to hire Josh Gibson in 1936 'cause he played with the Pittsburgh Crawfords in '35.

He hit the ball 20 miles! [Laughs] Griffith Stadium was the longest left field line in baseball. That hot dog stand back there—he hit *four* on us and people say, "You're kidding!" and I said, "No." It was 405 feet down that line; they had 25-foot fences and 25 rows of bleachers and a hot

Bill Cash (courtesy of Bill Cash).

dog sign on back of that. And he hit that hot dog sign four times. Center field was 484, 45-foot fence and trees in the back and he cut limbs out of those trees.

There was no greater hitter—Babe Ruth, you can call who you want. Josh hit the ball out of Yankee Stadium one-handed. I didn't believe it when Henry McHenry told me that the first time I went to Yankee Stadium in '43 when I was with the Stars. He said, "Come on, I'll show you where Josh hit one on me one-handed." I said, "Where?" "See that flag up on the end of the pavilion?" I said, "I don't believe it!" So he turned his back, he called Jim West, first baseman; he called Mahlon Duckett, the second baseman; he called [Little] Splo Spearman, the third baseman; he called [Gene] Benson, the center fielder; and he called Red Parnell, the left fielder; he said, "Where'd that ball go that Josh hit on me?" All five of 'em said. "Right by that flag."

He died when he was 36 years old. Nineteen forty-six we knew he was sick and he would go off and they would take care of him and they had other catchers catching. He had a brain hemorrhage. We think he died of a broken heart 'cause they chose Campanella before they chose him. In Campanella's book, he told us, he said he couldn't carry Josh Gibson's glove to the ballpark.

We had a shortstop named Frank Austin, Panamanian kid, and every time Josh comes up the infield moves back and Josh hit a line drive and Frank Austin, he jumped for the drive and it took his webbing out of his glove. [Laughs] When Benson, our center fielder, retrieved the ball, Josh had circled the bases and was sitting on the bench. I'm telling you, he was phenomenal.

We went to Newcastle, Pennsylvania, and in the field up there center field was 505 feet and he hit the ball one-hop against that 505 fence.

Is it true that he hit 70 home runs one year?

I was surprised he didn't hit more than that. He would hit that many easy. I tell everybody he would hit 60 before July the fourth if they pitched to him.

Sammie Haynes told a crowd at the All-Star game down in Dallas. One lady got up and asked about a guy named Josh Gibson and Sammie Haynes told her, said, "Lady, I'm just sorry you didn't get a chance to see him play. You people have lost a *lot* when you didn't see Josh Gibson play."

A lot of people look at little Luis Aparicio, the Chicago shortstop. They should've seen his father. His father played shortstop on the [Venezuelan] team I played for. He taught all the kids coming out of Venezuela. Boy, he could play! You talk about playing! Little Luis couldn't play with his father. That guy could hit, he could field; oh, he could do it all. He'd go in a hole, boy, when he went in that hole he got something to come out of there with. He'd take a streak over to first base. He was just

phenomenal. Luis [Sr.] taught 'em all.

[Chico] Carrasquel was one of the best. He was a 16-year-old kid when I played there. He played with the Venezuelan team. I was with Vargas. Quincy Trouppe caught for Magallanes. We only had four teams in the league.

You played against Leon Day and Satchel Paige. Was one of them the best pitcher or was someone else?

[Day] was great; not only a pitcher, he was a great ballplayer. If somebody was hurt on the team, he'd go play second base or play the outfield and he could hit, too. And run, throw—he had it all. He was an athlete. He was great.

He was about ten or twelve years late [being elected to the Hall of Fame]. There's a whole lot of lateness in respect to the black ballplayers getting in the Hall of Fame. So many of 'em were *so* good. Like they asked who I thought would be in the Hall of Fame, I named so many guys that should be in. It's a sin and a shame. Guys like Webster McDonald and Hilton Smith and Biz Mackey—those guys like that. Now here's a guy [Mackey] that taught Campanella how to catch and he's not in the Hall of Fame.

We had so many good pitchers. When I came through, Satchel was going over the hill, to tell you the truth. I don't know how old he was—nobody else knows—but the idea was, he was still good. But any time Satchel came to Philadelphia—Kansas City, 'cause he was pitching for Kansas City—we wanted to know who was following Satchel. They had nine pitchers on that team; they had six righthanders and three lefthanders. They had Booker McDaniels, they had Ford Smith, they had Theolic Smith, they had Hilton Smith, they had Connie Johnson, they had Satchel Paige—that was the six— and then they had [Gene] Richardson, [Gene] Collins, and Jim LaMarque. And if they say Connie Johnson's gonna follow Satchel, we'll try like the dickens to get something on Satchel, but you ain't gonna get none, but we can get some on Connie

Johnson. But if they say Hilton Smith is gonna follow Satchel — we always called Hilton Smith Satchel's caddy — you're not gonna get any on him. That's how great he was.

In the seven years I caught for the Stars, Kansas City come to Philadelphia and they never beat us. They have *never* beat us in Philadelphia. They beat us in New York, they beat us in Washington. Even when we played 'em in Briggs Stadium in Detroit, when Jim LaMarque beat us, 9-to-2, in the first game, Satchel pitched the second game and we beat him, 7-to-2. I hit in four of the runs in that 7-to-2 win.

First time I faced Satchel as a youngster — I was 24 years old — I tripled. I hit a ball one-hop against the scoreboard in Shibe Park. Next time I laid a bunt down third base, went down and hit the bag. I could always hit Satchel 'cause you can stand up there and dig in on him 'cause Satchel got perfect control. And he's not gonna throw at nobody, 'cause Frank Duncan told him, said. "Now, Satchel, you never seen this kid before. He's a young man just trying like the dickens to get by the best way he can." And he threw an outside pitch and that's where I hit it, in right center.

One thing, a fastball in our league, it really had to be fast. Most of the guys could hit that fastball, but you gotta finesse 'em, you know. That curveball was so hard to hit. [Laughs] If you couldn't hit that curveball, you had to go back home. The Dodgers, when they scouted Willie Mays down in Birmingham when he was a little 16-year-old kid, 'cause his father wouldn't let him go play with Birmingham during the week, and he came back and told 'em, said, "He can't hit the curveball." That man hit over 600 home runs!

Campanella, when he was in our league,

Bill Cash (courtesy of Bill Cash).

when he threw to second base his ball curved; 'course, he threw three-quarters side. And when he got with Nashua [New England League] in the Dodger chain, they taught him how to throw off his ear. That's when he learned that rifle throw to second base. I always had that rifle throw to second base. If Cool Papa [Bell] was living, he would tell you I'm the guy that stopped him from running.

You have a reputation for having one of the best arms ever behind the plate.

I did. In fact, I was in the Mexican Pacific Coast League and I broke my ring finger on my right hand and I finished catching that game — I broke it in the fifth inning — and came back at night and caught the night game with a broken finger. I went to the hospital the next day — I'm leading the team, hitting over .340 — so they found out it was broke; instead of putting a splint on my finger, they put a Band-Aid and I missed one ballgame. It healed but it's crooked now.

I played first base, third base, and the outfield in the Negro league, so I went to right field. They sent and got Clint Courtney, the catcher for the St. Louis Browns — this is 1953 — and he came; they made him manager, paid him twice the money they were paying me, and he sent and got Don Larsen; before he pitched the perfect game in the World Series he pitched for Obregon in the Mexican Pacific Coast League. And after he got Don Larsen, then he sent and got Frank Sullivan, who was pitching for the Boston Red Sox. Frank Sullivan couldn't get on the team 'til I left because you're only allowed five foreigners on a team. We had Buddy Peterson, shortstop for San Diego Padres [PCL]; we had Al Heist, center fielder; Don Larsen, Clint Courtney, and myself. We were the five guys on the team.

I was still hitting, but I wasn't hitting like I should hit. I went from .340 down to .258 and the owner put it in the paper that he was gonna get rid of me, so four teams were calling and said, "Bill, we want you to come with us." Now I'm the All-Star catcher in the league for four years and I said, "Now I don't know anything about it," and I didn't. One of the ballplayers called me the day it was in the newspaper; I speak Spanish and I can read it, so I read the paper and I went right to his [the owner's] office and I said, "How about giving me my release?" All the guys was up in a fishing town — they went up fishing. That was on a Monday. So Tuesday, Wednesday, and Thursday we'd practice, so I went and asked for my release. He said, "Wait 'til Clint Courtney comes back and we'll find out what's what."

So when Clint came, we practiced Tuesday and I went to the ballpark and Clint said, "Bill, what the hell are you doing? If I get hurt, you can go back and catch." I said, "I don't want to play for this team. All the time I played with a broken finger for this ballclub and the owner's gonna get rid of me because I can't hit? Hell, how am I gonna hit with a broken finger?"

That week my finger got a little better, a little better, and a little better. I didn't do so hot Saturday and Sunday morning. You only played four games a week down there — you played Friday night, Saturday night, Sunday morning, and Sunday night. Well, that Sunday night when I came up I gripped the bat pretty good. I hit a single and a double and a home run and I went in the office the next night, I said, "Give me my release. I don't want to play for this ballclub." So he gave me my release twenty minutes after six, I went over to the hotel, called Hermosillo and said, "Look, I got my release." He said, "I'll send a cab down for you tomorrow." So he sent a cab down for me and I went up to Hermosillo on Tuesday. They were out on the ballfield, so he took me to the ballfield and all the guys was congratulating me — I was gonna be with the ballclub.

I forget the name of the Mexican ballplayer — heck of a good ballplayer — he was hitting .258 and the manager told me, "Bill, you're gonna be my fourth-place hitter." I said, "Look. Can't nobody else hit fourth? I been hitting fourth all during my stay here in Mexico," even in Mexico City when I played with the Mexico City Red Devils. I went down there and the manager told me, "You're gonna hit fourth." I said, "You've got Bill Wright. He's a hell of a ballplayer." He said, "No, you're my fourth-place hitter." All during Culiacán, Obregon — all those teams — I hit fourth in the lineup.

He says, "I don't know what to do with him [the Mexican player]. He's so discontented." I said, "Put him behind me." And all during practice I was always encouraging him. I said, "Come on, come on. You can do it. You can do it." He was hitting .258 and I was at Hermosillo about three months; he raised his batting average up from .258 to .361 because I encouraged him.

We had the Obregon team up to Hermosillo; they was betting 4-to-1 they were gonna take four games from us. Well, Frank Sullivan beat us, 9-to-2, Friday night. Don Larsen had us, 6-to-nothing, going into the eighth inning [Saturday night] and I came up and he threw me a change-of-pace. I hadn't seen a change-of-pace in three years and, boy, Clint Courtney laid down on the ground laughing. He said, "You're so far out in front." If an experienced catcher would see what I did, he would know what to throw. I widened my stance, I said, "I'm not gonna try to hit a home run, I'm just gonna try to single." And I singled right over third base and we got three runs. This was in the eighth inning.

They didn't get any in their ninth inning, so we came up in the ninth inning. We had batted down to the pitcher [in the eighth] and our leadoff man led off [the ninth]. I always told Don Larsen when I was on the team with him, I said, "Don, don't try to throw your fastball by these Latin ballplayers. You can't do it." I said, "Satchel Paige couldn't do it. You gotta finesse 'em. Throw a curveball, throw it bad. Throw another curveball, throw it bad. Then you got 'em thinking; then you can bust your fastball by 'em." He wouldn't do that; he would always try to bust his fastball by everybody.

David Garcia was our shortstop. He came up and singled. Every time Larsen pitched, he'd get two, three, and four hits off him, just right over the infield. Chuckie Longbeers, our center fielder, he hit a long fly to left-center field and Al Heist went back and caught it. One out. Larsen was so sure he had the game won, so he looked over at first base and started pumping; well, David stole second base, no throw.

Ball one. He stood back and pumped again and he stole third with no throw. Ball two. And on the next pitch, Edgar Rodriguez hit a high hopper over Larsen's head that the second baseman and shortstop couldn't handle. David scored. 6-to-4. Rodriguez is on first and I come up. On the first pitch I hit Larsen across the scoreboard and tied the game.

When I got at home, I told—I forget the guy's name, he was a darned good ballplayer, a good athlete—"¡No espersa nada!" That means in English, "Don't wait for nothing!" And on the first pitch he hit across the left-center field wall and we beat 'em, 7-to-6. [Laughs]

The next morning—on Sunday morning—I had a Mexican pitcher; when I was there I tried to teach him how to hold men on, but Al Heist, he could fly! He could really run good. He was on first base and I said, "Now, look. When you get your signal from me, look at the first base runner, look back at me, and look back again." Well, he wouldn't look the second time. Al Heist caught that and when he looked at me, looked over at Al Heist, and looked at me again, Al Heist took off and he threw a curveball between the plate and the batter. The batter skipped and I got the pitch and stepped behind him and took the ball to second base eight inches off the ground. Clint Courtney stopped the game, came over, and told me, "Bill, that's the greatest throw I've ever seen in my *life!*" He said, "Bill, if I could catch, hit, and throw like you, I'd be the greatest thing the American League ever had."

I said, "I'm the property of the Chicago White Sox. They won't bring me up 'cause I'm black." I was the best catcher in their system in spring training. I beat Sam Hairston out for the catching job at Colorado Springs [Western League]. They lied to me and told me that the guy who show up tops at Victoria, Texas, in the spring training would stay at Colorado Springs and the next guy would go out. In spring training, I hit .375 to Hairston's .214. All the pitchers wanted to pitch to me because I had more knowledge of catching and my arm was stronger and everything, but they sent *me* out to Waterloo [3I League] and, boy, I was hot. I'll tell you the truth, I was *mad* because they *lied* to me. I tried to get my release; I said, "How about giving me my release?" He told me, "You play for us or you don't play." I said, "Well, I don't play."

I had a lot of outlaw leagues I went and played for making more money than they were gonna pay me and the thing about it was, they didn't pay me. I was making $750 a month up in Canada at Granby in the Provincial League. They bought my contract, sent me down to Victoria, Texas, in spring training, with Sam Hairston, and they cut my salary to $325 a month. I told the wife, "I'm going down to play, show 'em I can play. Maybe I'll get a chance to get to the major leagues." I could out-catch and out-throw Campanella, but he was a darned good hitter and I just started really hitting the ball like I knew how to hit when the majors started picking the guys out of our league.

That was in '53. Hairston and I caught against each other seven years. He was with the Clowns, I was with the Stars. We were both about the same age.

Didn't you break your leg when you were with the White Sox organization?

Yes, I did. It was in the southern swing that we went — Evansville, Indiana; Terre Haute, Indiana; and Quincy, Illinois.

Now you're talking about demoralizing. When you go into them cities, I can't stay with the ballclub; I'd just stay at a preacher's [house] because of the color of my skin. If you're the best ballplayer on the team and this happens to you, it's really demoralizing.

After I broke my leg, I came home for nine weeks and came back August the fifth. They didn't tell me I had to be back by August the first because the team was in the playoff. I got back August the fifth and I started working out and I thought I was in pretty good shape. Thursday I was out

working out and the secretary came out, said, "Bill, you're wanted on the phone." It was Skeeter Webb, our manager, called me, said, "Bill, we want you to go Superior [Northern League]." I said, "I'm not going!" Don Gutteridge and Glen Miller, he was secretary of the farm system, were there. I said, "They lied to me in Victoria, Texas; told me I'd stay at Colorado Springs." He said, "Well, look, Bill, I don't have nothing to do with that. Glen Miller's here now." So he put Glen Miller on and Glen says, "Look, Bill, both the catchers up at Superior are hurt. We need you up there. We got a 12½ game lead and Sioux Falls, South Dakota, and Eau Claire is breathing down our back and we don't want to lose." I said, "Look, Glen, you *lied* to me in Victoria, Texas. You told me that the guy shows up top gets the job at Colorado Springs and the next guy'd go out. You got the record. You know I hit .375 and Hairston .214."

When we was in Wichita Falls, Texas, the wind was blowing in from center field; you had the flag straight out. I hit a line drive three feet from the top of the wall and them guys was hollering, "Boy, look at the power that guy got!" and I nearly got throwed out at second base. That's how *hard* that ball was hit; the center fielder picked the ball up and almost threw me out at second base. He [Miller] said, "You go to Superior or we blackball you."

I had signed a contract to go back to Mexico, so, heck, I went up to Superior. I had my family back with me — my wife and two kids. I went up there and we won the championship by 6½ games, then we were in the playoff.

We had to play Eau Claire first. They had a little 18-year-old kid up there; boy, he could hit! It was the best three-out-of-five; we had won two games in Superior and we went down to Eau Claire and we were leading 'em, 4-to-3, with a man on second base. He came up and he fouled off about five or six pitches. I had a Cuban pitcher pitching and I went out to him and told him in Spanish, "I want you to start this slider at his ribs," 'cause his slider broke about a foot. He said, "Okay," so he started the slider at his ribs and the guy stepped back. He thought the ball was inside. It was a 3-and-2 pitch and when he stepped back, the ball broke across the plate and the umpire called him out. That little 18-year-old kid was Hank Aaron.

After we finished Eau Claire, we played Sioux Falls, South Dakota, and we won the championship of the league.

But it was really demoralizing to play for the White Sox. You know, you don't have to lie to the ballplayers. I told Glen Miller, "If you had told me the truth, I'd've fought just as hard to get into shape," 'cause I was in pretty good shape 'cause I was only out of the Mexican League, oh, about three weeks and I ran every day, went down to the park and run every day so I could keep my legs in shape. I was in the best shape I'd ever been in in my life and we had six of us Negro ballplayers down there. Connie Johnson was my roommate.

The thing about it is, it wasn't the idea they wanted us. To tell you the truth, it was the economics. See, the major leagues was going down; attendance was bad. We played in Philadelphia and the only time we could play in Shibe Park—Connie Mack Stadium, whichever you want to call it—was after the Athletics or Phillies played on Sunday. If they had 10,000 people in the stands, that was a big crowd. We'd come in Monday night and have 40,000 and the stadium would only hold 34–5 and they'd be sitting around all over everywhere. That was the whole thing.

Jackie Robinson was not the best ballplayer in our league. He was a substitute. He and Chico Renfroe was the double play combination substitute on Kansas City. Jackie had the athleticism, you may say. They knew he played with the white boys at UCLA; he was a three-sports man out there. That's why they chose him. His potential came out when he got in the major leagues.

Gene Benson was his roommate in Venezuela; he told him, "Jackie, where you're going is better than where you're coming from." See, nothing was outlawed in our league; they'd throw spitballs, they'd throw cut balls, they'd throw the shineball, everything. But in the major leagues, they had to throw straight.

In our league, they'd knock you down. Just like when Kansas City came to Philadelphia. Connie Johnson was pitching. First time up, I hit a home run in the upper deck and he was supposed to knock me down on the next pitch and he threw it high and I tommyhawked that one further back up in the upper deck. We was laying in bed one night, he said, "Cash, you 'member when you hit the two home runs on me?" I said, "Yeah." He said, "You know, you were supposed to go down on that second one." [Laughs] I said, "Yeah, I knew it." He said, "Frank Duncan," who was the manager of the team at the time, "said, 'Cash goes down or you're fined $25.'" So I went down the next time. [Laughs]

Is there one game from your career that stands out?

I was with Vargas when I stayed in Venezuela and the Yankees came down after their '47 spring training and they beat every team in the league and we were the only team to beat 'em and Hilton Smith pitched and I caught.

That was the first year Yogi Berra was with the Yankees; he came up from Newark. [Laughs] They put him in right field. Joe DiMaggio had an operation on his heel; he was the only ballplayer missing from the Yankee team. They had a kid named Cliff Mapes playing center field for 'em. We beat the Yankees, 4-to-3, that day. King Kong Keller was in left, Cliff Mapes in center, and they put Yogi in right. A fly ball went to right field and Yogi was hollering, "I got it! I got it! I got it!" Ball fell 20 feet in back of him. [Laughs] They told [Bill] Dickey, "Make a catcher out of him." Yogi could hit that ball, no question about it.

[His strike zone was] from his eyes to his toes.

That game against the Yankees in Caracas — I was elated to play in it. And then, too, the All-Star game in '49, which we played in Comiskey Park. I caught the whole game. The commissioner of baseball, Happy Chandler, was there, and Hank Greenberg; they sat in my box. My wife was sitting there.

That was a couple of 'em, but I played in a lot of All-Star games in all the leagues I played in — Mexico and I was in Cuba and I was in Venezuela and Dominican Republic. In fact, I was one of the guys in San Diego, Dominican Republic, that hit the ball over the left field wall. There's only two went over there; Alonzo Perry hit one and I hit the other one. The wind was very strong blowing in from left field and unless you hit it on the nose and a line drive — it was about 355 to left field and that's a pretty good poke.

A lot of people have never heard of you or the teams in your league.

I got on Buck O'Neil for the excerpts that he had on the Ken Burns episodes. After it was over, they had a big banquet up in the Marriott Marquis in New York. I was one of the honorees; we had 50 Negro ballplayers there. Buck and I are very good friends and he knows my wife and all; even before I signed in the hotel registry, he grabbed my wife and hugged her. "Get outta the way! Let me hug my girl."

I said, "Buck, you know good and well that we had six teams in the East and six teams in the West. You only mentioned four teams: Kansas City Monarchs, Homestead Grays, Pittsburgh Crawfords, and the Newark Eagles." I said, "What about New York Cubans, New York Black Yankees, Philadelphia Stars, Baltimore Elite Giants. We were all in the East." I said, "The Chicago American Giants, the Cleveland Buckeyes, Memphis Red Sox, Indianapolis Clowns, and Birmingham Black Barons. They were all in the West." I said, "You only got Kansas City, Homestead Grays,

Pittsburgh Crawfords, and the Newark Eagles." He said, "I mentioned them, but they turned it out." It seems like that would enhance it, letting people know that the league was comprised of six teams in the East and six teams in the West.

Did you ever appear on any baseball cards?

Three or four of the guys here — Philadelphia Stars — they were in the Ted Williams cards and I didn't get in it. Nobody asked me to put my name in it. I was the first-string catcher for the Philadelphia Stars; in fact, Stanley Glenn was my understudy and he's even in there. [Laughs]

Would you play ball again?

Well, I'll tell you, not with what I see right now. I'll tell you the truth, I would love to go back if I was younger to show those in the know that I could play and play a quality game. I would love to get up there and play with the guys who're getting all that money.

I only wish I was about 23 years old and know what I know about catching and baseball today. I see what's going on in the major leagues and it's pathetic. I don't see how these coaches could get these catchers to catch everything down the way they're catching it. That's why they have so many passed balls. We were taught anything below your belt, you turn your glove to *face* the ball. It's pathetic.

I saw a game the other night. A guy hit ball to right field and the guy kept running from first base and he's halfway to second and he threw the ball *behind* him, toward first base. Don't they learn fundamentals? Why does the outfielder throw *behind* the runner? That's a no-no in baseball, especially up in the major leagues.

The second basemen don't know how to pivot when they go across second base. That's how they get hurt. You hit second base with your left foot, go across, and put something on the ball going to first base.

And then, too, the pitchers don't set a batter up! Holy Christmas! They pitch just what they want to pitch. You've got to out-think these guys when you're hitting. It's between the pitcher and the batter and if the catcher's smart enough, he works with that pitcher.

The whole thing is, the coaches are making so much money and they're not teaching the ballplayers any fundamentals or anything about baseball. The guys just have got to have that good athleticism. I can look at television and see the guys, the things they do that the little kids aren't doing. I started two Little League teams and I'm telling you, sometimes the Little Leaguers'll be doing better than those guys be doing.

I go to churches, colleges, and schools and speak on Negro baseball and I got tapes I show the kids and one of the main things I tell the kids, "Stay in school. Education is the best thing you're gonna have in life and if you have the knowledge — you know, your athleticism is gonna leave you at a certain age — if you get that knowledge in your head, you'll be able to get through life."

I tell my kids, "I don't care whether you win or lose, but have fun. You're not gonna win all the time; if you lose today, you'll win tomorrow. Have fun. That's the main thing." And the parents want to put an adult head on a kid and you can't do it. I tell 'em, "Let the kids have fun."

WILLIAM WALKER "READY" CASH
Born 2-21-19, Round Oak, GA
Ht. 6' 1½"   Wt. 195   Batted and Threw R

Year	Team, league	Pos	G	AB	R	H	2B	3B	HR	RBI	SB	BA
1943	Philadelphia Stars, NNL	C	22	80		20	4	3	0		0	.250
1944		C	41	131	18	37	7	2	1	18	6	.282
1945		C	35	119	10	29	2	1	0	8	2	.244
1946		C	41	131	13	31	5		1	18	4	.237
1947		C		156	25	43	11		1		0	.276
1948		C										
1949		C	52	168	24	45						.268
1950		C										
1951	Granby, ProvL	C-OF	105	321	56	95	21	2	16	54	9	.296
1952	Superior, NorL	C										
1952	Waterloo, III	C	38	127	20	29	4	1	2	20	1	.228

Record in Latin America.

Year	Team, league	Pos	G	AB	R	H	2B	3B	HR	RBI	SB	BA
1947-48	Marianao-Almendares, CubWL	C		224	23	48	10	2	1	24	5	.214
1950	Mexico City, MexL	C	62	226	34	70	16	2	4	39	10	.310
1953	Cibaenas, DRSL	C		89	16	32			0	21	0	.360
1954		C		108	15	33			0	19	1	.306

Stanley Glenn

Pride in Defense

NEGRO LEAGUE DEBUT: 1944

The Philadelphia Stars of the late 1940s usually finished somewhere in the middle of the pack, but it certainly wasn't the fault of the catching. Example: The 1949 Negro American League All-Star squad had two catchers, Bill Cash and Stanley Glenn. Both were from the Stars. And both went into organized ball shortly thereafter.

Glenn was big and powerful, but it was his defense that carried him. He played on in the minor leagues through 1953 and then spent a few years more in a league unaffiliated with professional ball before deciding it was time to join the real world.

He went to college for a year and still attends required continuing education courses for his work in retirement as a lay speaker for the United Methodist Church. He's also active in his community with other former Negro league ballplayers, helping graduating high school students. He and his wife, a teacher, have put their two children through college, and he's eagerly anticipating her retirement so they can take off when the mood strikes.

You were signed while you were still in high school.

Seventeen years old. I was a player at John Bartram High School in southwest Philadelphia, and I had had two good years in high school of real production. At that time, there were only 11 high schools in the city of Philadelphia. There must be 30 now. I was having quite a productive year, home run–wise, and, of course, I could always catch. In high school I was six-foot-two, 195 pounds.

Who signed you?

Oscar Charleston. He might've been the best baseball player who ever played. He was a coach at the time for the Phialdelphia Stars. A fellow named Goose Curry was the manager. Charleston was a coach and the real man behind it, and in two years he was

manager and Curry was gone. Charleston was a baseball man all the way.

Was he still playing occasionally then?

Pinch hitting now and then, that's all. In the '43 season he played just a little bit, but mostly pinch hitting. He was a great hitter.

Your reputation was more glove than bat.

Yes. I don't think there was any catcher in the Negro leagues who was superior to me behind the plate, and I mean all of them: Campanella, Gibson, Noble, and Cash. And Mackey was still catching at that time. He was 48 years old when I came in. He was still catching every day and throwing runners out.

I always liked the defensive part of the game. I was always a good catcher, with a good, strong throwing arm. I liked the pitchers and I always worked my pitchers so that, when they got through a ballgame with as little amount of trouble as possible, I felt like I'd done my job. I just wanted to make sure a pitcher could throw strikes. If a pitcher could throw strikes, then we were going to be fine. I don't care who the hitter was; if the pitcher could throw me strikes, especially deep in the count against him, then we were going to win.

Who was the best catcher all-around?

Mackey was the best catcher and all of the fineness that Campanella gained was through Mackey. Mackey coached Campanella, taught him how to catch. Everything Campanella knew, Mackey taught him.

Mackey belongs in the Hall of Fame.

He's my first selection and I said that on an affidavit that someone sent to me about it for this year.

Who else belongs in the Hall of Fame?

After Mackey, I'd have to say Benson. Gene Benson. He was a singles hitter like Ashburn was; he was not the one that put fear in a pitcher's mind when he came up there. I played with him seven seasons. Line-drive hitter. If there was anything against him, it was because he didn't hit the long ball, but Gene was a great one. And he caught everything in center field, too. Outstanding. [His arm was] fair, not a Willie Mays arm. Accurate, but not truly strong.

And I'd have to say Henry Kimbro. A lot of people misunderstood Henry. He was quiet and he stayed to himself and he didn't talk an awful lot. A lot of people thought that he was evil because of that. I didn't find that with him. I found him a real fine baseball player.

Now, let's see. I guess I would have to say a guy named [Lazaro] Salazar, who played center field for the New York Cubans. I'm going to tell you something: He could pick it! He was a line drive hitter with power. A real good baseball player.

There was a guy that played shortstop for the New York Cubans. His name was

Horacio Martinez. He was a better hitter than Rizzuto; he was also a better fielder. He could pick it, my friend. He was there before I came in 1944 and when I left to go into organzied baseball he was still there, so he played a long time.

There was a guy for the Cleveland Buckeyes who was a catcher, didn't make an awful lot of playing time in America. His name was Quincy Troupe. He was a mighty fine catcher and in his late years became a good clutch hitter. Well, you're saying Hall of Fame. Maybe not Hall of Fame, but Quincy was a real fine ballplayer.

You've heard of a fellow named Clarkson? Bus Clarkson. Big Knockie. Knockie was a fine shortstop, even though he was a big man and, of course, he hit that ball out of sight.

The Hall of Fame selection process is lacking.

It has become political. Anytime Jim Bunning took all this time to get to the Hall of Fame — to have a man win a hundred games in each league and pitch a no-hitter in both, to leave him out 30 years is asinine.

He was tough. He'd knock your brains out. They had a guy from New York, a pitcher named [Bob] Turley. He could pick up pitchers; he knew what the pitcher was going to throw. Yogi Berra was at bat one day and when Turley whistled, it was a fastball. Jim Bunning yelled out, he said, "If you whistle, then Yogi's gonna get hit!" [Laughs] So Yogi said, "He's whistling, Jim, but I'm not listening!" [Laughs] Jim Bunning was tough. If Jim had had a real good ballclub behind him, then he would have been at 300 [wins], or close to 300.

In 1950, you joined the Boston Braves system.

In July of 1950. There was a guy named Honey Russell, who used to coach Seton Hall basketball, that was a scout for the Braves and he was following the Philadelphia Stars for, oh, I guess, two or three months. I was having a real fine year — fine years in '49 and '50. I think I hit about 12

Stanley Glenn (courtesy of Stanley Glenn).

home runs in one week in 1950. I guess he liked what I was showing and he recommended that they buy me. I was bought by the Braves and sent to Hartford in the Eastern League, and the Eastern League at that time was a pretty good league. It was a pitchers' league. We had some fine ballplayers on that Braves team; we had Gene Conley and Ray Crone amd George Crowe and Harry Hanebrink. Phil Paine. We had three or four guys that went from Hartford right to the big leagues. And the Red Sox, they were at Scranton at that time. They had Sam White and Frank Malzone and Dick Gernert. That was a real good league and we had a lot of fun over there. I enjoyed the Eastern League.

I was there the rest of '50, all of '51, and part of '52. Tommy Holmes was taken from us and he went up to manage the Braves when they got rid of Billy Southworth, and they sent a fellow down named Travis Jackson to manage us. He was at the end and somewhat of an alcoholic and they got rid of him and they sent a guy down named Del Bissonette. He and I didn't see eye-to-eye at all, so I think in the second month of the season they sent me up to Quebec in the Provincial League.

I played up there a couple of years and then it was time for me to get out of it. I was married then and ready to raise a family and I wasn't going any place, so it was time for me to get out of there. I was just about 30. I played a couple of seasons in the Inter-County League in Canada, and I was fortunate enough to play some winter baseball, too. Caracas, Venezuela. Maracaibo.

I always had a knack for electricity, so I went into the wholesale electric supply business. I stayed in there about 40 years and made a real good living for myself and my family.

Are there games from your playing days that stand out?

I hit five home runs in a doubleheader in Canada against the Phillies organization in Granby in the Provincial League. I guess that was my best offensive productive day.

I can't tell you how many great games I had behind the plate. My goodness, that was what I looked for — to catch. I caught Satchel and Leon Day. The Philadelphia Stars had a great pitching staff: Barney Brown and Henry McHenry and Wilmer Harris and Henry Miller and Bill Ricks. All of those guys were top-notch pitchers. Nobody, including the Homestead Grays

that had Gibson and Leonard and Easterling and Wilson and all those guys — none of them were eager to play Philadelphia. We had a great pitching staff.

I could sit back there and just what the hitter was thinking, I was always on the opposite side. I took an awful lot of pride in that.

Who was the one best pitcher who you caught on a regular basis?

On a regular basis, I would have to say Barney Brown, a real crafty lefthander. He didn't care if you were Josh Gibson or Buck. I think he loved it when I caught him because he had five different pitches and his *worst* pitch was the one I would call at a 2-and-0 or 3-and-1 pitch. [Laughs] No one was going to stand out there and say, "He's going to throw me a fastball," or, "He's going to throw me a curveball." Whatever his next two pitches were, that's what you were going to get. Josh used to say, "Where in the hell did you get that one from?!" And I'd say, "We saved that for you." [Laughs] Barney Brown was the best pitcher that I've caught.

Speaking of Josh, who was the best hitter?

Josh, by far. The best *right*handed hitter. The best lefthanded hitter I ever saw was Ted Williams. I'm going to tell you something. When you talk about hitters and somebody tells you that someone was better than Williams, then I don't know what world they were in. He was free and he said what he wanted to *whom* he wanted and he didn't fight with them, but his bat did all of the fighting. If he didn't want to talk to you, he didn't care who you are — he didn't talk to you. He was the greatest hitter that these eyes have ever seen.

Who was the best all-around ballplayer?

The best baseball player. I didn't see Charleston when he was in his prime. I'm going from just from what I saw and what the old-timers had told me. I'd have to say Charleston from that, but the best modern-day baseball player that I ever saw was Willie Mays. I played against Willie when he came up with the Birmingham Black

Stanley Glenn (courtesy of Stanley Glenn).

Barons. If Charleston could do things better than Mays, then they should've made another league for him. I think Willie might've been a little bit faster than Charleston in his heyday, but I never saw Charleston in his heyday, but Charleston had awesome power and they tell me that he and Tris Speaker just ran the balls down in center field. Charleston was a great left-handed hitter with an *awful* lot of heart. He just didn't believe anybody could get him out.

Mays's baseball instincts were better than anyone I've ever seen. He always knew where to throw the ball and it always got there on time. They say he never hit the

1949 New York Stars, Caracas, Venezuela
Back row (L. to R.): Stanley Glenn (Philadelphia Stars), Andy Porter (Indianapolis Clowns), Gready McKinnis (Chicago American Giants), Buck Leonard (Homestead Grays), Pat Scantelbury (New York Cubans), Bob Griffith (Philadelphia Stars), Art Pennington (Mexican League), Ernest Long (Louisville Buckeyes); Front row (L. to R.): Bus Clarkson (Philadelphia Stars), Lloyd "Ducky" Davenport (Chicago American Giants), Ray Neil (Indianapolis Clowns), Felix McLaurin (Chicago American Giants), Chico Renfroe (Indianapolis Clowns), Howard Easterling (New York Cubans) (courtesy of Stanley Glenn).

cutoff man, but nobody ever took any extra bases on him. [Laughs]

He was something. I saw him when he was a kid about 16 years old — 1948, I think it was — when his father wouldn't let him travel with the team. He only played when they were playing around Birmingham. Nineteen forty-nine he started to travel with the team a bit. I'll tell you, it was just unbelievable — a person of his age with all of the baseball instincts that he had. He was something.

Talk about the travel.

Oh, Lord. You don't want to hear about that! [Laughs]

I think maybe the Philadelphia Stars probably was the most sheltered team in black baseball. We played in the eastern league [Negro National League] here. There were the New York Cubans, the New York Black Yankees, the Newark Eagles in Newark, New Jersey, the Philadelphia Stars here in Philadelphia, the Baltimore Elite Giants, and the Homestead Grays, who played out of Pittsburgh and Washington, D.C.

From 1944 up until 1948, most of our travel was confined between those six cities and some small towns in between. Now, in 1948 we started to hit the circuit and go pretty far. I'm talking about just the time that I played. So we had it pretty nice. In 1944 and 1945 and 1946, most of our travel was on the train.

Then, of course, going to spring training and going down south was all a different thing. We'd go to North Carolina for spring training and travel was by bus, and it was nothing to drive 5- or 600 miles in a day and get out and play.

It was baloney or something that you would get at the store and make your own sandwiches, of course, because we couldn't go in restaurants and eat. Hotels were out of the question. There were few or no black hotels in the South, so either we slept in the bus or we stayed with some people in private homes. That part of it was terrible.

We went to Memphis for a series in 1948 and we were in Memphis five days. Of course, we played the Memphis Red Sox; they had their own ballpark. We played in towns like Clarksdale, Mississippi; Meridian, Mississippi; and Philadelphia, Mississippi; and we'd have to get dressed in Memphis, ride a hundred miles or 150 miles to wherever we were going to play, and the police would tell us when we entered the town that the ballgame had to be over by ten o'clock at night because they didn't allow black men on the street past ten o'clock. I'm just telling you like it was. We got the ballgame over soon as possible and if we didn't, they'd come out and end the ballgame. Then, of course, you'd have to ride back. I rode from Clarksdale, Mississippi, back to Memphis, Tennessee, which is probably 105 miles on those single-lane highways, and I had the uniform on all that time. And there was no place to eat.

I also stayed in Meridian, Mississippi, after I was in organized baseball. It was in a motel. I had to stay by myself. The rest of the ballclub didn't stay there. After breakfast I'd jump in the pool and they'd drain the pool. We would come in from practice around the middle of the day and I would eat lunch and I'd go in the pool and take another dip and they'd drain it again. And after dinner, they would do the same thing.

There was one man there, and he had two or three children with him and his wife. After the third day, he went up and raised hell. He said, "If you drain this damn pool again, I'm gonna blow it up!" [Laughs] It was funny and it wasn't funny to me. I was glad to get out of there.

All these sorts of things happened all the time. We talk about the South, but there were places right here in Pennsylvania — once you got outside of Philadelphia and Harrisburg and Pittsburgh you were treated almost the same way. It just wasn't in the South.

The year I went in organized baseball — 1950 — it hadn't changed a whole heck of a lot until this commerce thing came about where you had to serve people who came into your restaurant and so forth, or stayed at hotels. It was really pretty rough.

Would you do it again?

Oh, yes! I loved it so much I would *gladly* do it again. And I'm not going to regret where I was and what happened and as tough as it was, it was still a great time.

And the guys — we still meet once or twice a year. You see guys that you have known for 50 years. Some are in wheelchairs and some are walking with canes, but it's just a delight to see them. Even though we were competitors on the field, *off* the field we were great friends with each other. Even today, after all those years — more than 50 years — we're still great friends together.

STANLEY RUDOLF GLENN
Born 9-19-26, Wachapreague, VA
Ht. 6' 3"   Wt. 200   Batted and Threw R

Year	Team, league	Pos	G	AB	R	H	2B	3B	HR	RBI	SB	BA
1944	Philadelphia Stars, NNL	C										
1945		C	7	19	3	4	2	0	0	2	0	.211
1946		C										
1947		C		97	5	20	1					.206
1948		C										
1949	Philadelphia Stars, NAL	C	46	166	22	34						.205
1950	Philadelphia Stars, NAL	C	27	97	4	22	6	1	4	7	0	.227
	Hartford, EL	C	20	58	8	15	5	0	1	10	0	.259
1951	Hartford, EL	C	109	334	23	72	14	0	1	32	0	.216
1952	Hartford, EL	C	12	29	3	8	2	0	0	3	0	.276
	Quebec City, ProvL	C-OF	75	234	33	58	10	1	5	27	6	.248
1953	Quebec City, ProvL	C-1B	110	375	68	103	20	3	16	90	1	.275

Elbert Isreal

.300 Hitter

NEGRO LEAGUE DEBUT: 1945

Elbert Isreal's Negro leagues career was short: parts of two seasons when he was still in his teens.

Five years after his short stint with the Philadelphia Stars, though, he signed with the Philadelphia Athletics and began a five-year minor league career during which he batted over .300. Along the way, he played against the likes of Hank Aaron and Frank Robinson and was anything but overshadowed by them. But in those days — the early 1950s — a black ballplayer had to be outstanding, as Aaron and Robinson were, to advance. Isreal was very, very good but missed being outstanding, so he never got the chance it seemed he had earned. An injury led to a demotion, so he retired from the game as a young man.

Note the spelling of his name: Isreal. At least two recent publications about the Negro leagues spell it incorrectly. Both books also have the dates of his playing career wrong. What you will read here is correct.

I started out in '45. I tried out with the Homestead Grays. I stayed a while with them — about a month or so. It was '47 with the Stars. They got '50 in that book, but I didn't play that long with 'em no way. I was around 18 or so. On the Homestead Grays was Buck Leonard and Bus Clarkson. I didn't stay there that long. Buck Leonard was probably one of the best hitters I ever seen.

How much were you paid for your time with the Stars?

Two-fifty, I believe, for the short time I was there.

Why did you stop playing baseball?

I didn't like the long rides. I tried it twice. All night long, you know, and I was young. I just didn't like 'em. They didn't like young ballplayers no way 'cause most of 'em was old ballplayers. That's one reason they sent me back home, 'cause I was young. But I could hit the ball pretty good as some of them, but they said I was too young. I was 16, 17 — somethin' like that — with the Grays.

I tried playin' black ball twice and I didn't make it and I went on back in the government after that, then I worked into '52. A guy came by, wanted me to go play minor league baseball, so that's where I spent most of my time. I played for old Philadelphia [Athletics] in '52 in the minor leagues. I put my age back to 21 but I was 24, 25. I played in the minors for five years.

I started out with Harrisburg in the Interstate League. I won the battin' championship the first year. That was Harrisburg, Lancaster, Sunbury, York, Wilmington, Delaware, Salisbury, Hagerstown — eight different teams in a pretty good league. Class A.

I left there that year and I went to the South Atlantic League. Savannah. That was the year Hank Aaron was down there. Fifty-three. He was with Jacksonville and Felix Mantilla was down there. Shortstop. There was Macon, Augusta, Columbus, Charleston, Charlotte, Montgomery, Alabama; one more. There was eight teams down there. I wound up comin' in second behind Hank Aaron. I hit .316, I believe, and I think he hit .356.

That's pretty impressive. Anyone second to Hank Aaron is all right.

[Laughs] Yeah.

Then Kansas City took over 'bout this time. They [the A's] moved there. I played with Frank Robinson in '54. I played against him. In '54, I played in Venezuela and I hurt my arm. I played summer here and winter over there and I was supposed to come up with the big team in '55, but I messed up my arm and I just stayed home all that year. I played against Frank Robinson in '54 when he was with Columbia. I think he hit .291 and I hit .311.

I set out '55 and then I wasn't goin' back to play ball 'cause they wanted to send me to Class B ball down in the Texas League — with Abilene — because I skipped a year, but I went back down with Abilene and I think I hit .298 and I quit.

You had a .300-plus career average.

Yeah, but they wouldn't bring me up. They kept on tradin' with the Yankees and you know that's when they brought up Hector Lopez and Roger Maris, but they wouldn't bring me up so I quit.

The Yankees were one of the toughest teams for a black to advance with. They finally brought up Elston Howard because he was too good to deny.

Right. That happened to Hank Aaron, too. He wasn't even on the roster 'til that boy [Bobby Thomson] broke his leg. I played against Aaron and Aaron came through there and told me, "El, you know one thing. Don't feel bad. I wasn't gonna play, either. They was gettin' ready to send me back and that boy broke his leg."

They [white teams] wasn't willing to accept you unless you were extraordinary. That's what happened to me, so I gave it up. Fifty-six was my last year. I came back home. I was a presser and I pressed clothes until '60, then I went back in the government and worked from '60 to '83 and then I retired at 55.

Would you play baseball again if you were a young man?

If things were like thay are now, yes. But I went through the hard towns down in Savannah and Augusta and Montgomery, Alabama. That was before Martin Luther King — way before — and everything was rough. I used to sit out at the hotel in Savannah, Georgia, and they had to send a black cab out there to pick me up. I'd set out there and wait 25 or 30 minutes for the cab to come and pick me up. It was rough.

You played mostly in the South. Maybe if they had put you in the North it wouldn't have been so bad.

True. I only stayed up there one year. Playin' with the black teams now, I was in the North and the South and everywhere. It was just too much, man.

I had a brother play up there in that league from the '30s on up until '47, '48. Me and him played together in '47.

Any regrets other than the racial situation?

No, I don't have no regrets because I experienced a lotta life, including the racial thing. They told me and explained what was gonna happen and asked me could I accept it and I told 'em yes. Some things I didn't like down there that I kinda told 'em about it and didn't do it. I guess that got back up to the big office, too. They would try to segregate down there with water and buckets and I told 'em I wasn't gonna do it, I'd go home. Hank Peters was in charge in Savannah at that time and he came out there and put 'em straight. He said, "No more segregating. If you don't wanna play with Isreal, go on back home."

He was a good man, all but one thing. We were down there and I had led the club in hittin'. This boy named Tom Giordano— he's a scout now for somebody— he only hit .260-somethin' but he hit 18 home runs, or 20. They took him up to the majors the last of the season, didn't say nothin' to me. I led the club in hittin' and they took him up there.

But I enjoyed it. I liked it.

ELBERT ISREAL
Born 1928, Marietta, GA   Died 10-22-96, Rockville, MD
Ht. 5' 7"   Wt. 145   Batted and Threw R

Year	Team, league	Pos	G	AB	R	H	2B	3B	HR	RBI	SB	BA
1945	Homestead Grays, NNL	INF										
1947	Philadelphia Stars, NNL	INF										
1952	Harrisburg, InterstateL	INF										*
1953	Savannah, SAL	INF										.316
1954	Savannah, SAL	INF										.311
1955					Did not play							
1956	Abilene, TxL	INF										.298

Isreal played in the Venezuelan winter league in 1954-55; no records are available.

Minnie Minoso

Cuba's Greatest Export

NEGRO LEAGUE DEBUT: 1945

Jerry Reinsdorf, the White Sox owner, calls him "Mr. White Sox" and it's fitting. Minnie Minoso joined the Sox in 1951 and now he's nearing 50 years, on and off, as an important member of the club. It's public relations now, but he does that as well as he played, and very few ever played better.

His career in organized ball is documented, so we do not have to go into it here. Suffice it to say he was a great ballplayer. A couple of possibly lesser-known Minoso facts: (1) He played in professional baseball games in *six* decades. (2) He received two championship rings from two different Veecks. In 1959, Bill Veeck presented him with one after the White Sox won the American League pennant, and in 1995, Mike Veeck, Bill's son, presented him with one after Minoso played with that Veeck's Northern League champion St. Paul Saints. He played for that team on June 30, 1993, and his bat, the ball, and six-decade cap are all now in Cooperstown.

Before all of this, however, Orestes Minoso was a young man in Cuba who spoke no English but had a strong desire to come to the United States. Baseball brought him here, and both the sport and the country have been the better for it.

He played for the New York Cubans in the Negro National League from 1945 until late in the 1948 season, when the Cleveland Indians signed him and sent him to Dayton (Central League) for the last few games of the year. By 1951 he was in the majors to stay. He was an all-out player and no one ever hustled more; even Ty Cobb, known far and wide as a racist, admired Minoso's style and ability.

Minnie Minoso has given back to the fans and community in the many years he has lived in Chicago. Since 1987 he has been the cohost of a golf tournament in Chicago for the benefit of the Cystic Fibrosis Foundation, and he tours with Walter Payton's Sports Personalities, speaking and encouraging athletic involvement for kids.

Born in a dirt-floored shack in Cuba, when he was offered $30,000 in cash by Jorge Pasquel to play ball in Mexico he turned it down because he wanted to come to the United States. He was only 17 and had never even seen $50 at one time, much less $30,000.

Many, many ballplayers over the years have lied about their ages, taking one, two, even five or six years off so they would be looked upon more favorably. Minnie had years *added* to his age. He explains why in the interview.

When I was playing in Cuba — this was November of '44, somewhere in there — just when I was breaking in in the Cuban League, I came from Orientes to go over there and play with the semi-pro team.

They called me. They wanted to have me in Havana for Marianao baseball team. The second day I was there somebody got hurt — the third baseman — so he could not play. So the manager called me, "Okay,

Minoso, go in at third." And I went to third base. Later on, they tied up the score, 1-and-1, and in the ninth inning somebody got a base hit and he was sacrificed to second base. I was up and the first pitch I got a base hit and we win the ballgame, 2-to-1.

After the ballgame, Mr. [Jorge] Pasquel was over there and he took me to his hotel where he had an apartment and he offered me $30,000 for one year to go to Mexico and play for Tampico in the Mexican League. But I just told him, I said, "No, I'm not interested. I want to go to the United States."

I said, "Look. Anywhere you go it's tough and everywhere you go you have a little bit of discrimination — don't make any difference. Here and there and anyplace. But my dream is to go to the United States."

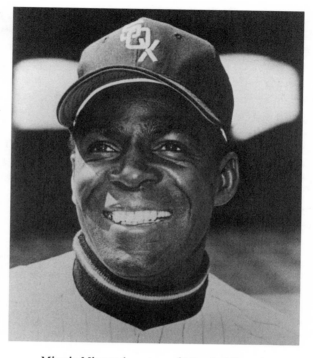

Minnie Minoso (courtesy of Minnie Minoso).

I just decided. I come to the United States and play for the New York Cubans. The team was owned by Mr. Alejandro Pompez and the manager was [Jose] Maria Fernandez. They used to call them New York Cubans because they had 12 Cuban and 12 American blacks.

The manager from the New York Cubans was coaching over there [in Cuba] for the team that I was playing for, the Marianao baseball team. Rodolfo Fernandez's brother, Maria Fernandez. They had a lot of guys that I know, like Ray Noble; they used to have Silvio Garcia. I'll never forget; he was the guy who taught me how to play third base because I used to play third base like I was catching — block the base like home plate. I have cuts on my knees two times, one for Monte Irvin and another one for [Hank] Thompson because I used to block over there. I no left the base open and Silvio Garcia teach me there and in the meantime he teach me how to high class dress. So I have two things from Mr. Garcia: He teach me how to be a good, high-class

expensive dresser and how to play third base. I had great respect for him. We was good, good buddies.

Fernandez was a good man and he always used to tell me, "Orestes, take it easy!" And I'd say, "Fernandez, this is my way."

When I came to this country I was 17, but you know what? Fernandez say, "Orestes, you could not go to United States because you need two more years to be inducted in the army." By this time, there was World War II. I said, "Fernandez, I don't care if you put a hundred years, I want to go to United States. What's the difference?" So I was in the army one year and I got a visa to come to the United States.

Fernandez, first he offered me $150 a month and two dollars to eat a day, but when Mr. Pompez came, before we left, he said, "Kid, I'm gonna give you $300 a month and five dollars to eat. Only two guys get that — you and Silvio Garcia — so don't say anything." I said, "Okay."

When I refused to take the $30,000, Pasquel said, "I'll put the money in a bank for you here in Cuba." I said, "No, Pasquel, I'm gonna go to the United States but someday, when I'm finished, if I make it, someday I'm going to Mexico." And those years went by and Jackie broke in.

Before I never dreamed it could happen, you understand. I just came over here because I liked the country and I used to have a dream to come to the United States, like most everyone. Maybe 99½ percent say they want to come to the United States. I fell in love with the United States when I come over here. I take the right road and it seemed like every move that I make I'm in the right place and never have any bad luck to be in the wrong place at the wrong time.

In '48, after Jackie, I signed and I went to Dayton. I went to Dayton because Cleveland had an agreement with it. The manager was [Henry] Bostick, played third base for the Brooklyn Dodgers long time ago. I signed on August 22nd and September I went to Dayton. Cleveland and a lot of people say I'm way ahead of the league because I hit 500-and-25 and probably Cleveland wanted to bring me in but Bostick says, "Look, this kid's ready to play there right now, but you fight for the pennant"—in '48 they win it—"and to have him to sit there you're gonna hurt him. The best is to let him stay here and then next year you do whatever you want to do with him."

They used to have a rule. You participate in the World Series, whether you play or not, you can only play one month after the World Series and you cannot play winter ball. Something like that. I have a chance to make extra dollars in Cuba.

Later, in 1965, I went back to Mexico for one year. I say, "Only one year." I went to Jalisco. I stayed there for ten years. [Laughs] I'm happy. I'm gonna be inducted to the Monterrey Hall of Fame.

You also belong in the Hall of Fame in Cooperstown. What about that?

I don't know. What can you do? I'm not mad. It's okay. [Laughs]

You have guys inducted to Cooperstown who never played in the big leagues. I played in the Negro leagues three, four years and I played in the big leagues and everywhere I played I hit .300. Only *one* place I no hit .300 — in the National League. I ran against the wall in St. Louis and was out three months. First time I get a home run in the Polo Grounds and next time I get a bean ball and I can't play for the rest of the year. That's the only league I no hit .300. I went to Mexico, I hit .300. In the Pacific League in 1967, only three guys — Hector Espino and another — had 100 hits, and I was the third one. I played in 90 games without missing one. I managed and played at Hermosillo and I beat Hector Espino for the first time in seven years with .341. Hector hit .339 and we played on the same team.

My fans are the people. Everywhere I go they love me and respect me. Even driving the streets, the police and the kids know me. I think that I'm happy. God gave me more than I was expecting and the fans, they were very, very great everywhere I go. I've got a great respect for them. Sooner or later, everyone will sit and think how wonderful it is to be nice and suffer for the fans because without the fans the game is no game. The baseball fans, they're the owners of the whole show.

What problems did you have when you joined the Cubans?

My first problem was that I wanted to speak better English because I don't know how to speak English at all. I never went to school to learn how to speak English, I used to buy the newspaper and act like I read the paper. I go to the movie and if people laugh, I laugh. If they did not, I didn't laugh. I didn't go to watch a Spanish movie because if I watch a Spanish movie I don't learn how to speak English.

I didn't let nothing bother me. They can call me any kind of name you want to call — black, nigger, or whatever. It didn't bother me. They *never* found out the secret word that bothered me. You know what

Minnie Minoso with Chicago White Sox, 1951 (courtesy of National Pastime).

would have bothered me if they would've called me? If they called me "whitey." I'm not white. They call, "Hey, blackie!" I say, "Yes, sir. That's my color."

I used to laugh. They'd say, "Geez, he no get mad!" In Cleveland, they used to say, "Hey, nigger!" "Hey, black!" I used to laugh and I'd get a baseball and say, "Here." "Really?" "Sure." "Can you sign it for me?" I say, "Sure," and sign it. They say, "Boy, you no get mad." I said, "No. You call me right. I'm black. My mother's black, my father's black." But you know what? I love everybody. White or black — we're all the same. I can change my name but I can't change my color.

Do any players stand out from your time in the Negro leagues?

You know [Josh] Gibson, the catcher? We play in Pittsburgh. This is my first year. We're leading, 2-to-1, in the sixth inning or so. Here he come to bat. Nobody out, man at first. I was third baseman. I was playing in so he wouldn't surprise me with a bunt. [Laughs] Fernandez told me, "Just a minute. Hey, Minoso — back!" So I back up. He say, "Back!" So he put me back at the end of the half moon of the infield. I say, "Well, if he bunts he's gonna walk to first base. I don't care."

This guy hit one! When it hit in my glove, it bumped through my hand and went over behind third base for a double!

So he's back up again later on and the pitcher was Pat Scantlebury from Panama. A lefthander. He used to pitch outside. [Laughs] He [Gibson] went after one outside and hit it in the upper deck in right field. He's running around and he says, "Hey, Pat, you Panamanian! Keep pitching me up there and next time I'm gonna hit one *over* the roof!" He laughed. "Hey, Patricio, keep pitching me up there!"

There's one thing I disagree. He was not the way they showed him in the movie. He was not a troublemaker like they show him. No. He was like a little baby when I saw him. He no bother anybody. He used to throw from his knees to second base. He was *strong!* That's the one guy — I saw him one year — that I don't think there was any question if he could play. He would play in Puerto Rico. You have many guys who were good over there who couldn't make it here. Like Rocky Nelson — he used to go over there and kill all those pitchers in Cuba. In the big leagues, it no matter who the pitchers. They get him out here. He couldn't make it.

I hit .320 here, go back there and I hit .300, .280. The people say, "Minnie, what's the matter? You no want to hustle?" I say, "I play every game and I broke my ribs against the wall and I play. I play with broken fingers." They think I should do better. But you put your own pressure. If you hit .320 here, you go to the league in Cuba, "I want to hit .400. I want to hit 40 home runs." You put pressure on because you want to do more than you can do.

Do you have any regrets from your career?

No. I'm a happy man. I have four children, I have fans and friends. I want to come to the United States and I do and I love the United States. Baseball has been good to me.

SATURNINO ORESTES ARMAS "MINNIE" MINOSO y ARRIETA
Born 11-29-22, Havana, Cuba
Ht. 5' 10"   Wt. 175   Batted and Threw R

Year	Team, league	Pos	G	AB	R	H	2B	3B	HR	RBI	SB	BA
1945	New York Cubans, NNL	3B										
1946		3B	33	123	22	32	7	3	3	16	1	.260
1947		3B	55	228	56	67	14	0	3		7	.294
1948	New York Cubans, NNL	3B										
	Dayton, CenL	3B-2B	11	40	14	21	7	1	1	8	6	.525
1949	San Diego, PCL	OF	137	532	99	158	19	7	21	75	13	.297
	Cleveland, AL	OF	9	16	2	3	0	0	1	1	0	.188
1950	San Diego, PCL	3B-OF-SS	169	599	130	203	40	10	20	115	30	.339
1951	Clev.-Chi., AL	OF-3B-1B-SS	146	530	112	173	34	14*	10	76	31	.325
1952	Chicago, AL	OF-3B-SS	147	569	96	160	24	9	13	61	22	.281
1953		OF-3B	151	556	104	174	24	8	15	104	25	.313
1954		OF-3B	153	568	119	182	29	13*	19	116	18	.320
1955		OF-3B	139	517	79	149	26	7	10	70	19	.288
1956		OF-3B-1B	151	545	106	172	29	11*	21	88	12	.316
1957		OF-3B	153	568	96	176	36*	5	12	103	18	.310

Year	Team, league	Pos	G	AB	R	H	2B	3B	HR	RBI	SB	BA
1958	Cleveland, AL	OF-3B	149	556	94	168	25	2	24	80	14	.302
1959		OF	148	570	92	172	32	0	21	92	8	.302
1960	Chicago, AL	OF	154*	591	89	184*	32	4	29	105	17	.311
1961		OF	153	540	91	151	28	3	14	82	9	.280
1962	St. Louis, NL	OF	39	97	14	19	5	0	1	10	4	.196
1963	Washington, AL	OF-3B	109	315	38	72	12	2	4	30	8	.229
1964	Chicago, AL	OF	30	31	4	7	0	0	1	5	0	.226
	Indianapolis, PCL	OF-3B	52	178	22	47	11	0	4	26	6	.264
1976	Chicago, AL	DH-PH	3	8	0	1	0	0	0	0	0	.125
1980	Chicago, AL	PH	2	2	0	0	0	0	0	0	0	.000
1993	St. Paul, NorL.		1									

Record in Mexico

Year	Team, league	Pos	G	AB	R	H	2B	3B	HR	RBI	SB	BA
1965	Jalisco,MexL	OF-3B-1B	134	469	106*	169	35*	10	14	82	7	.360
1966		1B	107	376	70	131	18	1	6	45	6	.348
1967	Jalisco, MexL	1B-OF	13	37	5	9	1	2	0	3	1	.243
	Orizara, MxSEL	1B-OF-3B	36	100	29	35	7	3	5	19	3	.350
1968	Jalisco, MexL	OF-1B	22	54	9	16	5	1	2	13	1	.296
	Puerto Mexico, MxSEL	1B-OF-3B	56	145	30	53	17	2	4	23	2	.366
1969	Jalisco, MexL	1B-OF-3B	36	103	18	33	3	1	2	14	0	.320
	Puerto Mexico, MxSEL	1B-OF	74	193	33	58	10	2	2	32	6	.301
1970	Torreon, MexL	1B	40	47	6	22	6	0	2	17	0	.468
1971		1B-2B	112	336	37	106	15	2	6	57	5	.315
1972		1B	121	425	48	121	24	1	12	63	5	.285
1973		1B-OF	120	407	50	108	15	1	12	83	10	.265

Record in Cuba

Year	Team, league	Pos	G	AB	R	H	2B	3B	HR	RBI	SB	BA
1945-46	Marianao, CubWL	3B-OF	37	143	14	42	7	2	0	13	5	.294
1946-47		3B-OF	64	253	36	63	9	5	0	20	7	.249
1947-48		3B	70	270	43	77	15	13	1	36	7	.285
1948-49		3B-OF	69	260	42	69	8	5	4	27	9	.265
1950-51		3B-OF	66	252	54	81	12	6	4	41	10	.321
1951-52		OF	42	144	19	39	6	1	2	10	1	.271
1952-53		OF-3B	71	266	67	87	9	5	13	42	13	.327
1953-54		OF	47	176	25	52	9	3	9	36	2	.285
1955-56		OF	64	252	47	69	10	3	8	35	8	.274
1956-57			50	218	40	68	13	3	7	38	0	.312*
1957-58		OF	58	238	37	60	9	1	8	34	3	.252
1958-59			55	233	33	60	8	1	5	25	6	.258
1959-60		OF	45	169	25	39	3	2	4	21	4	.231
1960-61		OF	35	128	12	32	7	1	1	12	1	.250

Warren Peace

Too Many Starters

NEGRO LEAGUE DEBUT: 1945

Twenty-five-year-old Warren "Bill" Peace joined the Newark Eagles pitching staff in 1945. World War II had taken many of the team's players and he benefited, gaining considerable pitching time that season even though the club still had Terris McDuffie and Don Newcombe.

In 1946, however, the war was over and the players returned. Rejoining Newark were Leon Day, Max Manning, and Rufus Lewis. Day is in the Hall of Fame, and an argument may be made for the other two. With a starting rotation such as this, Peace became a relief pitcher. And, again, with a starting rotation such as this, relief wasn't needed very often.

Frank Duncan, who pitched for Baltimore during the time when Peace was with Newark, summed up the plight of an Eagles reliever when he said, "I think [Day, Manning, and Lewis] went two or three months and a relief pitcher didn't get off the bench."

Maybe, then, on another team or at another time, Warren Peace would have had more of an opportunity than he did with this team at this time. He says, though, "We had one heck of a life." He really enjoyed playing baseball.

I won 15 the first year and I lost 5, I think it was. Then after the other guys came out [of the service in 1946], that's when I was relegated to relief 'cause the star pitchers were in the army and they came back out. I did mostly relief pitchin'. Like Leon Day and Max Manning came out of the service. And another guy, Rufus Lewis — he came out of the service.

And I also played with McDuffie, too — Terris McDuffie. You probably don't know him. A lotta people don't know, but he was the first black guy to put on a modern-day Dodgers uniform. He went to the Dodgers in 1945. We were in spring trainin' in Richmond, Virginia, and McDuffie and Showboat Thomas got a tryout with the Brooklyn

Dodgers at Bear Mountain, New York. Durin' the war the major league teams didn't go to Florida. They trained nearby to save gasoline and transportation and so forth.

A lotta the black newspapers — the *Norfolk Journal and Guide,* the *Afro-American,* and the *Pittsburgh Courier* — they were black newspapers — all of them got together and they decided that the Dodgers should give a black ballplayer a tryout, so the Dodgers broke down and decided they should take McDuffie and Showboat Thomas, which was two of the old guys, two of the oldest guys in the league.

They took 'em up to Bear Mountain. McDuffie was a pitcher and Showboat Thomas was a first baseman with the New

York Cubans; he couldn't hit the side of my house here with a trailer truck, but he could play first base. So they took those two guys for one day and gave 'em a tryout. And Leo Durocher was managin' the Dodgers.

They put McDuffie up to home plate to give him battin' practice. Now you know pitchers don't hit the ball. They're supposed to pitch, to stop the other team from hittin'. So they didn't give him a tryout at pitchin'. They pretty much gave him the bat and told him they wanted to see him do some battin'. Leo Durocher yelled to the pitcher and said, "Throw him the curveball!" So McDuffie — he's a righthanded hitter — he's standin' there waitin' for the curveball and the pitcher would cross him up and throw him a fastball — a high, tight one, you know, and knock him down. Then the catcher would say, "Okay, get ready. He's gonna throw you a fastball." So then the pitcher would throw him a curveball, crossin' him up so he wouldn't hit the ball. That's what they were tryin' to do.

And then finally, McDuffie, after three or four pitches like this, he realized what they were doin', so when the catcher told him to get ready to hit this pitch, he'd look for the next one. And he started rappin' the ball off the walls. McDuffie could hit! He started bouncin' the ball off the walls and after he hit four or five pitches off the wall like that, then they called him down, say, "Okay, sit down. Let the other guy hit."

Then they put Showboat up there and, 'course, like I said, he couldn't hit this house with a trailer truck. [Laughs] They didn't try him out at first base at all. He was such a darned good fielder. You didn't throw bad to him unless you threw the ball over his head. Now, these balls that the infielders throw across the diamond and the ball bounces in the dirt and the first baseman misses it and the ball gets past him and they give the thrower an error, you didn't throw bad to Showboat. Showboat could pick that ball up and put it in his pocket. That guy was one hell of a fielder.

He was fancy with it; everything he caught was one-handed. That's why they called him Showboat; he used to put on a show.

Then at the end of the day, they told the two of 'em that they couldn't make it. They weren't good enough. So they came back to their respective home teams, back to us. But they were the first ones to put on the Dodgers uniform. Most people don't know that.

The best all-around player — well, they could be several. Willie Wells was the best infielder. Then there was another guy, too, that played alongside of Willie who was as good: Raymond Dandridge. Wells should be in the Hall of Fame, but he had a drawback — he had a bad arm. He couldn't throw the ball across the infield. He could throw it across there 'cause he played shortstop, but he got rid of it fast. Most infielders, especially third base and shortstop, they can fire that ball on a line from over there to first base, but Willie Wells, he used to rainbow the ball over there. The ball had a big hump in it, you know, like a rainbow. I don't care how fast you could run, you couldn't outrun that ball. He would throw you out by one step. He got rid of it fast. But he could field his butt off. He and Ray Dandridge both. Those were the best two that I've ever seen.

Now for hittin', it would have to go to Josh Gibson. Josh was the best hitter and the longest ball hitter I have ever seen. Josh could hit that ball outta *Yellowstone* Park. [Laughs] I mean, in Wyoming. That's the truth!

I've heard that he once hit 70 home runs in one season.

I don't know that as a fact because he was playin' when I went into the league. He was a star then. I went there in 1945 and he died in 1947, so I played against him '45 and '46. He died durin' the winter of '47. He was 35, I think, when he died.

Monte Irvin, I guess you'd call him a Willie Mays before Mays came up. 'Course, Monte was gettin' up in age, too, when I came along. I think he was over 30 when he

Warren Peace (courtesy of Warren Peace).

Some baseball fans say that they had seen Satchel play in his heyday and two or three different people have told me this. They've seen him call his outfield in and have all three of 'em sit down on the ground right behind the infield and nobody could hit the ball out of the infield against him. He'd go on and pitch with these three guys sittin' back there and he struck out the side. Nobody even fouled the ball off. [Laughs]

He played year 'round. He'd go to Mexico and he'd go to the Caribbean islands — Puerto Rico and Cuba and so forth. Dominican Republic, Venezuela, Panama. Some of the guys I played with did the same thing, they played all year 'round, but I never got a chance to go down there.

Other than Satchel, who were the best pitchers?

Well, we had several good pitchers. Don Newcombe was a darned good pitcher. He went to the Dodgers. McDuffie was a darned good pitcher with us, and then they had Johnny Wright from the Homestead Grays — a darned good pitcher. The Dodgers tried him out in Montreal. He stayed with Montreal for a short time. There were a lotta good pitchers in that league. Rufus Lewis, he played with my team, and Lennie Hooker. Hooker was a knuckleball pitcher. And then there was Roy Partlow, who played with the Philadelphia Stars; Jonas Gaines, played with Baltimore Elite Giants; and then there was Barney Brown that played with the Philadelphia Stars. We had a lotta good pitchers. Dan Bankhead, that went to the Dodgers, used to play with Memphis.

Is there one game that stands out?

One that stands out above all the rest to me is when, in 1946, we were in the race to go to the World Series against Satchel Paige's team in Kansas City.

signed with the Giants. He never told us his age. I'm not gonna call him like Satchel, but nobody knew Satchel's age, either. Satchel didn't even know what year he was born. They claim he had it written down in the Bible and the Bible got destroyed so he didn't know how old he was.

Biz Mackey — he was the guy who made Campanella a star; he taught Campanella whatever he knew about catchin' — and Mackey was managin' our team in 1945, and he was the regular catcher and he was 45 then. And Mackey knew Satchel when they were little boys together and Mackey told us that Satchel was older than he was, at least five years older, and that was in 1945. They claim that when he was playin' with the St. Louis Browns or Cleveland Indians that he admitted to bein' 50, but he didn't know how old he was.

We were playin' the Homestead Grays. This is Josh Gibson and Buck Leonard's team, and Luke Easter was playin' with 'em, too, and Cool Papa Bell. This was the lineup they had. They had quite a team. [Laughs]

We were playin' against them in Newark and Leon Day was pitchin' for us. I don't remember who pitched for the Grays that day. This was near the end of the season and the winner of this particular game would win the second half. We had already won the first half. See, our season was divided into two halves. I was coachin' at first base. Leon pitched 15 innings against the Grays and the score was tied, 3–3.

Leon came to bat in the last of the inning and hit a home run to win the ballgame. When he came trottin' 'round to first base, I ran out on the field and trottin' along beside him. I'm trottin' around the bases with him, you know, and I'm pattin' him on his butt, congratulatin' him; I'm tickled to death 'cause we're goin' to Kansas City, we're goin' to the World Series — and he kept tellin' me, "Get back! Get back!"

And I ignored him. I kept trottin' along beside him. We got around to third base and he said to me, "If that umpire calls me out, I'm gonna beat the stuffin's outta you!" Only he didn't say "stuffin's"; he used that other "s" word. [Laughs] So then I realized I shouldn't be on that field. I turned off and went into the dugout.

He kept on to home plate and when he got to home plate, half of the people in the stands had come out onto the field and they were standin' there at home plate waitin' to greet him. If that umpire had called him out, he would've had a riot up there and I would still be runnin' from Leon. [Laughs]

He was all sweaty and tired and this was in late August and it was *hot*— 90 degrees. I couldn't blame him for wantin' to kill me if he'd been called out. [Laughs]

I'm gonna tell you a story that maybe your son would enjoy. One of the guys from the Philadelphia Stars told me this. It's true. It's about Goose Curry.

Goose Curry was the manager of the Philadelphia Stars. He was a playin' manager. We had playin' managers; we didn't have a manager to sit on the bench and manage; he played, too, to earn his salary. So Goose was the manager of the Philadelphia Stars.

All of us traveled in buses; we had our own buses, old raggedy buses. Everywhere the Stars went on the bus, Goose Curry wanted to drive the bus. Now my team, we had a chauffer to drive, but all the other teams the players drove the buses. Goose, he wanted to drive the bus but he didn't have a driver's license. So Goose would drive the bus anyway. Who's gonna argue with the manager?

One night he was drivin', speedin' along, and a cop came up behind 'em. So Goose pulled over to the side, parked it, jumped outta the driver's seat, and ran to the back seat of the bus and laid down on that long cross seat, like he was asleep. And one of the other guys with a driver's license sat in the driver's seat.

So the cop came 'round and knocked on the door and the guy opened the door to let the cop in. The cop wanted to see his driver's license, so the guy showed it to him. The cop say, "Do you know you were doin' 65 in a 30-mile zone?"

And Goose raised up from the back seat, said, "What did you say, officer?" The cop said, "This guy was doin' 65 in a 30-mile zone." Goose said, "Oh, Lord! My goodness! Officer, I'm glad you stopped us. You saved my life! You mean that he was doin' 65 in this ol' raggedy bus?!" And the cop say, "Yes."

And Goose said, "Officer, I'll tell you what. If you let him go this time, I promise you I'll drive the rest of the way myself." The cop said, "You promise?" And he said, "Yeah, I promise." The cop said, "Okay, go 'head on." Goose climbed back in the driver's seat and took off and didn't have a driver's license. [Laughs] That Goose was a funny man.

What kind of salary did you receive?

See, I came along in later years — in the mid-'40s — but in the early '40s they tell me that the average salary was $125 a month. But they gave me $200 to start with and my top salary was $225 a month, which was more than I was makin' workin'. Other guys, like Leon Day and Monte Irvin and Larry Doby, they got more money 'cause they were worth more. I think some of 'em got maybe $300 or $350 a month. I'm not sure 'cause they never told their salaries.

I heard that Satchel was makin' 'bout $1,500 a month. Satchel had his own airplane so he had to be makin' a whole lot more than anybody else was. Then, too, back then they played a lotta exhibition games, Kansas City did. They used to come out East and play all the teams in our league — six teams in our league — and Satchel used to pitch *every* night against one of these teams. He only pitched the first three innings. They'd come play us, then they'd go to Yankee Stadium and play the Black Yankees and the Polo Grounds and play the Cubans, Shibe Park to play Philadelphia, and all over. He'd pitch the first three and then another guy, his name was [Connie] Johnson — I don't know his first name; he was just as tall as Satchel — would come in and relieve Satchel and when they put Johnson out there, we thought we'd have it easy then. And he would come in and throw harder than Satchel did! Just like jumpin' from the fryin' pan into the fire. [Laughs]

They had more guys from Kansas City to go into the major leagues than any other team. Ernie Banks and Elston Howard, that went to the New York Yankees, used to catch — they came from Kansas City. Hank Thompson played with Kansas City in 1945. Lefthanded hitter.

What did you do in the off-seasons?

I was a printer for forty years. I worked in several print shops. Richmond, Virginia, is where I went durin' the winter time. My home is originally from North Carolina, a little town called Kitrell, North Carolina.

It's a little one-horse town. In fact, the horse died. [Laughs] I left there and went to Richmond when I was 20 years old.

I suffered with the asthma and my mama told me when I left home to wear my long underwear and keep my overcoat on durin' the winter and always wear a hat. [Laughs] I left for Richmond, Virginia, on December the fourth, 1941, and three days later the Japanese attacked Pearl Harbor and that whole winter I did just the opposite of what my mama told me to do. I took those long underwear off and threw 'em away and got me some boxer shorts and put 'em on and I went bare-headed all winter long and I didn't wear an overcoat. It would rain and snow and sleet and I was walkin' around bare-headed, had icicles hangin' down from my hair, and I haven't had asthma since. [Laughs]

Did you enjoy your baseball career?

All of us enjoyed our baseball careers. Every one of us. You see, we got paid for somethin' that we liked to do. We enjoyed playin' baseball. We played it for the *fun* and if you get paid it was just an added bonus for us. Plus they paid all our expenses, all our travel, and all our hotel bills — rooms and food. You had to like it. The only time we paid our own expenses was when we were playin' at home in Newark.

Was it a good life?

We had one heck of a life. I mean, we had *fun*. We didn't make a lotta money, but we sure had a lotta fun, and I'm not lyin'. Any of the black ballplayers will tell you that. We traveled under all conditions — old raggedy buses and everything, you know. I'd do it all over again. [Laughs]

Any regrets?

The only regret that any of us probably had — all of us wanted to eventually get in the major leagues because that was more fame and fortune, but that's 'bout the only regrets that we had. We were born too early.

Somebody told Cool Papa Bell that he was born too early and Cool Papa said, "No, that's not true. They opened the door too late." [Laughs]

WILLIAM WARREN "BILL" PEACE
Born 8-6-21, Kitrell, NC
Ht. 5' 9"   Wt. 160   Batted and Threw R

Year	Team, league	G	IP	W	L	Pct	H	BB	SO	SHO	ERA
1945	Newark Eagles, NNL			15	5	.750					
1946				3	1	.750					
1947				2	1	.667					
1948				1	1	.500					

Curley Williams
Punch at Short

NEGRO LEAGUE DEBUT: 1945

This is a story repeated often around 1950: A good, solid Negro league player was signed by a club in organized ball and did not advance because he was not given the opportunity.

Curley Williams was a run-producing shortstop with a little power, and shortstops with punch have always been in short supply. In his second year in the minor leagues, he got as high as Triple-A, but only briefly. Then he was sent back to Class A, and after that he was never given another real chance.

Earlier, he had played several seasons with the Newark (later Houston, and later New Orleans) Eagles and compiled a batting average in the .295 range with a home run about every 25 at-bats. What team wouldn't give a shortstop with that level of production a long, strong look today?

How did you come to join the Newark Eagles?

I was playing with a team in my hometown — Orangeburg, South Carolina. The name of the team was the Orangeburg Tigers, a local team. We were built around high school and college players. We had a little league there that played in Columbia and around, but mostly we played college teams.

A friend had played against a team from Lakeland that came up that way and the manager had pitched for the Newark Eagles in the 1920s. He called Monte Irvin and some more of the people up there and they got in contact with me. That's how I got up there. I started with them in 1947 and I played until they moved out to Texas and I played there, too.

When you left them, you played in organized ball.

My first year I played with the Colorado [Springs] Sky Sox in the Western League. That was a Chicago White Sox [Class] A team. I thought I had a pretty good season at Colorado. I hit .300 and I hit about 13 home runs there. The next year they sent me to the Toledo Mud Hens. I finished a half a season there and from there I went in the Eastern League with Scranton Miners. I played the rest of the season there — me and Leon Day. We did pretty good. I had a good season there.

I was supposed to go out to the [West] Coast one year. I got screwed around so much. I was supposed to go out to Sacramento and after I got to the airport I got a doggone page and they said, "Don't go to Sacramento." They changed their minds and sent me another ticket to go to Toronto, then they called Toronto and that's when they sent me back to Scranton. Junior Gilliam was going to Montreal and we were just running and passed each other and shook hands. He was running and I was running. He was one of my buddies; he was a great ballplayer. We played in the winter leagues together.

The following year I went to spring training and I didn't get a chance to play at all in spring training, so I got kind of angry about that. I had had a pretty good season and a guy that played all the games didn't have *half* as good a season as I did, but he was white. I got kind of [angry] about that — why wasn't I playing? They never gave me a reason.

I got mad that year. That was 1953, I think it was. I got in touch with some of my buddies that was playing in Santo Domingo, in that league over there on the islands. They sent me a contract for a lot of money, so I went down there and played. I had a really good year down there.

Before that I played in the winter league in Puerto Rico. This was in '50 and '52. We won the championship down there in '52. Bobby Boyd and Wilmer Fields and Bob Wilson were all on my team. And Lew Burdette. That's when the Yankees signed him and stopped him from playing down there.

A lot of ballplayers was blackballed, too. I had one of my buddies — his name was Green — he married a white girl his second year in organized baseball. The next year he was supposed to go to the major leagues and they blackballed him. I've never heard from him since. Nobody picked him up. I didn't think they'd blackball him — he was too good a ballplayer, a pitcher. But the major leagues, they got their heads together and that was it. Nobody signed him. I never tried to date a white girl. In fact, I didn't date much at all. I just wanted to play baseball.

Curley Williams (courtesy of Willie "Curley" Williams).

The next year after the Dominican Republic I was invited to spring training and they were wanting to send me to a Class D league. They had D and C ball then. I refused to go 'cause I thought I was a better ballplayer than that. That's when I started playing in Canada in the ManDak League. I played at Carman and I played out at Saskatoon. I played there about nine years and I did real good. I enjoyed it up there, too.

I had a guy on my team — Ron Fairly. And Don Buford. We were all teammates. My last professional ball was in Canada and I played from '47 to 1963.

You had pretty good power for a man who wasn't too big.

My playing weight was about 175 or 176

pounds and I could average between 15 and 18 home runs a year. I usually batted fourth or fifth.

The Eagles always had a reputation for having a good pitching staff. Who were the best pitchers when you were there?

We had Max Manning and Rufus Lewis and Leon Day. Leon Day was some kind of ballplayer, man. We had another guy named Bill Beverly; that's my real good buddy. We had another named Jimmy Williams. He left and he went out in the Mexican League and he stayed out there a long time. We had a lot of guys do that and I can understand that 'cause they was making pretty good money and they was treated better. They didn't get a fair deal here.

I don't feel bad about it. I did have a chance to play in organized ball. I was in my late 20s. 'Course, most of us at the beginning was in our late 20s when we went up there. I had a chance to play with most of those guys and I tell you, a *lot* of 'em *should* have been up there *years* before 'cause I seen guys when I was playing that was 35, 40 years old, man, and playing like a 16-year-old rookie.

Some places you got treated well and some places it was just ridiculous. You have to just take those things, you know — hear it, then don't hear it. Another thing, when I was in the [American] Association, we'd go out of town to play and you had to go live in a preacher's house or something like that. You couldn't stay with the team. That happened in the American Association.

We couldn't play in Louisville. We were playing in Louisville, staying down in some place they call the Brown Derby — it was an apartment house they had there for colored people — and me and Frank Barnes and another guy had to stay there. It was a two o'clock game and we didn't know it. We went to a movie; we had time to get a sandwich and go to a movie and be at the park at 5:30. We got out of the movie and caught a cab and went to the park and I said, "Boy, it looks kind of strange out here. It looks like a game has already been

played here," and, sure enough, that's what happened. We got back to our room and the coach — Rollie Hemsley — called us and asked what happened. I said, "We didn't know it was a day game."

That's when things really started changing a little bit. Our next round we were beginning to stay with the guys, you know. It changed just a little bit.

It was the same thing in the cafes. Even in spring training in Florida, they had a place set up in the back of the restaurant for me to eat. One table.

Florida was one of the tougher states.

It *was* tough. And my home state, too — South Carolina. It was bad then.

You didn't find those problems in Canada.

Not at all. In fact, they loved me so much up there they wanted to give me a job up there to run a big recreation center. I refused to stay up there because in Saskatchewan it's too doggone cold. That's the only reason I didn't stay — because of the weather. But I enjoyed nine *wonderful* years up there.

How were the traveling conditions with the Eagles?

Our traveling conditions was good. You know, we had a brand-new bus and it would seat 34 people. It had good storage for your luggage, but the only thing, when you're traveling like that you have to almost eat out of stores. We call it "dutching" — go on in and get your baloney and make your own sandwiches and get back in the bus.

Up North, they had a bunch of black hotels. We didn't have no problem in the North. The only problem you'd have was when you'd come South. Places like Philadelphia and New York, Baltimore — places like that — they'd have black hotels.

A lot of small towns, they wouldn't even let you use the dressing room. We dressed in the bus sometimes. Then you might have a place where they'd have one shower and you'd have to take turns — sit out and wait. That was kind of rough.

I enjoyed it. I loved baseball. Everybody I played with during that time just wanted to play baseball. Money wasn't nothing 'cause when I started with Newark I was making $250 a month. In 1947, $250 a month to me was a *whole* lot of money. I told my wife, "The average working guy is making about $40 a week." I remember in my hometown everybody used to say, "I'm going to Washington 'cause you can get $90 every two weeks working." So when I started playing and making $250 a month, man, I thought I was getting rich. [Laughs] It was fun, I'm telling you.

What was your top salary?

Believe it or not, in Triple-A I was making $550 a month. I was getting $550 there and Canada was sending me $250. They had part of my contract, so I was making about $800 a month.

In the winter leagues, I was making $850 down there. When you're not on the road you had to pay your own expenses. You get an apartment for maybe $175 or so a month. They'd take care of your expenses on the road.

We used to make a lot of money barnstorming. We'd get a percentage of the gate and we'd divide it. Especially when the guys got in the major leagues, we could make about $1,800 a month. Couldn't barnstorm but one month. The major league players made more but the minor leaguers would make about $1,800 that month. It carried us through the winter. Everywhere you'd go, you'd have a packed house.

Satchel Paige would take his all-star team out to California and play against the white all-stars out in that area, but they couldn't do it here in the South. That's why they went out there. Satchel Paige used to pitch against Dizzy Dean.

Who was the best player you saw?

Ernie Banks was one. He was with Kansas City while I was with the Eagles. [Gene] Baker was a fairly decent ballplayer. The old-timers, like Buck Leonard and Josh Gibson — those guys was kind of going out when I came, but they was still good. Then Satchel Paige — well, you know him. He played forever. I played against him maybe

10 or 12 times. The first time, I didn't hit the ball out of the infield on him and I was considered a fairly decent hitter.

I played against Monte Irvin and Willie Mays. He was in our league, too. He got signed for nothing. And Hank came a little later. He didn't stay in the league very long.

People talk about that catch Mays made in New York against Cleveland. Man, I seen him do that so many times — better than that.

If you could go back, would you do it again?

I think so. I dream about baseball almost weekly. I dream about some games, you know — I'm up there and the winning run's on second base. It's always there.

I have a lot of friends that are coaching now and in spring training I really have fun 'cause I go out to these games and don't have to pay to go in. Chicago trains here and right over across in St. Pete they got all those other teams there and Orlando and all's right around me. I know somebody on every team.

The biggest thing now is when we have our little gatherings maybe once every two years — like we met last year in Kansas City. Man, that was one of the happiest moments of my life. You were able to see guys you haven't seen in 35 or 40 years. That was really great.

Any regrets?

No. The only thing I regret was that things would have been a little better in the first year in organized baseball. It would've made it a *lot* better. You're afraid to say anything; you get out there, you play your heart out, and after the game you're just alone. Nobody to talk to — your teammates go their way, you go your way. That's sad. You're playing together with guys all week and then when the game's over you go your separate ways. That really hurt. You like to sit down and discuss things with ballplayers.

I'll tell you another thing that really [made me angry]. They'd have players — sort of light-colored players — from the

Dominican Republic and Puerto Rico and all and they could stay *any*place. They always put us someplace — in a black neighborhood. That kind of got to me, too.

That's just the way it was then. It shouldn't've been that way, but I'll tell you one thing — they missed out on some of the

greatest ballplayers ever lived. I seen some ballplayers, man. I used to just sit on that bench and here I am a young man, these guys out there 40 years old and I can't move 'em! [Laughs] I almost cried. These guys was playing like they were 15 years old.

WILLIE C. "CURLEY" WILLIAMS
Born 5-25-25, Holly Hill, SC
Ht. 5' 11½"   Wt. 176   Batted L Threw R

Year	Team, league	Pos	G	AB	R	H	2B	3B	HR	RBI	SB	BA
1945	Newark Eagles, NNL	SS	25	87	20	29	5	1	6	11	6	.333
1947	Newark Eagles, NNL	SS		200	36	43	7		2		3	.215
1948		SS							11			.288
1949	Houston Eagles, NAL	SS-2B	53	210	34	61						.290
1950		SS	65	250	59	73	15	5	8	32	2	.292
1951	New Orleans Eagles, NAL	SS		262	58	92			11	62		.351
	Colorado Springs, WL	SS										.297
1952	Toledo, IntL	3B	36	128	16	30	3	2	2	14	0	.234
	Scranton, EL	SS-2B	66	228	33	61	8	4	5	30	5	.268
1953	Carman, MnDkL	SS	57	199		57			12	40		.286

Williams also played in Puerto Rico in 1950 and 1952 and a portion of the 1953 season with Licey in the Dominican Summer League. Records are unavailable.

Part Two

AFTER JACKIE ENTERED ORGANIZED BALL

In 1946, Jackie Robinson entered organized ball and over the next few years other blacks joined him as the major league clubs recognized a good thing when they saw it. Some players were lured by dollars; others were sold by their Negro league teams to white teams.

The drain of talent from black baseball was so great by 1949 that the Negro National League folded and only the Negro American League and a few barnstorming clubs played on. The philosophy of the remaining black teams changed from one of signing talent to one of signing marketability. Could this young man be sold in a year or two for a profit?

Many point to Negro ball in the late '40s and early '50s as a minor league level of play, but look who began their careers in the Negro leagues during that time: Willie Mays, Hank Aaron, Ernie Banks, and Elston Howard are only a few. Well into the 1960s, Negro league graduates were still debuting on major league clubs. The black players were highly successful, in fact, that their own baseball died.

The end of professional Negro baseball is recognized as 1960.

Bob Boyd

"The Rope"

NEGRO LEAGUE DEBUT: 1946

Bob Boyd could hit. Here are his batting averages in professional baseball: Negro leagues (4 years) .362; minor leagues (6 years) .325; major leagues (9 years).293.

He was the first Baltimore Oriole regular to hit .300 (.318, 1957, fourth in the American League) and also the second (.309, 1958, sixth in the AL). His .301 career average for five years with the Orioles is the second-best in team history (to Bob Nieman's .303).

But Boyd was 30 years old before he made it to the majors to stay. Signed by the White Sox out of the Negro American League late in 1950 (when he was already 25), he hardly skipped a beat in making the transition, but he was a first baseman and first base in Chicago was under control. First, slugger Eddie Robinson was there. Then, when Robinson was traded to the Philadelphia Athletics in 1953, the man the Chisox got in return was two-time batting champ Ferris Fain, possibly the slickest fielding first sacker in the game at that time.

Boyd made an impression while Chicago property, though. Paul Richards was the White Sox manager from 1951 through 1954. In '55 he was named the Orioles' manager and at the end of that season, when Boyd was eligible for the draft, Richards took him.

He was 30, but he was in the majors to stay. He batted over .300 in four of the next five seasons. It would have been interesting to see what he would have done if he had been turned loose on AL pitching five years sooner.

You played four years with the Memphis Red Sox in the Negro American League. Even with a cumulative .362 average , you didn't lead the league once.

I had a good average but somebody just outhit me each time. I played regular, but I just couldn't never lead the league. After I got into Triple-A ball, well, I led the league [.320, 1952, Seattle, PCL].

Evidently there was no pitching too difficult for you. You hit wherever you played.

That's real true and I came up against some good pitchin'. They made it to the major leagues, guys like Bob Turley and Don Larsen and, oh, quite a few more. I was just a hitter, but I couldn't get my chance at the time.

Baltimore drafted you from the White Sox.

I was the first black that Chicago signed. Baltimore got me, yeah. I spent most of my time with Baltimore and I played for the Kansas City A's — Charlie Finley was there — and Milwaukee [Braves].

You were a lefthanded batter, but you could hit lefthanders as well as righthanders.

Bob Boyd (courtesy of Bob Boyd).

Yes. After Paul Richards — he was the manager — started switching, you know, righthanded hitters in against lefthanders, he set me down and started using me as a pinch hitter and he wouldn't let me play regular against the lefthanders sometimes. But, when he got in a jam, he always called me to pinch hit against the lefthanded pitchers, yet still he wouldn't start me most of the time. He'd just depend on me but I'd like to be in there regular against them. He got me where I didn't face them often like I used to and that's when I fell in my battin' average a little bit.

If you knock off a couple of early years with Chicago when you didn't play much, your career average is right at .300.

I didn't get to play too regular [with Chicago] because at the time they had a guy

named Eddie Robinson. He was the great long ball hitter and then they got rid of him and got ahold of the best first baseman in the American League. That was Ferris Fain. So they kept me on the bench most of the time as a pinch hitter, just breakin' me in. Then they sent me out to the farm team. Then Fain, he had a little trouble in Washington and he got his hand broke and that's the way I got my chance.

Is there one game, in any league, that stands out?

Mostly, in the major leagues, I broke up a no-hitter against the Yankees. Bob Kuzava, he was the pitcher — a lefthander — and I got a line-drive double off of him in the ninth inning. After the guy made the last out, I was comin' to the dugout and one of the fans threw a Coca-Cola bottle out there and hit me on the leg 'cause I broke up his no-hitter.

The thing about the majors, you know, I was just tryin' to make it to the major leagues. That's the only thing and it paid off and I was glad to do it. But they kept me down a long time and that's the reason I didn't last so long. I had to wait 'til my time come, you know.

What was your biggest thrill in baseball?

Nothin' really. I was just proud that I had a pretty good average when I was in the major leagues and I hit .300 there quite a few times. And also in the minors, too, so I did pretty good. I guess the biggest thrill was playin' major league ball.

Who was the best hitter you saw?

The best I saw was Ted Williams with the Boston Red Sox. We used to use the shift on him and I was playin' first base and he wouldn't hit the ball to left field — everything was comin' to right. He hit a ball one time — I was playin' first base, really kind of short right field — and he hit a ball so *hard*—at the time they had those

Bob Boyd with the Baltimore Orioles, 1957 (courtesy of Bob Boyd).

strap bags [a base was held in place by a strap on the underside that went through a ring in the ground] and the ball hit the bag and broke the strap and the bag come slidin' out to me and the ball stayed right there where first base was at. I never seed anything like it before. He hit that ball so hard it broke the bag and the bag was goin' on in the outfield! But the ball stayed there!

There was no way for me to get to it; he beat it out. [Laughs] He was the greatest hitter I *ever* seen.

Who was the best pitcher?

It's rough. I had trouble with some. You take Allie Reynolds, you take Bobby Feller and also Early Wynn and also Whitey Ford — oh, I can name a bunch of 'em. Frank Lary and Johnny Lindell — he threw a knuckleball. That was the ball that really give me trouble. I faced Lindell in the minor leagues, in the Pacific Coast [League], He had a butterfly ball. That's all he threw was a knuckleball. There's a *whole* lot of pitchers, I mean, that was *great* in those days.

Cleveland at the time had the best. They used four and every day you would see a good pitcher, like Bob Feller and Bob Lemon, Mike Garcia, Early Wynn, and [Art] Houtteman. The next would be the Yankees, but after the Yankees you'd only have two good ones on a club, you know. Just like Detroit or St. Louis Browns, like Ned Garver and them. The other clubs only had two, but those two clubs, they had four.

And that's why I make up a lot against those other pitchers. I was satisfied if I could get one or two hits off the four and when I met those not as good I'd run my average up. I'd hit them pretty good. [Laughs]

Who was the one toughest to hit?

Herb Score from Cleveland. I couldn't hit him to save my life. Bob Gibson, he was truly fast and the ball would rise when it get right at the hitter, but I hit him better than I did Herb Score. Herb Score, I just couldn't hit him at all. I faced [Sandy] Koufax and Warren Spahn and Lew Burdette; they was good back then.

Who gave you the nickname "Rope"?

A coach used to be with the White Sox, Luman Harris. I think he was a big league pitcher a long time ago. I was hittin' the ball hard, straight on a line. I wasn't a large man, you know, and I just couldn't hit no home runs, but everything I hit it looked like it was on a line. One day, in spring training, he brought a litle piece of rope about two feet long and had it in his back pocket. When I come to the battin' cage to bat he had pulled that rope outta his pocket and laid it at home plate. He says, "There's the rope," and so everbody starts callin' me "The Rope." [Laughs]

Someone said you'd have had a little more

home run power if you had not had such a level swing. You had the most level swing in the league and maybe if you had a slight uppercut you'd have driven more balls out.

Well, I don't know. I wasn't worried about home runs at the time because I was fast and all I wanna do is get the ball between somebody.

When you played, stolen bases were not emphasized, so your speed wasn't used to advantage.

They never would let me steal. I don't know why. The most stolen bases I had was 42 [Sacramento, 1951], I believe; that was in the Pacific Coast League. I think I led the league in stolen bases. That's the most I ever did any runnin'. Paul Richards never would let me go. I don't know why.

Did you save souvenirs?

I did — a few souvenirs — but I got rid of all of 'em. A collector came from California and he bought all of the stuff I had. I have my scrapbook. They tryin' to get that outta me [laughs], but I think I'm gonna have it for my grandkids, you know, 'cause they play Little League ball. I think I'm gonna save it for them.

Do you get much fan mail?

I do. Every day. I still get autograph requests in the mail every day and they call me to be on autograph shows. I'm in old-timers games. I'm gettin' around pretty good. They want me to travel around from city to city to play in the old-timers games this year. They have a new sponsor — it's called the Upper Deck Old-Timers game now. You get to see some of your friends and the guys you played against. You go out and have a good time. Everybody enjoys it.

As you said, you were not a very big first baseman.

No, I'm kinda small and that was against me, too, because I wasn't tall for the high ball somebody happens to throw. That's what they like — those tall first basemen. But I had speed and was a good fielder.

They tried me in the outfield a little while. In Chicago, Minnie Minoso was playin' third; Fain, he was playin' first; I was playin' left field. They brought Minnie in from playin' left field to play third 'cause the third baseman got hurt or somethin' and they tried me in the outfield and I wasn't used to playin' out there.

I played some there for Baltimore. In Cleveland, I tried to throw out Jim Hegan, used to catch for Cleveland. I tried to make that real strong throw and broke my arm. They sent me to Baltimore and they wired it up and durin' the winter they sent me to Cuba to play winter ball. The wire was still in my arm and I went over there and made a throw to try to get a double play and I broke the wire in it and I had to come back to Baltimore again. They opened it up and got the wire out of there, but the bone had knit back together. The wire was loose and when I pulled my arm up and down it was scratchin', so they opened it up and just pulled the wire out.

For a long time, they wouldn't let me throw, scared I'd hurt my arm again. I could hit, but I couldn't throw. When a play came up to do some buntin' and they had to force a man at second base, they'd put me in the outfield and bring somebody else in to play first base until after the play was executed.

Was this Paul Richards doing that?

Yes. Paul was a baseball man.

Would you go back to the mid–'40s and start over?

Ohh. I don't think so. [Laughs] We didn't make any money. We'd get two dollars a day [meal money] and mostly ride the bus — hardly ever slept in a hotel — drivin' from city to city.

I was a walk-on when I started in the Negro league. I guess I was good enough that they signed me and sent me to their farm club and I stayed there for a while and they called me back. My contract when I first signed was $175 a month. [Laughs]

Would you play baseball again?

Yes, I would, 'cause I really like the game and that's about all I have done.

Do you have any regrets from your career?

No. Not at all, because baseball has been good to me and I stuck with it. I'm just happy to get a chance to play. One thing I really liked about it, I fooled around and was there long enough to get on the pension plan. That's a help. We got a back-pay bonus not long ago.

ROBERT RICHARD "THE ROPE" BOYD
Born 10-1-25, Potts Camp, MS
Ht. 5' 9"　Wt. 170　Batted and Threw L

Year	Team, league	Pos	G	AB	R	H	2B	3B	HR	RBI	SB	BA
1946	Memphis Red Sox, NAL	1B										
1947		1B	73	283	54	96	0	0	4		0	.339
1948		1B	77	303	52	114	18	9*	5	51	4	.376
1949		1B	76	293	57	110						.375
1950		1B	63	250	54	89	27	8	7	58	2	.356
	Colorado Springs, West.	1B	42	158	39	59	6	5	9	39	3	.373
1951	Sacramento, PCL	1B	145	555	82	190	32	11	5	64	41*	.342
	Chicago, AL	1B	12	18	3	3	0	1	0	4	0	.167
1952	Seattle, PCL	1B-OF	161	641	100	205	29	18	3	75	33	.320*
1953	Charleston, AA	OF	49	198	33	64	8	6	2	22	12	.323
	Toronto, IL	OF	31	120	16	37	4	4	3	12	1	.308
	Chicago, AL	1B-OF	55	165	20	49	6	2	3	23	1	.297
1954	Houston, TxL	1B	94	358	59	115	22	2	7	68	3	.321
	Chicago, AL	OF-1B	29	56	10	10	3	0	0	5	2	.179
1955	Houston, TxL	1B	163*	635*	96	197*	39	6	15	04	13	.310
1956	Baltimore, AL	1B-OF	70	225	28	70	8	3	2	11	0	.311
1957		1B-OF	141	485	73	154	16	8	4	34	2	.318
1958		1B	125	401	58	124	21	5	7	36	1	.309
1959		1B	128	415	42	110	30	2	3	41	3	.265
1960		1B	71	82	9	26	5	2	0	9	0	.317
1961	Kansas City, AL	1B	26	48	7	11	2	0	0	9	0	.229

Year	Team, league	Pos	G	AB	R	H	2B	3B	HR	RBI	SB	BA
1962	Louisville, Ok. City, AA	1B	117	368	56	120	18	12	5	42	1	.326
	Milwaukee, NL	1B	36	41	3	10	0	0	0	3	0	.244
1963	Oklahoma City, PCL	1B	67	223	19	56	12	1	2	23	0	.251
	San Antonio, TxL	1B	55	229	34	77	17	4	2	25	3	.336
1964	Oklahoma City, PCL	PH	9	8	1	0	0	0	0	0	0	.000

Record in Latin America

Year	Team, league	Pos	G	AB	R	H	2B	3B	HR	RBI	SB	BA
1949-50	Havana, CubWL	1B	9	36	2	9	1	0	0	4	4	.250
1951-52	Ponce, PRWL	1B	72	305	55	114*	18	3	2	43	3	.374*
1952-53		1B		293	46	82	10	3	6	44	11	.280
1954-55	Cienfuegos, CubWL	1B	70	292*	38	90*	8	4	5	31	3	.308
1955-56		1B		285	43	89	11	2	5	42	5	.312
1956-57		1B		38	2	8	1	0	0	3		.211

Sherwood Brewer
Four-Position All-Star

NEGRO LEAGUE DEBUT: 1946

Sherwood Brewer, after playing baseball for the independent Harlem Globetrotters after World War II, joined the Indianapolis Clowns in 1949 and proved to be one of the most versatile players in the game.

In 1949, he was essentially the Clowns' right fielder, but he played infield as well. In 1950, he became the regular third baseman. In 1951, he was the shortstop. He moved to the Kansas City Monarchs in 1953, but they had a shortstop named Ernie Banks, so Brewer became the second baseman. In four seasons he played four positions, and he made the All-Star team at all four.

Defensively sound and a good baserunner, he had some punch and would put the ball in play. He played a little in "organized" ball when he was in his 30s, but he returned to Kansas City. Statistics show that he was evidently a .285 hitter, because that was what he batted, plus or minus, everywhere he went.

How did the Globetrotters come to sign you?

I was on Saipan in the army and after it was secured, they started a baseball club over there and I joined the baseball club. We played all over the Pacific and I played pretty well, so when I got out of the army and came home I had letters from different ballclubs from the Negro leagues and the Harlem Globetrotters, asking me if I'd be interested. That's how I got started.

Had you wanted to play professional baseball?

Oh, yes. All my life. That's all I did when I was a kid — play ball. My dad wanted me to be a ballplayer.

How did the Clowns acquire you from the Globetrotters?

I don't know. They pulled a deal, the Clowns and the Globetrotters. Abe Saperstein and Mr. [Syd] Pollock, who owned the Clowns, were friends anyhow. They were very good friends.

You played everywhere in the infield and outfield. What was your best position?

Oh, boy. Well, I'd like to think second base because I liked it better, but I don't know. I made the All-Star team four times at four different positions, but I think I was a better second baseman.

The best way to describe my play was just two words: I was fundamentally sound. When I was 15, I knew how to play baseball, I knew what was supposed to be done at every position because my dad had honed it in my head and when I went into the Negro leagues everybody was shocked that I knew so much about the game. I'd been watching it all my life.

You went to the Monarchs and then you joined "organized" ball for a while.

Sherwood Brewer (courtesy of Sherwood Brewer).

A guy down in San Angelo, Texas, in 1953, he came to the Monarchs and he had a chance to finish on top down there if he could find a second baseman. He came and talked to the Monarchs and got permission to talk to me. They told him, "If he agrees to go, you can take him." It was just about a month-and-a-half. So I went down to San Angelo, Texas. Let's see, what league was that? The Longhorn or something like that. I had a lot of fun playing down there.

That was the South. Did you encounter any racial problems?

One or two ballplayers in the league I had a little problem with, but the fans — no, I didn't have any. None.

You know what? When we were traveling through the South, we never had problems with the fans. Our problems were accommodations, such as sleeping and eating. But we never, *never* ran into problems with fans, even if we was playing a local team. Once in a while you'd run into a ballplayer you'd have trouble with, but our biggest trouble was sleeping, eating — such as that.

Most of our fans in towns in Nebraska and Iowa and places like that was all white because there's very few Negroes in those small suburban towns. Even today. And fans were always nice to us. We played league games in some of those towns, but we would also play local teams. That drew very well when you would go in and play a local team because a lot of the local clubs were the big factory in town or something like that and would have pretty good ballclubs. There were some pretty good semi-pro ballclubs around this country.

We went to Fort Wayne one time to play and they had a real strong ballclub and they borrowed Curt Simmons from the army to pitch against us. That's how tough the competition could be. It was a lot of fun. There was a lot of strong semi-pro teams around the country: the Bushwicks in Brooklyn; Fort Wayne; St. Jo, Michigan; the Coors out in Denver; Enid, Oklahoma. They had a lot of ex–Triple-A and major league ballplayers with those clubs. They were tough to beat.

I like TV, but I think it has hurt the game. And black kids just don't play baseball. This is a big city here and I could drive around this city all day Sunday and Saturday and I won't see four baseball games with black kids, but you can get up at 2:00 in the morning and you'll hear a basketball bouncing. All over this city, any time of night. I don't quite understand it.

Is there one game that stands out?

On the West Coast we were barnstorming against Bob Lemon and his group. Satchel Paige All-Stars barnstorming against Bob Lemon and I hit a home run and two doubles off of Bob Lemon and I'll *never* forget that. And I wasn't a home run hitter.

Lemon could throw that thing and he had terrific movement.

Oh, man! He'd scare you to death with that slider. [Laughs] What you did with him, you just didn't allow him to get ahead of you. If he got ahead of you, you were out. [Laughs]

How many exhibition games did you play against the white players?

Oh, my gosh. I have no idea. Let me see. We'd go on those 30-day trips 'cause the majors didn't allow them to play over 30 days. Sometimes I'd go straight to South America or somewhere. I must've played over a hundred ballgames against 'em.

Did you hold your own?

Well, I thought I did. [Laughs] We had a lot of fun.

There's something else I'd like to say. When Jackie Robinson was chosen to break that color barrier, it was not the major league ballplayers. They couldn't have cared less. It was management and society. I doubt if two percent of the ballplayers in the major leagues cared — objected — because most of 'em that I played against were all great guys. We had a lot of fun. Jackie said when he joined the Dodgers, he didn't even realize he was black the way those guys treated him. He had a little trouble out of Dixie Walker, but he didn't flat-out mistreat him; he just didn't have anything to do with him. I don't see anything wrong with that.

Who was the best player you came across?

The best hitter that I have ever seen in my life was Ted Williams, with Josh Gibson a close second. The best ballplayer I ever saw was a guy named Oscar Charleston. You remember Pete Reiser? If he hadn't gotten hurt, I think he, along with Willie Mays and Joe DiMaggio, would've been the best ballplayers I ever saw.

Did you see Bill Wright?

Yeah. I played against Bill. He could run. He could do everything. Big guy. He was a great ballplayer. He loved Mexico. He lives there now.

This may be an invalid observation, but blacks seem to have a greater ability to pick up foreign languages than do whites.

Well, let me tell you something. I am probably the only ballplayer that went to those South American countries that didn't learn to speak Spanish. I don't know why. When the Cubs decided to scout the South American countries, Buck O'Neil was going to recommend me to do so, and they were considering it, but the reason I didn't get it was because I couldn't speak Spanish.

I don't know. I guess because the guys spent so much time down there during the winter. How they pick it up so easy, I don't know. I can't explain it. They don't go to school for it — they just pick it up, but I couldn't do it. But I guess I really wasn't interested. All I wanted to do was play ball and just know how to ask for something to eat.

Who was the toughest pitcher?

For me, the two toughest pitchers I ever faced were Bill Greason and Bill Beverly. Both played with the Black Barons. Bill [Beverly] was mean besides. He'd knock you down and him and I are good buddies, but he'd stick it in my ear if I didn't get out of there. He respected me, you know, and he'd knock me down. I'd get up and look out there with that look, "Hey, man, this is me." But he never took that scowl off of his face. He was just like Bob Gibson. He would stick it in your ear, boy, and if he saw that it bothered you, you really were in trouble.

Bill Greason — I just couldn't hit him. He'd laugh at me sometimes. He told me one time — they were killing us, they had us beat real bad — he said, "Sherwood, I'm gonna lay one right down the middle." Right down the middle. Medium speed. And I popped it about a hundred feet right over the catcher. And I knew it was coming. [Laughs] It becomes mental, I think. Everything goes wrong. Instead of just relaxing I'd go up there and I'd squeeze the sawdust out of that bat trying to hit that guy. Those were the two toughest pitchers for me.

Would you be a baseball player again?

Oh, yeah! Without no question. The only thing different that I would do if I was going to do it again, in the winter time, instead of playing baseball, I'd go to school.

That's the only thing different I would do. I had no excuse for not going to school. I was a pretty fair athlete. I don't know how well I would've done in college but my dad was willing to send me the first year. But I wanted to work and then I got drafted in the army. I would do that a little different if I had to go over it again.

SHERWOOD BREWER
Born 8-16-23, Clarksdale, MS
Ht. 5' 8"   Wt. 168 Batted and Threw R

Year	Team, league	Pos	G	AB	R	H	2B	3B	HR	RBI	SB	BA
1946	Harlem Globetrotters, ind.	INF										
1948	New York Cubans, NNL	INF										
1949	Indianapolis Clowns, NAL	OF-INF										.279
1950		3B										.298
1951		SS										
1952	Ardmore, SoonerStL	2B										.238
1953	Kansas City Monarchs, NAL	2B										
1954		2B										
1955	San Angelo, LonghornL	2B										.288
1956		2B										.268

Jim Cohen

Coal Miner

NEGRO LEAGUE DEBUT: 1946

When Jim Cohen was drafted late in 1942, it was probably the best break of his life. It took him out of the coal mines, where he had worked and played ball on the mining camp team for five years, since high school. He was 24 years old, already a little late to begin a professional baseball career.

And it was even later before he got the chance, but without being drafted he probably never would have had that opportunity. He was able to play ball at Camp Lee, Virginia, and from there he was signed, at age 28, by the Indianapolis Clowns, for whom he played through 1952. Along the way, he pitched for two championship teams and appeared in the 1948 All-Star game. Before he retired, he was considered one of the top hurlers in the Negro American League.

I was in World War II. In 1942 I got drafted after Pearl

Harbor and I was discharged in '46. I was in a total of four years, five days.

I was in a replacement training center and I dealt with all the sports. I ran into a fellow who had played for the [Cincinnati] Clowns before the war. His name was Sloppy Lindsay and he was in the same company. He figured our team — our camp team — played real well, and the dominant factor [with the Clowns] was Syd Pollock; he called Syd and told Syd that he had him a pitcher. Along that line, I signed a contract before he ever seen me or I got out of the army. In 1946, I went to spring training as a Clown.

What had you done before the war?

My father was a coal miner and all coal mining camps are just about the same. They take pride in dominant [baseball] teams; all of 'em wanted to have a good team.

In fact, when I got a job in a coal mine, I went to the boss and I took my baseball glove and my baseball shoes — I wrapped 'em up and carried 'em with me under my arm. When I approached the boss, he said, "What can I do for you?" He was sitting down and looking down. I said, "I'm lookin' for a job." He started at my feet and started looking up. He got to my ball and glove before he got to my head. He said, "Are you a ballplayer?" I said, "Yes, sir." He wrote me up then, told me to go down and give this to the boss. They would take a chance on a ballplayer, wouldn't take a chance on *losing* a ballplayer. I started there and I played ball and I was the dominant player on the coal mining team.

When I went to [spring training] camp [with the Clowns] I was in good shape. I was in such good shape that my manager, which was Buster Haywood, let me pitch a whole game when I had my turn to pitch.

193

Jim Cohen (courtesy of Jim Cohen).

They usually pitch two or three innings, you know, and really that's enough, but I pitched a whole game. I was ready.

What pitches did you throw?

Fastball, fastball, fastball, control. I threw a curveball, then I threw a knuckleball, but the real asset is knowing where the ball's going. I learned that from Satchel Paige. Control — know where the ball's going. If you can throw high, outside and low, inside — if you can name those pitches and throw 'em, you got control. Then you study the hitters. So-and-so likes a low pitch; he'll never hit a low pitch from me.

And my catcher for that time was Sam Hairston. Sam was the first Negro the White Sox signed and we stayed together and went down to South America together. He was a smart catcher. I never did shake him off. [Laughs] If he called a pitch and I didn't think it was the right pitch, I'd throw it but I'd make it so bad that they couldn't hit it. He'd call me, he'd say, "Hey, Cohen!" He'd walk out to the mound. He'd say, "Man, I know darn well you didn't try to get that pitch over there. You better listen to me now; you're gonna get that thing hit outta here!"

I just talked to him the other day. He's assistant coach for the Birmingham Double-A team; that's a White Sox farm team. He told me when Michael Jordan came down there, he started out wrong. He should've gone to spring training with the major leaguers. Everybody had something to tell him and nobody told him nothing right. He said, "When I got him down here, I told him, 'Jordan, you got long arms. You take advantage of that. Get back off that plate and step into the pitch, because you come down here these pitchers down here will knock your block off.'" Sam had a lot of nephews and grandchildren and children and everything into baseball.

Jim Cohen (courtesy of Jim Cohen).

Do you know any of your season records?

No. They really didn't keep the records like they do now. On maybe Sunday, those were league games. These other games that we were playing, they didn't count in the league.

In '48, I went to the East-West game. That was the first year they had two games. I pitched in the second game in Yankee Stadium. The first game was in Comiskey Park in Chicago. Then we journeyed into the Yankee Stadium and that's where I pitched my three [innings]. I didn't give up but one hit in my stint.

That must have been pretty exciting.

Oh, it was. In Yankee Stadium, too. Oh, boy.

Are there other games that stand out?

I pitched a game against the Chicago White Sox and their ace pitcher and he beat me in 12 innings. His name has got away from me. I should never forget it, but I can't think of it right now.

The next-best game I pitched was in Baltimore against the Baltimore Elite Giants. I beat Joe Black in Baltimore. That was a two-hitter.

All those teams when I was playing ball had some standouts. In Baltimore, they had Junior Gilliam and Pee Wee Butts for a double play combination. Everybody tried to have the best double play combination. Pee Wee Butts and Junior Gilliam was Baltimore's; and Birmingham, they had Piper Davis and Artie Wilson — that was theirs and hard to beat; and then Newark had Larry Doby and Monte Irvin. That was their double play combination.

Who was the toughest batter on you?

Well, to me, the toughest for me to get out was Hank Thompson. Hank Thompson was tough. He could hit the ball. In '54, like Leo Durocher said, in that World Series, Hank Thompson was the best third baseman he had ever seen. When we used to play Kansas City, he was my real road buddy. We'd be going to play each other in the same town and he'd ride in the bus with me.

In our league, he played right field on account of his arm strength. He could throw. When he got up to the majors they put him on third base.

Hank [Aaron] played with the Clowns. He was my man. His mother had me lookin' out for him. [Laughs] She said, "This is my baby now. He's never been away from home. You see that he gets some sleep and see that he eats."

When Hank come on the team, he was unbelievable. All he says to you are "Shoot," "Shucks," or "Dog-gone." He's callin' you all kind of names. [Laughs] He didn't even know how to cuss. He was 17.

We played the little team in Mobile that he played for. The Clowns would go on a barnstorming tour when the season was over and we played this team in Mobile. Hank was playing shortstop and he would

go down on his knees to catch the ball, so when he threw to first base — you know, first basemen usually take a step toward the ball to help the throw — that first baseman was stepping back in the coaching box, gettin' back off. [Laughs] He could throw!

I lost some money on him. They had a scout in Buffalo — Ted Fisher — and he had a sporting goods store. Every time we played in Buffalo I'd go up to the store and get me some socks or something and I told him about Hank. He said, "If you ever get me a player that I sign to a contract, I'll give you $500." At that time, $500 was a whole *lotta* money. "And then if he ever plays a game in the majors, I'll double it."

So we played there in Buffalo. We were playin' Kansas City. We barnstormed with the teams in our league, like we played at Kansas City and we played in Buffalo. I went up to Ted and I told him, "I got a ballplayer for you," and he said, "No, I've gotta take my wife up in Canada." And I kept hounding him and hounding him and hounding him 'til he stayed there for the doubleheader.

Those pitchers knew what you liked and that's what you're not gonna get. Hank Aaron hit a home run over the right field fence and he hit *another* home run over the right field fence. I thought sure Ted would have notice of that, but he was still working for Branch Rickey — he was working for Pittsburgh then — and he said, "He's fine, but they like for you to pull the ball up there."

He didn't like him because Hank wasn't pulling the ball. If they don't throw you something to pull, they can't pull it. He said, "I'll talk to Rickey," and I said, "You better hurry up 'cause the others are after him real bad." And that's how I missed him. [Laughs]

Who was the best pitcher you came up against?

Quite a few of them. I batted against Satchel Paige but I don't count him 'cause he was never in a position to be really pitching. He did a lot of clownin' when he was playing on the barnstorming teams.

We played in Philadelphia one time and most of the people come to see Satchel. He was doggin' it and people said, "Let 'em hit! Let 'em hit!" During the last inning, he walked three hitters. Then one of our hitters — Speed Merchant — come up. He was a pretty good hitter. Satchel started bearing down. He struck Merchant out and my manager was standing in the dugout and he was hollerin' for Merchant, "Come on, Merchant! Come on, Merchant!" Satchel went into his stretch and he looked over to Buster and shook his head. [Laughs] He didn't throw but three [pitches].

That's what I tried — to copy after him with that control. You gotta have control and you get by with a whole lot of stuff.

Talk about playing in South America.

I went down to South America and played winter ball. They'd pay more money down there. I'd have a real good game, then I'd go to the boss. I'd say, "Look, I need some more money." "What you need money for, Mr. Cohen?" "It's the winter time. In the winter time in Pennsylvania it's cold! My kids gotta have clothes." And they'd give you some more money. [Laughs]

I'm going to my 60th high school class reunion up in Latrobe, Pennsylvania. I was the *only* Negro in my class. I played football, basketball, ran track, boxing team — I did everything in that school. We had a star from there. He went to Duquesne University. In 1937 through '41, Duquesne had a basketball team called the Iron Dukes and the coach was Chick Davis. They didn't have but six players. Pete Maravich's father played on that team. They had some kinda team. This boy — Lou Casparic — was there. We lived in the same coal mining camp. I was working in the coal mine with his father when his father got killed in the mine.

I wasn't born in Pennsylvania; I was born in the Southland. I was born in Alabama, but my father journeyed to Pennsylvania when I was 3 years old. That's where I grew up. I come outta high school in September and went right in the coal mine the next winter. My father was a coal miner. He didn't know anything else; he couldn't teach me anything. If he'd've been raised on a farm, I'd've been a farmer.

I learned this: The smaller your environment, the more effective you can be. When I went to Newtown, all the kids come around. "New kid in town!" You can only do what everybody else is doin' — basketball, football. When it came to choosin' up sides, everybody wanted to be on my side. I had a brother who was real good and they'd make me and him choose up so we wouldn't be on the same team. [Laughs]

You left baseball rather suddenly after the 1952 season. Why?

Jackie Robinson broke the barrier to give Negroes a chance to play in white baseball. Jackie and I were real close. Jackie had broke the barrier and I had a real good season in '52, so I said maybe I'll get a little raise and help me take care of my family, but before I could ask for a raise they asked me if I'd take a cut. I said, "No, I can't go back no further. I gotta get a job to help me take care of my family." I took some advice from some older ballplayers who had left baseball that the post office was a good place to settle. I came to Washington in '52 and got me a job in the post office and stayed in the post office 35 years. That's where I retired from.

Do you have any regrets from your baseball days?

Not a one. No. I'd go right through this same thing again.

JAMES CLARENCE "FIREBALL" COHEN
Born 5-26-18, Evergreen, AL
Ht. 5' 11"   Wt. 190   Batted and Threw R

Year	Team. league	G	IP	W	L	PCT	H	BB	SO	SHO	ERA
1946	Indianapolis Clowns, NAL										

Year	Team. league	G	IP	W	L	PCT	H	BB	SO	SHO	ERA
1947											
1948				3	8	.273					3.90
1949											
1950				2	3	.400					3.64
1951											
1952											

Cohen pitched for Vargas in the Venezuelan League during the winter of 1948-49.

James "Jimmy" Dean

The Original

NEGRO LEAGUE DEBUT: 1946

Back before prepackaged sausage patties, before Big Bad John, even before East of Eden, there was the first James "Jimmy" Dean. And, like the two other men of the same name, he was in the public eye. He pitched for the Philadelphia Stars, hanging up his glove in 1950.

He saw the writing on the wall. The major leagues were taking the Negro leagues' brightest stars and with them went the attention of the fans. Jimmy Dean saw the crowds drop to a mere handful and realized he must do something else to earn a living, so he returned to school to earn his college degree.

He spent the rest of his working life as a chemist for Merck and Company and did well. He put three boys through college and a fourth went on to a career on Broadway. "I know they're successful," he says, "because they never ask me for any money."

Jimmy Dean was successful, too.

A lot of the scorebooks never got into the paper. Say we had a game in Columbus, Ohio, and, shoot, the next day we may have been in another state — we may be in Springfield, Illinois — so, therefore, we couldn't get the clippings out there to find out. I got a few but I didn't get too many.

The newspapers didn't print the scores. We were really competition to the major leagues and they knew it. Judge Landis knew it, that's why he kept the blacks out of the majors. When they did play us we kicked their butts.

A lot of people claim the white ballplayers weren't trying when they played the black players. No pitcher wants to be hit. No one can say someone such as Bob Feller wasn't trying against batters such as Josh Gibson and Buck Leonard.

No. It was a feather in his cap to get them out. A lot of guys hit Bob Feller, although I've seen him strike out 16, 17 A's players. The Philadelphia Athletics. He was a good pitcher. They had quite a few good pitchers; they had Warren Spahn, Allie Reynolds, little Bobby Shantz. He only lives a block from me.

I started playing baseball at about 8 years old. From then on 'til I went to war I lived on a baseball field. I started out as a third baseman and then I played with a bunch of men called the Norristown Colored Elks and I played shortstop. I could field good and everything, but to hit grown men was a little tough. Then I shifted to second base.

I threw so hard, when I was about 13 years old the guys said, "You should be a pitcher." So I changed to be a pitcher and I learned how to throw curveballs and sinkers with a softball. I learned about the sinker — we called it the drop then — from Jim Taylor — Schoolboy Taylor — when he was with the Pittsburgh Crawfords. I watched him and when I started throwing it I did it like him. I threw over 90 miles an hour. If I got any rest, I was liable to throw it 95.

You ever see Satchel Paige pitch? You know that high kick? Just as that kick is on its way down to the ground, which only he knows, the ball comes right off the top of his foot, so between the kick and the speed, the ball will be in the catcher's mitt before the batter would know it. And he was tall — about 6-4 — and his arms looked like they went below his knees. He was one of the best pitchers I ever saw. Satch was a drawing card. What he used to do, if one team had a low attendance, Satch would come and stay there a week and pitch two innings, three innings. Then he'd take off in his long car or his airplane.

I can name two other guys I thought was just as good. That was a guy named Hilton Smith and also Leon Day. Leon Day's in the Baseball Hall of Fame in Puerto Rico and he's also in the Baseball Hall of Fame in Cooperstown. He was my buddy. I learned a lot from him. It really hurt me when he died because that man should've been in the Hall of Fame ten years before.

There's so many should be in the Hall of Fame. There's Hilton Smith, Double Duty Radcliffe, Wild Bill Wright, [Webster] McDonald — played with the Philadelphia Stars and the Pittsburgh Crawfords — and then you've got about three or four guys out of Kansas City. There's so many guys. Like I told 'em, Jackie Robinson wasn't the best. We had guys there way better than him. There should've been other guys before him. The first [black] player in the major leagues should've been either Satchel Paige or Josh Gibson.

My manager, the one who signed me, he's the greatest baseball player I've ever seen. That's Oscar Charleston. I'm telling

you, the man was awesome! He got chased out of Cuba 'cause he beat a policeman up. They hid him out until he got back into the States. But he was a good, fair man and he wasn't afraid of nobody. You mess with him you better be ready to fight. He could take a baseball and squeeze it and bust the seams. That's how strong he was.

I was 21. What happened was, the Philadelphia Stars were playing the New York Cubans in Shibe Park. A Cuban guy had seen me pitch because they brought a team to Ambler with mostly Puerto Ricans and Cubans. I think I beat 'em maybe like 4-to-nothing. The guy asked me, "How about having a tryout with the New York Cubans?" So I said, "Yeah, that'd be good." Then he said, "And we'll see if we can get you down in Havana to play in the winter league."

So when they came in [to Philadelphia], I went down there and I thought they knew. Nobody came over to me. Later the guy asked me, "What're you doing here?" I said, "I was supposed to have a tryout with the Cubans." And the guy said, "I don't know anything about it." I had my uniform and everything on. He told me to come back another time so I said okay.

I walked over to the Philadelphia Stars bench. Charleston asked me, "What do you do?" I said, "I pitch." "With your left or right hand?" I said, "Right hand. I was supposed to get a tryout with the Cubans." He said, "You be there Saturday at 9:00 and we'll take you up to New York." We went up there and I think I pitched six innings against the Brooklyn Bushwicks. I got tired and he took me out and put somebody else in, but I think we won the game something like 5-3. The Bushwicks were former major leaguers.

After that I barnstormed with a lot of teams. Every game I pitched they paid me $100. That was in Virginia, North Carolina, South Carolina, Connecticut, Massachusetts, New Jersey. In fact, I played for Jersey Joe's baseball team. Near the end of the season of '46, sometimes I pitched three

games in a week. That was 300
bucks. That was a *lot* of money back
in those days.

Then 1947 I went to spring training with the Philadelphia Stars and
we went down to Charleston, South
Carolina, and we trained down
there and we worked our way up the
coast. We went to West Virginia—
Wheeling—and Asheville, North
Carolina. Ohio. Played all through
there.

Then I got traded near the end of
the season because they needed a
lefthand pitcher. Most of our pitching was righthanded. Then I played
for Alex Pompez, the New York
Cuban owner. Somebody called up
and asked Alex Pompez did he want
a righthand pitcher and he said yes.

The Cubans and the New York
Black Yankees were the same team
really, so some nights I would play
with the New York Black Yankees.
When Willie Mays signed up for the
Giants, I was in the team offices
when they told me that they just
signed Willie Mays. I said, "Oh,
man, that's good!"

When he come out of high school, he
played with Birmingham. He was a good
outfielder 'cause he could chase fly balls but
he wasn't a good hitter. He couldn't hit the
curveball until he got in the Giants' organization. Leo Durocher was just like a father
to him and he taught him how to hit the
curveball.

Ernie Banks could hit. He could hit. He
played shortstop with the Monarchs. He
was good. The Monarchs had at least seven
or eight guys on their club that made the
major leagues. They're the team that put
the most people in the major leagues and
the high minor leagues.

In 1947, Opening Day in Kansas City—I
guess we had about 25-, 30,000 people, two
bands—and Kansas City beat us I think it
was 3–1 or something like that. It was real
close. That's when I really became good

Jimmy Dean (courtesy of James Dean).

friends with a lot of the Kansas City Monarchs players. They had a name for me—a
little cuss-word name—because I could
throw so hard. I threw my curveball the
same way, my curveball and my sinker the
same way. I placed two fingers on the ball
and everything I threw came off of those
two fingers.

Joe Black, when he was with the Baltimore Elites—he got into the majors—I
used to tease him. I said, "Joe, you know
one thing, man? You can't even throw hard
enough to break glass." He'd laugh. It was a
joke between us.

Roy Campanella, I played sandlot with
him before he went to Baltimore. And he
couldn't hit the curveball, either. See, what
happened to him—he really didn't know
how to catch good, he had a good throwing
arm—and I could get him out everytime I
pitched to him. He went to Baltimore and a

1949 Philadelphia Stars
(L. to R.): Herb Hill, Bob Griffith, Stanley Glenn, Art Hefner, Bill Ricks, Bill Cash, Henry Miller,
Wilmer Harris, Will Thompson, Marvin Williams, Jimmie Armistead, Barney Brown, Bus Clark-
son, Jimmy Jones, Ben Little, Jimmy Dean, Murray Watkins, Oscar Charleston (manager) (courtesy
of James Dean).

Baltimore catcher named Biz Mackey was one of the best catchers ever in the black leagues. That's another one should be there [in the Hall of Fame]. He taught Campanella.

My selection of best catchers I ever played with and against has to be Josh Gibson for hitting and Biz Mackey for catching, especially young pitchers. If they did like he called a game, they would win. And he had a good arm. And the next I'd pick was Campanella 'cause Biz Mackey taught Campanella how to catch. Then the next guy I thought was real good was Mickey Cochrane. He was the best in the major leagues.

Another catcher I thought had an arm as good as anybody was Bill Cash. There's some major league catchers played with Cash and they said they wanted to learn how he could pick people off. You got a man on second or third and if you didn't watch out, he'd pick you off. We had a special signal to throw. Usually we'd throw an inside fastball right in off the plate. When the ball comes that way and the batter is righthanded, the person that's on third base can't see as good, so all he did was make that one step and — Whip! — he had you. He's one of my best buddies.

The best first baseman I ever saw and played against who could hit and could field — he wasn't fancy but he could do everything perfect — was Buck Leonard. He could hit, hit, hit. Believe me. He didn't hit Satch too much, but all the rest of the guys he tore up. Satch even got Josh Gibson.

I knew Gus Greenlee, too, the owner of the Pittsburgh Crawfords, and I also knew [Cum] Posey, out there with the Homestead Grays, 'cause I had people that lived in Donora, Connellsville — all around that area.

I had a lot of people help me out. There was Barney Brown and Bill Byrd — he was a spitball pitcher — and Henry Miller, Bill Ricks, Wilmer Harris. They were good ballplayers and they would help you with things.

I played with Harry "Suitcase" Simpson. He was good. There's so *many* guys. There was Doc Dennis. I was a good friend of Jim West. Him and [Showboat] Thomas for the New York Cubans were the best fielding first basemen you'd ever see. They were fancy. Another guy who was good — he couldn't hit too well but he could play first base — was Tut. King Tut. He played with the Clowns. Speed Merchant played center field for 'em, then you had [Ray]

Neil playing second base and [Sam] Hairston was catching. They had a good team.

Gene Benson was a good center fielder. Good hitter but he was a slap hitter. He didn't take a full cut at the ball, he made connection. He faced the pitcher — his whole body was towards the pitcher.

The greatest team I ever saw was the 1946 Newark Eagles. They were even more powerful than the New York Yankees. In '46 they won the championship and every one of those guys could hit. A little guy named Jimmy Wilkes played center field — he could hit singles and doubles — and the other guys — [Lennie] Pearson and Doby and Irvin and [Pat] Patterson and Bob Harvey and Biz Mackey was catching for 'em. Man, those guys were awesome.

Leon Day, the first night game we played them in Shibe Park, pitched a no-hitter. No hits, no runs. And I always had something to say to Leon. I told him the darker he was, the harder he'd throw. He'd crack up.

The older guys taught me how to be a gentleman; they taught me how to dress, how to act. You never saw a baseball player raggedy; they were always dressed up. If we didn't, they would kick our butts.

We had a lot of guys carried great big, long knives and some of 'em even had pistols, so you had to be very careful that you didn't rub 'em wrong. Like if I hit a guy, it was because he got a hit off me but after the game he would forget all about it but during that game he was mad.

When I had the ball I'd look in the dugout to see what my manager Oscar Charleston wanted me to do and if he said, "Hit him," I hit him. Usually when I hit 'em they didn't come back for at least three or four days. If I didn't do that, he would fine me.

Willie Grace [of the Cleveland Buckeyes] got two out of four in Columbus, Ohio, and beat us and then we played the next night. Charleston would never tell you who's gonna pitch ahead of time. He said, "Jimmy, you got the apple tonight." I got the first two guys and then Willie Grace

came up. I looked in there and Charleston said, "Hit him." And I got him, too. I threw him a curveball — one of those sharp curveballs — right on his knee and he didn't get out of the way in time and that was it. He didn't play no more that week.

I don't know any of my records. After you win and lose a few you forget all about it. You're worried about going out there and winning. I know I beat Johnny Antonelli one night in upstate New York. I beat another guy named Johnny Gee; he was six-foot-nine. All he had was a fastball.

I played up to 1950. When you're used to playing before 25-, 30,000 people and you go to the ballpark and look and only see 2,000 people in the stands, you know it's time to get out. We would still be playing now if our fans had continued to stay to see us — support us — but they all went to the majors. By me having a pretty good scientific background, I went back to school and got my degree and then I worked for Merck for 33 years. I went to Morris Brown College down in Atlanta, Georgia. I've got buddies down around there now.

[Chico] Renfroe died not too long ago, but the best shortstop was Willie Wells, then next was Pee Wee Butts. He was the best fielder but he didn't hit with Willie Wells. Another guy that's in the Baseball Hall of Fame, the guy that stole the bases — Cool Papa Bell. He played out of St. Louis. Cash stopped him running.

Henry Kimbro was a hard man to pitch to. He could hit. He was evil but he could hit. And field. Joe Black, Junior Gilliam, [George] Hopkins — all those guys were afraid to talk to him. Don't make a mistake — he'd be on your case. He was a tough act to follow.

I had a lot of good roommates. I had Billy Bruton before he went to the majors, and I had Bus Clarkson, the shortstop who later played for the Braves, and I had Marvin Williams. He was one of the top second basemen in the Negro leagues. He was one who jumped when Max Lanier and those guys went down to Mexico. We were up in

New York — we were playing the Black Yankees that night — and when we came in there was a telegram for him. A moneygram. And he came over, he said, "Jimmy, guess what? What would you do if you had a check like this?" He showed me the check. It was from [Jorge] Pasquel; it was for $2,500. That's the first time I'd ever seen a check that big. I said, "Man, with that kind of money I'd take off." Sure enough, he left and went and played in the Mexican League maybe something like eight years. He married a Mexican woman down there.

I had a chance to go to Venezuela, Puerto Rico, Cuba, and Mexico but I wouldn't go 'cause I couldn't speak Spanish. I should've went like Cash did. He went down there and learned how to speak Spanish. We had a lot of guys on our team could speak Spanish. Remember Rafael Noble, caught with the New York Giants? I lived with him and his brother in New York when I was there playing with the Santurce All-Stars, which was Cubans and Puerto Ricans.

Once Robinson and Doby went in, the major league clubs just cleaned the top ballplayers out right away and sent 'em to the high minor leagues — Triple-A — and then our fans were gone. We used to play before 25,000 people, and 56,000 in Comiskey Park for the East-West game; that was money. And we had some of the top promoters in the world. We had Eddie Gottlieb, the owner of the Philadelphia Warriors [and Stars], and Abe Saperstein owning the Clowns and the Harlem Globetrotters, then you had Tom Baird, who owned the Kansas City Monarchs. Those guys were powerful and the thing about 'em, they were good to us. When it was time to pay you, you got that money and you got it right away.

I used to like to tail my fastball in to where the small part of the bat was and hit that. Boy, it would crack that bat right in half. And I threw a heavy ball. The harder you squeeze the ball, the lighter the pitch will be 'cause it'll sail, but the least amount of pressure you put on the ball and it comes off your fingers, it's dead so when it hits the catcher's mitt you got a swollen hand 'cause the ball feels like you're catching a shot-put. Our baseball gloves were just two pieces of leather and Cash used to fire that ball back to me! When I got done, my hands were as big as his. The harder I'd throw, the harder he threw it back to me.

You know, another guy that could've made the majors if he wanted to? You ever hear of Emlen Tunnell? Him and I ran around together every weekend — Friday and Saturday. Em was the first black football coach; he was assistant coach for the Giants.

What were some of your best games?

I beat Baltimore Elites, 2–1, and I think I had about nine strikeouts. I beat the Cleveland Buckeyes when they had Sam Jethroe. I think that was 6–3. They were my best [league] games.

Before I went with the Philadelphia Stars, I played against a team which Emlen Tunnell was on. They had a lot of guys that could have made black baseball. I think I had 21 strikeouts. I pitched five no-hitters. Three no-hitters were nine innings and the other two no-hitters were seven innings. These were high semipro teams before I went with the Philadelphia Stars. I guess that's one reason people got to know who I was and wanted to hire me to pitch a game.

We played the Trenton Giants. The team I played with then was a team called North Hills Giants. I pitched against Larry Doby, Monte Irvin, Jimmy Wilkes, Pearson — all them guys — and I beat 'em, 13-nothing, and I had 12 strikeouts.

Monte Irvin remembers that. They came and played with the Trenton Giants but weren't supposed to play with 'em because they were with the Newark Eagles. I got $165 for pitching that day 'cause there was a lot of gambling on that game and they were happy I won. That was the biggest pay

I ever got to pitch. I went to a place where they had men's clothes and bought me a complete outfit — hat, shoes, underwear, everything. It cost me $52.

Would you go back and be a ballplayer again?

Yeah. I loved it. Anytime you're out on the baseball field from sun-up to dark at the age of 8, you know you like it. I knew I could make the major leagues when I was about 15 years old. I just knew it.

JAMES A. DEAN
Born 2-25-25, Ambler, PA
Ht. 5' 10"   Wt. 175   Batted and Threw R

Year	Team, league	G	IP	W	L	Pct	H	BB	SO	SHO	ERA
1946	Philadelphia Stars, NNL										
1947	New York Cubans, NNL										
1948	Philadelphia Stars, NNL										
1949	Philadelphia Stars, NAL										
1950											

John Miles

"Mule"

NEGRO LEAGUE DEBUT: 1946

What is the record for home runs in consecutive games? Eight? Count again. In 1947, John Miles of the Chicago American Giants blasted eleven in eleven games.

Unfortunately, you can't look it up because what Negro leagues records were kept have, for the most part, long since been destroyed or otherwise disposed of, but there are people who remember it and talk about Miles's feat still today. Because of his power, his manager with Chicago, Candy Jim Taylor, told him, "You hit as hard as a mule kicks," and he became "Mule."

Miles, an outfielder/third baseman, was a big man (6' 3", 230 or so) and that home run splurge, although never matched by anyone before or since, was typical of his power. Although still hitting home runs, he left the Negro leagues early to be with his growing family, then returned to baseball for a partial season in organized ball to prove to himself that he could play there. Retired now from his post-baseball career, he has taken up golf but devotes much of his time to community service, working with children.

How did you come to join the American Giants?

John Miles: By a scout here in San Antonio, Texas, a fellow name of Mr. Webb. He knew the American Giants manager.

You were in your 20s when you signed. Had you been in the service?

Not exactly. I was civil service and the government sent me to Tuskegee. I was a part of the ground support but I was a civilian. I went to school there and I learned a trade — aircraft sheet metal worker.

You had been a good junior college basketball player. Was there any temptation to pursue basketball?

No, not really, because baseball was my desire. I played [basketball] at St. Phillips Junior College. They called me "Sonny Boy" in high school and junior college.

My most memorable experience in the Negro leagues was hitting two home runs in one ballgame and winning the game. After hitting the second home run, the manager said, "Miles, you hit as hard as a mule kicks." This is how the nickname "Mule" was originated and that year — 1947 — I hit a total of 27 home runs.

I heard that you once hit 11 home runs in 11 games.

Something like that. We're talking 50 years ago now. We don't have a legitimate record of that now because all the records were burned up or thrown away. I was a power hitter. I hit the two in a game against the Memphis Red Sox. Memphis had good pitchers. They had [Dan] Bankhead there and Lefty Mathis.

Was the two-home-run game your best game?

No, I had won other games that I hit only one home run. We were playing a white team in New Haven, Connecticut, and the score was nothing-nothing. In the seventh or eighth inning I hit a home run and won that game, 1-to-nothing. I hit a lot of home runs but some of the games we lost. It's more important when you win.

What was your batting average?

I hit my weight—.250, .270. I was a slugger; I wasn't a potential line drive hitter—I hit for distance.

How was the travel?

We traveled primarily by bus with very little time left for practice. The bus was our mobile home because there were not hotel or motel accommodations. We ate quite a bit of our meals on the bus. The accommodations for Negro ballplayers consisted of staying with various families and enjoying their extended hospitality. This was a sign of the times when everyone did not like the separate but equal facilities but accepted them.

We did play against white teams and won most of them; however those we won we did in a very sportsmanlike manner. I feel I have helped pave the way for black players of today. I did not come too soon to play in the major leagues because I feel I'm a part of Jackie Robinson, Hank Aaron, Willie Mays, Ernie Banks, Monte Irvin, Roy Campanella—and all the other Negro players in the major leagues today.

You left the Negro leagues at a young age—27. Why?

Because of my family. I was getting a leave of absence from my job so I could play. My wife said, "With two boys coming, are you gonna play ball or stay at home and raise children?" She kind of helped me make up my mind, so I decided to come back home. Now I have five boys and one

John Miles (courtesy of John Miles).

girl and 24 grandchildren. [Laughs] Now I can talk to them about my career in professional baseball. I take my grandchildren with me sometimes when I go to the reunions.

Who was the best player you saw?

We had a *lot* of good ballplayers. Every team had good ballplayers. We played hard for the love of the game, not the money. I got two dollars a day to eat on and $300 a month was my top salary. That was good money. Jackie was good, Satchel was good, Josh Gibson, Theolic Smith. Monte Irvin was playing; he was good. [Gene] Baker was playing with the Kansas City Monarchs. Willie Mays came after I did. Elston Howard. All those guys were good.

1946 Chicago American Giants
Back row (L. to R.): Clyde McNeal, Walter McCoy, Pep Young, Jacob Robinson, Clarence Locke,
Chet Brewer, John Miles, Jim McCurine, Ralph West, John Bissant, CandyJim Taylor (manager).
Front row (L. to R.): Walter Thomas, Harry Rhodes, Clyde Nelson, Chick Longest, William Charter,
Herb Barnhill, Red Howard, James Buckner, Willie Cornelius (author's collection).

You mentioned a couple of pitchers. Who was the best one?

Satchel was a great pitcher. He could throw hard and he was smart. Nobody could touch Satchel when he didn't want 'em to. You know the story about Satchel having all the guys come in from the outfield. He had 'em sit down and he threw nine pitches and that was it.

Satchel was good but we had guys just as good as Satchel. Leon Day was good. He's in the Hall of Fame. Hilton [Smith] was good. Don't cut him short. He was a good pitcher.

I've heard stories of Satchel's barnstorming teams. Whole towns would shut down for the day so everyone could go out and watch the game.

That's right. That was an outlet back then because you didn't have television. I played with Satchel's all-stars against Jackie's team barnstorming. I only played a few games because of my family. They came to San Antonio and I played with them while they were in Texas.

Would you do it again?

Oh, yes. Yes — because I loved the game. It was a pleasure and honor to be a part of

the Negro leagues. These teams had great players who played hard, not for the money but for the love of the game. Yes, I did enjoy playing in the Negro leagues. It was great to compete with a group of fine players. We shared the joys, the triumphs, tears, and losses as we played the game of baseball. I do not have any animosity for baseball players of today, nor for the enormous salaries paid to them. Although I never received a huge salary, it doesn't bother me because you never miss what you never had.

It would be easier to do it today if you were making that million dollar salary.

Tell me about it. I loved to play ball and that was my ambition — to play baseball. When I had a chance to go professional, I had no doubt in my mind about making it. I told my wife, I said, "I'm gonna try." "You're not gonna make it." I said, "Well, let me try." She said, "Feel free to go." Clyde McNeal was my roommate — he played with the American Giants and he lived here in San Antonio, too — and he enticed me to go, also. He just passed. He was my buddy and my friend.

I wanted to do something and I felt like

this was a chance to show my family, my boys now, that I did have the ability to play and I played and I made it. It's all history now.

When I came home in '50, we were integrated and I played with a team called the Laredo Apaches. That was in the Gulf Coast League here in Texas. I told my wife I still wanted to try to play. I was the only black on the team. I made the team and I hit a home run one night to win a game. The people gave me money, sports shirts; they gave me all kind of dinners.

We had a doubleheader that night and Laredo's only 150 miles from here and I told my wife, "I'm coming home after the game." I got halfway and I went to sleep. I went off the highway and I jerked my car back and I went across the highway and I went in a ditch and tore up my car. In the paper the next day they had, "Miles has accident on Laredo highway." So my wife said, "Well, what're you gonna do now?" I said, "I guess I'll come home now," so in 1951 I just came and got in a league here in San Antonio. I had the ability to play with a white team in organized ball and I made it.

A lot of people said, "How did it feel with a white team?" Yeah, there were a lot of abuses and people calling names, but the manager said, "Miles, don't worry about that. You're here to play ball. Don't worry about the spectators." That was the only harrassment; the players treated me just like I was another ballplayer.

There were incidents when we went to eat. One place wouldn't feed me and the manager said, "If you don't feed one player,"— there was 27 ballplayers on the team —"then 26 will walk out." So the manager [of the restaurant] came out and said, "Oh, we'll feed him." I felt like they were part of me and I was part of the team. They weren't gonna leave me and that made me feel good because they stood up for me.

The white fans, though, were rough. They said, "We're gonna have a nigger night tonight." They'd run a cat across the field. You'd find all kind of insults they'd say to you.

I showed I could play and compete with other guys as well as any other, white or black. I was trying to prove something to myself, not only to the other players or the other races. I wanted to prove to myself that I could do something and do it great. And I made it.

I've come this far by faith and every day I wake up, I say, "Thank you, Lord, for another day," because I appreciate it. I try to be a role model for the kids, not only my kids but other people's kids that don't have a father. They don't know what fathers are. When I go to church on Sunday morning, I say, "Lord, thank you that I can be a role model to these kids and give something back." That's the way I came up. People were nice and gave encouragement to me as we were coming up, so now I'm giving something back to the community. I go out and speak to the different classes in the schools, to the kids, and they're tickled to death. I made it and I can tell them that they can do the same thing I did. You have to think positive. We all once were kids and we came that way ourselves.

My motto for young kids is, "Winning ballgames is not by luck, it's how you play the game." That's my philosophy. Play hard and you win ballgames.

JOHN "MULE" or "SONNYBOY" MILES
Born 8-11-22, San Antonio, TX
Ht. 6' 3"   Wt. 230   Batted and Threw R

Year	Team, league	POS	G	AB	R	H	2B	3B	HR	RBI	SB	BA
1946	Chi. American Giants, NAL	OF										
1947		OF-3B							27			.250
1948		OF										.268
1949		OF										
1950	Laredo, GCL	OF										

Al Smith

Almost MVP

NEGRO LEAGUE DEBUT: 1946

Frequently in MVP balloting, the final vote count has been close, with one man edging another by only a few points, but number three is usually way back. It's a rare year when three men contibute so much that a three-way photo finish occurs in the race.

Beginning in 1938 and continuing through 1960, three sportswriters from each major league city voted for the award. Also beginning in 1938, 14 points were awarded for a first-place vote, nine for second, eight for third, etc., down to one for tenth.

It would seem to be a straightforward procedure. If a writer felt Player A contributed the most to his team's efforts, then that player would get his vote. The player he felt contributed the next most would get his second place vote, and so on.

Alas, were it only so simple. A lot more entered into it in many years. Items of concern at one time or another have been personality and territory. And, sad to say, race.

Consider those three elements. (1) Personality. Some players shrug off asinine questions asked by sportswriters ("Why did you hang that curve?" or "Why did you swing at that pitch in the dirt?") or even endeavor to answer them civilly. Others, guys such as Ted Williams and Jim Bunning, were not so polite and ended up offending and or alienating the writer who asked the stupid question. Come vote time, the writer remembers, "He called me stupid. I won't vote for him." It cost Williams at *least* one (1947) MVP award and delayed Bunning's berth in the Hall of Fame until he got off the baseball writers' ballots and into the hands of the Veterans Committee.

(2) Territory. This applies more to New York than elsewhere, but throughout the '40s and '50s and on into the '60s, it was *very* important to the New York writers for their team to have the winner if there was anyone who even remotely could be considered. If New York writers felt "their" man might be challenged by another, they would conspire to leave the other guy completely off their ballots, thereby giving him three zeroes in the final count. In 1951, when Yogi Berra won his first MVP award, the evening before the announcement was made it was conceded that Ned Garver of the St. Louis Browns had won. He was omitted from all three N.Y. ballots, though, and Berra won.

In 1954, when Cleveland won the American League flag and 111 games, it happened again. Larry Doby of the Indians led the league in home runs and RBIs, but once again the winner was Berra as the N.Y. writers placed Doby low on their ballots.

And (3) Race. This seemed to be an A.L. problem. When Elston Howard of the Yankees (who else?) was named the MVP of 1963, he was the first black to win in that league. Over in the National League, however, there had been *11* black MVPs in the 17 years since Jackie Robinson entered the league. This also was an obstacle Doby faced in 1954 and a problem that probably also entered the picture in 1955.

In most years, a close vote involved only two men, but in 1955, the closest three-man finish to that time in either league occurred. A blanket covered the three men: the ever-present Berra, batting champion Al Kaline, and Cleveland right fielder, leadoff hitter, and Negro leagues graduate Al Smith. There exist two vote counts and it is not known which is correct. In one, Berra had 218, Kaline 201, and Smith 200; and in the other, it was Berra 208, Kaline 202, and Smith 201. In either case, it was close.

Kaline had come out of nowhere to become the youngest batting champ ever and lead the Tigers to their first .500 record and first division finish since 1950, so his support is easily understood. Berra had the usual super year that had come to be expected of him: 27-108-.272, with 84 runs, as his Yankees reclaimed the pennant.

Smith, however, like Kaline in only his second full major league season, was the top leadoff hitter in the league, if not in the majors, with numbers of 22-77-.306, and a league-leading 123 runs. He led Berra in runs produced, 178 to 165.

The final result was brought about by the N.Y. writers not listing Smith above fifth on their ballots and — this is hard to believe — the *Cleveland* writers not voting him higher than sixth!

It was explained by the writers. "The Yankees won the pennant," they said, "and the MVP should be from the pennant winners." But in '54, Cleveland had won the pennant and Doby still finished second and Berra still won.

The 1955 season was only one of several good years enjoyed by Al Smith in his 12-year major league career. He was selected for the All-Star game in two years and played in two World Series — the only two the Yankees didn't play in from 1949 through 1964. (Here's a trivia question: Who are the only two A.L. players who appeared in both World Series during that time in which the Yankees did not appear? Smith and Early Wynn.)

In high school in St. Louis, you were a football star and Golden Gloves boxer in addition to being a baseball star. Were there options other than baseball?

Football was one of the options, but my coach — high school coach — said that I could last longer playin' baseball and that's the route I've taken.

This was 1946. Was there any interest from the white leagues?

No. I was in St. Louis but I started playin' with the Cleveland Buckeyes of the Negro league. Sam Jethroe was from East St. Louis and I had played on a semi-pro team and he went up playin' with the Buckeyes and he told them 'bout a short-stop — I was playin' shortstop then — and that's how I got with the Buckeyes. I was there '46 to '48.

Who were the best players you saw there?

Oh, boy, there were quite a few. Cool Papa [Bell], Biz Mackey, the catcher; and Frank Duncan [Sr.], Sam Bankhead — that's Dan Bankhead's brother; Willie Wells, Sr., Ray Dandridge, Buck Leonard — I can go on and on. Josh [Gibson], you know. The first team I played against he was on when I left St. Louis goin' with the Buckeyes.

Did he have as much power as the legends say?

Um-hm. He could hit the ball a *long*, *long* way. He died in 1947, right after I signed.

Who were some of your teammates?

Well, you had Willie Grace, Sam Jethroe, Quincy Trouppe, who went up with Cleveland [Indians]. Jethroe went to the Boston Braves.

Did you see Satchel Paige?

Yeah, I hit off of him. He was with the Kansas City Monarchs. Connie Johnson threw harder than Satch. He hurt his arm

Al Smith with Cleveland Indians, 1954 (courtesy of National Pastime).

just before he came to the big leagues. Sad Sam Jones, he was playin' with me over at Cleveland.

Did you travel the country playing?

If you was chosen on the All-Star team. I was picked on the All-Star team to play against the major league All-Stars. That was in 1947. I was 18, comin' outta high school. I played against Stan Musial, Dizzy Dean, Cliff Mapes, who was up with the

Yankees, DiMaggio—both Joe and Vince. I did fairly well as a kid, you know. It was more exciting than anything.

The Indians sent a scout to check out Sam Jones and saw you.

Yeah. They were lookin' at Sam Jones pitchin', and like I say, I was playin' shortstop. Eddie Plasick and Tris Speaker, I think, was scoutin' for Cleveland. We used to play at the old League Park, where Cleveland used to play at. They asked me to come down and work out and I went down. The same day that Satch signed up, that's the day I went down and worked out.

That day they asked me to stick around there for about two weeks. That was in '48 and they finally sent me out to Wilkes-Barre, Class A [Eastern League]. They were wantin' to send me to Oklahoma City, but, you know, during that time that would've been a problem. [Laughs] I don't know whether it would be any more of a problem than it was, 'cause up at Wilkes-Barre I got hell up there.

After I got playin' with Wilkes-Barre, you had guys from Mississippi and everything and after I played with 'em for a while, they was all right. There weren't no problem.

If it don't be for a fella by the name of Bill Norman — used to play for [manage] Detroit — he was the manager there and he just got up and said, "Hey! I'm the manager here. They sent him down. I don't care what color he is, I'm playin' him. If you don't like it, pack your bags." That was all he said.

Bill was a *very* nice fella. And then, I didn't know for a long time, he's from St. Louis originally. I was livin' in the county of St. Louis — Kirkwood, Missouri. 'Course, that's just the way he was. He was a hard-nosed fella but he was a good, sound baseball man.

In 1950, I went to San Diego [PCL] and I

Al Smith (courtesy of Al Smith).

played the full year in '50, then I went in the army in December of '50 and I got out on a medical discharge in July that next year. That's the reason I didn't play but a few games [in 1951].

The Indians called you up from Indianapolis in '53 shortly after the All-Star break. Cleveland was one of the first teams to integrate. Were there any problems?

No, I didn't have a problem when I went there. Like I said, in '48, by goin' up and stayin' up there two weeks workin' out on a homestand, I got to know quite a few of 'em and when I went back up I didn't have no problems.

Your first full year in the major leagues was 1954, and you guys couldn't be beaten.

Oh, that was a hell of a ballclub. That was a club you'd like to have every year. [Laughs] Especially bein' the manager.

They didn't have a leadoff man and durin' spring trainin' [Al] Lopez shifted me up to leadoff. I started watchin' the ball, you know; I didn't swing at bad balls, and he just told me to get on base and let them guys drive me in. So I started chokin' up on the bat and gettin' close to the plate and I wore a big shirt — an oversized shirt — and I'd get hit. I'd bunt, get my basehits. 'Course, we had a fella by the name of [Bobby] Avila playin' second base. He hit second and Avila and I had a bunt-and-run play that I'd give him a sign that I was gonna steal and he'd bunt to third base and I'd keep on goin'.

I scored 128 [runs], or somethin' like that, and l led the league in '55 and I scored over a hundred [101] in '54.

You hit several leadoff home runs.

I played against some good ballplayers and I found myself thinkin' more of the pitchers. See, they didn't wanna walk me because they knew that Avila was up next, then you had Doby and [Al] Rosen. I would get good pitches to hit, so I'd look for the fastball first pitch and I'd hit it out.

You took the place of a man who was an outstanding hitter: Dale Mitchell. How in the world did you beat him out when he was a .300 hitter year after year?

They said all Mitchell wanted to do was just get basehits, he wanted just the average. I could run, I could throw; they moved me over to right field and I think that was it. I could do everything he could do. I think he'd wind up sometime hittin' six, seven, maybe eight home runs.

You were very fast, but bases weren't stolen then.

Durin' that year, you didn't have to worry 'bout stealin' no bases 'cause we'd score eight–ten runs, you know. I knew how to run the bases. I knew the guys that I was playin' against in the outfield and like if Doby or Rosen hit one in the gap and I was on first base, they'd have to throw me out at home plate. A lot of times, [Tony] Cuccinello [third base coach] — I'd get to third base and I'd always told him close his eyes, don't wave, and that'd let me know that I had a chance, because if you wave, a lot of times that'd give a signal to the [fielders] that I was goin'. I'd get around

'bout, say maybe 15 to 20 feet from third base and I could look at him and tell if he wanted me to go.

You walked quite a bit.

Yeah. Eighty–ninety times. In 1954, Avila and I, we was, with walks and everything, 600-and-some times at the plate. I think that year I had close to a hundred walks. Our on-base was a pretty good percentage with Avila and I. [In 1954 and '55, Smith had an on-base percentage of .406.]

What about the 1954 pitching staff?

[Laughs] I'd take that any day. [Bob] Lemon — that was one fella I even hated to hit battin' practice off of. I didn't like him. Oh, he was tough! Damn, I'd say, "Lemon, throw me a curveball," and it looked like a slider. Well, I'd say, "Throw me your slider then," and it looked like a curveball. He was really tough! I could see why this man would win 20, 23, 20, 21 for about six, seven years.

And, 'course, [Early] Wynn was a hell of a battler. Wynn would knock you down, move you off the plate, changeups — and he threw hard. He knew how to pitch. He'd win 20, 22, 23.

But the guy that I think was the backbone of that pitchin' staff — any fellas that played durin' that time would tell you — was [Mike] Garcia. Garcia won 19 games that year and I'm pretty sure we never scored over two or three runs whenever he pitched, but with Lemon and Wynn we'd always get 'em eight, ten, twelve runs. [Laughs] I think Garcia was 19-and-8 or 19-and-10 or somethin' like that and the games he lost I don't think we scored maybe 11 runs, so he could've very easily won 25-27 ballgames that year if we had scored runs for him. He could throw hard, he had a hell of a sinker, and he could reach back and get it.

And, 'course, [Bob] Feller won 'bout 10 [13] games that year, pitchin' as the fourth starter every now and then to give them guys a rest. And then you had Art Houtteman that they got from Detroit. Houtteman won 15. And then we had a fella that I always did care about — he's one of the older fellas we got from Detroit. [Hal] Newhouser. He knew *how* to pitch. He would come in and he was a battler. He knew how to go. I think Newhouser won 'bout 10 [7] games or so that year.

And then we had [Ray] Narleski and [Don] Mossi, two relief pitchers — a righthander and a lefthander. Narleski'd throw hard. He'd come in like bases loaded, need to get one man out — he could do it. And then we had a relief pitcher, Dave Hoskins. He was a long reliever. Like I say, we had a hell of a pitchin' staff.

Mel Harder was your pitching coach.

Yes, sir. I saw Mel two years ago when they inducted me into the Ohio Hall of Fame over in Toledo. He knew 'bout pitchin'.

You played both infield and outfield. What was your favorite position?

Oh, I'd say, when I was in the minor leagues, infield, but they told me it was best for me to learn the outfield because Rosen was playin' third base and I could get to the big leagues quicker. I started playin' the outfield and when I got up there, Doby helped me out a hell of a lot. First, he'd sit you down and he'd tell you the pitchers on your ballclub and then the hitters off the other club and then he'd just say, "If I move to my right, I want you to move to your right." And if he'd shift over, he'd shift me over.

After a while, you get to learn the hitters on the other teams and like with Garcia, you're not gonna get the fly balls like you would off of Wynn 'cause Wynn was a high ball pitcher. Same way with Lemon. Lemon was a sinker ball pitcher, so you wasn't gonna get the fly balls like you would off of Wynn. So you get to learn those little things.

You had a 22-game hitting streak in 1956.

Let me tell you 'bout that. I had a 22-game hittin' streak and we was playin' New York and Allie Reynolds was pitchin'. Lopez always say that Allie never would move off the mound, and I push-bunted to first base

and Allie never covered first base. And do you know, the Cleveland writer give an "error of omission" [to Reynolds]. [In those days, the official scorer for each game was a different writer from the home city.] I had never heard of that. And I went on and had a 12 more game hittin' streak. I would've wound up with a 35-game hittin' streak.

And since we're on that, you look at the record. I never got a first place vote [for 1955 MVP] out of neither one of the sports writers there [in Cleveland]. And I could've won that thing. If one of 'em had give me a first place or second place vote, I could've won it. Look at the record. Kaline and I were right together and Yogi had a point or so more. Look back on the record and you'll find out that I don't think I got a sixth place vote from the Cleveland writers.

Yogi had 27 home runs. I had 22. Yogi drove in 108 and I think I drove in about 80 runs [77] and led the league in runs scored, 'bout a hundred walks [93], 180 or so hits [186] — only one thing he beat me in was home runs, by five. And, 'course, he drove in 108 runs, but, hell, he hit fourth place. They claimed that because they won the pennant — they beat us out — that's how come he got it. That's what they say.

I never lived that down. That's true. I go back there now and I see the older guys — the sportswriters — and I don't have too much to say to 'em. That year I got the Man of the Year award in Cleveland and I wouldn't even go to it. My wife and I come back to Chicago and I went to St. Louis. They looked for me and I would not go.

Cleveland traded you to Chicago.

I knew it was comin'. I can say that now. Nineteen fifty-seven, the last series that Chicago come there, Lopez told me, "Don't say anything," that he was tryin' to get me over there. And then durin' the winter of '57 I was traded.

You and Wynn for Minnie Minoso and Freddie Hatfield. Hatfield was a useful infielder, but that's about it. That does not look to be a very even trade.

He played part-time, but I think Wynn

had won quite a few games and I think what they were really basin' it on was that Wynn was gonna ask for money. And then Frank Lane [Cleveland general manager] was crazy 'bout Minoso. [Lane had traded for Minoso before.] That was the thing.

The Chicago fans did not take to you.

That's what I'm sayin'. Minoso was the fair-haired kid. It wasn't until '59 when they really stopped criticizin' every little thing that I'd do, or if I get a hit. In '59, we started playin'. That year I think I broke up 'bout nine or ten ballgames, drove in the winnin' run. And they started cheerin' me then.

Bill Veeck had an "Al Smith Night" for you in Chicago.

That was when he was tryin' to get the people to kind of forget. That night, when he had the Smith night, I think I dropped a fly ball and I think I went 0-for-4 or some-thin' like that. But it was a good gesture by him. Veeck was one hell of a guy. If he told you he was gonna do somethin', he didn't write it down. He did it. He had a mind of a elephant.

You went to Baltimore in 1963.

[Ed] Short, the general manager, and I, we had problems in Chicago. That year, Bill Veeck had promised me, said, "Al, if you have another good year, I'll give you some more money." I went and signed up for the '63 season, signed my contract. Short say, "Well, you already got your raise." I said, "That was the money that Bill promised me." So we got into a heated argument and I walked out. The next week I was traded. The year before, I tied the White Sox record — 28 home runs — and drove in, I think, 90-some runs.

How did you like playing in Baltimore?

It was all right. I felt that it was a ball-club that wanted me. I got the money that I wanted. And, 'course, they had [Luis] Aparicio and I both and they were tryin' to win a pennant down there but we didn't get the pitchin' until after I left. That next year, the guys started comin' in there like [Jim] Palmer and those fellas. If we'd had

Palmer and [Mike] Cuellar we'd've won that thing.

You were selected for the All-Star team two years.

We played two games in '59. I went in there in '55 runner-up to Williams — Ted — and '59 same way. [Laughs]

That's a good man to be runner-up to.

That's right. That's what I always tell everybody. "Hell," I said, "I was runner-up to a pretty good man." He's one of my best friends. He was sick there for a while and that kept me on the phone inquirin'. He's a real nice guy. He's doin' all right now.

People don't know the closeness that ballplayers have over the years. You go back to these old-timers games and everybody hits a home run and every pitcher wins 20, you know, and it's good seein' those guys. And then when one of 'em fall off by the wayside, it make you start thinkin' about yourself.

Is there one game that stands out?

Oh, I think the one game was that New York game in the Polo Grounds — the World Series in '54 — that catch that Willie [Mays] made. I think if he don't get the ball, we win that Series.

Did you think Mays had a chance at it when Vic Wertz hit it?

No, I didn't think he could catch it. I think that was 'bout 457 [feet] back in there — somethin' like that — and if the ball could've been like 30, 40 feet either right or left he'd never caught it 'cause it would've been up in the seats. Been up in the upper deck, rather.

Wertz hits the ball a mile and makes an out, then Dusty Rhodes comes up and hits a 250- or 260-foot pop fly for a home run.

That's what I said. [Laughs] 'Course, we had the same shot at it.

How about Wertz in that Series?

Oh, Wertz had a good Series. 'Nother thing, no excuse — Rosen didn't hit like Rosen of old and Doby didn't hit.

Who was the best player you saw?

Oh, let me see. I'm gonna tell you like this. I'm gonna take a 100-pound sack —

okay?— and I'm gonna throw about eight or nine players in this sack and then I'll tell you how it goes, all right? Okay, I'll throw Joe DiMaggio, Stan Musial, Willie Mays, Hank Aaron, Ted [Williams], Josh Gibson, Buck Leonard, and I would close it up, shake it around, and whichever one come out.

When you played against Leonard, he was an old man.

Yeah. Josh I think was 35. Buck was 'round 'bout 40. Satch was in his late 40s then, too, when Satch was playin' with the Monarchs. All them guys was up in age, but they was some hell of ballplayers.

Who was the toughest pitcher?

For me to hit off of? I'd say Allie Reynolds. He was really rough. Allie, Satch, Jim Bunning, Frank Lary. He's a guy that really give me problems.

You played with Nellie Fox. Does he belong in the Hall of Fame?

Yes, sir. Very good, steady ballplayer that gave his all. He had a certain amount of ability and used every bit of it. Most second basemen that you see, they hit like .220, .240. Nellie was always up around that .300, on base, gettin' hit by a pitched ball, things like that. Nellie was a better than average ballplayer.

Did you save souvenirs?

Some of 'em. Oh, I got the World Series film of 1954. I got all of awards — P. K. Wrigley Award and things like that — and a lot of pictures framed. Right now, I'm lookin' at where the beer spilled on my head.

That was the 1959 World Series. All I remember is that it was a home run by Charlie Neal.

What I did, I hustled back against the wall. The ball in Chicago was a lot of times dyin' down and I figured quick as I could get back to the wall, maybe I could jump and get it, but it made it to the second row.

It was hit like a line drive.

The guy that was reachin' up for it, he had set his beer on the ledge of the wall and when he got up, his coattail hit it and it hit down my head. I'd run to the umpire down the line and he told me what went on. I've got a sequence of eight shots of it. You see it when the guy gets up to get the ball, it was in the cup, then you see it startin' down, and then you see it when it hit me and when I ducked my head in the last picture and the cup was on the ground.

Do you receive fan mail?

Oh, yeah. I just sent out about 40 or 50. I get on the average over the course of a year probably 'bout 250 or 300. And I don't charge nobody anything. I've had people who send me money — checks — and I just put it back in there and send it back to 'em. I'm supposed to go to New York for a autograph session. I get paid for that, but as far as people askin' me to autograph, I do it.

Do you have any regrets from your baseball career?

Unh-uh. I wish I could go again. I enjoyed playin', the fans. I always feel like this here: The fans can boo all you want, long as they don't go down on the field and hit me. They got a right — they paid their money. That's the way I look at it.

We had one thing that happened to us. [Jim] Rivera and I, we was down there in the outfield in right field, catchin' fly balls, and some guy kept hecklin', callin' him a jailbird, and Jim wanted to go and we grabbed him. I told Jim, "Jim, there's no sense in that. That fella's ignorant." I said, "More likely he's had eight or ten beers and he's out here to let off his steam." We kinda talked to him.

I saw Jim at the Nellie Fox Society. They give us an award — Jim Landis, Jim Rivera, and myself — the outfield of 1959.

But, oh, yeah — I'd do it again.

ALPHONSE EUGENE "FUZZY" SMITH
Born 2-7-28, Kirkwood, MO
Ht. 6' ½"   Wt. 189   Batted and Threw R

Year	Team, league	POS	G	AB	R	H	2B	3B	HR	RBI	SB	BA
1946	Cleveland Buckeyes, NAL	3B										
1947		SS		214	38	61						.285
1948	Cleveland Buckeyes, NAL	OF	58	217	44	65	9	8	3	39	10	.300
	Wilkes-Barre, EL	OF-3B	68	231	37	73	8	8	1	30	5	.316
1949	Wilkes-Barre, EL	3B	139	521	112	162	27	17	12	82	11	.311
1950	San Diego, PCL	OF-3B-2B	104	326	73	81	13	4	10	50	11	.248
1951		OF	25	89	16	25	5	2	3	10	1	.281
1952	Indianapolis, AA	OF-3B	136	455	84	131	26	12	20	69	10	.288
1953	Indianapolis, AA	3B	86	313	72	104	20	7	18	75	9	.332
	Cleveland, AL	OF-3B	47	150	28	36	9	0	3	14	2	.240
1954	Cleveland, AL	OF-3B	131	481	101	135	29	6	11	50	2	.281
1955		OF-3B	154	607	123*	186	27	4	22	77	11	.306
1956		OF-3B	141	526	87	144	26	5	16	71	6	.274
1957		3B-OF	135	507	78	125	23	5	11	49	12	.247
1958	Chicago, AL	OF	139	480	61	121	23	5	12	58	3	.252
1959		OF	129	472	65	112	16	4	17	55	7	.237
1960		OF	142	536	80	169	31	3	12	72	8	.315
1961		3B-OF	147	532	88	148	29	4	28	93	4	.278
1962		3B-OF	142	511	62	149	23	8	16	82	3	.292
1963	Baltimore, AL	OF-3B	120	368	45	100	17	1	10	39	9	.272
1964	Cleveland-Boston, AL	OF-3B	90	187	25	33	5	1	6	16	0	.176

Record in Latin America

Year	Team, league	POS	G	AB	R	H	2B	3B	HR	RBI	SB	BA
1951-52	Ponce, PRWL	OF	64	242	54	71	9	5	9*	33	10	.293
1952-53		OF		210	39	56	15	7	4	28		.267
1953-54		OF	60	206	41	53	6	1	5	19		.257

Gene Collins

A Two-Way Player

NEGRO LEAGUE DEBUT: 1947

Gene Collins could pitch *and* hit. He was also fast and an excellent fielder, so to make full use of his talents, his managers would put him in center field on the days he wasn't scheduled to pitch.

He was a professional ballplayer from 1947 through 1961, and what records exist seem to indicate that the game held few mysteries for him as a pitcher or batter. He played in the Negro American League with the Kansas City Monarchs and had pitching records such as 9–3 and 7–1 and averaged more than 11 strikeouts per game (nearly 15 one season). In his only healthy season in organized ball, he joined Waterloo (3-I League) in mid-year and went 7–2 with 8.3 K's per game. Then, from 1953 on, he played in Latin America. Twice along the way, he led his league in strikeouts, once north of the border and once south of it.

But, as already mentioned, his bat would not let him only pitch. Some of his batting averages through the years were .299, .359, .336, .324, .317 and .356. He didn't show a lot of power in the United States, but he found a little in Mexico, belting 82 home runs in seven seasons down there.

Like too many, though, Collins came along at an awkward time. The Negro leagues were on their way out in the late '40s and early '50s, and white baseball was not yet ready to accept black players on an equal basis. Major league teams would give tryouts, even sign blacks, but most were doing it only in the token sense. "See, we tried. They can't make it," was said more than once by more than one team.

And that's too bad. There were many players like Collins who were probably good enough.

I got *many* a whipping all the way from the baseball field home because instead of doing what I was supposed to do around the house, I was out there playing baseball. We'd play until dark. Many times my mother would come down with a switch and she'd beat me all the way home. It was a standing joke around the neighborhood. They called me "Lefty" and they'd say, "Hey, Lefty, here comes your mother. You'll get your [rear] beat." And I knew it! And I couldn't outrun her. She'd run right

alongside of me and I was fast. [Laughs] She'd run right alongside of me whipping me with that switch. It still wouldn't keep me off that field.

How did you come to sign with the Monarchs?

I went to Kansas City to visit my father and I started playing with the Omaha Rockets, a semi-pro club, a traveling club. Mr. Barrett, he was connected with the Omaha Rockets. They used them sort of as a farm club where they would send players

1948 Kansas City Monarchs
(L. to R.): Buck O'Neil (manager), Connie Johnson, Jim LaMarque, Bob Thurman, Elston Howard, Gene Baker, Earl Taborn, Tom Cooper, Booker McDaniels, Willard Brown, Frank Barnes, Gene Richardson, Bill Breda, Herb Souell, Gene Collins, Curt Roberts, Mel Duncan. Bat boy in front (courtesy of Gene Collins).

to develop, and I was later signed by Kansas City after playing a short while for them. Earlier, I got my schooling playing in Detroit — the sandlots in Detroit.

You made your mark as both a pitcher and an outfielder.

Somewhat, yes, but mostly for pitching, but I was considered a pretty good outfielder, not much power but a good contact hitter.

Is there one game that stands out?

I pitched a no-hitter against New Orleans. That one stood out. In the later innings I noticed everyone was quiet in the dugout. I think about the eighth or ninth inning I realized that I was on the verge of accomplishing it. No one was talking to me and I didn't want anyone to talk to me. I was pumped up. There was a center fielder, Bill Breda; he made a diving catch in center field to save the no-hitter. That was in the ninth inning.

You played many years in Latin America.

One of the players — Earl Taborn, he was a battery mate of mine with the Kansas

City Monarchs — he was playing there in Vera Cruz and they needed a pitcher and he called Buck O'Neil to see if I was available. Buck O'Neil called me and I accepted.

How did the conditions differ in Mexico?

We were treated with more respect than we were traveling through the South. We encountered no prejudices in Mexico or other Latin American countries. It was quite relaxing to be able to play. We didn't have the tensions nor the stress. The children and the fans, they followed my wife and I around wherever we went, to a restaurant or wherever. We had to get used to it. We weren't used to people invading our privacy, but we enjoyed it. Sometimes it was rather annoying, especially when you were sitting down at a restaurant and people are standing out there watching every bite of food you'd take. [Laughs]

You mentioned lack of prejudice there. How serious was this playing in the South?

I'll tell you one incident I had. I was down in the bullpen in Tennessee and we had to run down our foul balls because of

Gene Collins (courtesy of Gene Collins).

You played in organized ball for a short period.

The White Sox bought my contract the last half of the season in '51 and I went to the 3-I League. I was the first black to play in the 3-I League, if I'm not mistaken, and then a week or so after that, a young pitcher from Providence, Rhode Island, Gideon Applegate, joined the team. I played for them for a little while. I was young, unschooled. I played at Waterloo for that season, then I had a little accident — a shoulder separation — and they sent me down to Superior, Wisconsin [Northern League]. I played there for a while.

Then, considering the treatment I was getting from Superior, I got an offer from Santo Domingo, Dominican Republic. The money was up front, they wired it to me right away, and the next thing I knew I was in Miami waiting for a plane. [Laughs]

I played in Venezuela and spent most of my time in Mexico after that. I didn't even bother about trying to get back to the States until I was about 27. San Antonio, they wanted to buy my contract from Poza Rica — I was playing there — but they wanted too much money for my contract.

You were an everyday player down there in addition to pitching.

Oh, yes. Even when I was with the Monarchs, there were times I would pitch one game, play the outfield the next game. In Mexico, I played outfield — center field — the first game of a doubleheader and then pitched the second game.

The White Sox were one of the more vigorous signers of Negro league ballplayers back then, but most never progressed. Today it looks as if it was only a token effort on their part.

That's exactly what it was. It was window dressing. Before the White Sox signed me, I had a tryout with a Yankee farm club.

economic reasons. I was down in the bullpen and a foul ball rolled to the fence and I had to outrun a young white boy and we reached it at the same time. He had part of the ball and I had part of the ball. He *demanded* that I give it to him and I laughingly told him to go ahead and try to take it. He tried to take it away from me; naturally I wouldn't let him. So he told me, he said, "You're supposed to call me 'Sir'! I'll tell my daddy on you!" I'm 21 years old and raised here in Detroit, so I said, "I don't care who you tell."

Buck O'Neil and the other older players who had been through that traveling through the South a number of years, they came down and talked to me. I never learned to accept it, but I just stayed away from those kind of people as much as I could.

There was myself; there was Luis Marquez, an outfielder, very fast, a Puerto Rican; there was Frank Austin, a shortstop, he was Panamanian. In spring training there, he outplayed this shortstop — his name was Aker, I think, or Acker, tall six-footer — but they released him and Marquez and sent me back to the Monarchs.

I developed a sore arm because of the weather in Florida — the breeze coming off the water, sleeping with no shirt on, and I developed a soreness in my elbow, so I had difficulty throwing as fast as I could. Bill Skiff was one of the coaches; he sent back word that I couldn't throw hard enough to break an eggshell. Two days later, after I arrived in Monroe, Louisiana, I pitched against the Chicago American Giants. I gave up one hit and struck out 13, but yet they said I couldn't throw hard enough to break an eggshell.

Now Frank Austin, they sent him back. Some team [Portland], I forget which team it was, in the Pacific Coast League, which was the next step — almost on a par with the majors — they picked him up and he won outstanding awards in the Pacific Coast League; I think he won Most Valuable Player, won the Golden Glove in fielding. Luis Marquez, I think he had a stint with the Boston Braves.

What it was, the blacks in New York were threatening to boycott the Yankees. They had gotten together and they were threatening to boycott the Yankee Stadium and demonstrate. They didn't want that, so they brought in myself and the two other players. They didn't try to help; they didn't try to teach or show us anything. No one ever instructed me on how to master my control or work with me. Window dressing, that's all.

The Yankees were reluctant to sign blacks, but the Boston Red Sox were the last to integrate.

That's Boston. Boston is *still* that way. [The blacks] are there, but they've isolated them. They kept them hidden. You couldn't progress unless you were a professional — a doctor, a lawyer, a teacher, something like that.

Who were the best players you saw along the way?

Well, let's see. Jackie Robinson was before my time. I joined them the last half of '47, so I missed Josh Gibson. I'd have to say Satchel Paige, Ernie Banks, Gene Baker. They were teammates of mine. Baker was a shortstop; after him was Ernie Banks. Elston Howard came out of high school and joined us as an outfielder, then we found out he could catch and we let him catch. I pitched against Willie Mays when he came out of high school for the Birmingham Black Barons. I pitched against him and played center field against him for Kansas City. Connie Johnson — he pitched for the White Sox for a while. I saw Buster Clarkson, Ray Dandridge, Cool Papa Bell, Dan Bankhead that had a stint with the Brooklyn Dodgers. We had some players that could play in the major leagues.

Did you see Bill Wright in Mexico?

I played against him in the winter league. He was living there; he had a restaurant and a family.

Did you become fluent in Spanish?

I wouldn't say fluent, but I can express myself; I can understand. I can go into Mexico right now and move around the city and talk to people and tell the people where I want to go. It's not fluent but it's passable.

I wouldn't trade my experience for anything in the world. We didn't make a lot of money but we met a lot of wonderful people. We had very little fighting among ourselves. I can count on my hand how many times I saw teammates fight one another. We played the game because we *loved* it. I would go anywhere, I would join any team to play baseball just as long as I made enough money to live off of. The experiences we had and the countries that we saw, the cities, it was educational in itself.

Who was the one best ballplayer?

Oh, boy. That's a tough one. There's so

many and to try to define one as the *best* I'd have to be able to sit down and look at their records, their production, their consistency. It's a tough question, but I'd have to go with who I knew and saw personally. I'd have to go with Willie Mays because he could do everything. He could hit, he could run, he could throw. He was a well-rounded baseball player. He could do everything.

I look at Barry Bonds. I see him drop some balls. We're all going to drop some, but I've seen some balls he should eat up. I look at these major league outfielders, how they *trail* balls. The balls are just a few inches from their gloves and they miss them. Here's a major league outfielder making millions of dollars and he's trailing the ball.

When I played, when Willie Mays played, when Cool Papa Bell played — I watched them play outfield. At the crack of the bat you'd look at it, you'd get your sound and you'd look at the ball — the trajectory — and you hear that crack and you know it's hit solid and you see the ball going up, you go back to the fence, then turn around and come back in if you have to. We were either there or we'd have to come in to make the catch.

These guys — they see the ball and they're looking at it and they're back-peddling or they're running sideways. Willie Mays and Cool Papa Bell, they used to turn their back to the infield at the crack of the bat — they'd take one look to see the ball leave the bat, they'd turn their back because they knew the sound of the ball off of the bat. That's the way I played. That's the way it's supposed to be played. You can't float.

I have few memories of crashing into the center field wall. Only three. One incident, the ball was hit over my head, I went back, back, went up to catch the ball and my foot went through the wooden fence. This was in Poza Rica, Mexico. I got back and I went up for the catch and my right foot went through the fence I hit it so hard. There I was. I made the catch, but I'm hanging by my right foot 'til the players came out — rushed out — and lifted me up so they could get my foot out of the fence. [Laughs] Luckily I wasn't hurt. I didn't even tear the skin. This is the way we played the game.

Would you be a ballplayer today if you were a young man?

Oh, yes. Without a doubt. It was my life. I get out now — I'm 70 years old — and play catch and field balls. I retired when I was 62, 64, and for three years in a row I played softball — slow pitch — and we won the championship three years in a row and I played *every* game. I can hit the ball. I can field; I still can move and field. I can pitch. Before I stopped completely, I played first base because I didn't like that slow pitch.

Do you follow baseball today?

Oh, yes. I'm a National League man because of the type of baseball they play. That's the type I played. You know — digging, scratching, getting down in the dirt, and hustle. That was me. I didn't believe there was a ball hit that I couldn't get to, I couldn't catch. I didn't believe anybody could get me out.

One of my favorite ballplayers was Pete Rose. Willie Mays. Jackie Robinson. Red Schoendienst. Stan Musial. The pitchers — Sandy Koufax, Bob Gibson. Those guys that could throw the ball and they fought you tooth-and-nail. They wouldn't give an inch.

Before we finish, I want to say this. There's been a lot said about John "Buck" O'Neil for the energy and the devotion that he's put into preserving the accomplishments of former ballplayers. I would say we've been exploited ever since we played. They're still doing it now. These different organizations are making millions of dollars and they're only sending the ballplayers a pittance. There's something wrong.

EUGENE MARVIN COLLINS
Born 1-7-23, Kansas City, MO
Ht. 5' 8"   Wt. 168   Batted and Threw L

Year	Team, league	G	IP	W	L	Pct	H	BB	SO	SHO	ERA
1947	K. C. Monarchs, NAL										
1948		17	93	9	3	.750	53	57	97		2.32
1949		18	117	8	9	.471	87	80	131*		3.38
1950		3	20	3	0	1.000	7	19	20		0.90
1951	K. C. Monarchs, NAL		74	7	1	.875			117		
	Waterloo, III	25	77	7	2	.778	45	93	71		3.27
1952	Colorado Springs, WL			1	2	.333					
	Superior, NorL			1	0	1.000					
1953	Colorado Springs, WL			1	1	.500					
	Superior, NorL			2	2	.500					

Record in Latin America

Year	Team, league	G	IP	W	L	Pct	H	BB	SO	SHO	ERA
1948-49	Caguas, PRWL			10	9	.526			157*		
1949-50	San Juan, PRWL		21	0	2	.000		34	19		7.29
1950-51	Pampero, VenL										
1953	Escogido, DRSL	4	13	0	2	.000					8.10
1955	Aguila, MexL	26	111	7	5	.583	121	104	82		4.62
1956		4	17	0	1	.000	7	17	21		3.18
1957		3		0	1	.000					
1958	Poza Rica, MexL	8	64	5	3	.625	40	53	47		3.09
1959		9	49	2	4	.333	58	44	45		5.51
1960		3		0	1	.000					

Batting Record

Year	Team, league	Pos	G	AB	R	H	2B	3B	HR	RBI	SB	BA
1947	K. C. Monarchs, NAL	P-OF										
1948		P-OF	18	37	7	9	2	1	0	2	0	.243
1949		P-OF	26	77	13	23						.299
1950		P-OF	72	242	33	55	8	4	3	37	3	.227
1951	K. C. Monarchs, NAL	OF-P		181	38	65		8	3	39		.359
	Waterloo, III	P-OF	25	59	9	9	4	0	1	4	0	.153
1952	Colorado Springs, WL	OF-P										
	Superior, NorL	OF-P	31	120	19	32	4	3	3	22	3	.267
	Wisconsin Rapids, WiSL	OF	79	310	47	88	17	5	6	57	6	.284
1953	Colorado Springs, WL	OF-P										
	Superior, NorL	OF-P	18	51	6	10	1	0	0	4	3	.196

Record in Latin America.

Year	Team, league	Pos	G	AB	R	H	2B	3B	HR	RBI	SB	BA
1948-49	Caguas, PRWL	P										
1949-50	San Juan, PRWL	P										
1950-51	Pampero, VenL	OF-P	28	104	9	37	9	2	0	17	1	.356
1953	Escogido, DRSL	OF-P		7	0	2	0	0	0			.286
1955	Aguila, MexL	OF-P	73	241	56	81	10	4	13	36	2	.336
1956		OF-P	99	366	53	101	17	4	8	49	4	.276
1957		OF-P	81	287	41	79	12	23	7	35	4	.275
1958	Poza Rica, MexL	OF-P	105	395	73	128	26	4	17	63	8	.324
1959		OF-P-1B	122	430	67	121	22	4	7	46	8	.281
1960		OF-P	103	353	62	112	26	3	13	50	5	.317
1961	Poza Rica											

Chuck Harmon

The Black Red

NEGRO LEAGUE DEBUT: 1947

Chuck Harmon had one of the shortest Negro league careers on record: five days. It began as an alternative to a summer job that didn't come through and ended when the job finally did materialize.

Later that same summer (1947), he became one of the first members of his race to be signed by organized baseball, but that career, too, sputtered initially. To retain his amateur status for college basketball, Harmon did not play professional baseball at all in 1948.

When he reentered pro baseball in 1949, he had to overcome a leg injury that had ended his college basketball career. He did, compiling a minor league batting average in the mid–.300s, and by 1954 he was in the major leagues, becoming the first American-born and second black to play for the Cincinnati Reds. He just missed being the first. In the seventh inning of the third game of the season — a loss to Lew Burdette and the Milwaukee Braves — Nino Escalera, from Puerto Rico, pinch hit for catcher Andy Seminick, the eighth batter in the order, to become the first official black Red. Harmon then pinch hit for pitcher Corky Valentine, the next scheduled batter.

Not allowed to stay in the lineup for any extended period of time, Harmon never got into a groove in his stay in the majors. There were a few times, though, when he did play a few games in a row and on those occasions he gave a glimmer of what he may have been able to accomplish. For instance, twice in his rookie year he was in the starting lineup for the better part of a week. The first time, in mid-season, he went 7-for-20 in a six-game stretch, then in September he went 8-for-20 in a stretch of five out of six games. On both occasions, he essentially did not play for the next two weeks.

Before baseball, you were a successful basketball player at the University of Toledo.

In the 1942-43 season, we were invited to the New York Madison Square Garden to play in the NIT, which was the big tournament back then. I think it started out with 32 teams and we ended up in the finals with St. John's of Brooklyn. They beat us, 49-to-29, or something like that, but it was a close game; at the halftime the score was 22–22 and they went on a spree. At that time you could goaltend and they had a big center — seven-foot or something like that — and he would swat everything off the backboard.

That spring of '43 I got drafted out of college — April. They drafted by numbers then and when your number came, you went. I was stationed at Great Lakes, Illinois, at the Naval Center. I stayed up there

'43, '44, '45. The last month I was in the service I was stationed in Virginia.

We had a basketball team at Great Lakes and also a baseball team. 'Course, this was a black team. Back then you couldn't play sports with the whites in the service. Of course, in college you did. That was the funny thing. You go in the service to fight for your country and then you're segregated. They had what they called the black navy and the white navy. The army was the same way. You played together in most of the high schools and colleges all over the country, except down south. Guys I went to school with, you go in the service and you couldn't play with 'em but you played with 'em in college. Your government segregated you.

I came out in '46 — the spring — and I went back to school that fall, back to Toledo. I got hurt in my final year of college — '48-'49 season — in basketball and I was out from around January on to March.

In the summer of '47 I signed with the Clowns. A promoter [Hank Rigney] from the Negro leagues lived in Toledo. I was trying to get a summer job; I was supposed to get on in Toledo on the playgrounds with the recreation department and when school was out it still hadn't come through, so this promoter — scout — asked me if I wanted to go play ball with the Indianapolis Clowns. I didn't want to sit around waiting for a job, so I signed.

I think my salary was $175 a month, or $200. I didn't exactly sign a contract. At that time, they gave you a letter introducing you to the team and the management, stating that Chuck Harmon has signed with so-and-so. That's all you had; you didn't really have a contract.

I met up with 'em on a Wednesday and we played Wednesday night in Indianapolis. We played the Kansas City Monarchs. Right after the game we left to go to Flint, Michigan, to play on Thursday. I think we played the Monarchs up there. You ride up there all night and part of the next day to get there and you get up there at nine or ten o'clock on Thursday, then right after the game that night you get on the bus and we went to Fort Wayne, Indiana, to play Friday night.

We got rained out, so we stayed in Fort Wayne overnight, then we went to Michigan City, Indiana, the next day — Saturday — and it was still raining, so we're rained out. We go on in to Chicago and we got a doubleheader with the Chicago American Giants at Comiskey Park that Sunday.

I decided that wasn't for me. Being in college, you traveled first class on trains and stayed in the best hotels, so I told the general manager that I was gonna leave the team. I told him I called back to Indianapolis to my sister's house and she said I had a telegram from the athletic director at Toledo stating that the job I was supposed to be getting came through and he wanted me to come back to take it. I was trying to quit gracefully.

Next morning, we left Chicago to go back to Indianapolis. They were trying to talk me out of it. When we got back to Indianapolis I called my sister and, sure enough, there *was* a telegram there from him so I wasn't a liar after all. [Laughs] You didn't want to be a quitter, but it just wasn't something that I wanted to try at that time. I was never used to anything like that. It wasn't right for me at the time.

I may have pinch run or I may have batted once, but I really don't remember what I did. You're a rookie, so you're exactly nothing on a team. The good thing about it, Goose Tatum was the first baseman; he was one of the superstars on the team and he knew about me from playing college basketball and he took to me right away when I joined 'em in Indianapolis. Goose was from around Toledo anyway and he played a lot of basketball with the Globetrotters all through there. We became good buddies.

When you're a rookie you sit in the back of the bus 'cause all the regulars, they get the seat by themselves. You know, you gotta sleep on the bus, so all the regulars, they

Chuck Harmon with the Cincinnati Reds, 1954 (courtesy of Chuck Harmon).

have a seat but if you're a rookie you just gotta sit where you can. He let me sit up front — he had the big seat in the front — so I had it pretty good. Nobody messed with me because of Goose.

It was an experience, but I just wasn't ready for it. I remember watching those guys play when I was a small kid back in Indiana; the team used to come down to Washington, Indiana, to play our semi-pro team. Oh, those guys could play some kinda ball and just to think: Here I am on the team. Am I really here? Am I good enough? That's one reason why I hated to quit.

Back then, if you played a pro sport you were ineligible for college in that sport, so I played under the name Charlie Fine. Goose Tatum gave me that name. He didn't want me to get in trouble and be ineligible to play in college. A lot of people played under a fictitious name. Monte Irvin did the same thing — he played under a fictitious name the first year.

When I got back to Toledo, my job was there waiting for me at the recreation department. This was June and I worked there about a month and then the same scout that got me the job with the Clowns, he scouted for the St. Louis Browns, too. Toledo was a St. Louis Browns farm club — Triple-A team. He asked me if I wanted to go play pro ball and, of course, I jumped at it.

I thought I'd go right with the Browns, but the same day I signed Willard Brown and Hank Thompson signed with them in St. Louis and they stayed with the big club. I signed in Toledo. Bill DeWitt, one of the owners of the Browns and the general manager, had seen me play in the service up at Great Lakes. The major league teams used to come into Great Lakes and play the white team. Mickey Cochrane was the manager up there and they had Virgil Trucks and all those guys. They really had a great team. He stayed over and watched our team play. Larry Doby played with us up there.

They sent me to upstate New York to play at Gloversville — Class C ball. That was around the first of July. I played out the season there.

In '48 they changed the rule about being a pro. If you're a pro in one sport, you're a pro in all of 'em. In '47 it was just the sport that you were playing that you were ineligible for. It didn't affect my college basketball, it just made me ineligible to play college baseball. In 1948, the NCAA changed the rules, said if you're a pro in one sport

you're a pro in all the sports, but they gave everybody in college that was playing another sport to go ahead and play and they wouldn't be ineligible, but they couldn't play any more pro ball. So in '48 I gave up pro baseball so I could finish basketball in college, in the '48 and '49 season.

So in 1948 in the summer, to make some money, my basketball coach, Jerry Bush, who played with the Fort Wayne Zollners — Pistons — which is Detroit now, he got me a job playing semi-pro [baseball] over in Fort Wayne with G.E. I went over there and tried out and made the team. I was the only black on there.

A lot of the guys worked for General Electric — I guess about half of 'em. The other half worked other places or didn't work at all. We played about three or four times a week and we had several guys that lived within fifty to a hundred miles of Fort Wayne and would come over after work and play. We had a pretty good ballclub because we had several ex–major league ballplayers.

When I was with Gloversville — Class C — I was making 175 or 200 a month. I was making 150 a month *more* playing semi-pro ball and you're still eligible for college. [Laughs]

We got invited to the tournament out in Wichita — semi-pro tournament. I think 32 teams were in it. Fort Wayne won it two years in a row. I think they were runner-up in '47; I know we won it in '48 and then they went back and won it the next year. I was just there in '48 and I was fortunate enough to win the Most Valuable Player award of the tournament.

I got hurt in '49 in college and that slowed me down some. I went back to play baseball at Gloversville. I didn't go to spring training 'cause my leg wasn't in good shape yet, but I joined the team after they got back from spring training and stayed there in '49.

My leg never did heal that good so they sent me down to Class D ball in Olean, New York. Down there we happened to

Chuck Harmon, 1995, in replica uniform (courtesy of Chuck Harmon).

have a trainer that was a physical therapist and he worked on my leg and got it back in good shape. I ended up having a good year the second part of the year down there and I got recalled to Gloversville at the end of the season.

The St. Louis Browns were sold during the winter and a lot of the players in the farm system were released. During the win-ter, Olean, since I had played down there the last half of the year and had a good sec-ond half — I hit about .360 — signed me. They went independent since the Browns let the franchise go. Some people there bought the franchise, so I signed with them.

I went back down there in '50 and '51 and played. In '50 we were runner-up for the pennant and won the playoffs, and we did just the opposite in '51. I had good years — .375 or something like that each year and around 140 RBIs both years. So for '52, they sold my contract to the Reds and they sent me to Toledo — Triple-A. I went to spring training with Toledo and I didn't make the ballclub. After spring training they sent me to Burlingfton, Iowa, the Reds' Class B ball team in the 3-I League.

The Reds elevated me up to Tulsa in '53 — Double-A ball, Texas League. Then the Reds bought my contract and put me on the Reds roster at the end of the season in '53, but due to the fact that the manager they had at Cincinnati — Rogers Hornsby, he was a pretty fair ballplayer — didn't really care for blacks so the Reds wouldn't bring me up and I didn't join the team. They fired him during the winter.

They sent me to winter ball down in Puerto Rico and I hit about .327. I think I was second in the league in hitting down there. That's when I ran into Hank Aaron. He finished about three points under me. He hit .323 or something and Luis Marquez, I think, that played with the old Braves, he hit .329, .330.

They had a lot of hard throwers down there. Bob Turley and Arnold Portocarrero were down there and Jack Harshman, left-hander for the White Sox, and Karl Spooner, lefthander for the Dodgers. We had Jack Sanford, Steve Ridzik. Howie Judson pitched for us that pitched here for the Reds. It was a really good league and that made it almost sure I was gonna make the Reds. All I had to do was do a little something in spring training and I was set. I went to spring training and I did all right, so I stuck with the big club all year.

Nino Escalera was Puerto Rican and I was the first black Afro-American to play for the Reds. He was the first modern-day because the Reds had some black ballplayers back in the early 1900s. [See note on pp. 257–258.] Jackie is credited as being the first modern-day black. The old Toledo team back in the 1800s had some. A lot of black ballplayers were playing under Spanish names. Look at the Washington Senators. They had a lotta guys.

You consistently batted in the mid– to high–.300s in the minor leagues as an every-day player, but in the major leagues you were never in the lineup on a regular basis. Did you get a fair shot?

Well, you know I'll say no. [Laughs] The thing was, I wish I could've got a shot. I played down there in winter ball against major league pitchers. The first couple weeks down there in Puerto Rico that first year in '53 I wasn't doing nothing — wasn't hitting — and they were getting ready to ship me out. I wasn't a home run hitter; I hit a few but I was an RBI man — I'd get you in. They were gonna send me home but one weekend I tore the ball up — hit a couple home runs, triples, everything — and then ended up almost winning the batting title.

With the Reds, you weren't in the lineup. The last part of the season in '54 or '55, I was in the lineup I guess the last 20-some games and I played straight and I did real good. But you were always in and out of the lineup. Bobby Adams and myself, we used to tease each other. You go out there and have a 3-for-4 day or something like that and the next day he'd say, "Well, I guess you're out of the lineup today." [Laughs] And, sure enough, you weren't in the lineup. You had too good a day, I guess.

I would have just liked them to say, "The job is yours," and that would've been it. I know what I could've done. I was one of them guys, I had to play. I never could get my eye platooning and playing here and there.

What was your best game? At any level.

I can recall one of my best and worst games was the same game, playing in Class D ball at Olean. We were playing Hornell and I hit three home runs, a double off the wall, and I struck out three times with the bases loaded. The score was something like 17-to-18. Hornell had a short fence and center field was the shortest part of the park, and all you had to do was hit a popup and it would go out. [Don] Zimmer played at Hornell [in 1950]. You go up there and you're swinging for that fence, you know, and, 'course, with the bases loaded I'm up there swinging from the heels every pitch. But I wasn't a home run hitter. That's why I hit for a high average; I just tried to hit the ball. You hit a home run when you meet the ball, not when you're trying to.

In the major leagues, against the Phillies on Charlie Harmon Day, I think I had 3-for-4. That was a good day, too.

I always thought it was a bad day if I didn't get at least three hits. You always wanted to stay over .500, you know.

Who was the best player you saw?

One of the best was Vic Power. You can't take anything away from Willie [Mays]. Willie was my buddy and he was one of the best I ever saw, but I really admired Vic Power. He did everything so easy. I played with him down in Puerto Rico and just being on the team with him and listening to him — I mean, he'd just go up there and say, "I'm gonna get me a hit. I'm gonna hit this ball this place, this time," and he could just hit that ball anyplace. He'd say, "I'm gonna get me four hits today," and he'd go up there and do it. [Laughs] And he could really pick it in the field.

It's too bad his off-field habits weren't up to snuff with some of these clubs. The Yankees, they should've brought him up. When he came up it was with the Philadelphia Athletics. Being from Puerto Rico, color didn't mean nothing down there. In Kansas City, he always had two or three girls on his arm riding around in a convertible and that's why the Yankees would never bring him up. He was one of the best I ever saw.

Who was the best pitcher?

I played with Robin Roberts. 'Course, there was Warren Spahn and then there was Ruben Gomez. He was a pretty good pitcher, too. I played with him in Puerto Rico. To pick out one, I don't know. I played with Curt Simmons, too, but Robin Roberts was about the smoothest. 'Course, I never played with Spahnie — I just played against him. In fact, I got my first home run off of Warren Spahn here in Cincinnati.

[Don] Newcombe and Sal Maglie were good, but I didn't play against the righthanders too much. But batting against Robin Roberts was the easiest of all the pitchers I have ever faced, but you didn't get a hit off of him. [Laughs] And I *hated* to go up against Curt Simmons. I hated it, but I hit him. I didn't want no part of Newcombe at all. He was mean and that ball was too fast. He'd throw that big foot — that number 13 shoe — up there in the air and let it come.

Would you go back and be a ballplayer again?

I certainly would. The only thing, I'd hope that I'd get a chance in the big show to do what I knew I could do.

That's the only regret I have. I didn't think I got a chance to really say, "This is your job."

CHARLES BYRON HARMON
Born 4-23-24, Washington, IN
Ht. 6' 2"   Wt. 175   Batted and Threw R

Year	Team, league	Pos	G	AB	R	H	2B	3B	HR	RBI	SB	BA
1947	Indianapolis Clowns, NAL	OF										
1947	Gloversville, CanAmL	OF	64	200	24	54	10	1	0	29	6	.270
1948					voluntary retired list							
1949	Gloversville, CanAmL	OF	14	51	3	11	1	2	0	7	0	.216
	Olean, PONY	OF-3B	31	134	20	47	12	1	1	21	0	.351
1950		3B-SS-1B	125*	551*	125	206*	47*	10	22	139*	17	.374
1951		2B	113	467	107	175	37*	10	15	143*	24	.375
1952	Burlington, III	3B-OF	124*	479	97	153*	34*	6	5	71	43*	.319
1953	Tulsa, TxL	3B-OF	143	566	86	176	24	11	14	83	24	.311
1954	Cincinnati, NL	3B-1B	94	286	39	68	7	3	2	25	7	.238
1955		3B-OF-1B	96	198	31	50	6	3	5	28	9	.253

Year	Team, league	Pos	G	AB	R	H	2B	3B	HR	RBI	SB	BA
1956	Cinc.-St. Louis, NL	OF-3B-1B	33	19	4	0	0	0	0	0	1	.000
	Omaha, AA	OF	58	242	50	87	17	6	10	49	4	.360
1957	St. L.-Philadelphia, NL	OF-3B-1B	66	89	16	23	2	2	0	6	8	.258
1958	Miami, IntL	OF-3B	36	126	12	26	2	2	0	11	4	.206
	St. Paul, AA	OF-3B	38	143	18	41	4	2	0	9	1	.287
1959	Charleston, AA	OF	20	65	5	15	3	1	4	11	0	.231
	Salt Lake City, PCL	OF	118	449	64	139	22	9	7	90	9	.310
1960	Salt Lake City, PCL	OF	136	415	57	119	15	7	4	35	10	.287
1961	Hawaii, PCL	OF-INF	7	23	3	4	0	0	0	1	1	.174

Record in Latin America.

1953-54 Ponce, PRWL		3B	70	269	36	88	5	7	1	23	9	.327
1955-56		3B		278		82			5	26		.295

Clinton "Butch" McCord

One Step Away

NEGRO LEAGUE DEBUT: 1947

Butch McCord should have had a chance to play in the major leagues. He earned it.

In 1950, his last season in the Negro leagues, he batted .368; then, joining organized ball, he didn't skip a beat, putting up averages of .363 and .392 in his first two seasons. All together, he played 11 seasons in the minor leagues, batting better than .300 five times and .298 another. He won two batting titles and two Silver Gloves, indicative of the best fielding first baseman in the minor leagues. Three of the years and a portion of a fourth, he played in Triple-A.

His teams were always in contention; three of them won their league pennants. And he was voted the most popular player and given a special night, almost unheard of in minor league ball.

But there were only 16 major league teams then and integration was a low priority with most, so Butch McCord stayed in the minors, being used as a drawing card in addition to his contributions at first base. A good, hustling black ballplayer with a good attitude proved invaluable in boosting attendance in cities where interest lagged. In those days—the 1950s—many (most) teams had never had a black ballplayer. White fans would come to see the novelty and black fans would come to see one of their own, so McCord was placed below his playing level for that purpose.

He was aware of how he was being used and it made him a little bitter. A lesser man could have stayed bitter, but McCord overcame it slowly and now encourages kids to play the game. Today the opportunities are there that were not when he played.

By all accounts, from what I've heard and read, you were a pretty darned good ballplayer.

By some people's standards. [Laughs]

By your standards?

Well, I stretched but I was unable to reach the mountain top.

Whose farm system were you in?

I never was with a major league organization until my latter years. I finally got in the Dodgers system, but that was about time for me to get out of baseball. Most of the time, I belonged to independent teams and they had major league affiliations and most of the time, the affiliation wanted to send their ballplayers to play with the independent teams and they wanted to get rid of you.

In those days, most of the white teams weren't too eager to promote black ballplayers.

I knew that.

In 1950, we played a ballgame — the Chicago American Giants played a ballgame in Paris, Illinois. A fellow was on first base — I can't think of his name right now but when we were at the 75th Reunion of the Negro leagues in Kansas City on October 26–29, 1995, he apologized to me and I said, "What are you apologizing to me for?" He said, "You remember the time you hit that long ball to right field and I went half way and the ball went out of the ballpark and I was coming back and you passed me up and you lost a home run?"

But that helped me. The general manager of the Class D team's park we were playing in saw me. He asked me would I come and play with the Paris Lakers [Mississippi–Ohio Valley League] next year and I told him I'd play with him if I could play first base because on the Negro league teams I didn't get to play first base. I played outfield. Then when he said, "Yeah, you can play first base," I never played another game in the outfield.

Butch McCord, 1957, Louisville Colonels, American Association (courtesy of Clinton McCord).

You were a very good first baseman.

I was fortunate enough to win two Silver Gloves in the minor leagues.

You don't win those unless you're doing it right. Who was ahead of you at first base in the Negro leagues?

See, I was a student at Tennessee A & I State University in Nashville. In 1948, I went to Baltimore Elite Giants and I went there as a first baseman but they had a fellow named Johnny Washington. I wanted to play, and so they put me in right field. The next year I went back and they had a fellow named Lennie Pearson, so I had to continue to play right field. Well, in 1950 — that was the last year the Negro league teams were organized, they began to break up — they sold me to the Chicago American Giants and when I got there, they had a ballplayer named Joe Scott, so I had to play outfield again. [Laughs] So that's the reason I said what I said when we played in that little town. I actually walked on in organized ball; no one from the major leagues signed me.

When you played for Paris, the pitchers must have dreaded seeing you come up to bat.

That's what they said. [Laughs] You see, I was beginning to get into my own. I was actually 25 years old but I put my age back a little bit.

When I went to Pearl High School in Nashville, they didn't have a baseball team and where I went to college — Tennessee State University — they didn't have a baseball team. The only black schools in those days — SWAC, I think, Tuskegee , Morris

1949 Baltimore Elite Giants, champions of the Negro American League
(L. to R.): Ed Finney, Henry Kimbro, Johnny Hayes, Leon Day, Pee Wee Butts, Vic Harris (coach),
Butch McCord, Junior Gilliam, Bob Romby, Frazier Robinson, Al Wilmore, Hoss Walker (manager),
Butch Davis, Bill Byrd, Lennie Pearson, Leroy Farrell, Joe Black (courtesy of Clinton McCord).

Brown — teams like that had baseball teams, but teams in the Midwestern Conference and other schools in the CIAA, they didn't have baseball teams at that time.

Did you serve in World War II?

Yes, I did, and that took another two years off my baseball years. I went in the segregated U.S. Navy and they wouldn't let me play ball in that, so I didn't pick up a baseball the whole two years I was in there, either, so you can see I had to fight my way up.

How did you get into the Negro leagues?

You can say I was destined to play baseball. See, the Nashville Elite Giants originally were here and they had their own ballpark, but I was too young at that time but everybody saw me on the sandlots playing hard ball.

Incidentally, in the early '40s, when I was still in high school, Satchel Paige — I guess it was Kansas City at that time — came to Louisville and the team they were supposed to play had a serious problem; the bus broke down and they couldn't get there. It was an exhibition game anyway and they had a lot of prizes and things they were giving away that day and they didn't want to cancel the game, so they came to Nashville and the guys picked me to go with them and I was only 16 years old.

When I got there, Satchel was on the mound and I guess he took for granted — you know, I was small and a little kid but I could swing the bat pretty good. I don't think he put his stuff up and he threw me a pitch and I hit a triple off of him. [Laughs] Then next time up, he let me know who Satchel Paige was. [Laughs] I didn't take the bat off my shoulder.

Just before 1946, I returned from the service. Tom Wilson — he was the owner of the ballclub, they had moved from Nashville to Baltimore — and he wanted me to play on his team but he died that year. That was 1947, the same year that Josh Gibson died, so the fellow that used to be Tom Wilson's secretary had a ball team in the Negro summer league here in 1947, so I played with the Nashville Cubs, known as the Nashville Black Vols before then — it was the same team that Junior Gilliam used to play second base for. I played with the Nashville Cubs until the death of Tom Wilson and the team was under the supervision of Mr. Vernon "Fat" Green, who asked me to play with the Baltimore Elite Giants. They would let me join the team when school was out in the spring and that's the way I got into the Negro leagues.

So you were playing about two-thirds or three-quarters of a season.

Except 1950. I played the whole season.

For missing spring training and being out of baseball those years, you more than held your own.

Well, like I said, I was a small kid. Like Hank said, we didn't have no idea we were going to get to play in the major leagues or anywhere. My ambition was to be a baseball player. Lou Gehrig was my idol because he was a clean liver; he had all the attributes that I aspired to be and I wanted to be like him. I would go to Sulpher Dell and watch the Southern Association Nashville Vols play and we would get in free. Every Saturday I would pick me out a player that I liked and I would try to imitate him. I would return home and my friends and I would get out in the lot and I would imitate those particular guys and that's the way I learned, through imitation, how to play ball.

But when you do that, you miss a lot of fundamentals. It's like Jim Brown carrying the football. They used to see him carry that ball in one hand, but when he was tackled they never saw him bring that ball into his body. Stan Musial would stand in that crouch, but they never saw him when he got ready to swing; he was just as normal as any other batter.

Who were the best players you saw?

I played against some great ones. I got to play against Roy Campanella and I got to play against Satchel; I got to play against later players like Monte Irvin and Buck Leonard. Leon Day played with me. Hilton Smith. All those guys that were still playing except Willie Wells; and Don Newcombe and Larry Doby — they had already gone or were getting ready to go to the major leagues.

Who was the one best?

You may not think it, but the most gifted player I saw wasn't the greatest

Henry Kimbro (seated) and Butch McCord, August 1996 (author's photo).

ballplayer. The number one player, you know who that was.

Willie Mays?

That's right. The best player I ever saw. But next best was Hank Thompson.

He could hit the daylights out of a baseball.

Right. And lefthanders, too. That's what I admired about him.

It's a funny thing, when I first saw Billy Williams — I got to see him when he first started. When I was at Victoria [Texas League], Billy Williams was playing left field at San Antonio. J. C. Hartman was playing shortstop. First time Billy came he was small and he really didn't want to play then. He wanted to play outfield and they were trying to make him a first baseman and I was giving him pointers how to play first base. He would hit the ball between me and the second baseman and I'd get on our pitchers and say, "What are you throwing this little man? You ought to be able to get this little man out." Until we went over to San Antonio and he caught one and went over that scoreboard — have you ever seen Mission Park in San Antonio? — well, it went *over* that scoreboard and he made a believer out of me. [Laughs]

I just think about how many Hall of Famers I've played with or against, counting the Negro leagues and the white leagues. I hit a home run off Drysdale when he was with Montreal. I played against Gaylord Perry, but he wasn't putting all that stuff on the ball then. Any pitcher that threw low, because I was a lefthand hitter, I could hit the low pitch — at spring training in intrasquad games I played against Koufax, Joey Jay, Juan Pizarro, and Ryne Duren. Bobby Richardson and Earl Weaver played with me. I played against Sparky Anderson. I just happened to play against some good ballplayers.

I had trouble with Pittsburgh. They always wanted to use their ballplayers. That next year in Denver they had five first basemen but they had to end up taking me and that's when I jumped to Triple-A. I played a share at first base and pinch hitting and I hit .358. Pittsburgh wanted to send me to Mexico and I told Branch Rickey, Jr., I said, "I'm not going to Mexico. My wife doesn't speak Spanish and I don't speak Spanish." So I went home again. I did that twice. [Laughs] So Mr. Cooper — Harold Cooper was the president of Columbus — called me, said, "I have two teams you can go to. You can go to Louisville or you can go to Minneapolis." I picked Louisville because I figured I could save more money because it was close and my wife could come up on weekends. But if I had gone to Minneapolis, you know who they would have sent out? Orlando Cepeda. [Laughs] They kept him and he caught fire and he hasn't looked back since. Hank [Thompson] was with that team, too; Cepeda was playin' first,

Hank was third base. Wayne Terwilliger was playing second, I believe.

When did the Dodgers get your contract?

The Dodgers bought my contract from Detroit in 1958 and they sent me to Dodgertown in Vero Beach, Florida. I was promised a Spokane contract in 1958. While in Lakeland with Detroit, my contract was purchased by the same general manager that I had started out with in Paris, Illinois. Hillman Lyons was currently general manager at Charleston, West Virginia. He also was at Buffalo at one time, but, anyway, I was over there and they decided to sell me to the Dodgers system and they bought me to play with Spokane. So I spring trained the whole spring with Spokane expecting to go to Spokane and when the bus left, I was still in camp. [Laughs] I went to Fresco [Thompson] and I asked him, "What's the matter?" He said, "We're gonna send you to Macon, Georgia, and try to increase the attendance at this segregated ballpark." [Laughs] And I said, "No, you're not!" He said, "We're going to give you the same money and everything," but what they wanted me to do was go down there and bring in some people.

So I went home and my dad jumped all over me. "Man, I don't know what you're back here for! You mean you're going to give up!?" "Yeah," I said. "It's the general principle of the thing." Then the general manager, Jerry Ware, from Macon called me and he asked, "When are you coming?" and I said, "I'm not coming." He said, "We're going to give you the same money." Then he hesitated and he said, "Now what would it take for you to come to Macon?" I thought, they aren't going to do this. I said, "Okay. You pay my expenses on the road and at home and make my salary clear and I'll come." He said, "Come on," and I had to go.

Your record shows you were well worth the investment, but you were at least a level below where you should have been.

Yes, they knew that, but that's where I won my first Silver Glove. And I hit .305.

That was the Sally League, the same league that Aaron played in. But the brand of ball at that time wasn't that much different because you had a lot of ballplayers playing then — D leagues, C leagues, and all that. Now A ball and Double-A is not what Double-A and A ball used to be. Nowhere near. Now it's just a bunch of college ballplayers who just got out.

You were in your 30s by this time.

[Laughs] Yes, I was in my 30s. My experience was beginning to take over, not my agility, and I always said that's when I really learned how to play the ball. Luke Appling helped me a lot when I was at Richmond. I was the first black to play Triple-A ball in Richmond [1955] and they were segregated, too. I really had the confidence, but, still, I thought I might, as Ray Dandridge said, get a cup of coffee or go to spring training because eveything I tried, I made.

A player today with your individual season production wouldn't have spent a full season anywhere.

I realize that. I think about it and I say, "Well, if I came along today, would I have been the same and had the same temperament and the same principles that I had then?"

If you were raised by the same parents with the same values, you would.

You know, the peer pressure's so much different. You can do everything right and it still might not work out. Your 11-year-old kid, when you tell him he can't do something, what's the first thing he tells you? He'll say, "So-and-so can do it!" [Laughs] "How come I can't do it?"

We — the ballplayers — were much closer, too. When we played in the Negro leagues, most of us, we got dressed in the ballpark dressing room — home and visitors, both clubs — and you got to know each other. It wasn't nothing for you to come in there and see a guy sharpening his spikes for the other team. [Laughs] But when the game was over, it was over. If a player needed something, we'd try to provide it. We'd tell him the best places to stay,

the best places to eat, where to stay away from. Every player is an individual now, and it seems to be about money or who can get the largest contract. There is no genuine love or concern for their fellow ballplayers.

When I got into organized ball, that's where I met Bill White and Maury Wills. They used to come to my house and eat breakfast with me every morning in the old Western League. Incidentally, Bill helped me out at a fundraiser to get baseball back on the athletic schedule at TSU. Bill White came to Nashville on September 19, 1995, to speak at the dedication of the baseball park to be named in my honor. The scheduled opening date is spring of 1997.

So you're immortalized.

[Laughs] If you want to say it that way. I still haven't got over it yet.

You were a very popular player wherever you went. Was that a result of your hustle?

And my temperament, too. I was easy to get along with.

Any special memories along the way?

I guess I'm the only man ever to participate in four triple plays. I hit into two and participated in two. I'll always remember the one that Don Demeter got me in. We were playing at St. Paul, Minnesota, and the hit-and-run was on and I hit one deep to left-center. Don went up on that fence and everybody's going and I'm right behind them and he caught that ball and doubled all of us off. [Laughs] Another one, I think I hit straight back to the pitcher.

What about the ones you participated in?

One was around the horn and the other one was an unassisted triple play.

Any real regrets?

I was bitter for about 10 or 12 years after I left baseball. I wouldn't even go to a pro game, but I found the courage to put my career disappointment behind me and to forgive those persons who were responsible for my nightmares. It wasn't baseball, it was the people managing the game.

I began to see the problems of the inner city kids and I'm endeavoring to help them and that's the reason I'm trying to get baseball back to TSU because everybody can't play basketball or football. Especially at the black schools, they can give 15 or 20 boys a chance where most white schools will give [baseball] scholarships to about two or three boys and if you look at all the tournaments like the College World Series, the NCAA, you don't see many black schools.

I think the worst enemy that any inner city has is progress. When you have progress, you take up real estate and they either build shopping centers or hospitals or condominiums or parking garages and they don't build any more playgrounds. It's easy to put in basketball courts and tennis courts — it doesn't take that much space — so the inner city kid has no place to play near home and he has to go to the suburbs to play.

The kids today, especially the black kids, they'll play basketball the year around for the same reason I say: the courts are there. When we came along, there were a few more vacant lots and city parks had baseball fields and you could go play *free* baseball. You could grab a bat and ball and go play a game of baseball. But today, the motivation is not there.

Looking at television, you've got to *taunt* a player or you've got to show off when you make a touchdown and all the fights they're having now. They're saying it's not that far from a jungle now. It's ridiculous when the man was pitching that perfect ballgame and the man threw a curveball and it hit him and he went out there and messed up his perfect ballgame. The man wasn't trying to hit him. Not on purpose. The kids see that and there's no way in the world that you're in the limelight — that you get your name in the paper or they talk about you on television — some kid's not going to take you as a role model. They think doing this will get them in the limelight and get them a certain amount of money. Somebody's gonna notice them.

Just like playing basketball. When black kids get past Little League, who brings them? The mamas. The daddies don't do it; the mamas bring them. Now if we could make coaches out of the mamas, we'd have some great teams. After Little League, unless somebody invites those kids to go over there to play, they're not going, so when they get to high school, who are the coaches? They're white coaches. In the meantime, baseball is still being played by white players and basketball is dominated by black players.

All right — what's your revenue sports? Basketball and football. In the meantime, you all are still playing baseball. So if basketball and football are my revenue sports, I don't have to worry about having enough players to play baseball. It'll be all-white, so I get these black kids to play basketball and football. I'll take the basketball player and put him on the track team; take the football player, put him on the wrestling team or the strength team and don't worry about the baseball team because I'll have white players for the baseball team.

And then you've got the black kid now, he likes to be seen. His girlfriend's not going to come out there and watch the baseball team. He wants to go out there and come down the floor and shoot it pretty for his girlfriend where everybody can see him. But we still shouldn't give up. We need somebody to motivate those kids that there's other sports besides football and basketball.

You know, that [Rafael] Belliard with Atlanta — I really admire that man. He's so small but he's such a great ballplayer. He hustles every lick! I've never seen him loaf. That's a role model. All kids are not goin' to be able to be pros. Basketball, you've got to be at least 6-7 — that's a small guard. Football, you're gonna have to be at least 260, 270, 280, so look how many kids are going to be missed.

And then, we've got to impress on them to get the education. Education is the main thing. The sports, if you happen to be a pro player, that's a benefit. That will help you to enhance your education. And the smarter you are, the better ballplayer you're going to be. You begin to think.

The things I see today — the guys can't bunt like we did and everybody slides head first. We had to wear a mouth guard. They would've knocked some teeth out. [Laughs] But, see, then, on a double play, you could go get him wherever he went. But today, you've got to slide close to the bag to take him out of the game.

Would you play baseball today if you were a young man?

Oh, yes. I would play. And I'd try to get me some of that money. [Laughs] But

you've got to have a place to play and that's what we need to remind these government people — the mayors and the councilmen and councilwomen — we must have space in the inner cities for playgrounds. If we had some playgrounds, you wouldn't have to talk about midnight basketball. They should be in bed at that time. How are they going to school the next day after playing basketball at night? How are they going to work the following day?

But, yes, I'd play baseball.

CLINTON HILL "BUTCH" McCORD, JR.
Born 11-2-25, Nashville, TN
Ht. 5' 10" Wt. 168 Batted and Threw L

Year	Team, league	Pos	G	AB	R	H	2B	3B	HR	RBI	SB	BA
1947	Balt. Elite Giants, NNL	1B-OF										
1948		1B-OF										
1949	Balt. Elite Giants, NAL	1B	55	182	29	49						.269
1950	Balt.-Chi. Am. Giants, NAL	OF	31	106	19	39	1	0	1	14	5	.368
1951	Paris, MsOVL	1B	121	476	132	173	38	12	16	118	22	.363
1952		1B	119	482	123	189	40	15	15	109	20	.392
1953	Denver, WL	1B	101	299	39	84	19	2	5	39	3	.281
1954		1B-OF	85	246	43	88	18	4	6	61	4	.358
1955	Richmond, IntL	1B	139	462	49	119	18	9	4	52	4	.258
1956	Columbus, IntL	1B	147	488	62	134	23	3	8	52	0	.275
1957	Louisville, AA	1B	140	554	73	148	30	9	7	55	3	.267
1958	Macon, SAL	1B	137	501	70	153	37	2	10	81	8	.305
1959	Victoria, TxL	1B	136	526	80	157	27	6	10	57	1	.298
1960	St. Paul, AA	1B	17	56	2	15	0	1	1	6	0	.268
	Victoria, TxL	1B	117	420	61	126	19	1	7	56	3	.300
1961	Victoria-Ardmore, TxL	1B	53	172	20	49	10	0	0	15	0	.285

Al Surratt

"Slick"

NEGRO LEAGUE DEBUT: 1947

Slick Surratt got a late start as a professional ballplayer because of World War II. He was 29 years old in 1949 when he joined the Kansas City Monarchs at a time when the Negro leagues were on the decline because of the talent drain by the major leagues, so he didn't get the exposure and recognition he may have gotten a few years earlier.

He was probably seen by more people on TV in 1994 than he was when he played. He appeared on Ken Burns's *Baseball* documentary as one of the commentators on Negro baseball. His enthusiasm for the game was evident. He's come a long way from his boyhood in Danville, Arkansas.

I was born in a little ol' town called Danville, Arkansas. That's about 65 miles from Fort Smith and about 70 miles from Little Rock and about, I'd say, 55 or 60 miles from Hot Springs, right down in between two mountains and two rivers. That's in the western part. The county seat of Yell County.

I came to the Monarchs in 1949. I started with the Detroit Stars in 19-and-47. I think I was about 27 'cause I had just got out of the service in '46. I played right field and center field.

I guess about the biggest thrill I can remember was playin' in Yankee Stadium. That was a thrill. As a kid growin' up in Arkansas I had listened to all of the great guys that the Yankees had and never would've dreamed of bein' able to play in Yankee Stadium. That was one of the biggest thrills that I had.

And then another one was the first time I had barnstormed with Satchel Paige. When he would pick you out, you had to be kinda an outstandin' ballplayer. I had a

lotta thrills, but those two stand out in my mind better than any I know of.

You barnstormed against Bob Feller's team. How did you do?

I did all right. I never will forget the third base coach once — you know, Feller could *throw* — and he give me the bunt signal. I said, "Well, this guy's *got* to be crazy." So I squared around to bunt and we was in Youngstown, Ohio, and the bat went almost up in the press box. [Laughs] Then he got to laughing, you know, and I looked around and everybody in the dugout was laughing, too. But I guess I got lucky that day and I hit one right back up the middle for a hit off of Feller. I didn't get a hit off him every time. Nobody did. [Laughs]

Who was the best pitcher?

Well ... I guess Satch or Bob. Satch was a heck of a pitcher. I just wish people could've seen him back in his heyday. Now that woud've been somethin' to see. And control! I'm tellin' you, I've never seen anybody had control like that.

Back in those days, there was so *many* good ballplayers. It was *amazin'* how some of those guys could play. You take Oscar Charleston — that was another one. They could do things and it just looked *natural* for them to do those things.

Who was the best player you saw?

By me bein' an outfielder and he was lefthanded, it would have to be Oscar Charleston or Cool Papa Bell. My last year we picked Ernie [Banks] up in Texas. That was another good ballplayer.

Did you play baseball after you left the Monarchs?

I played some semi-pro ball because I started workin' at Ford. They had a team over in Kansas City, Kansas, called the Kansas City, Kansas, Giants. I played for them and I also managed that team for years. I finally retired in the '70s.

When I started, I was only gettin' three dollars a day for meal money and $300 a month. There was one thing about it, you didn't have to worry about gettin' overweight. [Laughs]

It was a lot of fun. I had a chance to play winter ball in Mexico and Panama and Puerto Rico and Cuba. I didn't make a lotta money but I had a lotta fun. I played the game because I *loved* to play. From a kid growin' up in a little ol' town, that was a thrill to me just to play because I loved the game and in my hometown that was about the only thing goin' was baseball. You would live for Saturday and Sunday's games. And then in some of those little small towns the people was real religious and they didn't believe in playin' on Sunday and so Saturdays would be your big day in a lotta small towns. Every town had a team.

What helped me, I had two uncles there in Danville. They played ball so what really started me off was a fella didn't show up for

Al "Slick" Surratt (courtesy of Al Surratt).

a game. They was havin' a game and they didn't have nine men, so my uncle told my cousin, who was the manager, he says, "We can put my nephew out there. He can catch a ball." He says, "Oh, no." And sure 'nough, the first ball that was hit, it was hit to me and I made a good running catch so it kinda made this grown guy mad. When he did show up, the manager said, "No, I'm not gonna take him out. I'm gonna let him play." I was only 13 years old.

Would you be a ballplayer again?

Who wouldn't? Yeah, man. That would be something. Just think of all the money that the guys are makin' and the equipment and everything.

You were a good fielder. What would you do with the gloves of today?

I can count the balls that I missed. I didn't know what it was to make an error. That was *rare*.

I had a good arm. I was small and people, they couldn't believe what a good arm that I had and it was pretty true, too. I just *loved* to throw that ball if a guy was tryin' to go from first to third, I'd *gun* him down. And a lotta times we would be warmin' up and I would be in deep center field and I'd throw almost up in the press box just to be doin' somethin'. People would go, "Oooh!" [Laughs] That used to be fun. And I'm not braggin' but I didn't think nobody could outrun me.

Any regrets?

Noo, noo! No regrets. A lotta people ask me, they say, "You was born too soon." I say, "No, I wasn't. I wasn't born too soon because I got a chance to play against some of the greatest ballplayers that ever wore a glove. The door was just slow about openin'."

See, now, what better ballplayers would you want to play against than Ken Keltner, Joe DiMaggio, Phil Rizzuto, Stan Musial? Hey, they don't come no better. And I could just go on and on and name 'em, but I just named them few to let you get an idea of who we played against. It couldn't've been any better ballplayers.

ALBERT "SLICK" SURRATT
Born 1920, Danville, AR
Ht. 5' 8"   Wt. 155   Batted and Threw L

Year	Team, league	Pos	G	AB	R	H	2B	3B	HR	RBI	SB	BA
1947	Detroit Stars, Ind.	OF										
1949	Kansas City Monarchs, NAL	OF										
1950		OF										
1951		OF										

Thomas Turner

"High Pockets"

NEGRO LEAGUE DEBUT: 1947

Thomas Turner did not have a long professional baseball career, but he has spent his life in athletics.

He left college in 1936 and earned his living playing sports full-time: baseball with the Cincinnati Braves and Dayton Monarchs, football with the Cincinnati Stars, and basketball with the "Big Five," a touring team.

He continued to play all of these sports after he was drafted, and he also was his army post's champion bowler, one of the ranking golfers, and a superior roller skater. The officer in charge of recreation on the base, Lt. James Chambers, called Turner "the greatest natural athlete I've ever seen in my life." And at that time, Chambers had spent 27 years working with army athletes.

The Turner family was evidently very gifted athletically. Hattie Turner, a younger sister, once held the women's world records in both discus and baseball throws.

Turner played professional baseball again after leaving the service, in Mexico and briefly with the Chicago American Giants. For the past 38 years, he has coached women's softball teams in Ohio and Seattle, where he was a recreation supervisor for the Parks and Recreation Department. His teams have done very well; he has literally a room full of trophies and awards they have earned.

I started playing baseball when I was 11 years old. I started playing second base. My father managed the team. He bought me a glove, one of the best gloves that they were making. That was a Bill Doak. He admonished me from the day he gave me that glove, said if I lost it, that was it. So I slept with that glove. You know, those were the ones that would button; I could take it loose and put it on my pants and button it again. I kept that glove for years and years and years.

Then, in high school, I pitched — did real well as a pitcher. After I graduated from high school, I went to Tuskegee Institute for two years. I didn't play any sports

down there. I had a football scholarship, but Majors, the guy who was the coach at Tuskegee, he didn't like anybody under 200 pounds. I was weighing about 141 pounds, something like that. He didn't give me a chance because I wasn't what he was looking for.

So, in 1936, they organized this Indiana-Ohio League. All of these teams were major league farm clubs. A black man here in Cincinnati had a good thought. He put a lot of us guys together and we entered that league and I played in that league for four years —'36, '37, '38, and '39. In 1936 I was 21 years old when I started. I played shortstop the whole time in that league.

3/12/96
Thomas Turner
World War #2
1943
Nogales Mexico

Lt Chambers

Thomas Turner (L.), Lt. James Chambers (R.). Fort Huachuca, Arizona baseball team. Photo taken in Nogales, Mexico, 1943 (courtesy of Thomas Turner).

Then I was drafted in the service. We were sent to Fort Huachuca, Arizona. The first thing that I did there — we got there in February — they started doing intra-mural stuff, stuff like volleyball. I was in a heavy weapons company — 368th machine gun company. Right quick I made first sergeant. I had been a boy scout and we had a Spanish-American War veteran that was our scoutmaster and he taught us how to do close-order drill just like the soldiers, so I had all of that before I went into the service.

Then the whole infantry came in with the 368th. They started football teams, they started basketball teams, they started baseball teams. Each company had a team. I was "H" company. Then they picked the guys from each company to represent the whole infantry, so I made that team. That's when I started playing first base.

The nice part about the army—you got everything that you needed. They would have the equipment salesman to come in and you could pick out your glove, you could pick out your bat. Whatever you needed, we got it.

I was an expert marksman with the rifle, so I taught marksmanship on the range. I'd be out there for six weeks at a time with new recruits coming in. That's why I'm wearing this thing today [he pointed to a hearing aid]. I wouldn't put cotton in my ears—it bothered me. Eventually, it affected that nerve in my ear.

I was captain of the football team, I was captain of the baseball team the whole time I was there. I played basketball, I roller skated—ran the roller rink. Five years in the service I played sports, I had to practice every day, and in the evenings I was special services. I had to open the skating rink, I had to skate 'til 11:00 every night with civilians—people who couldn't skate, women who had never been on skates before, and I had to teach them how to skate. Man, you talk about a job! That was a job! My back felt like it had been walked on.

So I wouldn't play football the last year. I just quit. We beat everybody around there in Arizona and we all got gold footballs. Baseball the same way. We would go to Santa Barbara for the 9th Service Command tournament—Santa Barbara, California—every year and that's where I got that nickname "High Pockets." A whole lot of women would be there and they would be on the first base line and they would holler to me, "Hey, High Pockets!" so that's where that name came from.

Then we traveled to Mexico. They saw me play there, so Zaragoso asked me when I was discharged from the service would I like to come down and play in the Mexican League. I just said, "Sure"; I had no intention of going to Mexico.

I got discharged December the 23rd, 1945, and I came home here in Ohio and in nine days I had four long distance telephone calls from Mexico. I wasn't married, so I set down with my mom and talked to her. She said if I liked to, go on and play. They sent me my plane fare and everything, so I went back to Mexico.

First year I was there, we played in the Pacific Coast League; that was the winter league. Bob Lemon managed our team—Hermosillo. Herman Breech from Minnesota, he played. And I forget this guy's name—he was Chicago Cubs' shortstop, he played on the team. And when spring training time came, they had to leave.

The winter league consisted of four cities: Hermosillo, Guaymas, Culiacán, and Mazatlán. Bill Wright played with Mazatlán. I played against him; I was very anxious to see him. Bill was an excellent hitter. Bill was a long ball hitter and to me, when he did hit the ball, it looked like it would just suddenly disappear like a rocket. It would be gone! Over the fence, in the stands, wherever. He was a good outfielder; he had a good arm; he was a big man. He was an exceptionally nice person and he still is.

Do you think he belongs in the Hall of Fame?

Sure, I do. I think he belongs there. I doubt he'll get there. I don't think that would worry Bill. You see, the thing about it, they didn't keep good records. Just like when I wanted my records from Chicago, they didn't have a picture of me anyplace. My nephew lives in Chicago and he had to go to the newspaper office and get the write-ups. They didn't even have anything at the *Chicago Defender*—no pictures or anything. And [Walter] McCoy doesn't have any.

I learned how to speak Spanish down there. I'll be honest; the girls taught me. In most of the stores in Hermosillo, the clerks were women and you would never believe the enthusiasm that baseball created in the country of Mexico during those days. You'd have to see it to believe it. I would go to the post office from my hotel, which was about

Thomas Turner, 1995, in replica uniform (courtesy of Thomas Turner).

six blocks. It would take me a half a day to go from my hotel to the post office 'cause I would get stopped by everyone and everyone in every one of those stores and they wanted to talk to me. And they made me speak Spanish; they wouldn't let me speak English. They made me learn it. They would pick me up in their automobiles and

ride me to the park; it wasn't that far — you could walk — but they'd come by the hotel and pick me up in a car and ride me.

They paid me $700 a month, they paid for my laundry, they paid for my food, and they paid for everything. Only thing that I could spend money for was just for my personal effects. I couldn't spend money in a restaurant; I could go to the restaurant to eat and they wouldn't take my money. They were just that nice to me.

Bill Wright said the conditions for a ballplayer were much better there.

If you knew how to act. Some of the white guys had a rough time — a *real* rough time. I'll tell you why — because they came to Mexico with that American feeling, you know, and that didn't work too good.

I used to take kids — 40 or 50 of them — and play with them, take them to the ballpark. If one carried my glove and my shoes, he could get in free. Well, I'd give one my shoes and I'd give one my glove and they'd let them in free and they could sit on the bench with us. During warmups before the game started, I'd throw with them. Oh, boy, they loved that!

There were a lot of white businesses down there and they hired me to teach their kids baseball. During those days, they gave me, for an hour out in the field, five dollars for each kid. Five American dollars. That was good money. I had about 15, 16 kids. They would come to the hotel and pick me up in their limousine. The chauffeur would pick me up. This is the kind of life that I lived. Bill was telling you right.

One guy was putting up a creamery there. They didn't have pasteurized milk; you'd have to boil your milk to drink it, it was right from the cow. He had a son — he had two kids — he was from San Diego, and he struck up a friendship with me and when I got ready to leave he asked me to stay. They wanted to give me a home and they would furnish it for me if I would stay down there. I had married down there and my wife was pregnant with my first child. Well, I wanted my kid to be born in the States, so I left there in early '47.

When I came here, unbeknownst to me, Jack Adkins, who was our football coach in the service, had contacted Dr. [John] Martin, who was the owner of the Chicago American Giants, and recommended me to him to play with the team. And McCoy,

also. So that's how we got on with the Chicago American Giants. I never would've got on if it hadn't been for Jack Adkins. I wouldn't even think about it. In fact, I didn't know anything about them, really.

My daughter was born February the 18th and two weeks later we went to Jackson, Mississippi, to spring training. I met up with McCoy down there and another boy named [John] Ritchey. He was a friend of McCoy's and we were all three rookies that year. And [Benvienito] Rodriguez was a rookie that year and I didn't know this, but he was only 15 years old.

We made the team. I played with them until June, then I quit and came home. They were paying me $400 a month and our manager, Candy Jim Taylor, wanted to cut that in half. He wanted to pay me $200 a month. I told him, "No way." He says, "The only way we can keep you is you'll have to take that cut." So I came home.

I thought that cutting my salary in half was too drastic. If he'd've said maybe $300, I would've stayed there. In Chicago, I had to bear my own expenses and Chicago is no cheap town — never has been and never will be — so I couldn't very well take care of me and my wife and a kid off of $200 a month. I couldn't have paid for a place to stay.

We would be gone. We went barnstorming. We'd only play in Chicago on a Sunday when the White Sox wasn't there and at 12:00 Sunday night we was in the bus and gone. Evansville, Indiana; St. Louis, Missouri; Little Rock, Arkansas; Pine Bluff, Arkansas; Selma, Alabama; Memphis, Tennessee; Kansas City, Missouri; Wichita, Kansas; Omaha, Nebraska; and back to Chicago. Two weeks of that — that's what we did. We were barnstorming everywhere; that's how they made their money.

I got a job at Shillito's [in Cincinnati] parking cars for $30 a week. Then we started a semi-pro team called the Valley Tigers. We were good as professionals and I managed them until '51. Then in '51, G.E. hired me to play softball with their softball team. They had a good team. I played outfield and we won the industrial league two years in a row. Fast pitch.

I went to three tryout camps after I left Chicago. One of 'em was the Yankees, one was St. Louis Cardinals, and the other was Cincinnati Reds. The Reds offered me $250 a month if I would go down to their farm club in the Sally League, down there in Carolina. The Yankees, the only thing the guy asked me, do I think I could hit Triple-A pitching? That's the only word he said to me, and I told him, "I can hit major league pitching." Never heard from him.

Three days we were up there in Hamilton [Ohio]. If they didn't like you, they wouldn't invite you back the next day; they invited me back all three days. The last day we played intrasquad the whole day. I had 5-for-5, never made an error out there on the field. At this time, guys would bring ballplayers there and they would hustle them trying to get them hooked on. Everybody knew that I had a contract. I can't remember exactly what year that was, but it was in the early '50s. I never did hear from them, so I wrote them a letter — their headquarters were in Kansas City — and they sent me back a letter letting me know. The only problem was that I didn't weigh enough.

Do you know any of your individual season records?

In the Indiana-Ohio League, I was hitting .333. My batting averages never did go down under .300. In the service, I was hitting .4-something; I always kept a good batting average. No strikeouts.

We learned how to hit a ball with a broomstick and throwing a tennis ball. The distance, I would say, was about [15 feet] and me and my brothers would throw at one another like that and we learned to hit that ball as hard as they could throw it, with a broomstick. And we were able to watch it. I almost want to throw up sometimes watching these professional guys go up to bat and being suckered with these pitches. It's really something to be professional and be suckered like that with a pitch. They aren't watching anything! They can't bunt a ball; they can't do anything! Anytime a professional man strikes out four times in a row, there's something wrong. And continues to do so!

We talk about it all the time, this type of baseball. We played baseball because we loved to play baseball. I loved baseball. My mom and dad played baseball. My mom was a good hitter. And they were at every game we played.

Did you enjoy the reunion in Kansas City?

I never felt so good in all my life, just to see those guys and to know that they're still around. I proposed to our meeting, and I'm still going to follow this through — we're going to get checks, you know, from major league baseball — I've never gotten one yet but some of the players have been getting them for two years already. I suggested to these guys that we take our checks and give them to the guys who are less fortunate than what we are. Some of these guys, I understand, can't even pay their rent, don't have a place to stay.

Would you be a baseball player again?

Oh, yes. That's all I'd do. I was brought up that a man takes care of his family. I'd need to do that, but I would play again.

THOMAS "HIGHPOCKETS" TURNER
Born 6-22-15, Olive Branch, TN
Ht. 5' 9"   Wt. 155   Batted and Threw R

Year	Team, league	Pos	G	AB	R	H	2B	3B	HR	RBI	SB	BA
1947	Chi. American Giants, NAL	1B							1			.332

Turner also played in the Mexican League in 1946.

Tom Alston

The First Black Redbird

NEGRO LEAGUE DEBUT: 1948

From the outside, it looks great: paid to play baseball, paid more in meal money every day than many people earn who must feed a family of five; paid to stay in fancy hotels; paid to see the United States and foreign countries. Then there's the outside stuff: paid to wear certain shoes; paid to say you eat, drink, or recommend certain products; paid, in many cases, to sit and sign your name.

Sometimes, however, it's not all it's cracked up to be. Maybe it's the adjustments or the expectations (of your own or of others), or the stress of maintaining the schedule, but sometimes it just doesn't work out.

Tom Alston, college-educated (North Carolina A & T), big and strong, had everything going for him. A first baseman, he could hit a baseball often and far and became the first of his race to play for the St. Louis Cardinals. It was fun early, playing semi-pro ball and then briefly in the Negro leagues, but something happened and the fun, the glamour, left baseball for Tom. And then he left it.

I played semi-pro baseball in Kansas. I got a couple of contract offers from the Indianapolis Clowns 'bout '48 or '49, and I played with Greensboro [North Carolina, Negro Southern League, 1948] a little. I'd been in the military.

I signed a professional contract and I went to Porterville, California [Southwest International League, 1952], and I was leading the league in RBIS and home runs. I went to Las Vegas; it was my first time there. A teammate of mine said, "Come on. I want to show you a Negro Baptist gambling house." I was staying in a Negro Jim-Crow Baptist hotel. I was raised Methodist.

I just came from the All-Star game — Latins versus the Americans — and the Americans beat the Latins. I hit a home run and a single. I hit the home run off a 16-year-old Mexican boy. He was playing in Tijuana, Mexico. I didn't want to bat against the little fella because I thought he should be in school. Sixteen years old.

I had a good manager — one of the first black managers in baseball; I never read 'bout where he got credit for it. Chet Brewer, an old-timer.

So I went to the Baptist gambling house and I saw what I wanted to see. I just saw what it was — the slot machines and everything else — and walked right on by. I don't believe in gambling.

I saw the rooms and the restaurants for the white ballplayers. We had a room in the Baptist gambling house. We drove in from California, got there about seven o'clock in the morning. I said, "I believe I'll go upstairs and get me some sleep." So I went up there and I couldn't sleep. I tossed and

Tom Alston with St. Louis Cardinals, 1954 (courtesy of National Pastime).

turned, so I finally got up. I never had that problem, so I went downstairs and ate.

I went to the ballpark. I was so weak. My arm was gone — my throwing arm. It was dead. I was tired and weak. I couldn't throw the ball to the infielders. A teammate came out of the dugout — a white teammate — and said, "Tom, throw the ball to me. I"ll throw it to the infield."

I was batting over .400, leading the league in home runs and RBIs. The only hit I got [that day] was an inside-the-park home run. I went back to the hotel, ate my meal, and went on to bed. Next morning, I got up and went down to eat. My friend told me, he says, "Tom, come on and go with me to see the Brooklyn Dodgers' team doctor." See, Las Vegas was a Brooklyn Dodger farm team.

I said, "Okay." So I went to the doctor with him. He had a bad thumb; he wanted to see about it on the road. He walked up there and he [the doctor] said, "Come on in, Tom. I want to see you."

I said, "Doctor, I ain't come to see you. My friend come to see you."

"But you're the one I want to see." He examined me, checked my reflexes and everything. He said, "Tom, I'll give you one thing: you are a sick man."

We went on back to Porterville. I told my manager; they never sent me to the doctor. I went on playing. My arm was still bad. Later on, they sent me to Triple-A San Diego [PCL]. There I wanted to quit baseball. I went in the whirlpool about my arm.

I got so weak I couldn't hit the ball out of the park. Luke Easter was out there. I wanted some extra batting practice and nobody asked me to take extra batting practice the whole time I was there. I don't know why they didn't. I was too weak and I lost my power for hittin' the long ball.

I went to the offices at the end of the season. I told the general manager I wanted to quit baseball 'cause I could only hit .243. He asked me who did I think I was. He said, "You got nothin' to worry about." I just didn't want to be an obligation to the ballclub. I been used to battin' number four the whole time I been playin' ball, you know.

The next year in spring training I did pretty good. I was still weak and my arm was terrible when the season started. I finally finished the season and I was *tired*. One hundred eighty ballgames. I had a batting average of .291, 101 RBIs, and 23 home runs. But I didn't enjoy it. I didn't enjoy the whole season. I was weak. I used to hit the crisp line drives — singles, doubles, triples, home runs. I wasn't doin' those things anymore. At the end of the season I was *so* tired, man. One hundred eighty ballgames.

A teammate of mine with San Diego wanted me to play winter ball with him. I didn't want to go; I didn't have permission from my general manager or anything like that. So I go on down anyway — down for a while. I couldn't bat well at all. I was tired. I guess 180 ballgames wore me out, so I just went on back home to L.A.

I got a phone call in L.A. and it was my manager, my general manager, and owner. Lefty O'Doul was the manager. My general manager told me to come out to Hollywood, that Mr. [Gussie] Busch was out there. I ain't never heard of him before and he wanted to give me a contract with the Cardinals. He paid a hundred thousand dollars for me, Mr. Busch did, and five players.

I went to spring training and I was tired and I was weak. In spring training I couldn't do like I wanted to do, but I was on the team. I took Steve Bilko's job. Eddie Stanky was my first manager [in the major leagues]. Along about July they sent me to Rochester [International League] in Triple-A and bought Joe Cunningham. He was hittin' .300-something at Rochester. They brought him up; I went to Triple-A.

After the season, I was the Budweiser Beer Negro market representative from St. Louis to Wichita, Kansas. And I did public relation work for the Cardinals. I felt a twinge in my shoulder; I didn't think about telling the trainer or the team doctor.

I came back in spring training, accompanied the team north. I didn't start. Joe Cunningham started usually. I hung around; on cut-down date they sent me to Omaha [American Association], their other top Triple-A team. I did that for three or four years — hung around to the cut-down date and they sent me back to Triple-A.

In 1957, it was the same old thing — I got tired and weak and missed part of the season. That was goin' on since 1952. I got tired of playin' baseball so I just quit in 1958 or '59.

In 1954, you were the first Negro Cardinal. How were you received?

I didn't listen to them. Spring training was in Deland, Florida. There was Alex Grammas — they gave a hundred thousand dollars for him, too — and Harry and Dixie Walker. They were rough.

I hurt my back and got stiffer and stiffer and stiffer. I lost my powerful swing and my hip into the ball and turnin' on my swing. I went to camp and by the time I got to spring training my back was all right.

What did you do after baseball?

I got tired and depressed and everything and they took me to a mental institution. I stayed there ten years. I still go to mental health in Greensboro regularly.

I was never able to have a job. I came home in '59; I was not able to hold a job. I been on Social Security. I was disabled. I came back home and tried to work at night cleaning up offices and I got so I couldn't do that. I haven't been doin' anything since.

Do you receive a baseball pension?

Not much.

You get used to major league baseball — stayin' in nice hotels, eatin' nice food and everything. Come back home and go to a Jim Crow mental institute and the food was just terrible. I couldn't eat the eggs for breakfast — nothin'. Terrible food.

I don't feel like doin' nothin'. Don't feel like readin' a newspaper.

Do you hear from the Cardinals?

It was about three of four years ago before the Cardinals knew where I was. Joe Garagiola got in touch with me. Joe's in New York City.

You had a rough time. Would you go back and do it again?

Not under the conditions I had to work under, no.

Did you enjoy it when you started?

Early, yeah, in Kansas and the time in Greensboro. Not after that time in the Baptist gambling house. It wasn't too enjoyable. I wanted to quit and they wouldn't let me.

THOMAS EDISON ALSTON
Born 1-31-31, Greensboro, NC   Died 12-20-93, Winston-Salem, NC
Ht. 6' 5"   Wt. 210   Batted L Threw R

Year	Team, league	Pos	G	AB	R	H	2B	3B	HR	RBI	SB	BA
1948	Greensboro Red Wings, NSL	1B										
1952	Porterville, SWIL	1B	54	225	54	79	18	5	12	69	15	.353
	San Diego, PCL	1B	78	258	29	63	10	1	2	26	0	.244
1953	San Diego, PCL	1B	180*	697	101	207	25	5	23	101	8	.297
1954	St. Louis, NL	1B	66	244	28	60	14	2	4	34	3	.246
	Rochester, IL	1B	79	290	43	86	15	3	7	42	4	.297
1955	St. Louis, NL	1B	13	8	0	1	0	0	0	0	0	.125
	Omaha, AA	1B	117	430	68	118	21	9	6	58	7	.274
1956	St. Louis, NL	1B	3	2	0	0	0	0	0	0	0	.000
	Omaha, AA	1B	122	418	88	128	25	4	21	80	4	.306
1957	St. Louis, NL	1B	5	17	2	5	1	0	0	2	0	.294

Don Johnson

Groundhog

NEGRO LEAGUES DEBUT: 1948

At the age of 69, most people are either taking it easy or dead. Don Johnson is neither.

He has been recognized as the oldest active baseball player in the country. Baseball, not softball. In the winter, he coaches three basketball teams and is the scorekeeper five nights a week in the city league in Cincinnati.

He is a successful softball coach, so successful that he has been elected to the Hudepohl Softball Hall of Fame. Seven of the girls who played for him are also in there. In fact, it was softball that led to his career in the Negro leagues.

And all this after he was hit by a train and a doctor told him he'd have to give up athletics over a half-century ago.

Guys always ask me, "Can you still see the ball?" How many guys can see that baseball break and come in there at 69? I've been a lucky so-and-so all my life, knock on wood.

The doctor told me I'd never be able to play no ball. When I was 13 I got ran over by a train. My mom sent me to get a loaf of bread. She usually cooked when she come in from work; she'd usually make biscuits or cornbread and she asked me to get a loaf of bread, so she gave me the money and I went down and turned right on the street and they was choosin' sides for football. With her cookin', I said to myself, "Well, I got time to play a few minutes."

The train was sittin' there. We was playin' along the side of the tracks. The guy throwed me a pass and I turned and as I turned, the train started up and I got caught right between the cow catcher and the front right wheel, right there on the right side. Marvin McIntyre pulled me

loose and it tore my leg all up and hurt my head and shoulders. Cut my head, tore the muscle all outta my left leg. They done a good job on me. They got me down to the hospital, man, and patched me up pretty good. The doctor told me I wouldn't be able to play no more sports. Shoot, I made him out a liar. [Laughs] Hadn't been for Marvin, I wouldn't be here. He pulled me out.

You know, it didn't hurt until I got to the hospital and they went to workin' on me. That's when it started hurtin'. The guy carried me to the hospital on a motorcycle. They called the ambulance but this guy said, "Man, the way this guy's bleedin' he ain't got time to wait!" He carried me about three miles, I'd say, to the hospital on the back of a motorcycle.

I was lucky. I'm still playin' and havin' fun. We went out there at that reunion in Kansas City and I felt *bad*. I seen guys come in there in wheelchairs, one arm off,

Don Johnson, 1995, in replica uniform (courtesy of Don Johnson).

one leg. I felt like I wasn't supposed to *be* there. But it was great. The reunion was great.

When and where did you start playing professional baseball?

I was first signed by Cincinnati [Reds] in '47. They sent me to Ogden, Utah [Pioneer League]. I played that season. After '47, they released me. They didn't give me no reason. I was playing well, but they didn't give me any reason. I'm thinking it was a black reason. [Laughs] I batted in the low .300s, but I don't remember my record offhand. We trained in Columbia, South Carolina, and Allen University in Tennessee — a black college — and the black ballplayers had to stay at that college.

You were the first black signed by the Reds after Jackie Robinson entered organized ball.

Me and Charley Stewart signed in '47. He died here a couple of years ago. In fact, his father was the one that got us interested in that. Buzz Boyle was the one that signed us. Stewart also played with the Chicago American Giants later.

In 1911, they [the Reds] had the first two black players. [See note on pp. 257–258.]

Where did you go in 1948?

I went to the Chicago American Giants in the black league and I stayed in the black league on through to '52. That was my last season. I played with Baltimore Elite Giants, Chicago American Giants, and Philadelphia Stars.

You were Chicago's second baseman. Who was your shortstop?

Larry Raines. He lived right here in Cincinnati. In fact, we went to Chicago together. Then he went to Japan; he came back and that's when he went and signed with Cleveland.

They [Japan] wanted me to go — they wanted the keystone to go — but I got a little homesick and I didn't go. They had it figured that both of us was goin'. They asked Winfield Welch, our manager. I didn't go, he did.

Who was the best ballplayer you saw?

I've gotta say it's between Aaron and Mays. At the time, guys had *played* ball, you know. There wasn't no comin' up early. There was very few youngsters. When they came up [to the Negro leagues], the guys was in their 20s — 24 or 25 years old.

When I signed with Cincinnati I was two years out of high school, so I was 19.

Pat Patterson knew me from playin' fast pitch softball with Cincinnati Hottentots. I went to see them [Chicago American Giants] play baseball — they were playin' the Indianapolis Clowns at Crosley Field. I

lived in Covington, Kentucky, and I was sittin' right next to their dugout. They were warmin' up and Pat came by. "Hey, ain't you playin' no ball?" "No, I'm not playin'. I didn't sign with nobody. I'll probably play a little bit over in the city league." So he called, "Winfield, come here! You're lookin' for an infielder, here's an infielder."

He said, "Can you play ball, boy?" I said, "I don't know if I can or not. I would like to play, but I don't know what Mom's gonna say." I was in school; that was in late May and I didn't get out 'til the end of June. He said, "Pat, take him out there and put a suit on him and when the game's over we'll go over and talk with his mom." So I said, "Wait a minute! I paid a dollar-and-a-half to get in here. Gimme my dollar-and-a-half back." [Laughs] He laughed like hell and he gave me a buck-and-a-half back.

Durin' the course of the game, Indianapolis was winnin' like 5-to-2 or 5–3 or somethin' like that, so he sent me up in the late innings — I think it was the sixth or seventh inning. He told me to go up there and bat for the pitcher and I popped up. I took a big cut on that ball and I hit straight up. I came back to the dugout and he said, "Yeah, that boy can play." That's what he told me. He said, "I wanna meet you down in Louisville." He gave me the date they were gonna be there — they were goin' somewhere else — and after I got out of school, they sent me $300 and a plane ticket to Louisville. First, I had to okay it with Mom and she said, "Well, if he wanna play, okay." So I got the ticket and I got the $300 and I met 'em in Louisville and that's where I hooked onto 'em.

Anyone who can hit fast pitch softball ought to be able to hit a baseball.

That's right. That's the hardest game. I played it all across the country. I played out there [in California]; Joan Crawford had a team and they had a guy pitchin' called Charlie Justice. At that time, he was pitchin' from 45 feet. They done moved the pitcher's mound back a little now. Man, that guy — Charlie Justice — he was about

6-6 and, buddy, he could bring it! I had played that for half a season right after school one summer around '46. I was goin' on to 18. That's where Pat saw me playin'. I think they were in the same city we was one night.

Who was the best pitcher you saw?

The best I saw was Fannin, the guy that pitched with the King and His Court. He'd throw a strike from second base. [The King and His Court was a four-man (pitcher, catcher, infielder, outfielder) softball team that barnstormed the country.]

In baseball, that's pretty tough. I went against Whitey Ford. I faced Satchell once and then in '52 he was on my team. Oh, man, I saw so many guys. Booker McDaniels could really bring it and he had a lot on the ball.

In the Negro league you had to be a hitter 'cause them guys knew how to cheat. They'd cut the ball, they'd use spitballs, they done everything to you. [Laughs] You just had to go up there and hit. We didn't wear no helmets, neither. [Laughs]

What did they pay you, and did you get raises each year?

They started me out with $450 and I wound up with like $600.

See, I was just lucky. The old-timers on a team, when you come on a team and go to spring training, the manager don't cut you. The old-timers cut you. "Man, get him outta here! He ain't gonna help us!" They stand back, they don't do a damn thing. They sit back and watch them rookies and if one of 'em puts thumbs down on you, you can forget it.

I could pick it up pretty good. In fact, I still do, I still play baseball. I play in the city league plus I play in the senior league. Last year I hit high .300s, almost .400. In fact, *USA Today* found out I was the oldest baseball player in the U.S.

Did you encounter any problems barnstorming?

We didn't have too many. Sometimes we got stopped on the bus. The driver'd go through red lights and things like that.

We were barnstormin' down in Mississippi and the bus driver ran through a red light. This cop stopped us and pulled us over. "Hey, boy! You see that red light back there?" "Yeah, I saw it." "What in the hell you run through it for?" "Well, I'll tell you. I saw all the white people goin' through the green and you don't allow us to do what they do down here, so I went through the red." [Laughs] That guy laughed his ass off and just let us go.

I never had much problem. We'd go into the town and there were certain places you couldn't eat. People would stare you down a little bit, but I never had any problems. I never went lookin' for no problems. You can make a problem for yourself.

Any regrets?

No. I think baseball's been good to me. I learned a lot. In fact, I learned most of my baseball from Buck O'Neil 'cause whenever we played them I would go over and sit in his dugout and listen to him because Winfield was more basketball-oriented and Buck O'Neil, he was a great teacher. When we played against him, I would always be where I could hear him. I have a lot of success now with my team from things that he taught me.

They called you Groundhog. Where did you get that?

From Pat Patterson. Like I said, I could pick 'em up. I can still pick 'em up, man. Yeah. [Laughs] If that ball hits any part of that infield, it's gonna get picked up.

If you were a young man, would you play baseball again?

Shoot, yeah. You know I would if I'm playin' at 69. See, when I first started I lived in Kentucky and where I lived there wasn't but five black families and when I played ball I had to play with the white boys and if I wanted to play I had to catch and they didn't have no equipment. So did I want to play? All I had was the mitt and it belonged to somebody else. I caught without a mask and without a chest protector. I wanted to play ball.

Note: In 1911, the Cincinati Reds signed

two Cuban ballplayers, Armando Marsans
and Rafael Almeida, who were light-skinned
and it was sworn that neither had any black
ancestry, although both played with black

teams before the Reds signed them. Subse-
quent research indicates that each had black
heritage; Marsans is believed to have been
half-black.

DONALD "GROUNDHOG" JOHNSON
Born 7-31-26, Covington, KY
Ht. 5' 8" Wt. 160 Batted and Threw R

Year	Team, league	Pos	G	AB	R	H	2B	3B	HR	RBI	SB	BA
1947	Ogden, PioL											
1948	Chi. American Giants, NAL	2B										
1949		2B										
1950		2B										
1951		2B										
1952	Chi. American Giants, NAL	2B										
	Philadelphia Stars, NAL											

Melvin Duncan
Pitchin' and Guitar Pickin'

NEGRO LEAGUE DEBUT: 1949

Mel Duncan was raised in Centralia, Illinois, and one day when his team was playing there the town had a Mel Duncan Day. Naturally, he pitched.

Leon Kellman led off against Duncan and belted one more than 400 feet. The second batter hit one off the right field wall. Although he eventually got out of the inning, everything was hit hard. The second inning began no better. Manager Buck O'Neil came to the mound and asked catcher Earl Taborn, "What's the matter? What's wrong with Duncan's pitches?" "I dunno," Taborn replied, "I haven't caught one yet."

Mel Duncan had more good days on the mound than bad ones for the Kansas City Monarchs, Detroit Stars, and several Latin American teams from the late '40s through the mid–'50s, and had he come along a few years later he would have played in organized ball. But he didn't, so his name is unfamiliar to most baseball fans today.

Duncan's roommate in Kansas City was southpaw Gene Collins. A lot of teams now would like to have two pitchers like that in the same room.

I was born in Ann Arbor. My mother and father came here and I was born and they sent me back [to Centralia]. My grandmother and grandfather raised mostly all of us. I went to school in Centralia. Sherwood Brewer's from Centralia, and so is Gary Gaetti. You know where Belleville, Illinois, is? Okay, we're about 30 or 40 miles from there and we're also close around Red Schoendienst. We used to play against Schoendienst's brothers over there in Germantown, Illinois.

I was about 21 years old when I started playing professionally with Kansas City, but I also played with some older men when I was about 16 or 17 in Centralia, called the Centralia Colored Giants. We had a manager, he was my cousin; his name was Levi Lee. When I went to the Monarchs in '49, I gave him my contract to keep for me and a short time ago he mailed the contract to me. He still had it. It's beginning to get old, to deteriorate; it's still in good shape but it's just turning brown.

When I signed, I signed for $300 a month. It wasn't excellent; by the time you had your clothes cleaned from riding on the buses and all of this, plus with Buck O'Neil you had to tip and you had to dress properly. We didn't go around tramping and you couldn't harass the waitresses or the people in any place or anything like that. Whenever we'd go into people's homes, we treated their home just as though it was ours. He was strict on that.

He told me once, "When your mother sent you to me, that makes me your dad, your mother, your brother. I'm the only thing that you've got. I'm your boss, in other words." He said it with authority. He didn't say it and smile; he said, "And do you understand me, booger?" I said, "Yes, skip, I understand you." And you had to understand him 'cause he'd get right in your face and tell you. I never saw him have a minute's problem with anyone. He was a nice guy and he'd go along with you as far as he could, but if he had something to tell you or say to you he would do that.

Between him and the army and my grandmother and my grandfather, we had to say "Yes, sir" and "No, sir" to everybody. I grew up like that and that's the only thing I know and I'm still the same way. In our town, see, there was only 16,300 in Centralia and if you said something back — it didn't make any difference, black or white — they'd fan you, brother. And then when they'd tell your parents, it was worse then. It didn't take but a minute [for word to get back]. You'd get four or five good lickin's before you got home. I mean *lickin's*, too; there was no playing.

And it was $3 a day for food. If you drank beer or something like that, you couldn't make it. Beer was like 15 or 20 cents, but that still was a lot goin' out of your pocket. But then you had to tip. You had to eat one meal, skip one, and then maybe at nighttime eat you a sandwich and go to bed early, so you wake up just in time for coffee. Then you'd go out on the ballfield and you'd play ball.

We played hungry. The ballplayers now play full of steaks and lasagna and all that kind of food. We didn't see that. Plus, too, we were eating out of the back of restaurants most of the time if we wasn't in a mostly predominate black town, or we'd go to people's houses and they'd cook for us.

Through the South and some of the North we'd eat out of the back of restaurants. Detroit was one of the roughest places, and you know, also, was one of the last teams to accept black ballplayers to play in Briggs Stadium, let alone play *with* them. They didn't want us to play in there, period.

They used that phrase in 1949 — that the [Negro] league was dying out and all this. Now listen to this: Hank Aaron came in in 1950, Ernie Banks came into the league in 1950 or '51, Willie Mays, he was there in '48. Elston Howard — they got him from the league in 1950. And Frank Barnes. There was Bob Thurman, who played with Cincinnati; there was Willard Brown, who played with the old St. Louis Browns; there was Connie Johnson; there was Earl Taborn, he went with the Yankees farm club. In '49, '50, and '51 you can't say the league was dying because here's your major league home run champion and he didn't come in the league 'til the '50s. The talent was there.

But Willard Brown, he was in his 30s, I'd say. He could've played ball with anybody right then. I mean, major league or anybody. He could *mash* that ball. And, also, Lester Lockett could mash it. Oh, goodness. Lester Lockett had some age on him, too, but he could mash it. Those are two consistent hitters. I mean, *consistent*. Hit bullets!

Willard Brown, when he went to the Browns, he never would trot in off the field. He'd walk. So they told him in St. Louis, "You don't walk in off the field here. You run." He said he don't run anyplace he play. So I guess they released him. He didn't care anyway, 'cause he was making $2,000 a month in Puerto Rico, $1,000 for every home run he hit. He hit about 45.

And this guy Alonzo Perry — whew, he could mash that ball, too!

I played for Bill Wright in Mexico City. Wild Bill Wright. I saw him at the reunion in Kansas City and I said, "Do you know who I am?" He said, "Sure. Mel Duncan. You played for me." He's still got his wits. He was also a good ballplayer.

Who was the best?

Mel Duncan (courtesy of Mel Duncan).

Now you put me into a powerful situation. It's tough. You know, I never saw a second baseman could play with Bonnie Serrell. I never saw a hitter who could hit with Willard Brown and Lester Lockett. This is just me.

I've seen quite a few good pitchers, but one of the toughest was a guy with Baltimore Elite Giants called Spitball Byrd. I never saw a ball do the things he did. All he'd do was wet his two fingers and touch that ball. You know how you throw a bottle cap at somebody? You know how it sails — go up and down and up and down? That's the way the ball would go. And I'm a little country boy; I never saw anything like this.

A lot of people feel he should be in the Hall of Fame.

I think so, too, 'cause, listen, I don't know what that thing was he was throwing. It was unbelievable to me. He told us that we wouldn't beat him all season and we didn't. No, I don't ever remember beating him. I never got a hit off of him, I know that. I never got a hit off of Satchel and I thought I was a pretty fair little country hitter.

Also, one of 'em at Birmingham, too: Bill Greason. Everything he threw started not much over your knees — fastball, the curveball, and all. You'd swing at that ball and it would hit in front of the plate — it wouldn't even get there. That last one, he'd drop it over or either he'd blow it by you. He just kept you thinking, kept you thinking.

And Joe Black. If you couldn't hit the inside pitch, buddy, you got three of 'em. He could put it where he wanted to. He was late, too [going into organized ball].

To say about the best ballplayer I've ever seen, I really can't put that laurel on any one person.

Was Bonnie Serrell a better second baseman than Mahlon Duckett?

I never saw Duckett play, but I think so. To me, Jackie Robinson couldn't carry Serrell's glove. No, sir. He'd go behind second base and when he'd pick it up he'd flip it behind him. Like you hit a ball going over second to center field, he always had a thing with the shortstop where, if he'd go after a ball you come along just like it's a double play. When he'd flip it behind him, the shortstop'd catch it and fire it to first and you'd still get the runner. Just like getting a double play. Plus he could hit. He was a lefthanded hitter and he could hit that ball.

I've heard that you were a pretty good pitcher.

I wasn't as hard a thrower as Gene Collins, but I could bring it to you. Yes, I could. But Gene Collins—I'll say this, I couldn't see Willie Mays playing any more center field than he could. Listen, when he'd duck his head and turn his back and break for that wall, he *knew* where to go and he'd run into a concrete wall just like that! I thought the man was crazy. You know guys go back and feel for it? He'd just run on and he'd see that ball and he'd *leap* and hit up against that concrete wall, bounce off it, jump up, and throw a *strike* to second base. He could throw. Ah, he could throw!

With his strikeout record as a pitcher, he must've been throwing at least mid–90s.

Gene Collins was throwing close to a hundred. I believe he was one of the top pitchers in the league 'cause he could just bring it. And what made it so bad, he was just a little bit wild. Soon as the game'd start, the first pitch he might throw it three feet behind you. Get all up in a knot and throw it three feet behind you. Now the guys don't wanna stay in there.

And you knew whenever he was out on the mound you had a first baseman, second baseman, shortstop, third baseman, and a center fielder on the infield. We said two arm lengths either way, all them balls belonged to him. I don't care how it was hit. He was just like a cat. Aw, man, he could pounce on a ball so quick! The second baseman and them, they didn't have to play over in the hole and all this; they played their regular position 'cause they knew he had everything back through that middle covered. Now he's the best fielding pitcher I've ever seen, I'll say that. He was the best fielding pitcher *I have ever seen!* I mean, you'd hit a shot to him and with that righthand, all he'd do is flip that glove over like that and he had it. Just like a cat.

I just got back in touch with him since the last 30 years and I told him, "You know, sometime I thought you were just plain crazy. Things you do, sensible people don't do them kind of things." You'd hit a line bullet back through the box and he'd just—Pip!—just flip his glove like that and

look up and he had it. He was something special. Nice guy.

Do you have any of your individual season won-lost records?

In the Negro leagues? You know, I'm gonna be truthful. If they did, it's a miracle to me, but records wasn't kept accurately. Some nights they kept the score and some nights they didn't and to just up and say what it was I would be lying to you.

But I think about the first year, I was about 9-and-4, 9-and-5—something like that. You'd just came to the team and at this time there wasn't a seasoned pitcher on the team and most of the guys who weren't seasoned pitchers you didn't pitch in them big cities. You might pitch in "Boonville" before you get to Kansas City, but they had stars to pitch in Kansas City. At that time, kids wasn't as important as they are today. They want younger ballplayers now but during that time, I guess they thought if you'd been there a long time you were the seasoned ballplayer and they didn't worry about the rookie or the young guys coming.

Actually, I was 20 when I came in, not 21. I was born in 1929. Myself and Frank Barnes come in. He was a good pitcher. You know, his brother, Joe Barnes, passed—in Chicago, about maybe a month before the reunion.

How did you like the reunion?

Oh, you can't downgrade it 'cause you saw so many fellas that you knew, and we were treated royally. Just a wonderful thing like we were just one big family together.

Did you come up against many racial problems in your playing days?

In a few places we ran into a little. We ran into it a lot as far as eating was concerned. In New Orleans, they had a certain time for you to be in, so we were walking down the street and the cops stopped us. Gene Collins and I, we had just come back from Baton Rouge playing a ballgame there. They said, "Where you boys been?" "We been to Baton Rouge playing a ballgame." I knew what to say, you know. So they said, "Oh, you been out playing ball?" I said,

"Yes, sir." They said, "Who do you play for?" and I told him, "It's a Negro league team out of Kansas City. Missouri. We play for Mr. Berry."

Would you play baseball again?

I wouldn't wanna be anything else but a baseball player. I would go through the same things I went through before just to play baseball.

How did the attitudes in Mexico differ?

You didn't know whether you was black or white or Mexican or what. You were just a human being playing ball. That's the same way it was when Jackie Robinson sent me to Venezuela. You're just a different human being, like you're in another world. Well, you are in another country, but everything's just so different. You walk down the street, you think they're gonna call you black or so-and-so, they don't even pay you any attention. They don't even look at you. You're walking down the street with a light-skinned Mexican lady and she looks like she's white — they never look at you. I always wondered why is this like this.

In Venezuela I was treated royally; in Canada I was treated royally. Each town I went to in Canada didn't have one black in the town, period, and I'd go to restaurants and two or three young girls would come by and sit down and talk with me. Get ready to go home at night, maybe some guy would ask if I want a ride; he might live next door or down the street. I'd ride down to the house with him.

I was living with some white guy and his wife and two children and we never had a falling out or anything. Actually, I was living with a minister first; this guy came out to the ballgame and saw me. He said, "Why don't you come and stay with my wife and I. We got two girls and only thing they're gonna do is worry you to death. If you want to, you can come live with us." So I went over there and I paid them for a room and I just enjoyed being there with 'em 'cause they were young and plus they weren't ministers, 'cause if you wanna say

something you could say it but with the minister I had to be awfully careful.

Is there one game that stands out?

We were playing in Buffalo and I was pitching and I think it was against Peanuts Davis and the Indianapolis Clowns, but I'm not positive who it was against. They got a screen something like they have in Boston and I hit a line bullet up in the top of that screen and I was rounding second and he was just picking it up. I said, Well, I can make it to third. And when I got halfway there I kind of glanced and he was kind of like just picking the ball up nonchalant and when I hit third I never stopped going. But then when I got home, the umpire told me, he said, "Boy, you really circled those bases fast!" He said, "You know that's a ground rule double. You gotta go back to second." [Laughs] That's the reason why the outfielder wasn't hustling any more, 'cause he knew it was a ground rule double. But I mean, I was in top gear and I mean, I was coming! That was only about the first or second hit I'd gotten, but that was the first one I'd hit that far.

I won the game and Lionel Hampton invited us up to the Town Casino Bar that night. I've got a picture of him that same night with myself, Gene Richardson, and [Enrique] Borroto.

Do you have any regrets from your playing days?

No. Just regret that we wasn't able to make the amount of money that was being made and getting the chance to show whether or not you could play. But as far as playing in the Negro leagues, like I said, other than money-wise, I have no regrets.

I have no enemies. We didn't have brawls because all disputes were handled by Buck O'Neil or the captain, whoever the captain on the field was, and this was the way disputes was handled. If you were a batter and you broke for the mound, you'd be beat half to death with the mask from the catcher before you got there. We never had a bench-clearing brawl. I hate to even look at ball sometimes because of that. It's getting similar to hockey. It's because the owners have no control. If I'm paying you, I'm not paying you to fight. If I want to pay somebody to fight, I'll hire Muhammad Ali to play.

Sport is not sport anymore. You might as well say we played just to be playing 'cause we liked to play ball. They didn't have all them great big gloves they got now and all these beautiful uniforms. We had one road uniform and we had a home uniform. We'd go into towns, I'd collect mostly all the uniforms, take 'em to the laundromat, wash them — you got your number on your uniform and your pants, so stack 'em up there in a pile and guys'll come down and get their uniforms. Now they can change any time they want to. Put on new sweatshirts, they don't have to buy their spikes, they got three or four gloves in their lockers. They should be able to play ball without all this confusion.

We played in those ball uniforms in those little hick towns and sometimes the lights would be hanging off the posts but we just enjoyed playing, enjoyed being there. You know we couldn't've been playing for the money, we were playing because we *loved* the game.

A guy hit me in the elbow once and he writes me now. He and I are the best of friends. He kids me about that, he says, "I was tryin' to get your head." I said, "If you hit me in the head, then I shouldn't've been playing." His name is Bob Mitchell.

Today they're seeing fastballs and if it breaks a little bit it's a slider and if it breaks a lot it's a curve, and the split-fingered fastball and all this. What do you think if they'd been swinging at the wet ball that we used to swing at, the cut balls, the spitballs, the grease balls, plus when we played they didn't throw a ball out or throw it up in the stands like they do now. They used to have a man down there with a towel wiping the ball off. You've seen that. And the ball is still damp. These guys that can throw the spitter, this is something good for them — when it rolls into a mud puddle or some-thing. He wouldn't try to catch it, he'd just let the ball roll into the water and he'd pick it up and throw it back to the umpire. He'd throw it back to the pitcher. Well, this is all he wanted. Now he's going to work. They can work wonders with it.

But the fans want the home run. They lowered the strike zone. That strike zone's pitiful. They lower the mound, they decrease the velocity of the ball. Everything is taken away from the pitcher and taking it for the hitter.

But I never knew a better bunch of guys than I played with — not just the team I played on, the teams I played against, too.

Charley Pride was there in the league, too. He and I used to sing hillbilly songs together. Just truthfully speaking — he may not remember me — but he couldn't beat me singing 'em. No, sir. I still say that. He just pursued it. In my hometown, Grandpappy Jones came there and Little Jimmy Dickens came and I was the only black one sitting up there in the theater. I slipped in. The guy *knew* that I didn't pay, so he said, "Duncan, when did you come in here?" I was 11 or 12; I said, "I walked right by and I gave you a ticket." He said, "Did you give me a ticket?" I said, "Yep." He said, "Did you give me a ticket?" I said, "Yep!" He said, "*Did you give me a ticket?*" I said, "No, I didn't. I slipped in." He said, "What'd you slip in for?" I said, "I wanted to see Grandpa Jones and Little Jimmy Dickens." I never will forget, Jimmy Dickens was singing "Sleeping at the Foot of the Bed." Grandpa Jones was singing "Hey, Rattler."

I mean, I'd sing 'em, too. I'd sing 'em on the bus when we would be playing ball. Bought me an old guitar from a guy down in Oklahoma. He paid a quarter for it and I gave him five dollars. Had one string on it and we'd ride up and down the highway and I'd be pickin' my guitar and singing. Them guys would get so angry with me late at night; we'd be riding on the bus and I'd be pickin' and singing. [Laughs] Elston Howard used to jump on my back and say, "If you don't shut up, I'll break your little neck!"

We had fun and we respected everybody. We respected each other and everybody else. We didn't shun anyone for autographs and things like that; if people wanted to get our autograph on something, we'd sign it. Oh, it was great — great fun.

MELVIN L. DUNCAN
Born 3-31-29, Ann Arbor, MI
Ht. 5' 9"   Wt. 155   Batted and Threw R

Year	Team, league	G	IP	W	L	Pct	H	BB	SO	SHO	ERA
1949	K.C. Monarchs, NAL			9	4	.692					
1950											
1951											
1954											
1955	K.C.-Detroit Stars, NAL										

Duncan also played in the Mexican League and occasionally in the outfield in the Negro American League.

Walter Johnson
The Second One

NEGRO LEAGUE DEBUT: 1949

The most famous name in Washington baseball history is Walter Johnson. He pitched more than 20 years there, but the *Baseball Encyclopedia* tells us his last active season was 1927.

Yet, more than 20 years later, Walter Johnson again pitched in Washington, but the *Baseball Encyclopedia* doesn't mention him. You see, this Walter Johnson toiled for the Homestead Grays, the Negro leagues team whose home field was the same as the Senators': Griffith Stadium. Like the earlier Walter Johnson, this Walter Johnson was a good hitting pitcher, but unlike the first one, this one's career was not a long one.

A short stint in World War II wasn't enough for Uncle Sam. Johnson was recalled and sent to Korea at a time when he could have been establishing himself as a pitcher. Yet, when he came out, he was still good enough to be given a tryout by the Kansas City Athletics. This time it was an injury that stopped him.

This Walter Johnson left baseball then. Under other conditions, though, his story may have been very different.

I went to high school here [Baltimore] and I was an all-around athlete. I had about seven, eight scholarships, primarily to black colleges, but I opted to go to Richmond, Virginia, to start my baseball career. I played amateur ball here, but the Richmond team — called the Richmond Giants — was in the Negro American Association and most of the guys who went up with Newark and different teams — the Homestead Grays and whatever — they were down in this league. I was in my 20s.

I played with Richmond about three or four years and one year — '49, I think it was — the Grays were coming out of Miami and all the pitchers had sore arms and they were scheduled to play the Indianapolis Clowns over in Petersburg, Virginia. I was

asked by See Posey and the manager to go over and pitch and I beat the Clowns, 4-to-2. And I stayed with the Grays.

Then, in '50 when they disbanded, I was supposed to go down to Caracas, Venezuela, and I got as far as Miami and then I was called back into the service because I only had less than a year in the Second World War. When I came out, I had a tryout with the Kansas City Athletics. Lou Boudreau was there and spring training was down in Savannah, Georgia. I tore some ligaments in my thigh and they sent me to [Johns] Hopkins for some therapy treatments and that was the end of my baseball career because I decided, more or less, I wanted to do something else. I thought it was kind of late. I got some pretty nice reviews in the spring training camp, but the injury gave me a little food for thought and in the time that I had, I just decided that I wanted to do something else.

I became a professional bartender — mixologist — and I've worked all over the world, literally. I worked in Atlantic City, but after the Miss America Pageant they just rolled the sidewalks up, so rather than me going on unemployment, I had made a lot of contacts through my baseball playing and otherwise, and I just decided that every year, after the Miss America Pageant, I'd make contact and go different places to work. I've been in places like Miami; Milwaukee; Pittsburgh; Washington; New York; Aspen, Colorado; San Francisco; Lisbon; Portugal; Cleveland. As a matter of fact, I was in Cleveland when Luke got killed. Luke Easter.

Walter Johnson (L.) and Josh Gibson, Jr., at the 75th anniversary of the Negro leagues. Kansas City, Missouri, October 1995 (courtesy of Walter Johnson).

How old were you when you left baseball?

I must've been in my 30s. I was in my late 20s when I was contacted by Hank Peters. See, then, a buddy of mine was in the Athletics organization, Bob Trice, and I met him down in Havana and I think he was with Ottawa at the time. He recommended me to Hank Peters. That's when I had the tryout.

Bob Trice was an excellent pitcher. His control was phenomenal. I used to see him stand on second base and throw strikes all the time. He reminded me of Robin Roberts: always around the plate, always throwing strikes, not throwing *that* hard, and not wild at all — you could dig in on him — but he was exceptional. He's the closest thing to Robin Roberts I've ever seen. He didn't look intimidating at all. Bob Trice was slender and a modest-looking guy, modest-acting guy, had an even demeanor, never loud, never boisterous. He had an easy, loose windup — not a real high or big leg kick. I really liked him. [Trice had been a teammate of Johnson on the

Grays and later became the first black to play for the Athletics.]

There were some rewarding years. You know, I played with Josh [Gibson, Jr.]. Josh and I are very good friends — Josh, Jr. — because his father had died, I think, in '46 or '47 — something like that. I played with Buck Leonard, Sam Bankhead, Cecil Kaiser, Wilmer Fields. There were a couple other guys — Dave Hoskins and Luke.

Who was the best ballplayer you saw?

I did see Josh [Sr.] and I played with Buck [Leonard]. Buck, individually, is something special. He might not get the recognition that most of those other guys got.

The greatest ballplayer I ever saw was Monte Irvin. No question. They told me about Martin Dihigo and I've seen some other good ballplayers — Bus Clarkson, Oscar Charleston. I've seen those guys play.

I knew Monte Irvin's brother — he had a kid brother that went to Morgan University, he later coached at [North Carolina] A & T in Greensboro. I knew Monte had been with the Eagles and I liked him then when I had seen him. I hadn't seen that much of him, but after he joined the Giants and after I joined the Grays, I used to hear Buck and Luke and them talking and when they would discuss the greatest ballplayer — who *they* thought was the greatest ballplayer — Monte's name was always at the top of the list.

When I was growing up I didn't know too much about the black leagues. I was a New York Giants fan. You ask me about Hal Schumacher and Carl Hubbell and those guys, I could tell you everything. And when I found out about the Negro leagues I always wanted to play with the Homestead Grays, because to me they were the champions. They were absolutely the champions. I know they won three world titles.

Do you know any of your seasonal records?

In my first year with the Grays, it was simple because I was low on the totem pole. It was something like 6-and-2, 7-and-1. The next year was something like 13-and-4.

They didn't compile any batting averages. I was an extremely good hitter. As a matter of fact, when I didn't pitch I played outfield. I just ran into a guy in Kansas City who played with the Newark Eagles, named Jimmy Wilkes. He told me I didn't know my own strength, which was a compliment. When we saw each other, it was the first time I had seen him since 1948. On that occasion, we played part of a four-team doubleheader in the Polo Grounds. Monte Irvin hit one clean out of there. He and Joe Adcock are the only two that I know on record who have hit it completely out of the Polo Grounds.

I was fortunate. I got close to Satch because after his father died, both Sam Bankhead and Satchel Paige were very close to Josh, Jr. They were like godfathers and through my friendship with him, I gained a lot of knowledge of Satch. He used to take us down in the bullpen with a little piece of paper and he stressed control.

As a matter of fact, I hit three home runs off him and I think that's what caused Jimmy Wilkes to tell me I didn't know my

own strength, but the reason was he didn't throw at young ballplayers. We used to dig in on him.

He got even. After I hit the three home runs — the last one was in Offerman Stadium in Buffalo — the next night we played 'em in Shibe Park in Philadelphia. The first time I came to bat, he threw me three curveballs. They all looked like they were coming down the third base line and I was laying flat on my back and the umpire called me out. Satch shook his finger at me and said, "You little sucker, you'll never hit another one off of me!"

But my favorite pitcher at that time was Roy Partlow. He died in Philadelphia. I was working in Philadelphia at the time. It was ironic that I was in Philly when he died and I was also in Cleveland when Luke got killed. Luke was powerful; the only dislike I had for him, whenever we played, he used to beat the owner out of his money while we were on the road. When payday came, we may not be able to be paid. [Laughs] They played knock rummy. They used to cheat each other and Luke used to beat him. We prayed that we could get paid before Luke got to See Posey.

Speaking of getting paid, what was your salary?

I started off at $150 a month, just like Josh [Jr.]; $2.50 a day for meal money. The next year I was up to $280, then $300. To be truthful, they could've given me less than that; I was happy to be playing. It was something I always wanted to do, so I was grateful. I would've played for nothing. When I look at some of those guys nowadays hassling over a million dollars, it's ridiculous.

Any regrets?

No. The only thing I regret has to do with that old saying about being born too soon. No, I don't have any regrets. Every day that I spent in baseball, wherever I went, was very rewarding.

I never wanted to play with the Elites because in black baseball, with them only having 14, 15 ballplayers, the old-timers tried to play for as long as they could. As a result, when a young guy came along it was hard to find somebody to take him in hand. For instance, you hear the stories about George Kell and Brooks Robinson, how George Kell took Brooks Robinson under his wing and just taught him everything that he knew. Well, I was fortunate with Satch and Sam Bankhead being Josh, Jr.'s, godfathers and as close to Josh's father as they were, they just looked after Josh and, at that time, there were guys like Buck Leonard. Buck was very good to me. He taught me a lot. Satch taught me a lot. He didn't seek me out and isolate me, but he always took me along with the crowd. I was just another young guy that was trying to make it, and I'm grateful because that was never evident on a lot of other clubs.

Satchel always had the reputation of liking the young players.

No question. There are probably some others. Buck was one of the finest gentlemen I've ever met in my life. It was obvious about Satch in pre-game warmups and everything; anybody in the crowd could see how he used to take young guys down in the bullpen and pick up a little piece of paper or a bottle top and use it as a home plate. He'd have young guys surrounding him and he'd stress the significance of control. That was always his main topic: control, control, you gotta have control.

I learned more in spring training with the Athletics than I ever did in black baseball. They had Ray Hargroves and Boudreau was the manager. Nobody ever told me the significance of being like a ballerina on the mound and how to finish up and that you were the fifth infielder. Nobody really ever stressed that. The closest that they had ever come to that was when we had a shortstop out of Decatur, Georgia, named Dude Richardson, and one time he made an error and when he came back into the dugout when the inning was over, Sam asked him what happened. He said, "Well, Sam, the ball took a bad hop," and Sam told him, "Let me tell you something. There's no such thing as a bad hop. When the ball hops bad, you hop bad with it." That was the closest thing to anything like that that I had ever heard.

Most of the black ballplayers, they played to such an older age that they were always afraid a younger guy would take their position. For that reason, most of 'em were very aloof. I never reached my full potential, even to the point of knowing how to pitch, how to set a batter up. That came later.

I knew Leon [Day] real well. I know his whole family and we used to play cards together. The only three times I faced him, he struck me out. In later years—I guess three or four years ago—his nephew, he, and myself went out one night to play pinochle and I beat him seven straight games and I got up and quit. They begged me to play and I told Leon, I said, "No. This makes up for all of those times you struck me out."

Guys like him, they were fortunate in that they had more exposure. They were going down to South America, Mexico, Puerto Rico, and Panama *every* year and they were being exposed to a lot of guys who were in organized baseball, so I guess this helped them along with the things that they learned. But my game came slow and gradual and I think, by the time I was ready to grasp it, it was too late.

Would you play baseball again?

Oh, no question. We all think about that: "If I could just go back with what I know now." Of course I would play. That's one of the few things I knew how to do. If I had it to do all over again I'd do it, even if I had to go through the same routine the same way.

WALTER JOHNSON
Born 10-31-26, Baltimore, MD
Ht. 6' 0"   Wt. 170   Batted and Threw R

Year	Team, league	G	IP	W	L	Pct	H	BB	SO	SHO	ERAS
1949	Homestead Grays, ind.			6	2	.750					
1950				13	4	.765					

Bunny Warren

Stuck Behind Pee Wee

Negro League Debut: 1949

Ron "Bunny" Warren may have been beating his head against a wall trying to play professional baseball.

First, he's black and the early 1950s was a time when the Negro leagues were fading and there were fewer teams each year. But he was good, so good that the mighty Brooklyn Dodgers signed him to a contract.

And here came a second impasse. Warren was a shortstop, and possibly the most difficult spot for a kid to advance in all of professional baseball was at shortstop in the Dodgers chain. Pee Wee Reese was at the top and around 1950 wasn't about to go anywhere, so there was a logjam behind him. Among the shortstops between Reese at the top and Warren in Class D were no fewer than seven who eventually became regular major league regulars: Chico Carrsaquel, Don Zimmer, Billy Hunter, Bobby Morgan, Chico Fernandez, Rocky Bridges, and Stan Rojek. And, too, there were Jim Pendleton, Eddie Miksis, Tommy Brown, and Mike Rose. Being a low minor league shortstop owned by Brooklyn did not offer a promising future.

Family problems and insufficient pay added to Warren's difficulties, so he left the Dodger organization and returned home to Cincinnati, where he played for years with the Cincinnati Tigers, an independent team and one of the last Negro clubs. And years before, when still in high school, he had played some for the Detroit Stars and Indianapolis Clowns.

Today he's a birddog scout for the Astros.

When did you begin playing professionally?

Back in the '50s. I would say 1951. Before that, some Negro teams came through and I was underage and I was going under an assumed name, which was my brother's name: Elias Warren, Jr. By me still being in high school I couldn't hardly go under Ron Warren, of course. I played a little bit on teams that would come through, playing at old Crosley Field. I would hook up with them for maybe three or four games, go as far as Middletown and Dayton and even maybe to Columbus or Springfield. I would come on back home after maybe playing over a weekend — three or four days — under my brother's name. I was in about my third or fourth year of high school — 16 or 17 — when I was doing this.

The only thing about it, everybody kept calling me "Bunny." I had that ever since I was a child. My parents probably gave me that when I was a little bitty tot. It grew with me. In fact, most people here today, they refer to me like it's my given name. If they heard my name — Ron — they would say, "I don't know if I know that guy." [Laughs]

Then I signed with the Dodgers — Brooklyn Dodgers. They sent me to Sheboygan, Wisconsin [Wisconsin State League]. John Roseboro came there during that time. He came after me.

I had to come home because my wife was in a little pregnancy problem and the following year I tried to get back with them and they were reluctant to sign me or even give me my additional bonus. That kind of disturbed me a little bit, so I had another look-see. After that, things didn't quite go well for me because my family at that point in time was growing and I couldn't live on $154 a month. I stayed in Sheboygan I guess for about a month-and-a-half before things started looking bad for me again.

My high school coach, he was the one that gave me the opportunity — a fellow by the name of Clifford Alexander. He was the basketball coach at Willard High School, and football coach. I don't know why he didn't coach baseball with him being a scout and all. He had some minor league experience and he would be the man to do the baseball coaching but he never did.

It was that summer that I learned that he was looking for me to give me a contract to go with the Dodgers. He came to my dad's house and he signed me. This was back in '50, '51, and I was still trying to hook up with the Negro league.

Which Negro league teams were you trying to get on with?

Well, any of 'em, really. The majority of the ones that I played with coming through here were the Detroit Stars — they came here on a frequent basis — and another team I wanted to play with but they had enough with what they had was the [Indianapolis] Clowns. A friend of mine played with that team for years, a fellow by the name of Henry Merchant. Sam Odom also played with that team for years even though they were older guys, but they had the most notoriety of the guys that I had heard of.

But Detroit, they were average. They had decent ballplayers, but then, too, by that time in the '50s and going through the '50s, everybody was looking for minor league contracts and the Negro leagues was just about ready to fold. Every time they got a decent or promising ballplayer, it seemed like they would lose him to a minor league organization, so they became short *all* the time, you know.

[Bill] McKechnie and the Reds, they were having tryouts around here and a lot of guys would stay here, like for instance if some of the Negro teams would come through here maybe on a Saturday or a Sunday and they heard about a tryout, some of the younger ballplayers would stay for the tryout and see if they could connect to a major league club. A lot of these guys, they wasn't so much scouting a lot of the talent that was there in the Negro league because all the young talent was going from the high schools and other [amateur] teams to the minor leagues. They wasn't going towards the Negro leagues.

When Chuck Harmon came along, they were looking for another Jackie Robinson instead of a good ballplayer. There was only one Jackie but Chuck had all the good stats and credentials like Jackie — educated, a scholar and gentleman-type of personality, low profile, and, of course, a good ballplayer. They should've let Chuck play like Chuck plays. And at the time in the '50s, the major league teams could have done more to make these [black] players more comfortable, to give them another Afro-American player as a teammate.

That was the whole bad thing about the Negro league at that point in time. They were looking for another Jackie Robinson. They looked a hell of a long time, but then, too, the other teams were taking the talent as it came, *not* the whole package, and that kind of made it a demise for the Negro league as well.

I'll tell you something else that was really discouraging to a lot of black ballplayers. At that point, the major leagues, they were looking for bulk, like football players — the Kluszewskis, the Big

Ron "Bunny" Warren, 1995, in replica uniform (courtesy of Ron Warren).

Swishes [Bill Nicholson], the big guys who could get the ball out of the park. The guy 165 pounds, 158 pounds — they wasn't looking for these type of guys too much because they were going for the power stroke. Now baseball has come to the point where they're looking for the speed.

At that point, they didn't care if you stole 25 or 50 bases. All they wanted to know was if you could hit 18 or 25 home runs. Now, on the carpets, the speed's important and they're looking for it.

Back when you signed, Richie Ashburn was about it as far as that type of player went.

There's a man, it took him almost 30 years to get into the Hall of Fame. Something's wrong with that. Very, very wrong. I feel if it had not been for Mike Schmidt, this man would have been like a lost ball in the high weeds.

What did you do after you left the Dodgers organization?

I played with the Cincinnati Tigers. It wasn't in any professional league. I played 15 or 16 or maybe 18 years with them. Don Johnson played with that team, and Sonny Webb. Hank Boston, the Boston kid's daddy, was there. Daryl Boston—he went to the same school I went to.

Who was the best player you saw?

To be honest with you, I've got to be partial to shortstop because that's what I am. I think the best shortstop that I've seen is the one playing with the St. Louis Cardinals now—Ozzie Smith. If I had one play to make and I had one man to designate to make that play, he would be that man.

The greatest thing that ever happened to Barry Larkin is when he beat him out for the All-Star game a year ago [1994]. I know Larkin's a younger man and may have a little more pop in his bat, but if I had to play defense it's Smith. And as Whitey Herzog said, and I do agree, what's the difference in knocking in a hundred runs and stopping a hundred? That little man can play.

Who was the best pitcher?

I saw two pitchers that I really enjoyed watching all the time. One was Marichal—I *really* enjoyed watching him pitch. I thought he was a master craftsman. Everybody says Satchel Paige. I didn't see that much of Satchel when he was throwing the ball well; I saw Satchel when he was an older man and he was doing a fine job then, but I'm talking about someone who could bring the ball up there pretty good and there's two guys stand out in my mind, and that's Juan Marichal and Sandy Koufax.

Sandy was bringing that ball up there at least 95 [mph] and that curveball that he had! He brings to mind a little kid that played with the Clowns years ago by the name of Teddy Richardson. He was a left-hander and, man, he threw it *just* like Sandy did. He was a little guy; he was about 5-8 and maybe about 145 pounds. He could throw it so hard he'd make it whistle!

The Dodgers were in Cincinnati and Jackie Robinson was making his good-bye tour of the league. [Richardson] told me over in Covington [Ky.] ballpark, he said—he talked with a stammer, "I-I'm gonna th-throw four innings and I-I'm gonna l-leave h-here and I-I'm g-gonna go to the b-ball-park and s-say good-bye to m-my f-friend. Th-that's the only m-man that tr-treated ballplayers l-like th-they're decent." And, buddy, he made it whistle! He was out of there in a hurry. We got a cab and went down to the ballpark—Crosley Field—and we greeted Jackie. He was a gentleman. He was a great man.

How has baseball changed in the past 40 or so years?

Baseball's in trouble. They aren't promoting it. It's terrible when a kid goes up to a player and says, "Sign my glove," or, "Sign my cap," and the guy looks down at him and says, "My agent won't let me," or, "Give me $10." The sport is killing itself. And it's getting worse.

Guys say they don't have time. You go down to the ballpark and walk into the Redlegs' clubhouse and these guys got these little earphones on—Walkman—and they're in their own world. Nobody's saying anything, nobody's talking, nobody's trying to have a camaraderie with one another.

It's about the money. "I'm making mine, you make yours." You didn't have that in the Negro league because it was family. We didn't carry but about 16 ballplayers, or 17 at most, and everybody had a job to do. Pitchers played outfield and first base; some of 'em caught if they were righthanded. They had an old guy there called Double Duty Radcliffe and that's what he did—pitch and caught.

Nobody had the tendency to bask around for a fourth-day start. No, no, no.

Not when you're playing PC ball. PC ball in the Negro leagues is what they call percentage ball; you get paid by what you brought in. We were guaranteed so much and if we drew well and had a lot of fans, we made a lot of money, but now if we had a bad show and nobody showed up at all, we just got the guarantee and we kept moving.

A lot of these guys, unless he was a high-profile ballplayer, someone like a Satchel Paige or someone like that — these guys made *big* money — but if you was just a role-player guy or a middle infielder they knew that you weren't making no more than $60 or $70 a week, or a hundred maybe, if that much. You didn't sit around and talk about it. But they were satisfied with that; they just felt like, "Man, I want to play baseball. I know I'm gonna travel and I know I'm going to eat, and maybe if I make some money, fine. And who knows, I might even catch a break and go to the majors." That's the way we thought and that's what most of the guys out there were doing.

But mind you, too, a lot of those guys who stayed out there so long had nowhere else to go. They had black ballplayers who were out there for 20–25 years still trying to hold on to a job and some of 'em could. But, there again, by that time a lot of 'em had to because in the '40s — '47, '48, '49 — they almost emptied out the Negro leagues — all the best ballplayers — so the older guys were the only ones who could really stay 'cause they had nowhere else to go.

A few come to mind. One of 'em lives right here — Thomas Turner. He is a beautiful man — I'm telling you the truth. I've known him ever since I was a boy. He and my dad played baseball together. My dad played for the old team the Valley Tigers for years and also for the Cincinnati Tigers for a while and he played in that old K-O-I — Kentucky-Ohio-Indiana League. They had all these leagues around here at that time and I'll tell you what they did. Sometimes they had a mismatch in teams, maybe

they had a nine-team league or a seven-team league, so somebody had a bye every other Sunday. What they'd do is bring in a road team to play the team with a bye.

We went down several years to play in the Appalachian League because teams were dropping out because they couldn't keep it up financially. We used to go to Welch and Bluefield and all these places and we'd play these teams.

Some pretty good ballplayers came out of there. I'll tell you a kid that played for us and went all the way up to the majors — a kid by the name of Raines. Larry Raines. We called him "Hope." Died of a heart attack in Michigan. He played with us for years.

He played here in Lexington for a while.

For the Hustlers. We'd go through there and play the Hustlers sometime. Dave Whitney came from there, and Lou Johnson — Sweetslick Johnson — played for the Hustlers. I know quite a bit of those fellows there. Shoot, my daddy was born in Paris, Kentucky.

The worst thing in the world I've seen as I look at television about some of the Negro teams, like *The Bingo Long Traveling All-Stars.* That was not a credit to the men themselves, to be honest with you. It was a farce. I understand that actors cannot be ballplayers and maybe ballplayers cannot be actors, but by the same token, they could've gave a better portrayal of the Negro teams than what they did. It was entertaining but to me it was a slap in the face because once you've been there and you realize what you had to do and what went on, you can say, "This wasn't right." The only thing that I found that was halfway decent in there, halfway knowledgable, was the traveling aspect and what the guys did on the road and things of this nature.

You were a shortstop in the Dodger chain. That was a dead-end for years. There was no way to climb in the system at that position.

That's why I tried other positions. I played short, second, even third base, and even caught. I learned how to catch because my daddy wanted me to be a catcher because he was a catcher. It was no problem. The biggest thing about catching is put your mitt where the ball is at. If the guy misses, it's gonna be caught. [Laughs] And keep your eyes open, lose your fear of the ball.

But catcher wasn't much better in the Dodger organization. There was Bruce Edwards, Campanella, Rube Walker. The way that Roseboro got to play, Campanella got hurt.

Would you go back and be a ballplayer again?

What part of my body do I have to give up to do that? [Laughs] Yes, I would. I'm still waiting for the phone to ring. Who knows, somebody might like an old ballplayer.

RONALD "BUNNY" WARREN
Born 2-25-32, Covington, KY
Ht. 5' 9"   Wt. 160   Batted and Threw R

Warren played briefly for the Detroit Stars and Indianapolis Clowns in 1949 and 1950. He also played portions of 1951 and 1952 in the Brooklyn Dodgers minor league system with Sheboygan in the Wisconsin State League. After leaving organized ball, he played 16 years for the independant Negro team, the Cincinnati Tigers. No records are available.

Otha Bailey

Good as Campy

NEGRO LEAGUE DEBUT: 1950

When you think of a catcher, you think of a burly individual, probably six feet or so in height, usually slow of foot.

Well, Otha Bailey was none of the above. At 5' 6" and 150 pounds, he was one of the smallest men to ever be a regular backstop, but he had a great arm and he called a great game because he knew the hitters. And he was fast. He would often beat the runner to first base and he could steal the occasional base.

His talent did not go unnoticed, either. Both the Boston Red Sox and the Brooklyn Dodgers had interest in him. He spent his entire playing days in the Negro leagues, though, and his career spanned the decade of the 1950s.

How did the Birmingham Black Barons find you?

They came through [Huntsville] and gave me a shot in spring training. I didn't make the team at first. That was '49. I guess I was about 17, 18. They cut me loose outta spring training and the Cleveland Buckeyes picked me up in '50. I played with them a year and they folded and then the team outta Newark — Newark Eagles — they moved to Houston, so I went to them. Dr. [John] Martin in Memphis, he had connections, so he hooked me up with the Houston Eagles and I finished the season with them. That was in '51. In '52 I came back to the Barons.

The Boston Red Sox scouted you pretty heavily.

That was in '50, but the scout told me if I was two inches taller they would've signed me.

I was supposed to went to the Dodgers' training camp. That was in '51. I was in Miami, Florida, during the winter months and when they came to spring training, Campanella, he asked me to come to the Dodgers camp, but I overslept myself. I woke up and it was too late. They were gone. I seen 'em 'bout a couple weeks later back in Miami. Campy asked me what happened and I told him. He said I didn't wanna play ball, and I told him, "Yes, I do!" [Laughs] I figure I might've missed a little chance there. I might've got farmed out maybe.

The only thing [Campanella] had on me was some weight and some hitting. As far as the rest of it, I didn't think so.

You had the reputation of having a strong and accurate arm and of handling pitchers very well.

Yeah, I had a true-throwing arm. 'Fore I left Huntsville — I was playin' on a sandlot team — an older guy told me, I was his understudy, and he told me things I need to know — to know the hitters and catch the pop flies. I took that down, that stuck with me all the time.

To know the hitters — a team may come in and I might go to the cage, stand at the cage and watch 'em, watch the best ball he hits good and he don't get it in my game. Try to keep it away from him. He don't get that pitch unless we got a pitcher that can't throw it direct at the target, you know — a few inches higher or lower and he might connect. But I know what all hitters could hit, I never forget him. Once I see you swing good and you're hittin' that ball good — if it was low or high — you don't get it.

One man we couldn't get out. That was Hank Aaron. We'd shift the infield around, he'd still hit it through there. He's got good wrists.

We had some guys could run like a rabbit. I'd get some of 'em out. I'd get more of 'em out than they'd steal. If one'd get on, I'd be hopin' he'd run. One time I played for about three weeks and I didn't have to throw out nobody 'cause nobody run.

Talk about your Birmingham pitchers.

We had a guy named — they called him Jitterbug, I forget his name now; a guy named Menske Cartledge, Kelly Searcy, Hiram Gaston — he's a lefthander, Searcy and Hiram; and we had a guy named Hoss Thomas, Bill Beverly, and quite a few. [Elliot] Coleman came in '55. He was there 'bout a year or so. I worked with him lots. He improved a lot and he got a chance to go to organized ball. We had some nice pitchers, guys that would get you out.

Then we had Charley Pride. He was a good hittin' pitcher, too. He played outfield and pitched. His bat got so big, so we let him play outfield. We picked him up in Mississippi and he had a two-string guitar. He'd sit in the back of the bus singin' that country music and we'd jive him about it, say, "Man, don't be playin' that kinda junk! You ain't gonna get nowhere on that." But he did. He was a millionaire 'fore anybody knew who he was. I haven't seen him in a long time.

Otha Bailey (courtesy of Otha Bailey).

The best pitcher I ever caught in my life — you know who he was. Satchel. I caught him several times. He was goin' out but he still could pitch four to five innin's and he could get somebody out. Buck O'Neil used to ask me, "Who's the best pitcher you ever caught?" I've caught many good pitchers, but I'd have to name Satchel.

And a boy named Frank Barnes, he could throw that ball looked like 'bout 110 miles an hour. I used to catch him, too.

Who were some of the real good ballplayers you saw?

Ernie Banks for one, and Willie Mays and Hank Aaron and Elston Howard. I played against him in '50. We opened up in Kansas City in '50 — the Cleveland Buckeyes. We had about 25,000 and Buck O'Neil, he was there. And two or three guys out of Cuba. Frisco Herrera, he was an outfielder.

The major leaguers — I played against them, too. I played against Hank Thompson,

(L. to R.) "Doc" Wesley Dennis, Roy Campanella, Otha Bailey (courtesy of Otha Bailey).

Willie Mays, Suitcase Simpson, Campanella, Larry Doby, Joe Black. I played against Quincy Trouppe and Buster Haywood, with the Clowns, and Double Duty Radcliffe, Willie Grace, the Jefferson brothers. I think I played with and against some of the best ballplayers I know.

Who was the best one?

The one I thought was the best was Hank Aaron, as far as hitting, and he played outfield good. 'Course, Willie Mays was good, too, but his bat wasn't nothin' like Hank Aaron's. I ain't seen none like him. Willie, his wrists wasn't good as Hank Aaron's. Hank Aaron had good wrists. We were throwin' him curveballs that got by him and he'd wrist the ball outta the ballpark. Tough man.

There's so many ballplayers I played against and with, it's hard to name all of 'em. [Laughs] Some I don't even remember now.

Is there one game that stands out?

It's hard to say. I did good *all* the time. [Laughs] I was a hustling catcher. I played like I was really after it. I just loved the game. I played hard.

I hit one home run, I believe it was in Nashville, and the best was at Longview, Texas. I hit about three up against the wall. The next time I came up with men on base, they walked me and put me on intentionally. [Laughs] My bat was big that night. That made me feel good.

I couldn't hit the curveball but I could hit the fastball. I didn't strike out much. Very little. I'd hit it out there somewhere.

How was the travel?

We used to ride all night. We might play here and then we'd be on our way to Memphis, leave Memphis and we'd play in Little Rock, then we'd be headed to Kansas City. We might stop in Texas to play a game or two. We had maybe a 5- or 600-mile ride and not go to bed 'til after the game if we're staying the night there.

We got a keg sittin' up there by the driver for the look-out man to help him with the curves and stuff. Tell him you got a curve ahead, left or right or whatever it is.

One time we left Memphis goin' to Michigan. We played the House of David up there and then we'd leave there and go to Rochester, Minnesota. Just a long ride. We hadn't been to bed all night; we laid out in the ballpark 'fore the game. We got there, I guess, 'round 1:00, so we didn't go to bed. We stayed in the ballpark, slept around on the benches. People started comin' in and some guys were still asleep. Everybody got up and we's already dressed out. We played like mad up there.

We played practically every day. The only days we had off we was ridin' between. We might have a long jump, go from here to Houston and like that — down through Texas.

We played doubleheaders on Sunday. I'd catch a doubleheader on Sunday and then go from Memphis to Little Rock and catch another game that evening. I mean, I caught three games. I'd do five [innings] in the third game, but the doubleheaders in Memphis, I'd do both of those.

For backup, we had a boy named [Charles] Johnson. I had Johnson, one, 'course Pepper Bassett, he was there. When I came to Birmingham, Pepper was still there. Herman Bell, he had left, so when I came there in '52, Pepper was still there. Sometime they would start him. He'd catch four and I'd catch five, but then if the game get real tight, I would come in as a defensive catcher 'cause I could move faster and get a lotta balls that he don't get 'cause he's big and kinda old, too. He'd tell me he's gonna do four and I get the five. Later on, I was the startin' catcher.

Would you do it again?

If I could turn the years back I would. [Laughs] I figure I was good enough to go to the majors. I look at the catchers nowadays, they couldn't carry my glove. The balls gettin' off by 'em and between their legs. I didn't let none get by me hardly. I used to catch the knuckleball and all those trick pitches and I loved to do all that. We had a guy named Pee Wee Jenkins; he had a good knuckleball.

Did you enjoy your career in baseball?

Yeah, I enjoyed it. It was real nice. I loved the game. I used to go to the ballpark at 6:00 in the morning and stay out there all day — bunch of us boys when I was comin' up. We'd play all day.

OTHA S. "BILL" BAILEY
Born 6-30-30, New Orleans, LA
Ht. 5' 6"   Wt. 150   Batted and Threw R

Year	Team, league	Pos	G	AB	R	H	2B	3B	HR	RBI	SB	BA
1950	Birm. Black Barons, NAL	C										
	Chattanooga Choo Choos, NSL	C										
	Cleveland Buckeyes, NAL	C										
	Houston Eagles, NAL	C										
1951	New Orleans Eagles, NAL	C										
1952	Birm. Black Barons, NAL	C										
1953		C										
1954		C										
1955	Birm. Black Barons, ind.	C										
1956		C										
1957		C										
1958		C										
1959		C										

Bill Beverly

"Fireball"

NEGRO LEAGUE DEBUT: 1950

Bill Beverly came along at the wrong time.

In the first half of the 1950s, a black ballplayer was placed in limbo. His leagues were on the wane, and "organized" ball was not ready for him. Most blacks who signed with major league clubs were buried in the minors and not given a fair chance. "Look," said the parent club, "we've signed Negroes and they're still in Class B ball." Not all teams had this attitude, of course. The Dodgers, Giants, Indians, and Browns looked at a ballplayer's ability, not his color, but it was not the same with most of the other clubs.

But a young black, just like a young white, dreamed of being a major league player, so he signed with a team in "organized" ball. The drain on the Negro leagues was so great that they gradually disappeared.

Bill Beverly was one who chose not to be buried in a major league farm system and stuck it out with Negro league teams. He played for various black clubs from 1950 through 1955, with the exception of 1953, when he played in the Provincial League in Canada. Ten years earlier or ten years later he would have been better known, but in between the twilight of one era and the dawning of another, his career, and that of many others, is now just a footnote in baseball history.

And that's too bad, because some say he's one of the toughest pitchers they ever faced. He'd come inside, knock the batter down, "scowl at you just like Bob Gibson," one former opponent said. He could really throw a baseball.

How were you signed?

With the Houston Eagles, the old Newark Eagles. The Eagles were in town from Newark — came in '49 — and I was tied up in a tournament up in Waco, Texas, and I didn't get a chance to come out for them. In '50 I didn't go to the tournament in Waco and I went ahead and tried out for the Eagles. The very first day that I went there, they said, "Okay, we're playin' a team down in Victoria, Texas." I told 'em, "I'm scheduled to play with that team. That's my team that I play with here in Houston." They said, "I don't see how

you're gonna be able to do that because we accept you today with the Eagles." So that was one of the most happiest days of my life. I was playin' semi-pro up 'til then.

In 1950, your rookie year, your record was 5-and-1.

See, that's misleading. That 5-and-1 was league. We played every day — every night. We played in the major league ballparks every night. We [the league schedules] were up around 80–85 ballgames. We played a doubleheader on Sunday. We played four-team doubleheaders. We'd all meet up in Yankee Stadium. The Pittsburgh Crawfords would be there, the Chicago American Giants, the Indianapolis Clowns, and the Birmingham Black Barons. It was six teams in each league and on any given day we could be playin' league games in Winnipeg, Manitoba, up in Canada. Those games counted. And on the way to play up in Winnipeg, every night we would schedule a stop 2- or 300 miles down the road and play a local team. We was probably 110, 120 games a year, maybe more. We played every night; we never had a day off.

You also played first base and the outfield.

Let's say we came upon a team in Grand Rapids, Michigan, and they were a pretty good ballteam that had guys that were workin' for the steel mills and the automobile industry. These guys were guys that had came out of the major leagues and were older and were still playin' baseball and some of 'em weren't able to make it in the majors and they had jobs and had a good company team. They would always schedule us two and three years in advance for the owners of the club to get in touch with, "When you're comin' through here we'd like to play your team." They always tried to have some people that could beat us.

So when it come time to play against these teams, instead of pitchin' I'd play first base, the catcher would go to center field, the third baseman would play right field — you know, their favorite position. My favorite position was playin' first base. That's when we would play outta position and we always beat 'em that way unless'n they said "nigger." If somebody said "nigger" or somethin', we'd all go to our regular places and run the hell out of 'em.

Were you a good hitter?

Lemme tell you somethin' about baseball. You cannot say, "Okay, nine men

Bill Beverly (courtesy of Bill Beverly).

takin' battin' practice tonight." Every night you take battin' practice. If you're not pitchin', you run. We carried eight or nine pitchers. You get in the outfield and you run to keep your legs in shape so your arm'll be in shape, so when the eighth man bat and you know you're pitchin' that night — the night before they tell you, say, "Okay, here's a brand new ball. You're pitchin' tomorrow night" — that means don't go out and dissipate or go out an get drunk or go out and stay up late, 'cause you are pitchin' tomorrow night and you're a nine innin' pitcher. We don't look for you to need no help. So you go in, you go to bed, and you don't fool around.

Bill Beverly (courtesy of Bill Beverly).

So when you see the eighth man had hit, then you go grab a bat. They say, "What're you doin'?" You say, "Well, I wanna hit. I'm pitchin' tonight." They say, "You just stop 'em from gettin' some runs. We'll get you some runs. We just want you to stop 'em." See, and then you don't get a chance to take no battin' practice. No pitcher takes no battin' practice.

Then when the game get tight and you're pitchin' a two-hitter and they say, "Well, okay, you're ahead one run and you haven't given up but two hits, but we got to pull you for a pinch hitter." "What the hell you mean? I want this win! I'm pitchin' a two-hitter!" or a one-hitter or five-hitter. Well, it's the game and it's a professional game so you don't argue; you just come on out of the ballgame and the other guy go in there and know this guy's a damn good fastball hitter and he gives the guy a fastball right

down the gut and the guy ties up the ballgame and in an innin'-and-a-half he's won your ballgame 'cause he's gonna hold 'em now, after he gives up that run that ties the ballgame up or go-ahead. It doesn't look like it's being done intentionally, but that's the way the game is. That's the smartness of the game.

So when you say, "Was I a good hitter?"—I hit above average because I played first base and outfield. They wouldn't let me play first base because I threw too hard across the diamond and guys would pull their glove off on third base, "Damn that guy! He throw that ball across and damn near take my glove off!"

They called you "Fireball." Who gave you that name?

Pepper Bassett. Pepper was catching for Birmingham and I came to Birmingham. Pepper was supposed to take the place of Josh Gibson. He was a big man — 6-foot-4 — and he could blister that ball. He wasn't a very fast runner. He taught Roy Campanella how to catch; he's one of the guys instrumental in teachin' Roy Campanella. I came to Birmingham and he says, "Say, Beverly," he had a gruff voice, "I understand you're pitchin' tonight." I say, "Yeah, Pep." Well, I had admired him, pitchin' against him; I never played with him. "Okay," he said, "I'm gonna catch you tonight. In my hip pocket. About seven innin's we'll let the ball go through my glove and I'm gonna have my pocket popped up in the back. I'm gonna let the ball go through my glove and get it in my pocket. Then I'm gonna look around like I can't find it. The umpire, he's gonna go along with it 'cause the people gonna clap once we find the ball in my back pocket." I said, "Fine, Pep." So I was throwin' the ball seventh, eighth inning and I went down off the mound, 'cause he hadn't caught it in no pocket; I went down after him. "When are you gonna catch the ball in your hip pocket?" and he says, "It's comin' too damn fast, Fireball." That was where I got the name "Fireball," from Lloyd "Pepper" Bassett.

He's passed. There's two conflicting stories. One said he was killed in California with marked cards and another one said that he just passed. He was from Louisiana.

Do you know any of your seasonal records?

The *Pittsburgh Courier* carried 'em. That's the only way my wife could catch up with me. She could call the [team's] main office at night and couldn't catch up with us because the office closed at 5:00. If it was [Chicago American Giants owner Dr. John] Martin or [Birmingham Black Barons owner William] Bridgeforth who owned the team, they had offices for the ballclub, but the offices wasn't open at night. If an emergency came up, she could always get the *Pittsburgh Courier* and they would have where we were each night, so you could call the ballpark in that town. That's how all the ballplayers' families caught up with 'em because they could follow the *Pittsburgh Courier* and the *Chicago Defender*. These were standard newspapers that had been around for years and they had followed the Negro leagues and that's how you kept up with the stats in those days.

At the end of every game each night, the road manager would have to call in and tell the owner, or the secretary, what had transpired, what we had did against a league team, and call in that type of information — how much the gate receipts were and those type of things. So, it would wind up, the *Pittsburgh Courier* and the *Chicago Defender* would have most of the accurate records that were kept. Here, in recent times, people have tried to find who has the records for the old, now defunct *Pittsburgh Courier* and I think some people have been successful in getting some information.

The records are important. If it was possible, some people would try to suppress the entire existence of the Negro leagues, so consequently what happened is, there is information that is *available* and it's in the hands of people who are lettin' it out, not only begrudgingly, but they're gettin' big money. There's people sittin' on stuff now that shouldn't be in the hands of some people that have made some efforts to steal some stuff that almost went to jail. Someone thinks they can make money on it.

You went in the service in 1952. Did you play ball there?

Oh, yes. I played with the Camp Roberts, California, team.

I came back out in '53 and I went up to Canada — Thetford Miners, up in the Provincial League. I think that year I had a 10-and-7 record. Okay, same thing happened there. I wanna go on record as saying that, in the minor leagues — white minor leagues — if you were a good enough ballplayer that's how deep they buried you. They would take you, put you with these minor league ballclubs, and they didn't have any more place to put you in their system and they wouldn't let anyone else have you who was interested in you, so lots of guys lived and died right in the minor leagues and I didn't intend for that to happen to me because I was makin' enough money in the Negro leagues to be able to sustain my wife and three children.

It was pretty hard gettin' a job when I came in from playin' baseball because the companies figured if you're not havin' any longevity there's no future in it. When baseball season come, I don't care what they were payin' because it wasn't enough.

The most I made in the Negro leagues was $850 a month. At the time when I went up in Canada, I was makin' $375 and I think I went up there for less than $300. It just didn't balance out. I was 23 at the time. They go to lookin' at you when you're 25 to see if you're major league material, so I just felt like it was time for me to not be thinking so much about the major leagues. I was neglectin' my children and my family by just doing somethin' that I loved so much they didn't have to pay me to do, so I felt like I needed to come home and raise my children.

I was just tellin' the children — they was welcomin' us back and all — and I was lettin' them know I didn't regret that. Numerous times I felt like, Gee, I'm not doin' what I wanna do here and I've got a life to live and I need to go back to playin' baseball, but I'm glad I made the decision to stick it out and work for an oil well company 25 years. I don't ever regret that. I'm not a religious person but I do believe in humanity.

What it was all about was, if you had a good black ballplayer and the gentleman's agreement was you wasn't gonna have no more than three or four blacks at the most on the club and [if] you had good white ballplayers, there wasn't any room for you. If you were better, there wasn't any room for you. They thought it wasn't a good business move to bring in undesirables that the public didn't wanna see. It wasn't the public that was makin' the decision. They didn't try 'em. The public wants to win. The guy can be from Canada, but if he comes to Houston, Texas, and produces a winner — participating in a winner — they don't care where he's from 'cause he's representin' their city. His morals can be ever so low and they'll be behind him.

Take Pete Rose. I'm not a Pete Rose fan but I don't think what he did is so bad. I think a person like Marge Schott who uses the "nigger" word and says, "I'm payin' him a million dollars," this should be reprimanded more so than a man that has a hobby. Michael Jordan — he's a superstar; he gambles. What the hell do I care? It's his money. It doesn't affect me. If he bets on the other team and he throws a game, that's a horse of a different color. But you can't control other people. But Pete Rose was a hustler. This man was baseball.

What stands out most in your memory?

Let me put it this way. There's other things in my life that were more significant, for me to be truthful about it. Something that's very significant to me that happened to me was — and it stays in my mind — my dad and I were playing semi-pro ball. He

played in the Negro leagues, also, and my uncle and my first cousin. We had a long, illustrious career throughout the years in the Negro leagues.

He came back from playin' in the Negro leagues and he had retired. We were down in Victoria, Texas, 'bout 160-some miles from here in Houston and at the same place where I finally went and pitched against my old team, the Eastern Greyhounds, with the Houston Eagles. But, anyway, my dad hit a home run and I was pitchin'. He was hittin' eighth and I came up behind him and hit a home run. We hit back-to-back home runs. I danced all the way around that ballpark because I wasn't known for hittin' home runs. I was known for stoppin' people from hittin' 'em. He was elated and I was elated and we both broke down and cried. [Laughs] It was a moment I never will forget because he was so happy to see that I was finally comin' into my own. I musta been, at that time, 16 or 17 years old.

My dad was Green Beverly, my uncle was Charles. [My father] was illiterate; he was ashamed that he couldn't write and he deserted my mother and my sister and I to go play baseball. Quite naturally, my mother spoke against him; she vilified him. I don't know, some way or another, I don't care how thick she laid it on, it didn't accept with me, nor did it with my sister. Then I got to know the man. Years later he came to live with me and I found out that he wasn't the man that she portrayed him to be. That was very rewarding for me to find out.

Who was the best player you saw?

The best player that ever lived was Willie Mays. It would be a tossup with he and [Mickey] Mantle, but Mantle would have set records that would've been almost impossible to break had he not been hurt. He was a hell of a ballplayer. He could hit the curveball, the fastball; he could think. He was a hell of a good base stealer and runner, but he played hurt. It's tough to play when you're hurt. If you got anything botherin' you, it's tough and he played under those conditions so no one really knows just how great Mantle would have been. I put Willie Mays ahead of him because Willie played intact.

Ted Williams — you could put the shift on him and you could corral him. Joe DiMaggio — you couldn't corral him. He's gonna hurt you. If you throw out on the outside, he's strong enough to hit it out on the other side. Williams pulled everything.

Mays played the field; he runs better than well; he had a good arm when he left the game. And he could think, also. That's the only reason I put him ahead of Ty Cobb, Lou Gehrig, and all of these people. I didn't get a chance to see Cobb and them but I've researched it.

Mays is the toughest out that I ever pitched to because he could hit the fastball and I had it in my mind I could throw the fastball by anybody and he lucked up and hit that one, but he won't hit this one and there it is again. [Laughs] I wanted to get him out on the fastball and they said, "Just push your wrist and the man sees the ball and he can't hit it. Why you throwin' him a fastball?" I said, "It's me against him and this is my thing. There's nobody can hit my fastball." He's the greatest ballplayer I've ever seen.

They had a guy in Birmingham before I went there, Ed Steele. You can look him up. Steele was 'bout the best hitter that I pitched against. He didn't only hit me, he hit other pitchers. I don't mean Texas leaguers — bloopers — a *line!* Everything he hit, you could hang clothes on it. Line drives. He hit one back through the box on me one time. I said, "I'll get him out. I'll throw the ball outside, on the outside corner, as hard as I can throw it." He hit the ball right back up the center, hit me on the elbow and they thought he'd broke my elbow, but I shook it off and went on and finished the ballgame. He was one of the better hitters that I faced.

Who was the best pitcher?

The best pitcher I went up against was a lefthander, Kelly Searcy. We finally got on the same ballclub. You won't read too much

about him, but you ask ballplayers about him. He's from Nashville. He passed. He wasn't what you would call a flamboyant guy, but he was more like a ladies' man, but he could pitch.

Verdell Mathis. I saw him before I played baseball when I was a kid. He was a good pitcher. The first time I pitched against Memphis I pitched against him. "I don't wanna pitch against Verdell Mathis!" And he beat me. We didn't get any runs. But later I beat him. He was one of the best.

When you pitched against him, he was well past his prime.

Yeah, but he was still good. He knew how to pitch.

I never pitched against Jehosie Heard. Jehosie Heard was the best lefthander I ever seen pitch. He could throw hard for a little man like that. [Heard, in 1954, became the first of his race to play for the Baltimore Orioles.]

I'll tell you a little story 'bout Heard. You know 'bout "lights," don't you? You get around these guys and I'm gonna let you in on a great secret and it's only known by baseball players and close friends. A "light" is when you catch a woman in the nude. If it's a white woman, it's a "light"; if it's a black woman, it's a "shade." That's the dictionary of the black ballplayer. There's so many other words that's used that people don't know what you're talkin' 'bout.

So whenever we're goin' down the road on a bus, everybody's asleep and you've got a guy who stands up there and makes sure the chauffeur doesn't go to sleep. "Curve to the right, chauf." "Curve to the left." "Red light, chauf." All these type of things out on the highway you tell the chauffeur. So we were ridin' along and somebody says, "Light on the right." Well, that means that the bus driver's set to pass a car and the lady's got her dress up around her thighs. [Laughs] This is a great joy to a bunch of guys who've been away from home for a long time, to see something as colorful and nice as that.

So everybody'd just raise up, eyes half closed, and stand up in the aisle and look over the guys who were on the other side. And after they see the bus passed the lady in the car, they'd go back and sit down. And then everybody'd comment on it.

We went around a car and the chauffeur said, "Light on the right," so we got up and looked and Heard was sittin' over by that side and up jumps Charley Pride. Charley jumped up to look and Heard say, "Pride, what the hell is you lookin' at? If you seen anything you wouldn't know what the hell it is." [Laughs] Charley was country, just like he is now. He's more sophisticated now, but he was scared of everything. If anybody said anything to him he went into his shell.

Pride was with us in '54 and '55. He's a fine fellow. This is a truly nice guy. He is a hick. He's a country, redneck hick. He's one of the better guys that I've ever met, as far as humanity. He thanks everybody who claps for him.

Charley come from abject poverty. He had took us to see his family. Every time we'd get to Houston, my mother and them would bring out baskets of chicken, bring 'em out to the hotel where we lived, so every time you'd go in and a guy lived in that town, his family would always bring out some food. So we was goin' to Greenville, Mississippi, to play and that's not far from Sledge, Mississippi, so we came through Charley's hometown. His parents came downtown. We met them. They brought something to eat. Great, great meal — beans and chicken. That next mornin' when we were leavin', Charley pointed out where he lived. Shoulda seen the place. Couldn't believe how rundown it was. He goes back in the '80s and buys the sharecropper farm that he sharecropped on. He owns it now. That speaks well of America, when you come from a dirt-poor farmer — somebody else's land — and become as rich a man as he is. That's not total racism. The opportunities *are* here.

Speaking of food, what kind of meal money did you guys get?

I've got a book supposed to be comin' out January first. I'm gonna be talkin' about how the salaries varied, how the eating money varied. It was supposed to be a secret. The guys that were gettin' two dollars wasn't supposed to know that the guys were gettin' three dollars and 50 cents a day existed. I never kept it hid that I was gettin' $3.50 and I never got two dollars. I always got $3.50 and the reason that was, because all of the older ballplayers had been there paved the way for us was gettin' two dollars. We was gettin' $3.50 because the younger guys were all selected as potential white major league property, so they would give us more money, say, "Now don't tell the other guys. You're the only one gettin' $3.50." And then you come to some of the other ballplayers and they say, "I'm only gettin' two dollars. How in the hell am I gonna eat offa two dollars?" I wouldn't tell 'em I was gettin' $3.50. And some of the most intimate guys would say, "I'm gettin' $3.50 but I wasn't supposed to tell 'em, so don't tell 'em." "Me, too." [Laughs] The older guys, they wouldn't help you if you came in and tried to be arrogant around 'em and they don't like for you to make more money than they do.

Would you play baseball again?

Oh, man, I'd leave today! Oh, man! Look — you hear these guys, "Well, we played in cow pastures and cow dung was there and we had to move this," and all that. Sure we played in those ballparks, but that was one percent. We played in major league ballparks. We played in the best ballparks in the city where we were gonna play a local team. Some of 'em were better than major league ballparks because the entire community contributed towards it. That was their life. They wanted a decent ballfield.

You go to these towns. We were in Money, Mississippi. It was hot as hell. We were sittin' on the bus with our shirts off — I'd been to the movies — waitin' for 6:00 to go to the ballpark. We didn't get rooms and the bus was parked at the ballpark. When I got there, there was a white guy standin' up on the bus; he said, "Want up here?" and I said, "Thank you," and walked on by him, went back to my seat, pulled my shirt off, and sit down.

Eddie Brooks said, "Bev, you want a white wife?" I said, "What're you talkin' about?" He says, "This gentleman here's daughter is pregnant and he wants to send her outta town and she'll leave if any one of us guys want her, she'll go." I'm not interested in that. I don't know how he could do this. So she was pregnant and he felt so ashamed about his friends that he wanted to send her outta town—poor little thing had a suitcase—and stupid enough to think that any black ballplayer would want her.

These were the type of things that we ran across and didn't understand how a man could say, "Just take my daughter." She had no choice, poor thing. That's very sad.

But—oh, yeah—I'd leave yesterday. I loved the game. I don't sit down and watch it because there's too many inconsistencies from people who are gettin' huge amounts of money and can't play the game to perfection.

Baseball is really a game where, when one error is made, that's the game. If somebody don't make an error—and an error can be as minute a thing as throwin' the wrong pitch to the wrong guy that you know been gettin' him on. The other pitcher is throwin' him one that you don't know nothin' about and you've committed a cardinal sin against this man. You lose the ballgame and people say, "Well, it's just a hit." No—this guy had never been thrown that pitch because everybody in the league knowed he hits this pitch. So guys forget and go out there and make that error and throw a pitch up to a guy who can get the

ball out of the ballpark. Then they say, "That's just a coincidence." He been gettin' him out for months with the other pitch. Why do you throw him that one?

The managers can see all of this, 'cause every night they have to keep a record. If you're pitchin' the next night, you keep the book the night before. So if this guy hit a low, outside curveball, he don't get no hit tonight on a low, outside curveball. He got to hit somethin' else. He got to hit a inside curveball or a fastball inside or one down around his knees or he gets one in back of his head to scare the hell out of him if he's a home run hitter. He don't get up and wanna fight; he get up and say, "Well, I've got respect out of this pitcher. He feels as though I'm dangerous and he's gonna knock me down. I've got to hang in here." Really, he respects you and that's a compliment. These guys now, I don't know. I've gotta let you know I respect you. If I didn't respect you, why would I knock you down?

Would I be able to play now? I have no doubt in my mind. We had mediocre ballplayers, too—we had to have nine—but they were average. But I see some guys who are below major league quality. They're just there. They don't know how to play the game.

You gotta have individual ballplayers the public come to see. They don't come to see nine ballplayers, really. They come to see one guy who rattles the boards or steals *way* more bases than anyone else. That's what you got to have. You got to have exciting ballplayers. Nine of 'em ain't gonna be exciting, but every team has to try and have two, or one, exciting ballplayers. You know, Mantle was exciting; Maris was dull. Same power, great ballplayers, but Mantle, man, you just couldn't beat him. He's colorful. That's the game.

WILLIAM "FIREBALL" BEVERLY
Born 5-5-30, Houston, TX Died 9-11-96, Houston, TX
Ht. 6' 0"   Wt. 185   Batted and Threw R

Year	Team, league	G	IP	W	L	Pct	H	BB	SO	SHO	ERA
1950	Houston Eagles, NAL			5	1	.833					4.63
1951	New Orleans Eagles, NAL										
	Chi. American Giants, NAL										
1952	Chi. American Giants, NAL										
1953	Thetford Miners, ProvL			10	7	.588					
1954	Birm. Black Barons, NAL										
1955	Birm. Black Barons, ind.										

Ollie Brantley

Red and White Sox

NEGRO LEAGUE DEBUT: 1950

Seventeen-year-old Ollie Brantley joined the Memphis Red Sox of the Negro American League in 1950. His record in Negro league play has not been recorded, but it must have been a good one because the Chicago White Sox purchased his contract a few years later *and* gave him a $15,000 bonus. That was a huge outlay in the early 1950s.

Brantley gave a good return on the investment. Moving steadily up the minor league ladder as a starting pitcher, he had seasons of 22, 18, and 15 wins and reached Triple-A San Diego (PCL), one step away from the major leagues, when he hurt his strong right arm.

Moved to the bullpen, he continued to pitch well, especially in 1965 with Orlando (Florida State League), where he led the league with 61 appearances and compiled a 15–8 record with a 1.63 ERA. The previous year, at Bismark, Manitoba (Northern League), he had been 6–3, 1.50.

Playing until he was nearly 40 years old, Ollie Brantley won 135 games in organized ball and lost only 99 (a .580 winning percentage) with a 3.54 ERA (2.83 *after* he hurt his arm). His Negro league record is not known, but he may have more than 150 wins altogether. That's a good career for anyone in any league.

I played in '51 and '52 for the Memphis Red Sox. Then I went in with the Chicago White Sox. I got traded and played in the Twins organization, too, 'til 19-and-71. I got traded from the White Sox over to the Twins in 19-and-61. I played Double-A, Triple-A.

Did you spend spring training with the parent club?

I did a couple of years. We were playin' in the same place in Sarasota and I worked out with them. I played Triple-A and usually you go to spring training with 'em and the last few days or so they send you back out to Triple-A.

How did you join the Red Sox? Are you from Memphis?

No, I'm from Arkansas. Marianna — little small town 'bout 40 miles out of Memphis. They scouted me and I started playin' with the Memphis Red Sox. A guy by the name of Goose Curry, he'd go around and he'd check around all these sandlot teams and that's how he found me over there playin' Sunday baseball and he brought me over there just as I got out of high school. I played two years with the Red Sox and then I guess they sold me to the White Sox. I don't know how they did that. I got $15,000 bonus.

You played until you were nearly 40 years old.

Yeah. I hurt my arm. When I was with San Diego I was in Tacoma, Washington, one night and I was pitchin' and it stays kinda cool there and rainy. I don't know what happened. It looked like I pulled a muscle in my elbow and I never did get back to really like I shoulda been. That was in 1960. I played on for a while.

Do you know your record with the Red Sox?

I had a winnin' record with 'em the years I played there. You know, I was just a young man then, 'bout 16 or 17 years old. I was winnin'; I don't know what kind of record I had, but I could throw the ball pretty good. I was mostly a fastball pitcher.

I had good years [in organized ball]. I won 15 games in Class A ball and I went to Double-A ball and I won up there 16 or 17 games and I went out to the Northwest League and I won 20-some games. I always had a winnin' record.

My best year was, I believe, 1959. I was at Charleston. That was in the South Atlantic League. I think I won 18 ballgames, but that was a tougher league. I won 20 ballgames in Class B.

I've had several good games I pitched 1-to-nothin'. I never pitched a no-hitter but I've been close to it. I pitched a one-hitter. Every game to me was a big game when you're winnin'.

I barnstormed with the Willie Mays All-Stars when they played against the Mickey Mantle All-Stars, and I pitched against those guys and I played winter ball a lot, played against a lot of major league ballplayers down in the winter league, down in Venezuela and Nicaragua and Columbia, South America, in the '60s.

Who was the best player you saw?

That's kinda hard to say 'cause there was a lot of good ballplayers at that time. I don't know really who was the best ballplayer . I played with [Luis] Aparicio before he went up. Rod Carew—he was my roommate for two years. He was a good ballplayer, [but] he wasn't the best. I played against Willie Mays and Mickey Mantle and those kinda guys. Those were tough ballplayers in those days. I don't think the guys today can play with those guys, Hank Aaron and those. They were great hitters.

They've got good ballplayers today, too, but you don't have a lot of finesse pitchin' like you did back then. Now you don't have to worry 'bout gettin' hit with the ball; you just stand there and take your cuts. The game is a lot different now; it's played differently. It's not as rough as it was back then in those days. They've got better facilities now and a livelier ball, I think, and everything else. Weaker pitchin'.

Who were some of your Memphis teammates?

Bobby Boyd was one. I was a lot younger than those guys. They was gettin' ready to get out when I came in. Verdell Mathis, he was there. Verdell was mostly a teacher for the younger guys. He was a great pitcher. His better days were behind him when I came up. Most of these guys are up in their 70s now.

The league was almost ready to fold at the time we came in. I think they existed 'til about '55 and that was it. They just dissolved. They were strong when they were playin'; they had a lotta good ballplayers, a lotta good ballplayers that never got to the big leagues. They never did get their chance, but just about every ballplayer you'd meet could play then—run and hit. Those guys had a rough time—traveled on the bus, stay on the bus all night and get a dollar-and-a-half for meal money. You couldn't hardly eat for that. That's what I got when I played for the Red Sox.

It was rough. A guy had to be a heck of a ballplayer then to stay up and sleep on the bus, not get proper rest, and make all them long trips. They were playin' every night, town to town. Some were league games and some of 'em weren't.

Who was the best pitcher you saw?

At that time, Verdell Mathis was one of the better pitchers that I saw. I didn't see everybody in the Negro leagues. I saw most of the guys on the Birmingham Barons, I saw some of the Kansas City Monarchs,

Chicago American Giants, Indianapolis Clowns. At that time, all those pitchers could throw hard. Most every pitcher you'd meet could throw the ball hard. They had good hitters, guys could run and hit. They had a lotta good ballplayers.

I've seen so many good pitchers when I was in organized ball. Billy Pierce was in the White Sox chain, Dick Donovan — all those guys. We were down in the minor leagues hopin' that we'd get a chance to get a shot up there, but those guys had a set team at that time, in the '50s. Most of the major league clubs had their pitching staffs almost set. Maybe one position, then you'd have so many guys competin' ahead of you — D, C, B, and A, Double-A, Triple-A ball. You usually had to come all the way up the ladder.

Did you enjoy baseball?

Oh, yeah. I wouldn't take anything for

the time I played. It's a lot better facilities now but I wouldn't take anything for the time that I went through. I enjoyed it and I learned a lot. I learned to respect the game and know what it's all about. Some of these ballplayers today, I don't think they really know what it means for them to be there makin' the kind of money they're makin'. We didn't make any kinda money. Guys like Mickey Mantle, Willie Mays, Hank Aaron — if they made a hundred thousand dollars it was good back in those days. That ain't no money today.

Any regrets?

No, I don't have any regrets. If I could just call time back to today I believe I could be up in the major leagues, but that's just one of those things. Some people weren't even around to enjoy what we enjoyed. Like bein' here [in Kansas City] and gettin' together again, man, that's great!

OLLIE BRANTLEY
Born 1932, Lexon, AR
Ht. 6' 2½"   Wt. 178   Batted and Threw R

Year	Team, league	G	IP	W	L	Pct	H	BB	SO	SHO	ERA
1950	Memphis Red Sox, NAL										
1951											
1952											
1953											
1954	Waterloo, III	3		1	1	.500					
1955	Bisbee, AzMxL	49	157	10	11	.476	180	65	124		6.02
1956	Waterloo, III	36	114	7	9	.438	125	49	70		3.87
1957	Eugene, NWL	42	264*	22*	15	.595	243	98	166		3.65
1958	Colorado Springs, WL	39	193	15	6	.714	201	54	126		3.40
1959	Charleston, SAL	46	198	12	11	.522	207	64	121		3.91
1960	San Diego, PCL	3	5	0	0	.000	4	4	0	0	1.80
	Charleston, SAL	27	143	7	9	.438	142	43	91		3.65
1961	Columbia, SAL	15	66	4	5	.444	74	13	31	0	3.82
	Topeka, III	8	35	2	1	.667	34	12	30		3.96
1962	Bismark, Man., NorL	38	109	7	2	.778	111	30	99		2.81
1963		41	76	7	6	.538	76	20	64	0	4.03
1964		31	60	6	3	.667	39	23	52	0	1.50
1965	Orlando, FSL	61*	144	15	8	.652	113	21	105		1.83
1966	Wisconsin Rapids, MWL	56	91	5	6	.455	87	18	70	0	2.67
1967		37	48	8	2	.800	53	9	30	0	2.81
1968	Wilson, CarL	31	71	2	3	.400	81	13	38		3.30
1969	Orlando, FSL	22	24	5	1	.833	32	4	13	0	4.88

Charlie Davis

"Lefty"

NEGRO LEAGUE DEBUT: 1950

Charlie Davis played professional baseball for five years in the early 1950s. Today he lives in Cincinnati. He moved there in 1960 when he lost a job in Atlanta because he owned a new car. He was told, "You don't need no job. You got a new car."

Davis was then only a few years removed from his Negro leagues playing days, and he still had his pitching ability. He joined a local team, as did a few other Negro leagues veterans (Ted Richardson, Eddie Stankie, Larry Raines), and the team became so successful no one would play it.

His playing days are well behind now but he loved his time as an active player, during which he played against the likes of Satchel Paige, Ernie Banks, and Buck O'Neil.

I was 19 when I started. 1950. Before that I hadn't played nothin' but city league ball. I lived in Atlanta and I worked at Simmons Bedspring and Mattress. They had two company teams — one white team, one black team. We only played one another on the Fourth of July.

It was a bunch of city league ball around there in Atlanta. We played all the cotton mills, like LaGrange. All those different places had teams, they all had maybe two teams, and we'd always play one another. I really never thought about playin' in no other league.

One of the guys played in the Negro league practically all his life was Pee Wee Butts. He saw me play one day and he came over and asked me on the weekend, he said, "Look, I think you can make a livin' playin' baseball." At that time, I said, "Oh, I don't think so." He said, "I'm gonna see can we get you in spring trainin' with us."

At the same time, we had another friend of mine play with me at Simmons Bedspring. He couldn't hit or he couldn't throw as good as me, but he could always outrun me and I felt he was a better player — a boy named Lloyd Ramsey. It was 'bout eight brothers of 'em.

Birmingham sent me money to come to spring trainin'. We took spring trainin' down in Montgomery, Alabama, at the college and the guy called me and said, "You gonna be there?" and I said, "Yeah, but I got a friend that's a better ballplayer than me." He said, "You pay his way and we'll give you the money back when you get here." So I took him along with us to spring trainin'.

I had never took exercise — nothin' like — to play baseball full time. We checked in the hotel. They gave me a uniform the next day and said, "At 7:00 we want y'all to be ready to take the field."

Well, I went and eat everything I could eat, drunk a quart of milk. I said, "Man, these guys are gonna work me hard so I gotta be able to take it."

Well, I went out to take exercise and 'bout 9:00 I was layin' flat out — done fell out. I mean, I never did that before. So I'm layin' out and I woke up, I said, "Well, I know I'm goin' home," but I happened to look down the line and there's about four or five old ballplayers layin' down there with me, so I felt I had a pretty good chance.

Well, my friend, he's steady goin'. So when time come to go in that afternoon, the man said, "All you guys that fell out durin' practice, you gonna have to stay out here and catch up. You gotta stay out here and do what the other guys done done." I did that and then one of the coaches came to me and told me, "You can't eat that kinda food on the kinda exercise that they gonna give you."

About the third day, they had guys runnin' by the speed. Always the fastest guys always was further ahead at the end. My friend, by the third day I'm runnin' about fourth guy behind him and I thought he was much faster than me, but I'm gettin' in shape and I found out I could outrun him a little bit. I guess we went on 'bout two weeks; the guy came in and told me, said, "Well now, Davis, I'm gonna have to let your friend go home. He ain't gonna make it." Well, I was wantin' to go home, too.

He said, "No, we're gonna trade three of y'all to Memphis and I think you got a good chance." I wasn't interested in stayin' then. My friend went home and I was ready to go home.

So they traded me and a boy named Higgins and one named Eddie Reed. Higgins was the onliest one was really mad 'cause he's from Alabama and he was mad that he got traded. Me and Reed, it didn't make us no difference long as we got a chance to play.

We goin' on over to Memphis and I talked to Butts that night. He said, "I'm gonna tell you what they gonna do. They gonna keep you, but they gonna hassle you. They gonna try to get you to play as cheap as they can get you to play. What do you think you could stay for?"

And I said, "If I made maybe $400 a month that'd be more than I was makin' on my job." He said, "I'm sure they can give that, but they're gonna run you through the thing. Say you want $400 a month and stick by it."

So we goes in to talk to Dr. [John B.] Martin [Mempis Red Sox owner] and Goose [Curry, Red Sox manager] and Martin say, "Well, I got this ol' country boy here. I think we can teach him how to play ball a little bit. We gotta go through all this trainin' with him, we gonna furnish him food and a place to stay and all that." He said, "We'll give you $250 a month. You can send some money home."

I said, "I can't play for that."

"What you mean you can't play for that? How much you think you could play for?"

I said, "I gotta have $400 a month. I got some people back home."

He said, "We ain't gonna give no country boy that kinda money. You ain't proved yourself. You wanna stay and play or you wanna go home?"

I said, "I wanna go home."

So we kept arguin' and finally he told Goose, he said, "We gonna give him that. If he don't turn out, I'm gonna send him home. What we tryin' to do is teach you how to play baseball."

'Bout two weeks later we's in New Orleans playin' Birmingham and Birmingham had really good righthanded hittin' lineup. All I'm thinkin' about is when can I slip off and go home. Goose told me, "I'm gonna start you tonight. If you go past five innin's and you do a good job, I'm gonna let you go home."

That was fine with me, so I went out there and I shut 'em out for seven. So here come Goose and I'm wantin' to go all the way after I got through seven innin's. He's takin' this *long* walk and it took him

(L. to R.) Lonnie Harris, Satchel Paige, Charlie Davis, Kansas City, Missouri, 1953 (courtesy of Charlie Davis).

forever to get there. He said, "Lefty, you done did pretty good. I'm gonna take you out."

I said, "Yeah, but I got a shutout."

He said, "That's okay. I got Buddy Woods and [Isaiah] Harris. They need to throw some. I'm gonna use them behind one another. I'm gonna take you out. You earned a trip home."

So after the game I went to the hotel, packed up *all* my stuff. He took me down to the bus station and bought two tickets. He bought me a ticket from New Orleans to Atlanta and from Atlanta to Birmingham. He said, "Gimme your luggage."

I said, "What's that for?"

He said, "I know if you carry all your luggage you ain't comin' back."

Well, I was thrilled. I didn't care. I made up my mind then — I don't care; if I get home, I ain't goin' back no way.

So I came on to Atlanta and all my friends plus the guy they had cut loose, they all ridin' me 'bout, "Yeah, they done

cut you loose, too. You didn't make it," and I said, "No, I gotta go to meet the team in Birmingham." "No, no. They done cut you loose." I think that was the only thing that got me to go on back — to show them.

I went on back and met the team in Birmingham and that year my complete season I had about a 14-and-2 record. At 19 years old. I never did get a chance to relieve no more than maybe one innin' some-times. They expect you to go nine, but I was one of them guys, I had a really good arm. They teased me a lot 'cause if somebody's in trouble in the ninth innin' and the score'd maybe be tied, I'd say, "Hey, skip, lemme go see can I get these guys out," and I'd wind up with a win. That's what they teased me about: "You get all them wins on two innin's or one innin'."

That same year I made the East-West game. The East-West game was always in Chicago and when I was picked I couldn't believe it. Really, 'cause guys like Satchel Paige, Menske Cartledge, the guy right here in Cincinnati, he's dead now — a guy named Lefty Richardson — they was there. Me and Richardson played here in the city two years after I came here to live. He was a lefthander for the Clowns, weighed about 145 and he could throw 95. Ever'body wondered where he get the speed from. In fact, in our league I think him and Marshall Bridges was the hardest throwin'. Two lefthanders.

Marshall was the guy that the whole team used to wonder when do this guy sleep and when do he eat. We never saw him do nothin' but drink beer, smoke them cigars, and he'd be the last guy you'd see at night. And he wasn't a guy chased a lotta women. He would just stay up and drink. Never was a startin' pitcher, he was frankly the only relief pitcher on our team. Him and Charley Pride.

1953 Memphis Red Sox
Back row (L. to R.): Leroy Hancock, Isaiah Harris, Ray Higgins, Eddie Reed, Buddy Woods, Eddie Hancock, Jehosie Heard, Willie Patterson, Charlie Davis, Pat Paterson (?), Pepper Bassett. Front row (L. to R.): Arzell Robinson (?), Willie Sheelor, Fate Simms, Clay Cartwright, Zeke Merrick, Joe Chisholm, Berry (?), Goose Curry (manager) (courtesy of Charlie Davis).

Charley Pride always wanted to be a starter, but if we was killin' a team they'd let him come out and get somebody out but he wasn't that much of a pitcher. Charley Pride tried everywhere. He tried first base and all the guys teased him. Our team was payin' him $175 a month and the team kept him 'cause he could play the guitar and play that harmonica. He had a regular hair comb he put a piece of paper 'round. He'd play that.

Charley went to Birmingham as a first baseman. He'd admit he wasn't goin' back to Sledge [Mississippi]. They just give him eatin' money, he would stay.

In Waco, Texas, the guys on the team, we chipped in and bought him a guitar. Fifty-eight cents apiece. I heard him talkin' about he don't remember that. We bought him the guitar and if he didn't sing spirituals, we'd take it. He always loved Ernest Tubb and he'd play that kinda music and we'd say, "Man, if you don't sing some spirituals we gonna take the guitar!"

There was a spiritual group outta Memphis called The Spirit of Memphis. They offered him at that time a hundred dollars a week, furnish his clothes. He refused to go 'cause he wanted to play baseball.

He had a brother; I think he's a high sheriff down there somehwere and he's a better ballplayer. When we was in Memphis on the weekends he'd come out and take practice with us and he was just a much stronger ballplayer than Charley was.

He always played [guitar] just like you see him play. I 'member when we was in Battle Creek, Michigan — they had a independent team and we used to go out and play them. They had a couple ballplayers on the team had birthdays so they had a big celebration. You hear these people talkin' 'bout home run contests, see we had all that then. We battled 'em for home runs, we battled 'em for speed. Well, we had a couple of guys on our team could just flat-out *motor*. We had this guy named Perry — he's from Grand Rapids — and Perry had bad feet and all the guys claim he ran fast 'cause he didn't wanna touch the ground. He was probably one of the older guys on the team.

They lined us up. They had three crates of chickens. They ask, "Why they got these chickens?" Well, the chickens was for the relay team. The one win the relay was gonna get all these chickens. What we did, we put Perry on the last leg 'cause the guys thought he was too slow and they put their fastest guy on the last leg, not knowin' that Perry could fly. So when this guy got to third base, Perry was crossin' at home. We won the chickens.

So now they wanna know could any of us sing. We said, "We got a guy can play the guitar. Charles, go get the guitar." "Man, I ain't gonna do that out here before these folks." So we begged him. He went and finally got the guitar — he's missin' a string — and he got there and started playin' that guitar and they start throwin' money at him and that night ever'body on the team wanted to sleep with him to divide that money up.

I worked after the season every year. They used to barnstorm against the all-stars and always picked the best players. They picked players could play other positions other than pitch. They would just carry so many guys on there. In fact, you'd make as much money on that tour as you probably made all the season.

They started the tour always in Baltimore. When I got home if I got a job they had to hunt me to go. They'd finally catch me when they came to Atlanta. I'd join up with 'em then.

The major league ballplayers got 55 percent off the top, bookin' agent got 20, and the minor league Negro ballplayers got 25 percent. They split it up every night, whatever your money be. Some of the major league ballplayers, like Jackie Robinson, Campanella, Monte Irvin — I 'member Minnie Minoso one year — they gave their cut. You know, whatever they made they just put it in the pot with the minor league ballplayers. Your cut might be $3- or 400 in different cities every night. They paid for your hotel but you had to pay for your own food.

They had this secretary — he was a old guy then and I wonder if he's still livin'; he's from Texas and he's named Ligon. Ligon would always look up on a day like today and he'd say, "Man, it's gonna rain that game out tonight. I'll give you $200 for your cut."

Well, the guys didn't know that he already knew that they'd done sold out the ballpark. Some of 'em would fall for it. They claimed I was so tight, they say I saved my eatin' money, but I said, "Unh-unh, I'm gonna take a chance." Well, if you took a chance then all of a sudden you got a big piece of money and the guy done blowed that little $200 if he done sold the share.

The season would always end up by playin' two games in Miami. That would be the end of the road trip and I 'member every year I got home with $4-, 5,000 after that. That's what I had made in the season. That was great money.

And what we would do, like, you know, tonight I might pitch, but I could play outfield and I could play first base. Marshall Bridges could do the same thing. We always wanted Marshall to pitch to guys like Larry Doby 'cause he'd make Larry mad. He'd throw at him a couple times and he could bring it. Campanella, all them guys'd get mad, but we didn't worry about beatin' 'em. Several times we coulda beat 'em. People don't realize that.

Monte Irvin was one of the greatest guys. And Campanella. We had hard times with Don Newcombe, Junior Gilliam — some of them guys. I 'member we'd go out in Texas and those Triple-A ballparks a lotta times we all had to change clothes in the same dressin' room, but some of them guys would change clothes in their hotel, have somebody bring 'em out. But Monte Irvin was always one of them great guys.

There's a lotta guys talk that said they played in that league didn't play in that league and they don't know none of the guys and that shocked me when they start talkin'. Some of 'em are goin' by what they read, you know. I was talkin' to a guy the other day and he was tellin' me, "Well, we got paid today and then we didn't get nothin' to eat." That never happened with me. I got my paycheck first and fifteenth. If you wanted to choose to get your eatin' money every day, you got it every day. If you wanted to choose to get it once a week, you got it once a week. Two-fifty a day down south; now when you come north they'd always raise it a dollar.

In some instances, we played like in Cincinnati on a Monday night. By the time you got through gettin' dressed and get outta there and get somethin' to eat it's 12:00. They would tell you, "We're goin' to Louisville and if you wanna ride tonight we'll give you two dollars. If you wanna check in a hotel, we'll check in a hotel." Well, the guys said, "Let's ride tonight." If you stay at the YMCA in Cincinnati they didn't have air conditionin' — it was hot — so you'd ride. You'd probably get to Louisville early in the mornin' and they'd have somewhere for you to stay and you might play there Tuesday night.

Some of the guys look at it and tell you how hard it was. I'm tellin' you, I don't think I coulda had it no better. It *sound* rough but it was *great*. I wouldn't gave it up for nothin'.

Talkin' 'bout ballplayers, Pee Wee Butts was the greatest shortstop I've ever seen. They had a guy named [Eddie] Brooks —

he's dead — played second base. That was the greatest combination I had ever seen.

I'd have to say Pancho Herrera was one of the best hitters. I'd say Ernie Banks was the really best hitter but defense-wise, they had another guy named J. C. Martin played defense in front of Banks. I was able to see him in Kansas City [at the reunion]. I was sittin' there askin' about him and looked and there he was.

They had another guy that played with Detroit Stars was named [Ray] Miller. Left-handed hitter. I never was able to make him miss the ball. I got him out most times but he'd sit down and hit line drives somewhere. He had bad ankles; he couldn't play but about two or three games a week. He was a *great* hitter. He made the East-West game every year he was there and he didn't play regular.

[Henry] Kimbro was one of the great hitters. All the guys at Kansas City, his teammates, say, "I ain't speakin' to him." "What do you mean?" "Man, that old man give me such a hard time playin' with him." I said, "Man he's a hundred years old." "I still ain't speakin' to him." He would get mad at me 'cause he didn't wanna never hit at no changeups. If I got two strikes on him I'd throw him four changeups and he'd walk halfway to the mound and call me a name. He just meant he wasn't gonna never hit at a slow pitch.

And the Simms brothers — 'bout four of them played in that league. We had Fate Simms with us. He was a good catcher, good infielder, and he could fly. *Good* speed.

I would have to say the best pitcher was Satch. There was quite a few. Menske was good. I saw a little lefthander at Kansas City I didn't know what he had. Norm Gaston. Ev'ry chance he get he'd slip off and go home and some guy'd find him up in Canada. He could throw I believe harder than Marshall. They clocked him one time at 98.

[Berto] Nunez was a little pitcher — 'bout 5-11, couldn'ta weighed a hundred and seventy. He could throw as hard as Marshall. Ever'body worried about him gettin' two strikes 'cause then they figured here come his fastball and they wasn't gonna be able to catch up with it.

One of the other guys that played with me named Buddy Woods, a righthanded pitcher. I talked to some guys in Kansas City; they say he livin' in Las Vegas, lost one of his arms.

Satch, it seemed like he didn't throw hard. Seemed like you'd be ready: "This pitch ain't comin' that fast," and it was just like a plane — right by you.

You see that picture of me and him and Lonnie? I'm 6-2 and a guy says, "It look like you gotta look up at him." He had to be 6-4 or 6-6. You see him throw his sinker. He would come underhanded and his hand would drag the ground. That ball would just take right off. He'd say, "God, son! Didn't you know I was tricky?" He'd be talkin' to you. "Son, I'm gonna throw you the best curveball you ever seen in your life." Then he'd throw you somethin' like that and he'd say, "Well, you know, Satch is tricky."

His condition kept him so long. A lot of these young guys don't realize that. He never drinked or smoked and he always got him somethin' to eat and some rest.

I never did drink, never did smoke. I'm a country-raised guy. I never knew what it was to get in condition 'til I started playin' in that league. You know, I played once a weekend. We didn't have nobody to train you 'bout gettin' in shape to play.

Back in '76 I was playin' softball with some guys. First time in my life I ever had a pulled muscle. I got to the ballgame late and when I got there the bases was loaded and they said, "Hurry up and put on your shoes and come hit!" I came up there and hit the ball in the gap and roundin' second base and somethin' say "Bip!" I say, "Oh, my god, what was that?" First time in my whole career that I had a pulled muscle. But, see, playin', you know what it took to get you in shape.

Today I have so much respect for [Greg] Maddux 'cause he pitch somewhat like I did. I could strike certain guys out but I never thought about that. I thought about gettin' him out easy. And that's what Maddux do. I mean, Maddux throw some stuff up there — you wanna hit at it, fine, but he don't be worryin' about how many times he strike you out.

When you reach a certain age, you gotta stay in shape. You gotta stay in shape year-'round to keep playin' baseball. I'm watchin' [Ryne] Sandberg tryin' to come back and I said, "Boy, he's got a test on his hands."

The one best game I ever played in was in Topeka, Kansas. That was the onliest no-hitter I ever had. Against Kansas City. Ernie Banks was on the team. And, believe it or not, you know who could really hit at that time? Buck O'Neil. We worried about that.

In the ninth innin' Goose came to me and told me — they wouldn't tell me I had a no-hitter — but he told me in the ninth innin', he said, "You know Banks is comin' up." That's the only way you kept Banks in the whole game was they didn't have a lead on you 'cause he'd always come out for Martin. He said, "Banks is comin' up. How you gonna get him out?"

I said, "I'm gonna try to get him out tight." Goose said, "Okay." Well, I got one right in on his hands. He hit right up to center field.

I walked the next guy, which was — what was this guy's name? He played third base for them 'cause we always felt like they oughtta knock the glove off his hand 'cause he never kept it on his hand. But he was always a pesky good hitter. Hank Bayliss! I walked him. I wouldn't have to worry 'bout him stealin'.

And then here come Buck. And Goose called time. He came out and told me, "Now look. You keep that ball low if you have to bounce it." But I had made up my mind Buck was lookin' for me to keep it low 'cause I had good control. I got two strikes on him and threw him one right in his wheelhouse and he missed it. I struck him out. Next guy bounced out and Goose came out. If you ever saw Goose, his eyes looked like two big eggs. "What was on your mind?" he said. I said, "I was ahead of him, skip, and he was lookin' for me to keep it low." And Buck O'Neil told me the next night that's exactly what he was doin'. He said, "Lefty, you had pretty good control. I was *never* thinkin' you were gonna throw me nothin' right where I wanted it."

We won the game and about two weeks later we had this little boy from Waco, Texas. Goose picked him up. Little righthander. If we was on a long winnin' streak, Goose would let the pitcher that pitched the night before go out and talk to the other guy; he'd stay on the bench. And we did play jokes on one another, so I goes out to talk to this kid and he says, "Hey, Charlie, Buck's comin' up. I believe I can get him out. I throw hard as you do. I believe I can get him out up around his chest."

I said, "Do what you wanna do with him, but Goose had told me to tell you to get it low if you have to bounce it." Before I got back in the dugout, he wind up and threw one high and Buck hit it and told the guy on base in front of him, "Hold up. I done took ahold of that."

And the dugout was all kinda low, you know. You had to bend over to come out and Goose jumped up and bumped his head. Ever'body's scared to laugh. He said, "What did you tell him, Lefty?" "I told him you said throw it low if you have to bounce it."

Here comes this guy after he got 'em out. He comes walkin' in the dugout and Goose's standin' there with both hands in his back pockets. He said, "I …" Goose said, "Every time you open your mouth, that's ten dollars." And he was tryin' to tell Goose that I told him to throw it up high and he couldn't even get his words in 'cause he was scared he was gonna get fined.

'Bout two days later, he said, "Lefty told me to try it up there!" I said, "Wait a minute. No, I didn't."

I tell you, I wouldn't miss that time playin' for nothin' in my life. I was there five years.

CHARLES "LEFTY" DAVIS
Born 3-15-29, Fort Valley, GA
Ht. 6' 2"   Wt. 190   Batted and Threw L

Year	Team, league	G	IP	W	L	Pct	H	BB	SO	SHO	ERA
1950	Memphis Red Sox, NAL			14	2	.875				1	
1951											
1952											
1953											
1954											
1955											

Ira McKnight
There to the End

NEGRO LEAGUES DEBUT: 1952

The Negro leagues began dying that day in late 1945 when the Brooklyn Dodgers signed Jackie Robinson, but it was a slow death. Final interment didn't take place until after the 1960 season, and maybe it wouldn't have occurred even then had it not been for expansion.

Whatever the reason, the 1960 season was it for professional black baseball. Some of the stars from the 1940s and even earlier were still playing. They were in their 40s and even 50s, too old to be signed by organized ball but too good to not play.

The legendary Satchel Paige had returned to the Kansas City Monarchs and he was there at the end. There with him was a young catcher who had played briefly in organized ball. His name was Ira McKnight, and he was Satchel's last catcher in the Negro leagues.

With the final demise of the Negro leagues, McKnight played on a touring team and then went to Canada to play in a semi-pro league there that was the equal of the lower minor leagues.

I started out in 1952 and then I came back in the league in 1956 through 1960 — at the very end. I was 20 when I came back. I had been playin' semi-pro ball in South Bend a little bit and then I was with a White Sox farm team. I took spring training in Hollywood, Florida. I was signed by the White Sox in '55 but I got cut in spring training.

Originally I signed with Memphis. I was about 15 but I put my age up to 16 so I could leave home. Goose Curry was the manager of Memphis and he come through there lookin' for a catcher and a couple friends that knew Goose told him about me. Goose asked me to try out. The secretary, Rufe Ligon, he tried to get me to come back the next two years — '53 and '54 — but I wouldn't go. I went back to high school.

In '55, I started playin' with an amateur team, then I saw an article in the paper Kansas City [Monarchs] was formin' a new team. Mr. Ted Rasberry, he bought everything from Kansas City 'cause they sold everything but the bus and one player. That was Bob Mitchell. That was '55. I saw the ad, so I wrote him and went to Chicago and met up with them. We went down south to Birmingham to train and I tried out and made the team in 1956. Ted Rasberry owned Detroit [Stars] and Kansas City.

I caught. That was my main position. In 1957 I played with Kansas City and then I signed with the Yankees and I got hurt and I got released. I came back to the league in '58 and I stayed on 'til '60. I was with

Auburn, New York [in the Yankees system].
New York-Penn League. I hit about .315 —
it's in the *Blue Book*— but I got released
anyway. I don't know what happened. I
could have signed on with another team in
the league, but I just came home.

I came back to Kansas City and I caught
Satchel Paige. He'd come pitch three
innin's. He was throwin' great. Age — I
don't know, but I know he had to be in his
60s 'cause he was in his 40s when he went
up with Cleveland. He could throw the ball
hard even then and he had great control.

Was he the best pitcher you caught?

Well … no. At that time he was great,
but he wasn't the best pitcher I caught.

A guy named [Marion] Sugar Cain — he
was up in his late 40s when he was playin'
then. He had a great curveball. Cain was
kinda old, but he went on a tour one year
against the major leaguers — Harmon Kille-
brew was one — and he had good success
against them on that tour. The White Sox
wanted to sign him, but I think somebody
that knew him told about his age and they
wouldn't sign him. He was a great
pitcher — good control, great curveball.

Then I had a guy named Bill Jones out of
Jacksonville, Florida. He was younger; he
was a good pitcher. Willie Smith — I batted
against him and he went up with Detroit
and became an outfielder. He was a great
pitcher in the league. Good curveball. He's
from Birmingham. Eugene Williams — he
was a good sidearmer. I think he went with
the White Sox but he didn't stay too long.

Joe Ferguson — this was up in the Cana-
dian league now — he went up to the
Dodgers as a catcher. They converted him
to a catcher, but he pitched up in Canada,
where I played semi-pro ball. He was a
good pitcher.

There were a lotta good pitchers, but
these were some of the best I batted
against. Another guy was Willie Harris; he
was out of Chicago.

Who was the best player you saw?

I would say the best player — there's
quite a few, but one of the best — was Frank

Williams, Billy Williams's brother. He was
a good hitter, could run, good outfielder —
he had all the tools. He was in the Pittsburgh chain, then I think the Cubs signed
him. He was older than Billy. They released
him and I think he went out to Sacramento
to live.

*Are there games that stand out from your
career?*

It was 1961 and can't remember the
place, but one game we had a no-hitter. We
had three different guys pitch. Satchel
pitched three innin's; I think a guy named
Aaron Jones — he was out of Chicago and
he was a good pitcher — he pitched three
innin's. We had three guys pitch three
innin's apiece. I can't think of the other
pitcher. I caught the whole game. I think I
got two hits. I was a pretty good hitter for a
catcher.

We was tourin' and went to Danville,
Illinois, and then to Michigan City, Indiana, and then went to Fort Wayne. We was
playin' against semi-pro teams and I think
I went 3-for-3 in Danville and we went
over to Michigan City and I went 5-for-5.
Altogether, I think I went 8-for -8. Eight
hits in a row. Then we went over to Fort
Wayne and the streak stopped; I went 1-
for-4 there. I remember that pretty good.

What type of hitter were you?

I had good power, but I was mostly a
line-drive hitter. I didn't go for power. I
think my best year was '57; I think I hit
about 13 or 14 home runs. I had some
power but I didn't like to strike out too
much, so I hit mostly line drives — a contact hitter. I'd bat two sometimes and I'd
bat three and then I batted four and five. I
had good speed for a catcher.

*When you left the Negro leagues after
1960, what did you do?*

I went up to Canada, up in
Saskatchewan. They were allowed to have
two imports from the States. It was a pretty
good semi-pro league. Curley Williams
played up there. He was there when I left
the [Negro] league in 1960 and went up
there.

Ira McKnight (courtesy of Ira McKnight).

Then in 1961, '62 we was tourin' up in Canada and Satchel was with us then. He toured with us about two years. Goose Tatum was there, too, with the Detroit Stars as a drawin' card. In 1961, I think. He'd do his tricks.

When you were playing in the Negro league, a great many changes were taking place in society but there was still discrimination. What problems did you encounter?

When we came in the league it wasn't really noticeable. We didn't have the kinds of problems the older players did. We didn't pay too much attention to it. The older guys noticed it more than we did. It was rougher back before I started.

How were the travel conditions?

It was better, but we still traveled by bus, though. It was rough. When I got hurt in '56, I got my finger hit by a bat — double swing — and we were in Omaha, Nebraska, and we rode all night goin' to Kansas City, Missouri, and I didn't get nothin' done to my finger. Rode all night and on the next day they took me to a doctor and he gave me a shot in my rear. My finger is still

messed up right now. It grew kinda crooked. I went to a Yankee Stadium doctor; he said I'd have to have it broken to straighten it out. It's crooked to this day.

We had a lot of 5- or 600 mile trips. We'd leave somewhere and drive all day and play at night. Sometimes I'd catch doubleheaders and one time I caught three games in one day. It was rough travelin'.

What about meal money and salary?

In those days, we got three dollars a day [for meals]. I was paid maybe two-fifty a month.

How many games did the team play in a season?

About 80. We'd play every night and I caught most of 'em. In '56, I shared the duty with another catcher, but in '57 I caught most all of 'em 'til we picked up another guy in Florida and I started playin' the outfield. Then '58 and '59 it was just every game.

Any regrets?

Not too many regrets, but I should've went higher in pro ball. I think at times my owner, he sold some of the players' contracts pretty cheap. Quite a few of the players got manipulated out of a little money.

I regret that I didn't go higher in baseball. I should've went higher. I think I had major league potential, but at the time with the Yankees it was pretty rough. They had Elston Howard and Yogi Berra and other guys in the minors. Johnny Blanchard. I met Jim Command; he was up in Grand Rapids, Michigan, after I came back in '58 and he was catchin' with a semi-pro team — the Grand Rapids Sullivans — and I thought I had as good potential as he did.

I should've went higher. When you get dejected your confidence suffers. You give up a little bit. You play just enough to keep playin' 'cause you want to play baseball. In different circumstances, I should've went higher.

Would you do it again?

Play ball again? Oh, yeah. I would. It was a good experience. In fact, I'd do it again because at the time when I was comin' up in South Bend, there wasn't nothin' else to do in South Bend. You could get a job with Studebaker at that time and I'd just been stuck in South Bend. Baseball helped me get away and it was a good experience. I would do it again.

IRA McKNIGHT
Born 8-5-35, Trenton, TN
Ht. 5' 10½"   Wt. 180   Batted and Threw R

Year	Team, league	Pos	G	AB	R	H	2B	3B	HR	RBI	SB	BA
1952	Memphis Red Sox, NAL	C										
1956	Kansas City Monarchs, ind.	C										
1957	Kansas City Monarchs, ind.	C-OF							13			
	Auburn, NYPL	C										.315
1958	Kansas City Monarchs, ind.	C										
1959		C										
1960		C										

Dave Whitney

Baseball's Loss = Basketball's Gain

NEGRO LEAGUE DEBUT: 1952

Dave Whitney is one of the best all-around athletes ever to come out of Lexington, Kentucky, and when the time came to chose one sport to pursue, his choice was baseball. He began as the property of the Kansas City Monarchs and in 1954 succeeded Ernie Banks as that team's shortstop.

Organized ball wanted him, and offers were made to the Monarchs for his contract. Historically, when a player was sold by a Negro leagues team to a major league team, a portion of the purchase price was given to the player, but this was 1954 and the Monarchs, indeed all of black baseball, were struggling to survive. The money, all of it, was needed to stay in operation, so Whitney was told he would receive nothing if the sale came to pass.

Married with a child, he needed the assurance and security not available in baseball, so he retired from the game. He became a high school basketball coach, later moved to the college ranks, and eventually retired as Alcorn State's all-time winningest coach. Then, when the need arose again in 1996, he returned as the basketball coach at Alcorn State.

But he'd play baseball again.

I went to high school in Lexington, Kentucky—Lexington Dunbar. I played baseball for the semi-pro team there in Lexington and I guess I was about 17, 18 years old and I was playing with 25-, 26-, 27-year-old guys. I played shortstop with them.

You know the tournament they used to have out in Wichita, Kansas? The ABC. We made that at least three times and went out there. That was my introduction to the Negro leagues because I played one ballgame against Hank Aaron and the old great Negro catcher, Josh Gibson, who played with the Homestead Grays, and we played the House of David, the Indianapolis Clowns—all those guys—and we were on a semi-pro level but we had some hell of a sponsor, you see.

Bill White, who became the president of the National League, was in the service then, in Fort Knox, and he would come up on Sundays or when we played at night during the week and he would play for us. Larry Raines, who played for Cleveland, and I'm trying to think of the tall left-handed pitcher that went with the Yankees. [Steve] Hamilton. He was a hell of a basketball player with Morehead. We all played on that team. We had a heck of a baseball club.

I went to college and I went on a basketball scholarship. I played baseball and basketball and football, and my senior year the Indianapolis Clowns wanted me to stop school and my dad wouldn't let me. The

Dave Whitney (courtesy of Dave Whitney).

day I left college — graduated — the Kansas City Monarchs had already been talking with me and they sent me a ticket and I met them in Dayton, Ohio, and I played that night. Played left field. This was '52.

Buck O'Neil was my coach. He was the one that found me. Ted Rasberry — he was the guy that really tried to get me to go with the Indianapolis Clowns when I was in college.

I had a good season with the Monarchs. I had a *very* good season with them and a lot of scouts got on my case. I hit .325 and stole a lot of bases and had a good arm and everything and I was able to barnstorm up until October. The funny thing about it, when I got home I had greetings from Uncle Sam. [Laughs] I had to go directly in the army.

I played basketball and baseball in the army and the scouts just followed me all the while I was in — two years. I got out in '53 and in '54 I was definitely going back with the Monarchs because they kept in contact with me the whole time. Dizzy Dismukes, who was the traveling secretary during that particular time, he was a kind of personal friend of mine and he kept in contact with me during that time.

When I got out that October [1953], they sent me a little money to tide me over 'cause I was married then, then I went to spring training with 'em. Everything happened there pretty good and I had a lot of scouts interested in me. Somewhere in late August we were in South Carolina and I don't know whether they ever got the story true or not, but they came down to sell me to one of the major league teams and I don't think they could get the money right, but I wasn't going to get any of the money. I said if I wasn't going to get any and somebody was going to make some money on me, I had a college education so I can go on and try coaching. I never wanted to coach or teach school. I wanted to be a professional baseball player, but that's what I did.

At that time, the organized ball teams would contact the club directly. When I

replaced Banks, I think there was some kind of binding negotiation that they wouldn't raid.

What was your salary with the Monarchs?

I think it was about $1,200, $1,300 a month, something like that. They were so sure they were going to sell me, that's why I got paid that kind of money.

When I left, I went to Burt High School in Clarksville, Tennessee, and started coaching basketball. I guess that's where I've gotten my greatest success — in basketball — because when I went there I stayed there nine years and I was 219-and-79, something like that, and I won the national high school tournament in 1961. During that time they would bring 16 teams in from 16 different states — the black champions — and we won. I went there four years. We won it once, placed second once, placed third once, and placed fourth once in the consolation game.

A few colleges got interested in me in my fifth year and I decided I was not ready to go to coach college basketball so I stayed on and the year after we won the national tournament I went on to be the head coach at Texas Southern University in Houston, Texas. I was there five years. Had a poor record there. When they hired me, we were in a rebuilding situation and I'm almost sure, and I guess everybody agreed, that we started back on the path to success because within two years after I'd left there, they had won the national NAIA. [Laughs] I figured I had a little part of putting 'em on the right track.

I was a little dissatisfied. I wasn't getting the things that I needed there at the university, and Alcorn made me an offer to come there and I tendered my resignation and I went to Alcorn in 1969.

I had almost 400 victories and 200-some-odd losses and we played everybody in the United States — the Indianas, the Minnesotas, Georgetown, Louisville. You may have been down there when Louisville beat us one point in the NCAA tournament. They sent the wrong man to the foul line. I

never will forget that! Of course, there's
nothing you can do about it. I knew what
kind of situation we were in and we were
kind of breaking a little bit of ground, you
see, and I just couldn't do the things that I
would ordinarily have done if I was already
in that atmosphere. After that, we went to
four NCAAs and three NITs.

I guess the biggest break I ever had,
Coach [Bobby] Knight asked me to come
up on the 1984 Olympic selection committee. We got to be pretty good friends 'cause
we were invited to his tournament at least
four times. We were treated very well at
Indiana. He's a great coach and a great man.

*Who were the best baseball players you
saw?*

Oh, man. The best one I ever saw was
Willie Mays. We played against Willie Mays
about three weeks before he went to organized baseball and we played about a month
before organized ball got Hank Aaron. But
Ted Williams was my favorite player.

The best pitcher?

Oh, man. Oh, man. Being from Lexington, I was kind of sentimental towards
Cincinnati and I guess my opinion would
be colored—isn't that a hell of an expression?—because I was always partial to when
they had [Paul] Derringer, Bucky Walters,
and that bunch over there. But I would say
that Feller was a great pitcher and a kid that
I played against at Redding, Pennsylvania,
was Herb Score. I don't know how good a
baseball pitcher he would've been if he
hadn't had that injury. He could throw it.
Bob Gibson was a hell of a pitcher. There's
so many, I guess it's just a personal opinion
who they think is the best.

Who was the toughest you ever faced?

I believe Score and Sad Sam Jones.
When I was a youngster, when I played on
that team in Lexington, I faced all those
guys. Jones was quick and he made an
impression on me.

*Who was the best basketball player you
saw?*

Oh, man! Geez! Well, Michael Jordan is
the best I've ever seen, but that played

against my teams, it would have to be
Patrick Ewing on the college level and a
kid at Jackson State—Purvis Short. You've
asked me a hell of a question there. We
played against almost everybody in the
United States. We played out of our competition because we were trying to do some
things that no other black teams had
done.

Who was the best player you coached?

I've always refused to name one. I know
who he is, but I kind of feel like if I say he's
the best player I ever coached, I'm relegat-
ing some other players who played great for
me and I never would do that. I'd always
call three or four names.

*What do you think of the three-point
shot?*

I kind of like it, but I think it should be
out just a little bit. I think it should be
international rules because kids are getting
so proficient now in shooting the basketball
it's almost a gift for some of 'em. I don't
think the game should be made easy. If it's
made easy, you'll have too many people that
can excel that are not really equipped to
play an all-around game. If you make it
difficult for 'em, then only the true per-
formers will excel.

*Would you go back and be a professional
baseball player again?*

I certainly would.

Would you try to make it a longer career?

Not necessarily. I think my circumstances warranted that I do the things that I
did. I was married and I had a kid and that
was my first commitment, to my family. If
it had been the other way, if I hadn't had a
family, I may have made a different choice,
but I've been perfectly happy the way it
turned out. My wife asks me all the time
don't I regret it. No, I do not regret the
decision I made because I made a decision
that was important to me and what I
believed in.

DAVID WHITNEY
Born 1-8-30, Midway, KY
Ht. 5' 8"   Wt. 138   Batted and Threw R

Year	Team, league	Pos	G	AB	R	H	2B	3B	HR	RBI	SB	BA
1952	Kansas City Monarchs, NAL	OF										.325
1952-54						military service						
1955	Kansas City Monarchs, NAL	OF										

Dennis Biddle

In and Out by 19

NEGRO LEAGUE DEBUT: 1953

The record for wins at the age of 17 in the major leagues is five, set by Bob Feller in 1936. In 1953, Dennis Biddle, pitching in the Negro leagues, equaled that number, then turned 18 and and won ten more, giving him 15 wins in his rookie season.

An injury derailed Biddle's baseball career when he was only 19, but he got himself back on a successful track a few years later by returning to college. Although the fame that may have come with baseball escaped him, he has enjoyed a long and rewarding life as a social worker, working with young people.

At the time Biddle's career began —1953 — blacks were making inroads into organized ball, but, all else being equal, most major league teams still preferred white kids. These were the days of the bonus babies, when money was spent by the hundreds of thousands of dollars on young talent; interestingly, not *one* bonus baby was black.

So it wasn't surprising when 17-year-old Dennis Biddle didn't receive any offers after his senior year in high school, even though he had hurled *seven* no-hitters. Negro baseball was dying then as the top Negro league players were being taken by organized ball, but the last of the Negro league teams were still operating and developing players such as Ernie Banks, Gene Baker, Elston Howard, and a raft of others.

Biddle signed with the Chicago American Giants, and had not a fluke baserunning accident ended his career after two seasons, he may well have joined that list.

You played for the Chicago American Giants in 1953 and '54. How old were you when you began?

Seventeen. I've been put into the Congressional Record as the youngest to play in the Negro baseball leagues. I played two years in the Negro leagues, then the Chicago Cubs were interested in purchasing my contract. Matter of fact, they were purchasing it and I reported to spring training and I broke my leg the first day of spring training, 1955. I jammed the bag sliding into third base,

broke my ankle in two places. I was an excellent slider [but] somehow cut my slide short and jammed the leg. It was one of those freak accidents.

I still limp. When you look back 40 years ago, they didn't have the modern-day medicine they have now. They didn't operate on it like they would do now and make sure that everything was okay.

How did the American Giants get you?

I was playing in the state championship in Arkansas for the National Farmers'

Association. That was the conference that we were in. We couldn't play in the regular state conference because that was white. I pitched a 1-to-nothing no-hitter in the championship against a team named Eudora, and a scout — he was a scout and booking agent for the Chicago American Giants — saw me pitch and asked me if I would like to try out with the Chicago American Giants.

Now, when he told me this I didn't know anything about the Negro baseball leagues. I thought it was a team that would be traveling down through there and I would try out for the team nearby. I said, "Sure, I would like to," and he said, "I'll have somebody call you." I gave him my telephone number. This was on a Friday. That Sunday I got this phone call as we were getting ready to go to church. The guy said, "My name is Frank Crawford from the Chicago American Giants. How would you like to try out?" I said, "I would love to." He said, "Well, be in Chicago Tuesday morning, 10:30, Washington Park, diamond number seven."

I'd never been hardly out of my hometown — Magnolia, Arkansas. I told Mom, I told my dad and my sister. I told my mom and dad, "I gotta go." We didn't have any money. My dad, he was crying; my sister was crying, but my mother gave me the strength I needed and also the money. I don't know where she got the money, but she gave me twenty dollars. It cost me fourteen dollars to catch the bus from my hometown to Chicago — one way. She hugged me and she said, "Baby, good luck."

I caught the bus, got off the bus in downtown Chicago — Randolph Street. They had the roving steps — the escalator stairs; I'd never seen them before. I saw these steps and I was afraid to get on them, so I walked up the stairs to the street. I saw a bus and people were getting on it, so I got on there. I asked the bus driver how to get to Washington Park. He said, "I'll tell you where to get off because you've got to transfer." So I got off where he told me and

he told me what bus to catch and I got on that bus and he let me off right by the park. The name of the street now is King Drive, but it used to be called South Parkway. Fifty-first and South Parkway is where he let me off.

I walked across the street and there was this guy sitting there. I asked him could I leave my bag there, would he keep my bag 'til I came back? I told him I was looking for diamond number seven, I had a tryout. He said, "Sure."

I got my glove and my spikes out of my bag and I left it with him and I walked across the street. I didn't have to walk too far before I saw diamond number seven, so I sat there, waiting for Crawford. That's all I knew — Mr. Crawford. Two or three guys showed up and then finally Mr. Crawford came.

We started throwing and about six or seven other guys came down and I tried out for the team. He had a contract right there already typed out. I've got a copy of the contract now. I signed my contract and three days later I was pitching my first professional game in Memphis, Tennessee.

Something happened that [tryout] day that followed me for a long time. This gentleman that I had left my bag with became like a father to me. Crawford had a room for me on 47th and South Parkway. He said, "Where's your bag?" and I said, "Across the street over there." He said, "Where?"

I went over there and I was lucky. A lady said, "Are you the young man that left your bag here? Mr. Washington had to go to work and he said you would be back for it." I said, "Could I have his telephone number?" I took it to the hotel with me and I didn't sleep all night long. I have never heard so many sirens!

I couldn't wait 'til daybreak so I could call him. I called him, he came down, picked me up that morning and he said, "Get your bag. You're going with me." Twenty-eight years later, I buried him. He went through everything with me.

How much were you paid?

Five hundred a month. Six games a week. We played a lot of money games. A money game is where the booking agent would book us in a town with the local team. Twenty thousand people would come out to see that game. Paying a dollar apiece, that was a big payday for us. That money was split 60-40 by the teams.

'Course, the league games — it was hard, it was really hard, riding that bus from city to city and playing all those games. Only 16 players — you played every day. Besides pitching, I played center field and first base. I batted left and right.

Do you remember your first game?

Oh, yeah. I got my game ball. I kept the ball. I didn't know the significance of it. I gave it to my son when he was 6 years old and he kept it.

For years we didn't even talk about the Negro leagues. The only time I talked about it was with my kids and my grandkids. It was something that was a part of my life that had come and gone. Nobody was talking about the Negro leagues; everybody was talking about the guys that were playing in the majors.

[My first game] was against the Memphis Red Sox. My catcher was Double Duty Radcliffe and he was an old man but he was still good. [Laughs] I struck out 13 batters and I gave up one home run. The score was 3-to-1. I didn't know the guy's name; all I knew is they called him "Big Red." He hit a home run off of me that's still going today, I think. I had struck him out twice and Double Duty had come out and told me to throw him a curveball. I saw him step up in front of the plate so I knew he was waiting for my curveball 'cause that's what I struck him out with, so I was going to cross him up and throw the fastball. Double Duty said, "Throw the curveball!" and I

Dennis Biddle (courtesy of Dennis Biddle).

shook him off. I threw the fastball and this guy hit it! [Laughs] Double Duty came out and yelled at me, "Boy, I've been in this league 25 years! When I tell you to do something, you do it!" [Laughs] He still remembers it.

"Big Red" is what they called him and he was a big guy. He had to weigh close to 300 pounds; he was big and tall and every time he'd swing that bat and miss the ball, it looked like I could feel the vibration of the bat out there. [Laughs] He could swing hard! [Note: "Big Red" may have been catcher Pepper Bassett. He fits the description: 6' 3" and probably 240 pounds at the end of his career in 1953.]

I won my first five professional baseball games, all while I was 17. The second game was against the Philadelphia Stars in

Racine, Wisconsin, and that's how I got my nickname as "The Man Who Beat the Man Who Beat the Man." I was pitching against a guy by the name of Lefty McKinnis. He was a legendary pitcher; everybody was talking about how good he used to be. He had been around a long time and he was one of the very few pitchers that ever beat Satchel Paige. I found that out after the game.

During the game, he was always talking to me, telling me, "Hey, kid! You're telegraphing your pitch." And I'm saying, "I don't know what he's talking about, telegraphing my pitch." My manager told me, "The batter knows what you're gonna throw before you throw it." I said, "So. They still can't hit it." [Laughs]

But he said, "Son, let me tell you something. A batter's trained to watch the ball all the way from the pitcher's hand. The longer you keep it covered up, the more effective you'll be because it'll take him time to pick it up."

He showed me how to do it and every game after that — and even today when I teach young pitchers how to pitch — I use the same technique that he showed me that night in Racine, Wisconsin.

I won the game, 5-to-1. After the game, they said, "Hey, kid, you just beat the Man." I said, "What are you talking about?" "He's one of the very few pitchers ever to beat Satchel Paige. He's the Man." From that night on, they called me "The Man Who Beat the Man Who Beat the Man."

I had 30 wins in two years, 30 wins and seven defeats. The first year [the schedule] was 71 games, the second year was 73 games. The first year I played in 18 games and I had a 15-and-3 record. My second year I had a 15-and-4 record.

The Cubs were following me. As I look back, those days and nights we were riding the buses and we'd get to a stadium, the scouts would be all over me and I could see the older guys sitting there with a sad look on their faces. Being a social worker and

taking psychology, I reminisce back to when this was happening and I know they were happy for me, but there was some resentment. You know, the fact that they had passed them by and there was always two or three young guys on the team — these are the guys the scouts would be talking to.

And these [older] guys were great. They were great *then*. I saw this with my own eyes and I was only a kid. I can imagine what they were like when they were kids. If you talk to the older guys now, they will tell you they have no bitterness; this is the way things were.

The older guys were training us. Cool Papa Bell trained me. I was fast — I could run real fast — and I remember distinctly Cool Papa Bell coming to the Chicago American Giants, coming to our games and traveling with us on the bus. He was too old to play. He was like a mentor. I think the major leagues were paying him a salary. I can't prove that, but he didn't only talk to me, he'd be talking to the other guys on the other team, too. He would always find something somebody was doing wrong and he would correct them. Like me; I was fast but I would round the bases and lose a lot of time. After the games or early in the morning, he would take me out to the park and he would walk through it with me.

He didn't smoke and drink and after the game the older guys, they'd be going to parties and stuff. I was too young to go and Cool Papa would always stay with me and he would tell me stories about some of the guys. I learned a lot from him about some of the great players that played down through the years that you don't read about in books because they didn't set any records and stuff.

Is there one game that stands out as your best game or biggest thrill?

The first game was my biggest thrill 'cause I was in a daze for a couple days. [Laughs] I had a terrific curveball; I didn't believe people could hit my curveball and my sinker and when I started playing professionally, it was the same way. I would set them up with the fastball and throw them that sinker and if they didn't swing at it, it would hit the ground but they'd swing at it every time. [Laughs] I was proud of that. I'd hear talk was going around the league: "Is that that boy with that curveball?" Word was getting around.

I remember I struck out Buck O'Neil in Omaha, Nebraska, one night. We were playing the Kansas City Monarchs; he was player-manager. We went to the eleventh inning. I came in in the tenth inning to pitch and we scored a run in the eleventh inning. I think I walked a guy, then somebody made an error. The guy was on second base and Buck came up to pinch hit and I struck him out. I didn't know him then. I didn't know he was *the* Buck O'Neil 'til years later. That ranks up there with the biggest thrills — striking him out. The score was 5-5 going into the eleventh inning and we scored that run, then I struck Buck out and that was the end of the game. He was the last out.

Who was the best hitter you saw?

I saw a lot of good hitters. The guy I was with a lot was Double Duty. Ted wasn't a young man anymore and he could still hit that ball. A lot of guys could tear the cover off the ball but Double Duty, I remember him distinctly hitting long home runs.

There was a guy named Dick Vance; he was a catcher and he could hit some long balls. I don't know; I saw a lot of guys and I don't remember their names. I saw some great ballplayers, some guys that were too old to go to the majors and they were still playing and they were great. They could hit that ball and I wonder sometimes why they were not in the majors. It had to be their age. Jackie was 28 but he was exceptional.

What about the best pitcher?

I saw some great pitchers, too. I saw some pitchers I modeled myself after and when I look back, you know, you play them tonight and you didn't see them again for a few weeks. You never came to know them personally. Lefty McKinnis was good. That night he faced me he struck out a lot of men, but they made some errors behind him and we scored some runs.

A guy that I remember was with the New York Black Yankees. He was a Cuban guy and he did go to the majors. His daddy played in the Negro leagues, too, they tell me. Tiant! Boy, he could throw that ball! I got a picture with him in New York. They really talked about his dad. Cool Papa told me about his dad — he was awesome.

You went back to school.

That's the reason I'm in Wisconsin. I went to the University of Wisconsin. I became a social worker and I worked for 24 years with the State of Wisconsin as a social worker. I retired four years ago. I was working in the corrections system and you can retire early, but I couldn't relax so I started working for this social service agency called C.Y.D. — Career Youth Development — working with the same type of youth I was working with when I was a social worker. I'm like the principal of a school now. I'm enjoying it.

I went to school in '58. I thought my leg was going to come around. The doctors kept watching it and I thought it healed. I could still run, but being a pitcher I kind of favored that leg on my landing. I couldn't get the ball across much anymore; I still had the speed, but it just wasn't there and I saw the light. I said, "I better get my butt back in school."

That's what I really wanted to do when I graduated from high school. I had two scholarships; I had a scholarship to Grambling College to play football and I had a scholarship to Arkansas A. M. and N. — which is now the University of Arkansas — to play basketball, but nobody recruited me for baseball. At that time, at the black schools baseball was not one of the money sports.

I went to [visit] Grambling. Mr. [Eddie] Robinson took me down to visit the campus and I spent the night with Willie Davis. We're good friends today because of that. We played football against each other in high school.

Mr. Robinson told me then, "If baseball is your dream, you should go after it, son." This is a week before the Chicago scout talked to me. You know, I saw Mr. Robinson last year in New York — they had a tribute there to the Negro league baseball players and he was there. I went up to him, I said to him, "Mr. Robinson, do you remember me?" He said, "No, I don't remember you." I said, "You recruited me right out of high school back in 1953. You remember Willie Davis?" He said, "Oh, you're that skinny boy!" [Laughs] That was the highlight of the whole thing, so we had a picture taken together. That was great.

Would you be a ballplayer again in the same situation?

As I look back, I would have gone to college, paid my way, and played baseball. But I'd play [professional] baseball again.

I play now. They've got a league here they call the Old-Timers League. You have to be 30 or more and some guys 60 years old are playing. I'm 61; I'm the oldest one on the team. Last year we won one game and I won it. [Laughs]

You're working with the Negro league players now.

When we were in Kansas City and I saw the guys that came, some of them were in pretty bad shape. Some of them were literally poor. Some of them just had the clothes they had on their backs.

We had a meeting. Fay Vincent, the commissioner of baseball, had ordered the Negro league players to be insured. Joe Black was given six months to find all the Negro league players. That wasn't fair because these guys are all over the country and he only found a little over a hundred — about half — and that was what the meeting was about — the insurance. They said, "This was two years ago and Joe had six months to do it. After he didn't do it in six months, the rest of the guys were left out."

On the way back home, I felt that was wrong and something would not let me rest until I did something about it. Personally, I didn't need the insurance. One day I might. So I started investigating why the other players did not have it and as I got deeper into it, I found out a lot of other things that were not conducive to us. Period.

I was a member of the Negro League Players Asssociation. I'd never got much correspondence from it and I didn't know why. I never knew much about it. I heard that the guy that ran it was a millionaire that put up a lot of money to bring the Negro leagues back to the forefront, bring back the players. For years, nobody talked about the Negro league players. This guy got an attorney and he filed some papers and he claimed to be representing all of us.

I called New York. I knew it was supposed to be nonprofit and I wanted to know what was the charter under and I found out that it was filed under someone else's name, not the Negro league players.

So I said before we can get insurance, we've got to get organized, so this is why I started this organization. We're organized now and we're legal. It's called Yesterday's Negro League Baseball Players LLC. LLC means Limited Liability Company, which means the players will get paid.

I'm in the process of setting up a pension fund for them. We'll get a pension every month; we'll get insurance. Other people made 2.4 billion dollars on us and we're going to have some say on that now. We've just organized.

Fay Vincent ordered Major League Properties to look out after us. That includes licensing and anything else. There are several companies that have applied for licenses through Major League Properties that paid money to sell memorabilia. That money goes to the players — 50 percent of it. Thirty percent goes to the museum, 20 percent goes to the Jackie Robinson Foundation. 'Course, that's not right, either, because it all should go to the players first and then to the Jackie Robinson Foundation after the players are all gone.

The *New York Times* reported that, on sales alone, they made 2.4 billion dollars. The players didn't get any of that money. Those little checks they send us every six months is nothing compared to what they are making up there.

These guys, all they have that's worth anything is their little signatures on their pictures. This is all they have.

DENNIS "BOSE" BIDDLE
Born 6-24-35, Magnolia, AR
Ht. 6' 0"   Wt. 180   Batted B and Threw R

Year	Team, league	G	IP	W	L	Pct	H	BB	SO	SHO	ERA
1953	Chi. American Giants, ind.	18	112	15	3	.833	35	18	32		1.64
1954			121	15	4	.789	30	21	38		1.65

Elliot Coleman

"Junior"

Negro League Debut: 1954

Probably the two most famous graduates of the Birmingham Black Barons are Willie Mays and Charley Pride. Both had many hits over the years, albeit of a quite different nature.

There were other first-rate ballplayers who left the Barons for organized ball, among them Piper Davis, Artie Wilson, John Kennedy, Jehosie Heard, Bill Greason, Kelly Searcy, and Elliot "Junior" Coleman. The fans of today know very little about these men, but there is lot of talent represented there.

The last two Barons to enter organized ball are the last two on that list: Searcy and Coleman. They were half of Birmingham's starting rotation in 1954 and '55 and were it not for injuries may well have been in a major league rotation a few years later. Searcy is generally regarded as one of the best pitchers of the latter days of the Negro leagues and Coleman was on his way to that acclaim when he signed with the Baltimore Orioles, where he was moving his way up the minor league ladder when Uncle Sam summoned him for military duty. Returning two years later, Coleman sustained an arm injury at Triple-A Vancouver that effectively ended his promising career. But baseball was a pleasure for Junior Coleman.

You had a pretty good team in Birmingham. Was Jehosie Heard still there?

No, he was gone by then. We had a catcher named Otha Bailey, a little short fella that I thought had a lotta good. He didn't weigh much. Otha weighed 'bout 155, which was small for a catcher. We had Doc Wesley Dennis, who played first base who had been in that league, oh, I would say a long time with three or four teams. We had Eddie Brooks, who played second; Curley Williams played short; and we had Jessie Mitchell and who else did we have in the outfield? We had Jessie Mitchell, I know, and, 'course, Charley Pride, he was an outfielder/pitcher, and we had a kid— well, he really wasn't a kid—named Pijo King, which was probably the best player that we had and probably the highest paid. Doc Wesley Dennis, our first baseman, was probably second.

We had a pitching staff—'course, Kelly Searcy and I later signed with the Orioles, and Kelly was a lefthanded pitcher. Kelly was tough. He was, I would say, one of the better pitchers in that league. And in '55 I opened up the season against Satchel Paige with Kansas City in Birmingham. I guess it was one of those things where Satch was a little older and he was, I guess, pretty well not really in his prime.

We had Bill Beverly—Wild Bill Beverly. I think he called himself "Fireball." We had a kid named Menske Cartledge, was from

South America, I believe. He was a tall righthander. We had another kid — I call 'em kids — Horse Thompson; he was from about 30 miles from here. So we had a pretty good pitchin' staff.

I thought we had a pretty good team. In fact, Kansas City gave us, I would say, the hardest time, and Memphis Red Sox was competitive. The Indianapolis Clowns had a fairly decent team. I felt that we were second to the Kansas City Monarchs as far as a team goes. We had a pretty good team.

When did you sign with the Orioles?

I signed with Baltimore after the All-Star game in 1955 at Comiskey Park. I pitched a couple innin's in the All-Star game. That was on a Sunday. I was also bein' looked at by the Dodgers and the Yankees durin' that time, too, but there was a [Baltimore] scout there in Chicago at Comiskey Park that wanted to see me pitch and I think I pitched again that Monday for him. Then I came home and talked to my mom and signed a contract. I flew to Baltimore and I was up there basically at the end of the season, so I guess I had the advantage because, during that particular time, the minor league managers was there so they had an opportunity to see me throw a little bit and the next year I really didn't have a problem tryin' to go with the teams because the managers had already seen me.

So I went to Aberdeen, South Dakota, in '56 and '57 I went to San Antonio. Fifty-eight and '59 I was in the service and I came out in '60, went to Vancouver in the Pacific Coast League and I hurt my arm in San Diego. I pulled a muscle and from '60 to '64 I couldn't get anybody out. I ended up bein' released in 1964. I can imagine if they would've had the surgery then that they've got now, I probably would've been out about three weeks. But, you know, it didn't happen that way so I guess that's the

Elliot "Junior" Coleman (courtesy of Elliot Coleman).

way the ball bounces. That pretty well ended my baseball career.

Do you recall any of your seasonal records?

With the Barons, what did I have? I had a 12-and-5 and a 16-and-6. And with the Orioles, I played with Aberdeen, South Dakota, and I had a 14-and-8 record with a 1.56 ERA and 1957 at San Antonio I had a 12-and-15 record and a 2.56 ERA. I was pitchin' well but our team really wasn't that good. However, in '57 I had gone to spring training with Baltimore and, personally, I thought I was gonna stick. I pitched against Cleveland four innin's and I think Early Wynn was pitchin' for Cleveland. I came in with the bases loaded and somebody popped up and somebody hit into a double play. I was taken out in the eighth innin' for a pinch hitter.

Paul Richards, who was the manager durin' that particular time, felt that I didn't have enough experience so I got sent to the Texas League. I did pretty good down there but after that season I was called into the army—'58 and '59. Went to Vancouver in '60 and, as I said, that's where I developed arm problems.

How did you get started in baseball?

Well, I guess, actually, comin' from a church-goin' family, I had to go to church on Sunday but I've got an older brother who's three years older than I and he had an interest in maybe goin' to college and to become a teacher. In fact, he's a principal now at one of the high schools here, but he was a third baseman — he had a pretty good arm — and there were teams who were in the process of scoutin' him, but he didn't like baseball. So he showed me how to throw a curveball, you know, and that sorta thing, and I thought I was pretty good.

The team that he played with only played on Sunday, which meant that we would slip off from church after Sunday school and go play ball. 'Course, I got a spankin' because Mother told me to stay at church, but I didn't stay at church. I would slip off and go play. Actually, I was goin' with my brother and whoever was gonna pitch that particular day I would not let him pitch unless I could warm up with him because I wanted to throw my curveball.

One Sunday, their pitcher did not show up, so the fellas on my team told my brother, "Why don't you make your little brother pitch? He thinks he's a pitcher." So I did pretty good; I think we won somethin' like 12-to-1. I had about 16 or 17 strikeouts and everybody, said, "Hey, li'l Coleman! Boy, you're tough! You gonna be a pitcher!" I thought I was, too. [Laughs]

About two Sundays later, we had a team that came to Nashville to play and they had asked me about pitchin' and I went down and warmed up — pretty chesty — and I

think that team scored about nine runs in the first innin'. [Laughs] So then I decided that I really wasn't a pitcher. Maybe I should do somethin' else, but about two or three weeks later after that I pitched and then I never had any more troubles as a pitcher.

I just pitched in and around the city and each area had a team — north Nashville, south Nashville, east, and west — and we would go to little towns that was in and around, playin' against teams. *Every*body would hear about you, so if there was any-body who was supposed to be pretty good, then people knew it.

There was a fella that lived up the street from me named Sidney Bunch who asked me to come and try out for Birmingham, because we had gone to Waverly, Ten-nessee, and Waverly was somethin' like a farm team for the Black Barons. He had played with Birmingham. That was on a Sunday and that Monday he came by my house and picked me up and we had gone down to Sulpher Dell, where the Birming-ham Black Barons was practicin'. They asked me to warm up, so I warmed up.

They had a player named Eddie Brooks; I guess he was what I would call a Punch-and-Judy hitter, which is a good double and single man, so they asked me to pitch against him. They said, "We want you to pitch just like it was in a game." I didn't think too much about it, but I don't know if it was the beginnin' of the season — maybe Eddie wasn't really that sharp — but Eddie just didn't hit anything that day. I don't know; I guess it could've been me but I'm not necessarily sayin' that because later on Eddie was the fellow who played second base and I thought he was a pretty good hitter. He was our leadoff man.

I guess they just selected me that day and I took off. I think I signed a contract for about $175 a month and $2 a day to eat on and, believe you me, you could eat with about 90 cents and you can save a dollar and a dime in those days. That was pretty good money, I thought. I'd never really had any jobs or anything and right outta high school, I thought that was pretty good. School teachers, they were makin' somethin' like $125 per month — some of 'em might've made 150 — but I thought I was doin' pretty good for a kid just outta high school. I enjoyed the travelin' and I enjoyed baseball. I would've played free.

To tell the truth, I did not know that you got paid to play baseball. [Laughs] When they talked about, "We'll pay you …", I said, "Wait a minute. You got to be kiddin'!" There was a lotta things I was naive about because, believe it or not, I just found out somethin' two years ago. Charley Pride came through and he wanted to see Soo Bridgeforth. Soo Bridgeforth was the owner of the Birmingham Black Barons, so we were on our way out there and we also picked up another fella named Jim Zapp and we were talkin' about the All-Star game and somebody mentioned that when you were selected on the All-Star team, then you got $250. I said, "Wait a minute!" Here I am, 38 years later. I said, "Soo owes me $250!" I didn't get it and I did not know that you were supposed to have gotten $250 if and when you were selected on the All-Star team.

Now if you think about those times, most of the baseball players was old and the older players did not cater to the younger fellows. They wouldn't tell you anything because the younger fellows had not paid their dues. Now, it seems like it's in reverse because my son, who attended Tuskegee, he tried out with the Braves and he tried out with Kansas City and he tried out with the White Sox. The last time they sent him anything for a tryout camp, they wanted players between 16 and 21. He was 23. Now, you don't have to tell the truth about your age, but everything has reversed now. They've got an interest in the younger players and when I started, I was too young. Nobody would really help me. They would not tell you anything. That's how I got the name of "Junior." If you wanted to know anything, you had to find out yourself 'cause they wouldn't tell you.

You're one of the youngest former Negro leagues players.

I'm pretty close. At this meetin' in Kansas City, there was one fella there who was 55. There was an article in the *Nashville Tennessean* and it's been about two years ago that was written and a fella came out and was talkin' to me and it had somethin' to do with Jackie Robinson and him signin' and the players started leavin', but, anyway, I thought the Negro leagues broke up in 1958, but we found out this time that the Negro leagues broke up in 1960 or 1961.

As I said, I only played about a year-and-a-half, then I signed [with the Orioles]. The first meetin' that I attended in 1989, I was so enthused because I wanted to hear about the Satchel Paiges and the Josh Gibsons and those guys and then it seemed that something really hit me: Hey, you're one of those guys! Even though I've only got about a year-and-a-half, I would still like to be considered as one of those people who participated in that league.

I thought it [the reunion in Kansas City] was great. I thought it was amazin' because I met fellows that I had not seen in 40 years — Jessie Mitchell and Curley Williams. Jess and I were friends with Birmingham and Jess is two years older than I am. I can remember goin' to New York and we walked about 60 blocks to go see a movie. That's how I know that Central Park is 55 blocks long. [Laughs] I won't ever forget that and I told Jessie, I said, "I think you owe me an apology for askin' me to attend a movie when we were in New York. You didn't tell me that Central Park was 55 blocks long."

There was a different unity in that baseball league than anyplace that I have ever been and I guess the reason bein' was that, when we talk about the love of the game, that's why we really played it. We really wanted to be better than the other team, we really tried to beat them, we were determined that certain teams were not gonna beat us, so it was a competitive thing versus, "Hey, how much money you gonna get?" 'Cause none of us made any money, not anything to brag on. It was just fun playin'.

How much did the Orioles give you?

I got, I think it was $800 a month plus air transportation home at the end of the season. I think the next year, I might've got somethin' like a two or three hundred dollar raise.

What they did, the team was owned by a doctor out of Memphis when I signed and Soo Bridgeforth had sold it and we had always said that if anybody got signed, that the players would get X amount of money. My contract was worth, I think they said, $7,500 — what the Orioles had paid for me. I think I was supposed to have got somethin' like $2,500, they was gonna divide $2,500 among the players, and the man who owned the team was gonna get the rest, but everybody on that team said, "Now, Junior, you're gonna be leavin'. How do we know that you will give us our money? Why don't you let the owner of the team settle us?" "That sounds okay." So that's what I did. The players didn't get any money; I didn't get any. [Laughs]

That's what happens when, I guess, your mom and dad are church people. You don't know anything about tryin' to negotiate. The only thing that I knew was that somebody said, "Make sure you ask for air transportation home at the end of the season. If you don't, you could end up walkin'."

There was a lot of things I didn't know. I was green and, as I said, the players on the team would not tell you anything because they was older and they knew. But it looked like it might've been a little jealousy. You know, "He's signin' and I'm not. He's only been here a year or two, so I'm not gonna tell him anything to really help him."

I didn't know that you could negotiate your contract. When I heard anything from the Orioles, I thought that whatever they offered me, that's what I had to take. I did not have any advice at all. I feel that, actually, I was taken advantage of 'cause I had

some pretty good seasons. I made the All-Star team; in spring trainin' I'd go and we would play in L.A. and Paul Richards would call, "Hey, send me Coleman and so-and-so over here," so I felt like I was doin' pretty well in the organization.

I guess what really happens is that once the people in the organization who like you or maybe could help you, when those guys lose their jobs and a new bunch come in, you can just forget it. We had Luman Harris, who was a scout, and Paul Richards and Harry "The Cat" Brecheen; all those guys was pretty high on me. But after I hurt my arm, after about two or three years, I couldn't pitch anymore. I guess when you hurt yourself, they don't have any choice. There's too many sound bodies to worry about somebody that's lame.

When I stopped pitchin' I was still goin' to a Dr. Hillman, who was an orthopedic surgeon out at Vandy, tryin' to get my arm back in shape. When I left the Orioles — I retired with the intentions of tryin' to get my arm in shape — Harry Dalton, who was in charge of the players, had told me, "If you can get your arm back in shape, give us a call and we'll see what we can do." After about three years, I knew that I would not be able to get my arm back in shape. I had gotten married, I really could not afford to pay an orthopedic surgeon to look at my arm, I was 26, 27 years old — gettin' old — and I felt, well, maybe I need to look at somethin' else.

Later, I was the pitchin' coach at Tennessee State University for two years and I thought I was very fortunate. There was one youngster there named Carlos Thomas that signed with the Dodgers the first year. The next year, we had a kid named Everett Stull, who signed with the Expos, so both years that I was there, I felt that I did somethin'.

To tell the truth, I really don't have any regrets. I've had a good life, I've got a good wife, I've got a daughter that's in Chicago and she makes commercials for McDonald's, and I've got a son who's got a chemical engineering degree, so I don't have any regrets. I think that baseball was a steppin' stone. It was great while it lasted.

The only regrets that I've got, and sometimes I have dreams about it, I can go in the bullpen, I can warm up, but I never get into the game. I guess in my subconscious mind, I still wonder if I could have played in the majors. If that question was answered in my baseball career, I would be completely satisfied.

I do know that the four innin's I pitched against Cleveland I didn't have any problems. I had four strikeouts and I was very well pleased with my performance, but I felt that I could've played in the majors and that's one question I never will have answered. Other than that, I'm very well pleased with the way my life has turned out.

Would you be a baseball player again?

Yes, I would. The only thing about it, I would really like to know the ropes and I guess I would like to know how to take care of my arm better — you know, what I need to do after I finish pitchin'. See, nobody told me that; nobody told me you need to put this on your arm, or don't hang your arm outta the window without a coat. I don't know if the Orioles felt that I knew all of this.

But I thought that baseball was great. I've had an opportunity to see most of the world; I've met a lot of what I would consider important people, great people; I've made a lotta friends that normally I would not have been able to. Even now, it still opens doors for me at work; different things that happen in and around the city I get invited to, I can go down to McDonald's and the people say, "I saw your picture on TV. They interviewed you here and there." Those are the things that had happened from baseball that I figured normally certainly I would not have had an opportunity to do. Speaking with you tonight, had it not been for baseball, you never would have made this call, so it's been great as far as I'm concerned. There's a lot of things not

as important as money and even though I did not make any money in baseball, there's some other things that it was able to do for me.

When I would go out and pitch, if the third baseman missed the ball, if the center fielder didn't hit, the next day in the paper you'd see where old Coleman lost the game. A lot of people my age still don't know how to lose. I do. I don't like it. You know, baseball was inspiration for me along those lines.

Who were the best players you saw?

If I had to talk about the Negro leagues, I would put Kelly Searcy at the top of the list. He was a lefthand pitcher. I've had the privilege to see Herb Score and some of the great lefthanders, and he was in the category with all of those guys. I thought he was tough.

I thought that Doc Dennis was one of the great hitters that we had. We had Eddie Brooks, who was a very good hitter. We had a fella named Jim Zapp, who lives here in Nashville who was a great fastball hitter. He was a pretty good-sized man. There were good players in the Negro leagues.

After I signed with the Orioles, I would think that Brooks Robinson probably stands out in my mind more so than any player. He had gotten hurt and they sent him down for about a month to San Antonio and to have a man like him playin' third base when you're pitchin', it was an honor. To me, he didn't look like a ballplayer; he wasn't that fast, but he was quick. Anything that was hit down the third base line he was gonna get it.

I also had a chance to see the McNallys and the Jim Palmers and those guys. It's amazin'; when they first came to the Orioles, I was the fella that they came to. Everybody had heard about Junior Coleman, you know. [Laughs] I was the one with all of the lip service and now, I guess, it ends up with me really admirin' those guys.

ELLIOT HOYT "JUNIOR" COLEMAN, SR.
Born 12-27-34, Nashville, TN Died 7-6-96, Nashville, TN
Ht. 6' 0"   Wt. 180   Batted and Threw R

Year	Team, league	G	IP	W	L	Pct	H	BB	SO	SHO	ERA
1954	Birm. Black Barons, NAL			12	5	.706					
1955	Birm. Black Barons, ind.			16	6	.727					
	Baltimore, AL					did not pitch					
1956	Aberdeen, NorL	28	193	14	8	.636	139	108	160	1	2.56
1957	San Antonio, TxL			12	15	.444					
1958-69				military service							
1960	Vancouver, PCL	20	61	3	4	.429	66	34	24	0	5.75
1961	minor leagues										
1962											
1963											
1964											

Bibliography

Charlton, James, ed. *The Baseball Chronology.* New York: Macmillan, 1991.

Clark, Dick, and Larry Lester, eds. *The Negro Leagues Book.* Cleveland: The Society for American Baseball Research, 1994.

Marazzi, Rich, and Len Fiorito. *Aaron to Zuverink.* New York: Avon, 1982.

Riley, James A. *The Biographical Encyclopedia of the Negro Baseball Leagues.* New York: Carroll and Graf, 1984.

Thorn, John, et al., eds. *Total Baseball.* 4th ed. New York: Viking, 1995.

Wolff, Rick, ed. dir. *The Baseball Encyclopedia.* 9th ed. New York: Macmillan, 1993.

Index

Numbers in italic indicate photographs